BOUNDARIES AND JUSTICE

BOUNDARIES AND JUSTICE

DIVERSE ETHICAL PERSPECTIVES

Edited by

David Miller and Sohail H. Hashmi

PRINCETON UNIVERSITY PRESS   PRINCETON AND OXFORD

Copyright © 2001 by Princeton University Press
Published by Princeton University Press, 41 William Street,
Princeton, New Jersey 08540
In the United Kingdom: Princeton University Press,
3 Market Place, Woodstock, Oxfordshire OX20 1SY
All Rights Reserved

Library of Congress Cataloging-in-Publication Data

Boundaries and justice : diverse ethical perspectives / edited by David Miller
and Sohail H. Hashmi.
   p.   cm.—(Ethikon studies in comparative ethics)
Includes bibliographical references and index.

ISBN 0-691-08799-7 (alk. paper) — ISBN 0-691-08800-4 (pbk. : alk. paper)

1. Ethics. I. Miller, David (David Leslie) II. Hashmi, Sohail H., 1962–
III. Series.
BJ1012.B598   2001   172—dc21   2001021155

This book has been composed in Goudy

Printed on acid-free paper. ∞

www.pup.princeton.edu

Printed in the United States of America

10 9 8 7 6 5 4 3 2 1

10 9 8 7 6 5 4 3 2 1
(Pbk.)

Contents

Nine
Islamic Perspectives on Territorial Boundaries and Autonomy

Acknowledgments

THIS BOOK is the result of a dialogue project organized by the Ethikon Institute in collaboration with the Carnegie Council on Ethics and International Affairs and the University of Wisconsin Center for International Studies. The trustees of the Ethikon Institute join with Philip Valera, president, and Carole Pateman, series editor, in thanking all who contributed to the success of this project.

We are especially grateful to Joan Palevsky, the Carnegie Council, and the Center for International Studies for major financial support, and to other generous donors, including the Sidney Stern Memorial Trust, Harold Guetzkow, the Carl N. Karcher Trust, and the Stanley K. Sheinbaum Trust.

In addition to the authors, the project was greatly enhanced by the active participation of other dialogue partners: Brian Barry, Richard Friedman, David Kennedy, Friedrich Kratochwil, Andre Liebich, David Little, David Lumsdaine, David R. Mapel, Terry Nardin, Joel H. Rosenthal, Mark Tessler, and Michael Walzer.

Special thanks are due to Joel H. Rosenthal, president of the Carnegie Council, and his colleagues Eva Becker and Ulrike Klopfer for hosting the dialogue meetings at Merrill House in New York, and for their gracious hospitality.

Five contributors to this book were not present for the Merrill House dialogue meetings, and we thank them for agreeing to join the project at later stages: Nigel Biggar, Robert McCorquodale, Raul Pangalangan, Daniel Philpott, and Jeremy Rabkin.

We are particularly indebted to David Miller and Sohail Hashmi for taking on the challenging task of editing this book. We are also grateful to Ann Himmelberger Wald, editor-in-chief, and Ian Malcolm, our editor at Princeton University Press, for their valuable guidance and continuing support.

About the Sponsors for This Volume

The Ethikon Institute, a nonprofit organization, is concerned with the social implications of ethical pluralism. Its dialogue-publication programs in intersocietal relations, civil society, family life, and bio-environmental ethics are designed to explore a diversity of moral outlooks, secular and religious, and to clarify areas of consensus and divergence between them. By encouraging a systematic exchange of ideas, the Institute aims to advance the prospects for agreement and to facilitate the accommodation of irreducible differences. The

Ethikon Institute takes no position on issues that divide its participants, serving not as an arbiter but as a neutral forum for the cooperative exploration of diverse and sometimes opposing views.

The Carnegie Council on Ethics and International Affairs is a nonprofit organization founded in 1914 by Andrew Carnegie to affirm, explore, and nurture the interrelationship of ethics and foreign policy. The Carnegie Council strongly believes that ethics, as informed by the world's principal moral and religious traditions, is an integral and inevitable component of all policy decisions in the realms of economics, politics, and national security. By promoting a greater understanding of the values and conditions that ensure peaceful relations among nations, the Carnegie Council hopes to contribute to a better life for people everywhere.

The Center for International Studies of the University of Wisconsin–Milwaukee is a National Resource Center funded by the United States Department of Education. National Resource Centers are intended to ensure that the United States possesses the expertise and knowledge to carry out its responsibilities in world affairs.

Contributors _____

Nigel Biggar holds the Chair of Theology in the Department of Theology and Religious Studies at the University of Leeds, where he specializes in the field of religious ethics and public life. He has a long-standing interest in the conflict in Northern Ireland and has published for the Belfast press on the peace process.

Joseph Boyle is professor of philosophy and principal of St. Michael's College at the University of Toronto. He has published extensively on applied ethics and moral theory, and is co-author with John Finnis and Germain Grisez of *Nuclear Deterrence, Morality and Realism*. A past president of the American Catholic Philosophical Association, he has been part of the contemporary effort to understand and develop Catholic natural law theory.

Joseph Chan is associate professor of political theory at the University of Hong Kong. He has published articles in major journals including *Ethics*, *History of Political Thought*, *Journal of Democracy*, and *Oxford Journal of Legal Studies*. His current research focuses on Confucian political philosophy, human rights in Asia, liberalism, and Aristotle's political philosophy.

Russell Hardin is professor of politics at New York University and a fellow of the American Academy of Arts and Sciences. He is also a trustee of the Carnegie Council on Ethics and International Affairs and a former editor of the journal *Ethics*. His publications include *Collective Action* and *One for All: The Logic of Group Conflict* as well as many articles in major journals.

Sohail H. Hashmi is assistant professor of international relations at Mount Holyoke College. He is the editor of *State Sovereignty: Change and Persistence in International Relations*, and the author of numerous articles on Islamic ethics. He is currently completing a book analyzing the contemporary Islamic discourse on war and peace.

Will Kymlicka is professor of philosophy at Queen's University, Ontario. He is author of *Liberalism, Community, and Culture*, *Contemporary Political Philosophy*, and *Multicultural Citizenship*, which was awarded the Macpherson Prize by the Canadian Political Science Association and the Bunche Award by the American Political Science Association. He is also the author of *Justice in Political Philosophy* and *The Rights of Minority Cultures*, and coeditor (with Ian Shapiro) of *Ethnicity and Group Rights*.

Loren Lomasky is professor of philosophy at Bowling Green State University and contributing editor to *Reason* and *Liberty* magazines. He is the author of *Persons, Rights and the Moral Community*, for which he was awarded the

1990 Machette Prize. His most recent book, co-authored with Geoffrey Brennan, is *Democracy and Decision: The Pure Theory of Electoral Preference*. He also coedited (with G. Brennan) *Politics and Process: New Essays in Democratic Theory*.

Robert McCorquodale is professor of international law and human rights at the University of Nottingham School of Law. His books include *Cases and Materials on International Law*, and he has written articles on issues such as the right of self-determination, globalization, and international human rights law. He is an editor of the *International Journal of Human Rights*, the *Federal Law Journal*, and the *Australian Journal of Human Rights*.

David Miller is official fellow in social and political theory at Nuffield College, Oxford University. He is the author of *Principles of Social Justice* and *On Nationality*. He is also the editor of *Citizenship and National Identity* and coeditor (with Michael Walzer) of *Pluralism, Justice, and Equality*. His research interests include theories of justice and equality, and ideas of nationality and citizenship.

Richard B. Miller is Finkelstein Fellow and professor of religious studies at Indiana University, where he teaches courses in religious ethics and the philosophy of religion. He is author of *Interpretations of Conflict: Ethics, Pacifism, and the Just War Tradition, Casuistry and Modern Ethics: A Poetics of Practical Reasoning*, and essays on war and peace, medical ethics, casuistry, and the study of religion.

David Novak is the J. Richard and Dorothy Shiff Professor of Jewish Studies and Director of the Jewish Studies Programme at University College, University of Toronto. He is a founder of the Union for Traditional Judaism, vice president of the Institute on Religion and Public Life, and a fellow of the Academy for Jewish Philosophy, the Jewish Policy Center, and the Woodrow Wilson International Center for Scholars. His books include *The Theology of Nahmanides, Jewish-Christian Dialogue*, and *Jewish Social Ethics*.

Sulayman Nyang is professor of African Studies at Howard University. He is a specialist in Islamic Studies and the sociology of religion in Africa. His publications include *Religious Plurality in Africa* and *Islam, Christianity, and African Identity*. A former diplomat, he served as Gambia's deputy ambassador to Saudi Arabia and several other Middle Eastern and northwest African states.

Michael Nylan teaches in the Department of Chinese Studies at Bryn Mawr College and has been the recipient of awards from the National Endowment for the Humanities, the American Council of Learned Societies, the Fulbright Program, the American Association of University Women, and the Linkback Award for Excellence in Teaching. She is the author of *The Shifting Center, The Canon of Supreme Mystery, Constructing the Confucian*

Classics, Then and Now, and numerous articles on classical learning in China.

Raul C. Pangalangan is associate professor of law at the University of the Philippines in Manila. He was the Philippine delegate to the Rome Conference that created the International Criminal Court, and was also a Philippine participant in dialogues among claimant states in the Spratly Islands dispute in the South China Sea.

Daniel Philpott is assistant professor of political science at the University of California, Santa Barbara. He is the author of *Revolutions in Sovereignty* (forthcoming from Princeton University Press) and of articles on sovereignty, self-determination, and ethics in international relations.

Jeremy Rabkin teaches international law and American constitutional law in the Department of Government at Cornell University. His most recent book is *Why Sovereignty Matters* (AEI Press, 1998).

Hillel Steiner is professor of political philosophy in the Department of Government and the School of Philosophical Studies at the University of Manchester. His book, *An Essay on Rights*, was recently awarded the W.J.M. Mackenzie Prize by the Political Studies Association.

M. Raquibuz Zaman is the Charles A. Dana professor and chair of the Department of Finance and International Business at Ithaca College. He has authored and edited four books and contributed articles to numerous books and scholarly journals. He has also served as director of publications for the Association of Muslim Social Scientists, consultant to the World Bank, and consultant to the Food and Agricultural Organization of the United Nations.

Noam J. Zohar teaches moral and political philosophy, rabbinic thought, and courses in ethics and *halakha* at Bar Ilan University. He is also a fellow at the Shalom Hartman Institute in Jerusalem and has taught at both Princeton University and the University of Pennsylvania. His published works include *Alternatives in Jewish Bioethics* and several articles in related fields. He is coeditor (with Michael Walzer and others) of *The Jewish Political Tradition* (Yale University Press, 2000).

BOUNDARIES AND JUSTICE

Introduction _____

DAVID MILLER AND SOHAIL H. HASHMI

THIS BOOK is an exploration of the boundaries that divide human communities from one another. That such boundaries exist, and moreover appear to have existed from time immemorial, is not in dispute. Indeed, since most species of higher animals are communal and territorial, we may speculate that the need for boundaries is built into our genetic makeup. But humans are also rational and reflective creatures, and as such we must ask ethical questions about what justifies the boundaries that we have drawn between us: what purposes they serve, where (if anywhere) they should be drawn, how permeable or impervious they should be.

These questions take on especial urgency in a world where existing boundaries are being challenged from a variety of directions. Very often these challenges have the effect of weakening boundaries. Thus states find it increasingly difficult to control the movement of people and goods across their borders, partly because of the growth of a global economy, partly because of population movements that they cannot prevent, partly (as in the European case) because they have entered into international agreements which entail relaxing their control. As the principle of humanitarian intervention develops, states are less able to claim sovereignty as a shield for massive violations of human rights. Once the boundary of sovereignty has been breached, humanitarian interventions frequently lead to prolonged periods of international stewardship. Cultural communities, too, find it harder to preserve their own identity and distinctiveness in the face of the massive impact of global media of communication.

But this does not mean that we are moving rapidly toward a world without boundaries, for there are powerful counterforces at work. Nationalist movements, for instance, attempt to carve out areas within existing states within which they can exercise political hegemony, indeed sometimes even attempt to secede altogether and create new states, and in doing so they necessarily create new boundaries between themselves and the remainder of the preexisting political community.

The boundaries in question fall into two basic categories. First, there are social boundaries, dividing lines that run between groups of people, so that they recognize themselves, and are recognized by others, as falling into two or more categories. These may be established in a number of different ways, depending on the criteria used to place people in the various categories, and the degree of formality involved. Class divisions, for instance, are usually created by informal means, using characteristics such as social origin, occupation, lifestyle, accent, and so forth to determine whether someone belongs to the upper, middle, or working class, and then enforced by social practices that encourage people in each class to interact mainly with people of their own kind (working with each other, enjoying leisure together, intermarrying, and so forth). Ethnic divisions operate in much the same way.

Other boundaries may be marked more formally, for instance by legal rules that assign people to particular categories and prevent them from moving easily across the dividing lines. Citizenship provides an obvious example here. Each state divides the world population more or less neatly into two categories, those who qualify as its citizens and those who do not, and since falling inside the boundary of a wealthy and stable state usually brings with it considerable benefits—the range of goods and services that citizens (and sometimes legal residents) are entitled to—access to citizenship is fiercely guarded. Only those who meet the (often quite demanding) conditions are allowed to cross the boundary. In the case of repressive or poor states, boundaries often serve the opposite role, that of preventing people from exiting.

Boundaries in the second category are territorial boundaries, boundaries in space that demarcate a portion of the earth's surface as forming a certain territory. These boundaries can in turn be subdivided into two main kinds—those that mark out areas of property, and those that mark out political jurisdictions, that is areas within which a particular political authority holds sway. In the case of property, the boundary serves mainly to define an area within which the owner, whether one person or a collective, is entitled to make use of physical objects and to exclude others from that use. In other words, the function of property boundaries is to assign things to persons in such a way that it is reasonably clear who has control over a house or a farm or a factory. Boundaries of the second kind serve to identify an area within which someone—again this may be a person or a collective—can wield authority over whoever is physically present in that area. This will typically involve laying down rules of law and enforcing them, and the significance of the boundary is that it tells people which system of law applies to them when they stand or reside in any given place.

In the modern world, this distinction between property boundaries and jurisdictional boundaries is relatively clear, but it has not always been so. In feudal systems, for instance, the person who was given dominion over a piece of land by his superior recognizably held it as property—he could decide what use should be made of it, who would work it on his behalf, and so forth—but in many cases he was also granted a large measure of jurisdiction in the sense of wielding authority over those who resided on the land, settling disputes, punishing certain crimes, and so on. So although when thinking about territorial boundaries it is useful to distinguish between property and jurisdiction, we should recognize that there is in fact a range of ways in which territory can be controlled, with pure property relations and pure authority relations standing at opposite ends of that range.

If we look now at how social boundaries are related to territorial boundaries, we should begin by noticing that social boundaries need not take a territorial form. For instance, two ethnic groups may live side by side in a certain region, preserving their separation through the use of different languages or adherence to different religions, but having no distinct space which belongs to one group rather than the other. Yet at the same time there are powerful forces which tend to make social boundaries crystallize as physical boundaries in space. As a simple example, consider a religious group which needs a place of worship— a church, mosque, or synagogue. In order for this portion of space to serve the function that the group requires, it must be able to control sufficiently what takes place within it—it must be able to exclude people who are acting in a way that disrupts services, it must be able to designate certain places as holy, as accessible only to certain religious officials, and so on. An obvious way to do this is for the group to own the building as property, and use its property rights to exercise the necessary degree of control. So the social boundary between the community of faith and the outside world is expressed as a physical boundary between the area that is under the community's control and the rest of the neighborhood.

It is a distinctive feature of the modern state, an institution that first emerged in Europe in the fifteenth and sixteenth centuries and has now become the dominant form of political organization worldwide, that it should attempt to make social boundaries and territorial boundaries converge. It does this first of all by claiming sole political jurisdiction over the territory it claims as its own—in other words, it tolerates no rival political authorities in the territory in question, but insists that its law and its policy should prevail throughout—and second, by attempting to make *nationality* the paramount form of social identity. The principle is that everyone who resides permanently in the territory should share in a common national identity, and that this identity should override other characteristics that might cause social boundaries to be drawn differently, whether within the state or between states. So nationality is to take precedence over class, or ethnicity, or religion, features which potentially can divide people inside state boundaries, or unite them across these boundaries (think of international workers' movements, pan-Islamism, etc.). If these identities were to prevail, then social boundaries and territorial boundaries would no longer map neatly onto one another.

Where states have succeeded in becoming nation-states, in the sense just described, whether by setting their borders in the appropriate places or by carrying out a nation-building program among their populations, they have certain undeniable advantages. Because their citizens are bound together by a common identity that overrides their differences, it is relatively easy to

mobilize them for common projects such as national defense or rapid economic development. Citizens are also more likely to have confidence in the
legal system, and in the readiness of their fellow citizens to comply with it.
Because of the solidarity that exists within the nation, redistribution carried
out in the name of social justice becomes more feasible. But the cost associated
with these benefits is a suppression of other forms of identity that conflict with
the nation-state model. Thus ethnic groups whose members straddle the
boundaries of two or more states may have to choose whether to acquire separate nationalities, or struggle for political recognition as nations in their own
right; in the meantime, their lives within the existing states may be made
uncomfortable, as they suffer from hostility and discrimination. Transnational
forms of solidarity, for instance those grounded in adherence to a common
religion, are prevented from developing fully, for fear that they would undermine loyalty to the states system. Such costs have led a number of contemporary thinkers to argue that the nation-state model is fast becoming obsolete,
and that we should aim to return to a world in which social boundaries and
territorial boundaries are no longer tightly linked. This would mean, in particular, downplaying the significance of the existing "hard" borders between
states in favor of a new world order in which boundaries still exist, but they are
"softer" and do not necessarily mark the limits of exclusive political jurisdictions. People living in any one place might be subject to several different
systems of political authority, none of which claimed the kind of monopoly
that states have traditionally claimed for themselves.

But ought we to move in this direction? This depends, of course, on our
ethical assessment of boundaries of both kinds, social and territorial—whether
we value them, and how we understand their purpose. And this in turn will
depend on the underlying ethical perspective from which we ask such questions. The rationale for the present book is precisely to see how different
ethical traditions, religious and secular, have dealt with the boundaries issue.
Our contributors were asked to reflect on a number of key question that arise
when boundaries are being debated, and to see how the tradition they represent would answer them. The questions cluster around two separate but closely
related concerns: boundaries as delimiters of property rights and boundaries as
delimiters of political rights. Under the first heading, a number of questions
arise. What does it mean to "own" something from a moral point of view?
What, if anything, justifies the holding of private property by individuals?
What resources are not properly subject to private ownership? When should
rights to private property give way to the interests of the wider community?
How far, for instance, should we require individuals to redistribute some of
their property to those in need, and by what means do we implement distributive justice, private or public?

Under the second heading fall questions relating to jurisdiction. Should
territorial frontiers mark jurisdictional boundaries at all, and if so, what can

justify them? Or should we ideally aim for some form of more inclusive community than that afforded by modern nation-states, perhaps even a world political community? If territorial boundaries are going to exist, how "hard" or "soft" should they be? In other words, how difficult or easy should it be to move people and goods across them, to travel, to migrate, and so forth? And how far should territorial boundaries be made to coincide with social boundaries, particularly where these take the form of ethnic or national divisions? More broadly, how does each tradition understand cultural diversity: is it a deeply embedded feature of human identity, or something that can and should be submerged in a common humanity? Finally, since what nation-states claim above all is *autonomy*, the right to self-determination within their territorial borders, we asked contributors to record whether this demand has an ethical basis, or whether it should be seen simply as an aspect of power politics in the contemporary world.

The ethical traditions surveyed in this book fall broadly into two groups. On the one hand, we have three traditions—international law, classical liberalism, and liberal egalitarianism—that took shape in the era of the modern state, and in large measure in response to its existence. Of the three, international law has traditionally been the most "statist" in orientation. Its origins lie in the writings of seventeenth-century writers such as Grotius, whose aim was precisely to lay down principles to govern the interactions of the emergent states, and it has received its definitive form in the various documents and treaties agreed upon by state representatives during the past century. It is not surprising, therefore, that international law provides a defense of state sovereignty, of the inviolability of established state boundaries, of states' right of control over the natural resources found in their territory, and so forth. But as McCorquodale and Pangalangan both point out in their chapters, this interpretation of international law is increasingly being challenged by those who argue that an interdependent world requires new principles, principles that would pare down the rights of states in the name of human rights, the international redistribution of resources, and environmental concerns that transcend national boundaries. Both authors concede that the practice of international law has so far mainly served to consolidate the nation-states system, but they claim that international law as an ethical tradition is more open and flexible than this suggests, and has the resources to adapt to a changing balance between the international protection of human rights and traditional state prerogatives.

As for classical liberalism, this also emerged under the aegis of the modern state, and its main concern has been to understand how such states can be constituted in a way that preserves the greatest possible area of human freedom. Historically, classical liberals rarely addressed the issue of jurisdictional boundaries directly: they took state boundaries for granted and sought means to limit the power of governments within them. On the other hand, they had a great deal to say about rights of ownership, sometimes going so far as to see jurisdictional boundaries as created simply by property holders contracting together to transfer their rights of enforcement to the state. This heavy emphasis within classical liberalism on individual rights leads to ambivalence about the justification of boundaries among present-day exponents of the tradition. On the one hand, as Lomasky points out in his essay, jurisdictional boundaries may be seen as serving valuable functions, provided they are "soft"—allow easy passage of goods, services, and people across them. On the other hand, as Steiner argues, any border may compromise the rights of those who are excluded by it, especially their rights to an equal share of the earth's natural resources. So although classical liberalism is frequently regarded as offering the main justificatory arguments for the nation-state as a form of political organization, the ethical principles it espouses turn out to be quite critical of state borders in the form that they currently take.

We have used the label "liberal egalitarianism" to describe the liberalism of recent authors such as John Rawls whose commitment to liberty is combined with a strong defense of social justice and state-sponsored redistribution of goods and services. Like its classical predecessor, liberal egalitarianism has emerged and flourished within nation-states, and of all the traditions discussed in this book, it can offer the most systematic ethical defense of the boundaries that exist in the contemporary world. Yet even here there is a paradox. As Kymlicka points out, liberal egalitarianism begins by assuming the moral equality of all human beings, and it therefore seems difficult within this tradition to justify borders whose inevitable effect is to privilege some groups of people at the expense of others. But he goes on to show that a kind of liberal nationalism—and in particular the practice of liberal nation-building—can be justified in liberal egalitarian terms, so long as this is accompanied by a program of redistribution from rich to poor countries that guarantees people everywhere a decent life. Hardin also thinks that a consequentialist defense of liberal nationalism can be given, but he is highly critical of attempts to extend this to ethnic and cultural groups within states. Assigning rights to such groups, he argues, is to privilege collective autonomy—the claim of groups to determine their members' way of life—at the expense of individual freedom. For Hardin, then, territorial boundaries are less offensive to liberal principles than social boundaries, which threaten to trap individuals in impoverished and stultifying cultural enclaves.

Whereas international law, classical liberalism, and liberal egalitarianism are ethical traditions formed in the modern period, the remaining traditions described in this book are considerably older. They first took shape in societies that were very different from those of the contemporary world—in particular, their political systems were significantly different from the modern state, and as a result, boundaries were not defined and enforced in the way that is now familiar to us. So these traditions have had to adapt their ethical thinking to a world in which nation-states have become the primary form of political organization, and they have done so with a greater or lesser degree of discomfort. By the same token, however, at least some of these traditions may be better placed than those in the first group to guide us in thinking about the ethics of a post-national world order, precisely because they do not assume that social boundaries and territorial boundaries should be made to coincide with one another.

The oldest traditions are Confucianism and Judaism. The former has traditionally been associated with the writings of Confucius, a Chinese philosopher who sought to propagate his ethical teachings among the political leaders of the fifth century B.C. As the essays by Chan and Nylan indicate, however, scholars are divided on the origins of the ethical system known in Chinese as *Ru jia*, which is commonly translated as "Confucianism." The extent to which *Ru jia* should be associated with Confucius and his early followers remains highly controversial, as do the questions of when and by whose efforts a "Confucian" tradition developed.

Confucian ethics has a strongly cosmopolitan flavor. Although Confucian scholars recognized the *de facto* existence of territorial boundaries, they never attributed ethical significance to them. While Confucians contrasted the civilized people living in the central area of China with the "barbarians" living on the margins, as Chan and Nylan point out, they had no notion of ethnic or national self-determination. Instead, the barbarians were to be brought peacefully under the benevolent rule of the Chinese emperor. According to Chan, the highest form of political rule was universal kingship, whereby a virtuous ruler would draw all the peoples of the world—"all under Heaven" (*tian xia*)—into his jurisdiction. In contrast, Nylan suggests that the idea of universal rule is a modern, Western-influenced reading of Confucian sources, whereas a strict reading of the earliest texts indicates a more restricted understanding of the ruler's domain.

Nonetheless, both authors agree that in Confucian philosophy neither social nor territorial boundaries finally matter, when compared to the moral quality of human relationships—relationships which begin with the family and extend outward to encompass the whole of humankind. This unbounded understanding of human relationships also colors Confucian attitudes to rights of property. Confucians accept private property but couple this with a strong ethical obligation to succor the needy. Moreover, although this obligation is strongest with respect to those connected by familial and other such ties, in principle it applies to strangers, too, and so to human beings worldwide.

In Judaism, boundaries of both kinds take on much greater significance. The picture here is complicated by the fact that the Jewish ethical tradition has evolved over a long historical period, in the course of which the situation of the Jews themselves has changed radically (original settlement in the land of Canaan, exile, return to Israel, the Jewish Diaspora, the modern foundation of the state of Israel). These changes have meant that Jewish understanding both of social boundaries—between Jews and gentiles especially—and of territorial borders of the two kinds we have distinguished (jurisdiction and property) have altered significantly, as Novak's essay makes clear. In general, we can say that for Jews, as a people who see themselves as having a special relationship to God, it has been a matter of great significance to preserve their distinct identity, especially in those periods when they were deprived of their own territory. So although the Jewish ethical tradition contains principles governing the rightful treatment of gentiles, it also includes rules designed to regulate admission to the Jewish community through conversion. As for territory, Judaism famously includes the belief that the Jews' right to occupy and control the land of Israel was conferred directly on them by God, though it is worth underlining that this grant was conditional on Jewish adherence to moral law. Judaism does contain certain cosmopolitan elements, as Zohar reminds us in his essay: it includes prophetic visions of the human race eventually being reunited in a single polity. Nonetheless, its central vision is of a religiously defined community rightfully asserting its primacy in a particular territory—the vision that has made the politics of Israel so fraught with conflict.

In Christian ethics, we discover a series of underlying tensions that have allowed Christians to answer questions about boundaries in quite different ways. On the one hand, Christianity is a universal religion which commands us to see all human beings as God's children, and therefore to treat them equally. On the other hand, Christian thinkers have recognized that imperfect humans need to live in communities of more limited scope, with the political capacity to organize their common life, and this entails differentiation between insiders and outsiders. They have also at various times drawn sharp contrasts between the faithful and infidels, and have sanctioned forceful ways of defending the former and proselytizing the latter, in defiance of existing political boundaries—thus Christian writers have justified crusades against infidels and heretics and the imperial conquest of non-Christian peoples. More recently, however, Christian universalism has taken a humanitarian form, stressing the obligation to protect the human rights and meet the human needs of people worldwide, and opposing the idea that states have absolute rights of sovereignty over the resources that lie within their borders.

In the two essays on Christian ethics included here, Miller lays most emphasis on the cosmopolitan aspects of Christianity, documenting both its bellicose and its humanitarian faces, while Biggar shows, in contrast, how the Christian understanding of human nature can lead naturally to a liberal form of nationalism that recognizes the value inherent in bounded political communities. Miller also looks closely at Christian attitudes to private property, demonstrating a recurrent belief among thinkers in this tradition that property rights must always yield to the urgent needs of others and the common good of the community.

A similar emphasis on the contingent nature of private property is evident in Islamic ethics. As Zaman and Nyang both indicate, Islamic law (*shari'a*) upholds the right of individuals to private property. Muslim scholars frequently point out that the prophet Muhammad himself was a leading businessman of Mecca before the beginning of his prophetic mission. Yet ownership and the use of property is circumscribed by moral obligations toward one's family and the needy in the community. Distributive justice is not simply an ethical demand upon Muslims; it takes the form of a religious-legal institution, the *zakat* (tax on surplus wealth), which is one of the five pillars of the faith. As Zaman points out, *zakat* and the general Islamic principles enjoining social welfare have led many modern Muslims to argue for the creation of an international redistribution mechanism, whereby the oil-rich Muslim countries would share their vast wealth with the poorer countries. These appeals are made in the name of the continued relevance of the Islamic concept of a universal community, the *umma*. So far such claims have been resisted by those interpreting Islamic ethics to fit the reality of more circumscribed Muslim communities, those residing within modern states.

Distributive justice claims are only one of a range of issues relating to boundaries that divide contemporary Muslims. Islam, like Christianity, defines itself as a universal mission. Unlike Christianity, it developed a theory of international relations that formed an intrinsic part of its legal system—a theory that was far more complex in its approach to the problems of religious pluralism and territorial sovereignty than the traditional division of the world into *dar al-Islam* (land of Islam) and *dar al-harb* (land of war) would allow. Indeed, both Zaman and Nyang suggest that these terms had less to do with territoriality than with jurisdiction. *Dar al-Islam* was any area or any community that accepted the supremacy of the *shari'a*. In the case of non-Muslim communities, such acceptance in theory conferred a wide area of autonomy— territorial and jurisdictional—into which the Islamic state could not intrude. Conversely, *dar al-harb* implied any area where the jurisdiction of the *shari'a* was absent, leading by implication to lawlessness and insecurity for Muslims and non-Muslims residing there. Of course, this medieval Islamic worldview was never fully realized, and today it faces obsolescence as Muslims accommodate to the reality of international boundaries. Yet, no one would deny that Islamic ethics continue to inform the controversies among Muslims on how and when they should make such accommodations.

The natural law tradition was for many centuries associated with Christian ethics, but its origins lie in classical antiquity, and specifically in the writings of Greek and Roman Stoics. Whether in its religious or its secular guise, it postulates universal norms by which to judge human institutions, and by the same token it does not regard cultural differences between human groups as having deep ethical significance. Yet central to the natural law tradition, as Boyle emphasizes in his essay, is the idea of a human community pursuing the common good of its members under a system of authority, and this means that boundaries are acceptable when they help to facilitate this. Commonplace features of human existence—the fact that people who live in close proximity to one another need rules to govern their interactions, for instance—mean that political jurisdictions must be primarily territorial. Natural lawyers do not take a principled stand on whether political authority should be national or international in scope, but they do recognize the need for discrete local juris-dictions if authority is to be exercised effectively.

Thinking about questions of property and distributive justice in this tradi-tion has evolved significantly over the centuries. Private property has always been justified as an essential component of the common good, but from Aqui-nas onward natural lawyers have recognized that when human beings are in urgent need, they are permitted to set aside established property rights. In the present century this principle has been elaborated by Catholic natural lawyers into a defense of social justice and the welfare state.

In his response to Boyle, Rabkin develops a strand of natural law thinking associated with seventeenth- and eighteenth-century European and American liberals, that of natural rights. Natural rights theorists, he suggests, view the state primarily as a vehicle for the securing of the widest possible range of individual freedoms, constrained only by constitutional limitations that per-mit the flourishing of a civil society. On the theoretical level, this means that such a state bears obligations only toward its own citizens. The state's obliga-tions to ensure social welfare, for example—minimal in any case—are con-fined to the needs of those residing within its jurisdiction. Any assistance to those beyond its boundaries is altruism. On the practical level, a natural rights approach dictates for Rabkin that a state's borders be relatively "hard." The right of immigration, for example, is tempered by the state's foremost obliga-tion to preserve the social and economic welfare of its own populace.

We shall not in this introduction attempt to draw extended comparisons between the ethical traditions included in the book, leaving this task for Philpott's concluding overview. There are two questions, though, that may trouble the reader and that deserve an answer here. First, why treat secular and religious traditions together in the same volume? Second, why choose these particular traditions, and not others that may have an equally strong claim to be included? In answer to the first, we reject any claim that secular and reli-gious modes of thought are wholly distinct. At least as far as the issues dis-cussed in this book are concerned, we find a great deal of common ground between the ideas and arguments of thinkers whom we would classify as secu-lar and those whom we would classify as religious. Indeed, the secular/religious distinction is difficult to apply in some cases: how are we to classify Confucianism and the natural law tradition, for instance?

A further consideration here is that in today's world it is possible to combine political ideas drawn from secular and religious sources in creative ways. For a large part of the world's population, moral discourse is conducted from within religious value systems. Indeed, such religious values may permeate the legal and political orders under which they live. Yet they may also appeal to universal principles of predominantly secular origin that have become a lingua franca in contemporary international politics — the idea of human rights, for instance, or of the self-determination of peoples. Religious thinkers have grappled with such ideas to see how far they are consistent with, or even derivable from, the traditions they represent. Thus any notion that we have two hermetically sealed forms of ethical discourse, one secular, one religious, must be rejected out of hand.

If we ask what, in general, are the relevant differences between religious and secular modes of thought, in cases where the distinction is reasonably clearcut, we find three principal ones. The first has already been mentioned: The religious traditions first took shape in a world where the modern state had not yet become the predominant form of political organization, and, although they have found ways to accommodate this institution, they are less closely tied to it than the three main secular traditions surveyed here. The second difference is more philosophical: The religious traditions ground their political morality in a fuller, more substantive understanding of human good, deriving ultimately from their understanding of human beings' place in the Divine order, whereas the secular traditions begin with the idea that human beings have certain generic interests—interests in liberty, material resources, and so forth—but try to avoid taking a stand on questions of ultimate value. (This contrast is explored much more fully in Philpott's concluding chapter.) The third difference is that religious traditions must draw a distinction of some kind between those inside the community of faith and those outside; there is evidently no secular equivalent to this dividing line.

Yet these differences, important though they are, do not translate into a clear contrast between a "religious" and a "secular" perspective on boundaries, as readers of this book will discover. On the contrary, within both camps we encounter reasons to attach greater significance to social and territorial boundaries, but equally, reasons to attach lesser significance to such boundaries in the name of common humanity. Religious traditions, for instance, do characteristically counsel members of the faith community to observe different rules of conduct when dealing with fellow members than when dealing with outsiders, and may even recommend that the faith community should form its own state; but at the same time they may impose obligations toward humankind as a whole, such as obligations to help needy strangers. Where the balance between these two imperatives is struck varies as much within traditions as it does among them, as the essays in this book demonstrate.

As to the second question, "Why these perspectives and not others?", we can be more succinct. We have chosen perspectives that have had, and continue to have, a major impact on the shape and conduct of political communities; in that practical sense they are significant perspectives. But we are also aware that other traditions might equally well have been chosen: Marxism, Hinduism, and Buddhism are obvious examples. Moreover, different, equally important questions about perspectives on boundaries may be posed to all the traditions. We anticipate these possibilities being taken up in later volumes in this series. A companion volume to this book will focus on the making and unmaking of boundaries, including the question of how rights to territory are created and transmitted, and the difficult issue of political secession. What we hope to have done here, in the spirit of the Ethikon Institute, is to encourage dialogue and debate among proponents of diverse ethical perspectives on questions that have taken on a new urgency in contemporary national and international politics. In particular, we have attempted to breach some of the boundaries that have kept these traditions apart: religious vs. secular, eastern vs. western, classical vs. modern. Voices other than those found here will no doubt join the discussion, as we search for ways in which human communities can live together on a rapidly shrinking planet.

One

Christian Attitudes toward Boundaries

METAPHYSICAL AND GEOGRAPHICAL

RICHARD B. MILLER

CHRISTIANS began to think systematically about the ethics of land, territory, and boundaries within a specific set of historical circumstances. European claims to dominion in the New World during the sixteenth and seventeenth centuries generated a new range of questions in moral theology for Catholics and Protestants alike, theology developed most notably by Cajetan, Vitoria, Soto, Suarez, Molina, Las Casas, Gentili, and Grotius. Yet these authors did not generate normative principles for addressing questions of dominion and boundaries *de novo*; they drew on a tradition of categories, distinctions, and concrete practices that give substance to the Christian imagination regarding political and social issues.

Here I want to identify elements of that tradition, focusing on broad themes and distinctions that frame much of what western Christians have presupposed in various discussions of boundaries, ownership, distribution, diversity, mobility, and autonomy during the early modern and modern periods. We will see that Christianity asserts the priority of metaphysical boundaries over geographical ones. Central to this priority is the belief that God is the highest good, a source of love and order in this-worldly affairs, requiring loyalty that transcends the divisions of political life. Moreover, although some Christians articulate a clear rationale for boundaries, dominion, and regional loyalties, such a rationale stands in tension with obligations to love the neighbor, near or distant, irrespective of political affiliation. Whether (or how) Christians are to reconcile their duties to others, given the importance and corrigibility of borders, remains a contested issue in the tradition today.

With these thoughts in mind, I will pursue three goals in this chapter, which is largely descriptive and analytic: first, to represent Western Christianity's various responses to the issues before us in this volume; second, to call attention to tensions within those responses; third, to identify how some Christians have sought to resolve those tensions by specifying the practical requirements of duties to their neighbors. In this last capacity I will discuss how Christian social critics have defined the scope and weight of their obligations to others as these duties connect with cases of individual or collective conscience.[1]

Boundaries

How Christians assess territorial boundaries is largely a function of how they conceive the boundary that distinguishes creation from its Creator. Ethical and political questions are framed by an understanding of the relationship between an unchanging God and the changing, finite, natural order. Traditionally, God and creation have been understood as ontologically different, constituting separate orders of being. Christians believe that God is the source and sustainer of natural life, and this belief leads to important ethical and psychological consequences. Individuals who trespass the boundary separating finite from infinite being, extending themselves beyond human limitations, are judged as guilty of the most fundamental wrongdoing, the sin of pride. Accordingly, the religious and ethical life must be shaped by the virtue of humility, in which the believer gratefully acknowledges her dependence on God for life and salvation.[2] Boundaries are important because they define an order of being and value, along with corresponding attitudes that should structure the Christian's life.

Marking off the boundary that distinguishes God from creation, of course, does not say much about how Christians are to understand regional or other boundaries that provide the specific contours of social life. In general, one measure of an individual's relationship with God is how she relates to her neighbor. Love of God and love of neighbor, while distinct, are not irrelevant to or independent of each other. Mainstream Christianity typically believes that failure to love God properly, a life that lacks the grace necessary for *humilitas*, will generate disordered relationships with one's neighbors—relationships affected by *libido dominandi*.[3] Those who deify their own needs and desires are prone to violate the boundaries that require Christians to respect the needs and desires of fellow creatures. Ignoring one set of boundaries leads prideful humanity to ignore other limits as well; a wrongly ordered moral psychology is illusory and dangerous. Conversely, honoring one's limits before God ought to produce a corresponding set of behavioral limits with respect to oneself and the created order. For Christians, matters of political ethics are informed by considerations of moral and religious psychology. In personal and political affairs, the Christian life is marked by an understanding of finite freedom, of bounded love.

Various subtraditions within Christianity have sought to specify in greater detail how individuals are to understand the patterns and processes of the created order, the laws of nature that ought to give direction to individual and collective decision making about this-worldly affairs. God is not only the source and sustainer of natural life; the deity also has ordered creation according to principles that are discernible to human reason and that stand apart from positive law or social convention. Principal among such natural law tenets is the claim that individuals have an innate tendency to develop a common life, that membership in community is a natural human good.[4]

Such natural tendencies nonetheless rely on various customs, which serve instrumentally to facilitate the terms of social cooperation, among other goods. On this basis, Christians can sanction geographical boundaries, for such conventions are necessary to mark off one human precinct from another. Territories have their own identities and autonomous jurisdictions; they provide useful ways for human groups to establish their own habits, loyalties, and practices for common living. As a natural fact, human beings seem to need a sense of place.

How Christians are to view territorial boundaries is a function, then, of how their affections or loves are ordered, and how individuals make practical arrangements in their natural quest for a common life. These ideas derive, respectively, from Augustine and Aquinas, and they inform much of what Christians say about social and political conventions like geographical boundaries. Moreover, when considered together, these ideas frame the ethics of borders in Christianity, for they alert us to a tension between duties to near and distant neighbors. Natural law considerations lend credence to the notion that borders help to fulfill basic human goods, which, as a practical matter, involve regional loyalties and fellow-feeling. For this reason, at various times Christians have affirmed the importance of location and particularity: the feudal kingdom, Calvin's Geneva, the New England commonwealth, and the national or ethnic church are familiar examples. At the same time, Christianity requires an indiscriminate, unconditional love of others, irrespective of political, social, or national affiliation. Borders ask us to privilege local solidarities, but Christian *agape*, exemplified by Jesus's teaching and example, is altruistic and cosmopolitan.[5]

Given these competing demands between the natural law and the law of love, various theologians have sought to define an "order of charity," a hierarchy of loves and loyalties required by the complex relationships of everyday life.[6] All else being equal, may I love my wife more than my mother-in-law? My son more than my nephew? Fellow educators more than affluent stockbrokers? The living more than the dead? These questions are a function of how our loves are constrained by nature and circumstance, requiring us to define our responsibilities toward others. But Christian thinkers differ widely over whether such a ranking is permissible, and, if so, how individuals should concretely order their loyalties.[7] To many Christians, allowing believers to develop a hierarchy of responsibilities accedes too much to everyday custom, thereby dulling the edge of Christianity's capacity for social criticism, its radical message of selfless, indiscriminate love.

However such debates are sorted out, metaphysical boundaries in Christianity do not directly inform the ethics and politics of geographical borders. That is because, in Christianity, political developments are conceived as part of an order that is present but passing away. Christian thinking about the ethics and politics of boundaries takes into account not only the difference between the Creator and creation, but also the difference between time and eternity. The Kingdom of God—communion with God and the saints—is relevant to life in this world in that it represents an ideal of friendship and equality, but it is an object of hope, never to be identified with any specific political or social arrangement.[8] Christians believe themselves to be on a pilgrimage in this life, and no temporal reality is to be elevated to the status of an unchanging good.[9]

This distinction between eternity and time has clear implications for Christian politics and ethics, especially among those who wish to preserve Christianity's radical message, for it suggests that borders are ephemeral phenomena, and that regional loyalty might weaken the demands of neighbor-love. Conventions that encourage us to localize our commitments may also encourage us to find eternal satisfaction in temporal activities, thereby generating disordered attachments toward the passing realities of political and social life.[10]

Boundaries in Christianity, then, help define a hierarchy that distinguishes between absolute and relative goods. God, the eternal, unchanging good, is the only object of unqualified loyalty. All other relations are to be framed by an understanding of how temporal, created reality relies upon and remains subordinate to the immutable good.[11] Those who order their lives by these distinctions understand (1) the duty to respect the boundaries that distinguish natural life with its intrinsic integrities, and (2) the mandate of universal love and unconditional solidarity. Christians traditionally embrace the second of these two claims, and sometimes the first as well. In any event, the extent to which territorial boundaries have a place in Christian politics and ethics is a function of whether borders can function within an overarching theocentric cosmology.

Within this cosmology, Christians typically view regional boundaries as one feature of life in the Earthly City, complete with local loves and what Augustine calls a "shadowy peace." The goods associated with civic life have a real but relative status, and boundaries may find sanction in Christian belief insofar as they contribute to these lesser goods. Like political authority, coercion, and (for some Christians) war, territorial boundaries function as an instrumental good. So long as they are not used to the disadvantage of others, boundaries may enable groups to coordinate their political and social arrangements toward a common good, one that is bound together by temporal attachments and practical needs. But these needs are relative and provisional, enjoyed by Christians as fugitive goods when compared to the hopes and ideals represented by the Kingdom of God.

Ownership and Distribution

In Christianity questions of ownership and distribution of land and resources are informed by a special concern for the poor. In the Gospel of Mark readers are told that, in response to a man who asked how to attain eternal life, Jesus responds, "Go, sell what you have, and give to the poor, and you will have treasure in heaven" (Mark 10:21). The Great Judgment in the Gospel of Matthew describes Jesus as saying: "Truly, I say to you, as you did it for the least of these my brethren, you did it to me" (Matt. 25:40). The Gospel of Luke adds,

> Blessed are you poor, for yours is the kingdom of heaven.
> Blessed are you that hunger now, for you shall be satisfied. . . .
> But woe to you that are rich, for you have received your consolation.
> Woe to you that are full now, for you shall hunger.
>
> (Luke 6:20–22, 24–25).

On these grounds Christians are sometimes suspicious of worldly goods and attend carefully to substantive issues of distributive justice.

Moreover, questions of ownership are framed by the boundary that separates Creator and creation, eternity and time, as well as by the patterns and processes that provide integrity and direction to the created order. That means that Christians often approach matters of ownership according to two general requirements: (1) to have rightly ordered loves, in which relative goods are loved relatively, and absolute goods are loved absolutely, and (2) to make practical arrangements that enable individuals to flourish according to their natural tendencies and endowments. As a result, Christians possess distinct and, at times, competing orientations for addressing issues of ownership: love of God and the neighbor in need, on the one hand, and considerations derived from the law of nature, on the other.

Attention to rightly ordered loves, as I have suggested, focuses attention on matters of moral psychology. How, Christians often ask, should individuals attach themselves to the material world? How should the will be ordered? What priorities ought to shape the religious and moral life? This attention to rightly ordered loves has traditionally implied a set of limits for ownership, and such limits typically have been understood in light of the common goods of creation. Many Christians believe that the goods of creation are given by God to be enjoyed by all (see Lev. 25). In early Christian times this conviction meant that, ideally, no one was to be left wanting or denied resources that are basic to human life and well-being. One measure of rightly ordered attachments is the extent to which an individual succeeds in putting private property to good use, given the requirements of living in community. In this respect, Christians from the earliest times distinguished their beliefs from the Roman view of absolute ownership, which imposed no limits on the right to private property.

Belief that the goods of creation are to be held in common led to two specific approaches toward property in relation to the poor in early Christianity. The first, recorded in the book of Acts, is one of communal sharing. We are told that first-generation Christians in Jerusalem "sold their possessions and goods and distributed them to all, as any had need" (Acts 2:45). But early Christians did not create a communistic commune. Peter tells Ananias that he is not obligated to sell his property, and having sold it he still has the proceeds at his disposal (Acts 5:4). Among the Jerusalem Christians, the over-riding principle was that "no one said that the things which he possessed were his own, but they had everything in common (Acts 4:32)." How material goods were actually shared depended on the needs of some and the free generosity of others.

The second approach, based on the writings of Paul, requires almsgiving. Here the idea is that the blessings given to some oblige them to assist others who are not well-off, that private property is to be voluntarily redistributed. Paul instructs the church in Corinth to contribute liberally to him so that he may distribute funds to needy Christians in Jerusalem (1 Cor. 16:1–4). Macedonian Christians have contributed generously, he observes, and he urges those in Corinth to give similarly: "Each one must do as he has made up his mind, not reluctantly or under compulsion, for God loves a cheerful giver" (1 Cor. 9:7).

In either case, the idea is that private property is not an absolute good, that there are limits to property as a value and source of satisfaction. For early Christians, the needs of fellow believers defined those limits in practical, tangible ways. The goal, as Paul describes it, is to produce equality within the community, so that "your abundance at the present time should supply their want, so that their abundance may supply your want. . . . As it is written, 'He who gathered much had nothing over, and he who gathered little had no lack'" (2 Cor. 18:13–15). For other Christians, the central question surrounding private ownership was one of degree or, more accurately, proportionality. Clement of Alexandria (c. 150–215), for example, argues that accumulating wealth is not intrinsically evil, for the test of virtue is whether material possessions are the center of value. Clement thus understands Jesus's instruction to "go, sell what you have, and give to the poor" (Mark 10:21) as a command to renounce materialistic passions, not material wealth per se. Indeed, individuals who are relatively impoverished may be guilty of avarice; the question is not *whether* but *how* one relates oneself to property and dominion. So Clement writes, "A poor and destitute man may be found intoxicated with lusts; and a man rich in worldly goods temperate, poor in indulgences, trustworthy, intelligent, pure, chastened."[12] Here the issue of ownership is framed not so much by the needs of others, but according to the character of the owner. Much of Christianity has taken this route, focusing on the dispositions involved in owning property. Virtue and vice pertain not to redistributive principles or the neighbor in need, but to self-referring properties, the internal ordering of the soul. Accumulated property is dangerous not because it contributes to an unjust or uncharitable economic order, but because it draws the soul away from the love of God.

Yet even this emphasis on character and virtue implies limits, a social mortgage on private property. Clement argues that the most virtuous way to relate to one's possessions is to give them away, that ownership beyond sufficiency is contrary to the natural, created order. All humanity is meant to live in harmony; failure to share is inhuman. Indeed, if Christianity required material renunciation, Clement observes, then it would be impossible to exercise Christian charity to the poor. "How could one give food to the hungry, and drink to the thirsty, clothe the naked, and shelter the houseless," he asks, "if each man first divested himself of all these [material] things?"[13] Virtue requires not the wholesale rejection of property, but temperance and generosity. Possessions are provided by God "for the use of men; and they lie to our hand, and are put under our power, as material and instruments which are for good use to those who know the instrument."[14]

Subsequent to these developments, responses to questions about love, virtue, and material attachment took more radical shape, interpreting Jesus's instruction to renounce worldly goods in literal rather than figurative terms.[15] In the fourth century of the common era, Christian monks fled in desperation and social protest to the deserts of Egypt. Followers of Antony and Pachomius, two central figures of Egyptian monasticism, held that faith and private ownership were incompatible.[16] Those who followed the tradition of Antony followed an ascetic ideal of absolute poverty, living in the desert with only the barest essentials. The chief idea was that, to be authentic, spiritual detachment from worldly goods must be incarnated in tangible, material ways. Poverty to the point of deprivation was a virtue; love of God involved radical self-denial.[17]

Those who followed the example of Pachomius socialized rather than renounced the institution of property. Pachomius's rules for cenobitic monasticism included common possession of all goods. As Justo L. González writes, "In this rule, all things were to be held in common, not only in the sense that they must be at the disposal of the needy in the community, but even more in the sense that no one would be able to dispose of them."[18] The goal of communal monasticism was not to abandon property, but to put a high regard on communal life, including partnership in owning material goods.

Thomas Aquinas's (1227–74) treatment of ownership and theft develops with characteristic clarity the limited right of private property. In the *Summa Theologiae*, Aquinas argues that it is natural for humans to possess external things as regards their use. "Man has a natural dominion over external things," he claims, "because, by his reason and will, he is able to use them for his own profit, as they were made on his account: for the imperfect is always for the sake of the perfect."[19] Private property is necessary, Aquinas adds, because individuals are likelier to care for things when they own them privately rather than collectively. Moreover, as a practical matter there are fewer occasions of disorder and strife when property is privately owned.[20] For Aquinas, the more radical route of selling one's property and giving to the poor is a precept rather than a command, a "counsel of perfection" that obliges only those Christians with a special calling.[21]

But dominion and ownership are not absolute rights for Christians who possess property, as Aquinas argues in his discussion of the Sixth (or Seventh) Commandment, "Thou shalt not steal." Among other reasons, theft is wrong because it is "contrary to justice, which is a matter of giving each person his due."[22] Yet for Aquinas the prohibition against taking property does not hold universally; there are some impoverished individuals who have no alternative but to take another's possessions. About such circumstances, Aquinas writes, "everything is in common. Therefore a person who takes somebody else's property which necessity has made common again so far as he is concerned does not commit theft."[23] The notion of "theft" implies circumstances of moderate provision; in those circumstances, it is possible to justify the institution of private property. But such a justification is relative to circumstances that are not applicable to those who suffer from extreme deprivation. Indeed, to take property that necessity has rendered "common" is to acquire one's just due. Private ownership of external goods may be conducive to order and peace, but such goods should also be used "as common, so that one is ready to communicate them to others in their need."[24]

By the Middle Ages, then, the limited right of private property and the criterion of right use were recognizable features of Christianity. These concepts became mainstays in Christian thought and practice during the early modern period, providing a platform from which to develop arguments about the connection between rightful ownership, territories, and access to natural and human resources. In the sixteenth century, the issue of private property in relation to territories and boundaries generated cases for practical deliberation when questions arose about the right of Spanish conquerors to the land and territory of indigenous Americans.[25] However, in this context traditional ideas were designed more to protect individuals from encroachment than to require individuals or groups to share in common goods. Francisco Vitoria

(c. 1483–1546) argues that many Spanish claims to dominion were false pretexts to acquisition—that alleged heresy, sin, irrationality, or madness on the part of native Americans were all insufficient bases for acquiring their land. Dominion is granted by God and cannot be denied for these reasons. Addressing his views directly to Charles V, Vitoria held that territorial dominion is only a temporal, natural good, distinct from supernatural matters of faith, religion, and salvation. Amerindians have dominion owing to the natural fact that they inhabit their land and "have judgment like other men." Vitoria writes:

> This is self-evident because they have some order in their affairs: they have properly organized cities, proper marriages, magistrates and overlords, laws, industries, and commerce, all of which require the use of reason. They likewise have a form of religion, and they correctly apprehend things which are evident to other men, which indicates the use of reason. Furthermore, "God and nature never fail in the things necessary" for the majority of the species, and the chief attribute of man is reason.[26]

Natural reason is the great leveler, putting indigenous Americans morally and politically on a par with the Spanish invaders.

Complicating this line of argument, Vitoria adds that the Spanish have a natural right to seek conversions, that "Christians have the right to preach and announce the Gospel in the lands of the barbarians."[27] In his mind, this right can be inferred from the natural law, because "brotherly correction is as much part of natural law as brotherly love."[28] This right likewise permits the Spaniards to use force to defend themselves if they are attacked by native Americans or to protect Christian converts if they are attacked by others who reject Christian teaching.[29] Although Vitoria claims that Amerindians have the right to their land, he acknowledges limits to that right: They may not obstruct Christian evangelization. Truth has rights, and native Americans' right of dominion may not bar Spaniards from exercising their rights of evangelization, free passage, and self-defense. The indigenous population is thus bound by the natural law to allow the Spaniards to travel, teach, and preach. However, Amerindians are not obligated to accept Christian tenets, and war cannot be used against them to force conversions.[30] The main point here is that natural rights and the natural law allow for both dominion and the freedom of religious preaching; the latter might at times limit the former. In Vitoria's mind, this tension is not between revelation and reason, or religion and natural law; it is a tension within the natural law itself. In this way, Vitoria crafts a basis on natural law grounds for using force to protect some religious interests—so long as the use of force is subsumed by the justice of self-protection.

Owing to the work of Vitoria and others, the idea that lacking religious orthodoxy is a sufficient condition for forfeiting rights to dominion has disappeared in the modern period. But the idea that private ownership and dominion are limited rights has survived. This fact is especially apparent in the tradition of papal encyclicals, beginning with Leo XIII's *Rerum novarum* (1891) and continuing throughout the twentieth century, a tradition that emphasizes universal human rights and the dignity of all persons as images of God.[31]

Witness as one example the writings of Paul VI. Drawing on the principle of the universal purpose of created things and the commandment to love the neighbor, Paul VI writes that "private property does not constitute for anyone an absolute and unconditioned right."[32] When others lack what is necessary for basic well-being, "no one is justified in keeping for his exclusive use what he does not need."[33] But Paul VI does not repeat the early Christian notion that excess property should be voluntarily relinquished. Rather, coercion may be used in some circumstances: "If certain landed estates impede the general prosperity because they are extensive, unused or poorly used, or because they bring hardship to peoples or are detrimental to the interest of the country, the common good sometimes demands their expropriation."[34] Echoing the views of Aquinas, Paul VI suggests that the needs of humanity outweigh the rights of dominion when these two claims conflict and that, as a matter of justice, one may take possession without consent of the owner. Moreover, for Paul VI the problem has less to do with how materialism might corrupt the virtue of the wealthy than with how the disparity of resources has produced inequitable economic arrangements worldwide.

Two features of Paul VI's statements stand out. First, the right of expropriation does not permit individuals to secure basic provisions vis-à-vis a common set of goods, whatever Paul VI might say about the universal purpose of created goods. Rather, he argues that those in need have claims only to goods that others have in surplus: Excessive goods become "common" for those in dire need.

Second, Paul VI's permission of expropriation is confined to participants who are active in the internal affairs of a nation-state. One nation is not permitted to intervene to produce equitable arrangements in another sovereign state's domestic affairs. Relations between states must be regulated by the principle of solidarity with the needy, but coercion is not an appropriate method to acquire territory or other possessions. Rather, he suggests, boundaries remain sacrosanct, allowing for only noncoercive measures to satisfy competing goods. In particular, states should turn to the redistributive and relief efforts of international agencies that rely on a World Fund. Such a fund would use money otherwise spent on military arms, and its aim would be "to relieve the most destitute of this world."[35] Echoing the views of the early church, Paul VI sketches a vision of international sharing, in which the needs of some are met by the voluntary generosity of others.

Liberation theologians—Christians informed by Marxist analysis—typically insist upon a "preferential option for the poor," adding that mainstream

Christian approaches to territory and ownership wrongly proceed by criticizing the institution of surplus wealth rather than poverty.[36] In liberation theology, issues of land and territory include two items typically ignored in standard Christian accounts: first, a critical discussion of the modes by which property has been *acquired* (rather than how it should be redistributed); second, an insistence that discussions of redistribution operate within a liberation rather than a developmental paradigm. Developmentalism, liberationists allege, presumes a situation in which Latin American countries remain dependent on and subservient to the capitalist enterprises of First World nations and corporations. As Gustavo Gutiérrez (1928–) remarks, satisfactory assessment of land and boundaries will not occur until social analysis is framed by the ideal of liberation, focusing on "the aspirations of oppressed peoples and economic classes," and emphasizing "the conflictual aspect of the economic, social, and political process which puts them at odds with wealthy nations and oppressive classes."[37] Emphasis falls on sharing ownership of the means of production, recalling the tradition of collective ownership in early Christianity.[38]

For ecologically minded Christians, issues of territory and ownership call attention not only to duties to the disadvantaged, but also to responsibilities to the natural world itself. Typically such responsibilities are developed under the idea of stewardship. Briefly described, stewardship requires Christians to accept land and natural resources as a divine gift. The goods of creation are to be used with an eye to future generations and to the divine purposes of creation. Stewardship may thus require humans to subordinate their interests to the needs of the biosphere; nonhuman life imposes claims on human decision-making. Accordingly, landed property and natural resources are to be developed not only with human but also with wider natural needs in view—although Christian ethicists are often vague about what those natural purposes are.[39]

Diversity

Territorial boundaries serve an instrumental, functional role, marking off groups that seek practically to coordinate the terms of a common life. Such groups will doubtless be culturally, linguistically, and religiously different, developing codes and habits designed to make their common life more convenient.[40] Insofar as we understand such differences as a function of relative, fugitive goods, they may find sanction within Christian belief and practice. Having separate living spaces is a necessary condition for communities to develop their respective histories, customs, and identities.

Yet even if boundaries may serve some general human function, their exact lines are drawn in specific social and historical circumstances. Providing the social contours of civic life, boundaries are the fruits of contingency and political constraint, not lacking in self-interest. When seen as products of circumstance or accident, and when recognized as potential sources of division among humans, they appear arbitrary from a theological point of view.

One critical question for Christians is whether membership in and loyalty to such communities becomes a final object of value. Temporal communities demand commitment from their citizens; the danger of idolatry is not remote. And idolatry can bring intolerance toward differences, a sense of superiority toward members of other communities. (I will provide examples of such intolerance in Christianity below.) When regional boundaries contribute to overweening collective pride, they produce tendencies that have religious and ethical dimensions: self-righteousness, divisiveness, dogmatism, intolerance, inequality.

Within Christianity these dimensions have been subject to withering criticism, especially (but not only) from twentieth-century Protestants. H. Richard Niebuhr (1894–1962), to take a prominent example, protested against provincialism of all kinds—cultural, national, ethnic, and religious. Niebuhr articulated what Paul Tillich calls the "Protestant principle," a form of religious and social criticism that "contains the divine and human protest against any absolute claim made for a relative reality. . . . The Protestant principle is the judge of every religious and cultural reality, including the religion and culture which calls itself 'Protestant.'"[41]

In Niebuhr's mind, this principle has relevance to two problems. First is the replacement of a disinterested, nonpreferential perspective by partial loyalties and preferential loves. Boundaries that mark off different groups are problematic because they represent the sinful tendency to elevate the particular to the status of the universal. For Niebuhr, the remedy rests in the faith of "radical monotheism," faith in a transcendent object of loyalty that relativizes humanity's cultural and social achievements.[42] Radical monotheism demands a loyalty to "the universal commonwealth of Being," and particular loyalties have meaning only by virtue of their affirmation of and subordination to the "One beyond the many."[43]

Second is the tendency of religions to rationalize rather than criticize forms of provincialism. Drawing on the writings of Max Weber and Ernst Troeltsch, Niebuhr observes the tendency of religious movements, including Christianity, to be more affirmative than critical of cultural practices, especially religious nationalism and patriotic zeal.[44] Religions tend to accommodate themselves to local customs and then rationalize those customs in light of a higher principle. In Christianity, this tendency has led to fragmentation along social, racial, and class lines, in which the earlier unity of Christian belief has given way to a tragic series of internal divisions, all sanctioned by religious claims.[45]

For Niebuhr, the solution to the dangers of parochialism and fragmentation lies not in the Christian affirmation of political, class, or other divisions, but in solidarity with those who suffer innocently. Such solidarity is the distinctive response required by the cross, Niebuhr argues, a unique angle of vision implied by Christian faith and practice. Rather than celebrating the identities formed by boundaries and territories, it is incumbent upon Christians to join in common cause with those who are being crucified by power politics—children, the poor, the infirm, "the humble, little people who have had little to do with the framing of great policies."[46]

Diversity is tolerable, then, within limits established by a theocentric point of view. Individuals need recognizable practices and traditions according to which they interpret themselves and the world around them, and communities serve an important role insofar as they nurture a sense of identity and membership. But for Christians, human life is marked by sin, the temptation to privilege local loyalties and loves. Hence the need for a critical principle, one that scrutinizes local customs from the perspective of transcendence. Religious criticism thereby reveals a range of persons whose needs are the object of attention and care: the innocent victims of history and politics.

Mobility

"Amongst all nations it is considered inhuman to treat strangers and travelers badly without some special cause," Vitoria writes, "humane and dutiful to behave hospitably to strangers."[47] Boundaries that mark off territories have a real but relative value, given their instrumental status in a world marked by finitude and sin. As a general rule, the value of borders and territory should not trump the (stronger) value of hospitality to strangers when those strangers pose no danger to the community.

Mobility across borders involves at least two cases: (1) travel and (2) immigration with subsequent application for membership. Travel is the easier case: Within Christianity, one test of the relativity of boundaries would be the extent to which they are permeable. In the beginning of the world, Vitoria argues, all things were held in common, and "everyone was allowed to visit and travel through any land he wished." Such rights are not eliminated by the institution of property; free human intercourse, itself a natural good, should not be impeded by the rulers of local jurisdictions.[48] Assuming that strangers impose no great hardship on a community, allowing them to enter and exit would seem "humane and dutiful."

To the more difficult question of immigration and membership, Christians (to the best of my knowledge) have not given much systematic thought.[49] At a minimum, however, the Christian imagination is informed by two duties: the obligation to protect the natural inclination for community and participation, and the commandment to love the neighbor, including enemies and strangers.

These two demands generate competing responsibilities, returning us to questions about near and distant neighbors, the order of charity. The need for community and identity would seem to allow for some restrictions across borders. To maintain a sense of "us," political communities must distinguish their members from "others," and such distinctions imply a form of discrimination. Moreover, the formation and continuation of communal identity presupposes that citizens are trained in civic practices, complete with rituals, the recollection of history, and the transmission of local customs in schools and popular culture. For such civic formation to be effective, communities need a relatively stable population, not one that is in flux and flow. For these (and perhaps other) reasons, the requirements of a common life involve restricting the terms of membership.[50] Internal order and local flourishing require limited access; subsequent membership requires that emigrés acquire civic habits that bear the stamp of a community's history and self-understanding.[51]

But as Niebuhr's remarks make plain, Christian responsibilities go beyond near neighbors and civic membership to embrace all humankind, especially those in acute need. The requirement to love the neighbor indiscriminately would suggest duties that transcend borders. How these duties are fulfilled in tangible ways is difficult to specify, but the cosmopolitan aspects of Christianity imply that borders should be opened for those seeking refuge from political and economic oppression. Cosmopolitanism likewise alerts us to the unseemly events that often prompt mass migrations: tyranny, intolerance, famine, or lack of hope at home. For these reasons Christians have cause to consider issues of mobility in tandem with issues of diversity and distribution. Restricting mobility across boundaries can reinforce local prejudice and global economic disparities.

Migration across regional and other borders is also a reminder that our understanding of "near" and "distant" neighbors is subject to change over time. Boundaries are not insuperable barriers, and individuals who were once foreigners can become friends or fellow-citizens within a generation. In this vein, Karl Barth (1886–1968) writes of the fluidity of borders and the idea that groups are bound to absorb others or dissolve into new configurations. Barth observes: "Whole languages of what were once very vital peoples are now extinct, or can live on amongst other peoples only as 'dead' languages. No frontier, however 'natural,' has ever proved stable, nor has any history, however distinctive, been able to guarantee the continuance of a nation."[52] In Barth's mind, the duty of the Christian is to affirm her given language, locale, and history—but only provisionally. The overall impetus is universalist: "to unite loyalty towards those who are historically near with openness towards those who are historically distant."[53] Nations and groups come and go, Barth remarks, and thus "we must not confuse the contrast of near and distant neighbors with the creation of God and its immutable orders."[54]

Autonomy

Christians teach that freedom is found in faithful obedience to God—that true autonomy is actually "theonomy," living under the authority of God's gracious power.[55] Typically addressed to individual consciences, such ideas have also taken on militant political dimensions, leading Christians to expand the geographical region of God's sovereignty. Whether in the context of the medieval crusades, the suppression of minority sects, the encounter with the Amerindians, the wars of the continental Reformation, or the Puritan revolution, Christians have freely invoked religion to justify the use of force to protect if not expand their territorial boundaries. Such justifications, privileging God's law to any set of human conventions, pay little heed to territorial borders or local autonomy. Central to such appeals is the honor of God and the concomitant duty to defend God's justice in the face of alleged infidelity or heresy. Frequently Christians cite various depictions of God-as-warrior in the Hebrew Bible to support the idea that religion, war, and the violation of communal boundaries are compatible (see, e.g., Deut. 20).

Seeking to justify war as a religious crusade, Christians have argued that righteousness should be visible in personal and social institutions: The holy commonwealth tolerates no exceptions or impurity, and war may be an instrument to purge the world of idolatry. In a letter to Christian knights leaving for Jerusalem, for example, Bernard of Clairvaux (1090–1153) writes that "for our sins, the enemy of the Cross has begun to lift his sacrilegious head there, and to devastate with the sword that blessed land, the land of promise. Alas, if there be none to withstand him, he will soon invade the city of the living God, overturn the arsenal of our redemption, and defile the holy places which have been adorned by the blood of the immaculate lamb." Reminding knights that self-sacrifice for the crusade merits an indulgence, Bernard writes that God "puts himself in your debt so that, in return for your taking up arms in his cause, he can reward you with pardon for your sins and everlasting glory."[56]

In the sixteenth and seventeenth centuries, religious justifications for war were used on behalf of killing other Christians rather than "infidels." Advocates for holy war such as Henry Bullinger argued that religion justified war against heretics near and far, believing that God commanded such wars and fought alongside holy warriors.[57] For such Christians, the reign of God, while still a distant hope, must become more clearly manifest in political arrangements. In a holy war one could distinguish clearly between the just and the unjust, and the duty of the former is to enforce the justice of God. Catholics, too, embraced these views: William Cardinal Allen, a seventeenth-century English bishop exiled in Flanders, thought that the defense of Catholicism justified the use of force, and that Protestant rule was to be resisted under the authority of the pope.[58]

In these cases we see the importance of metaphysical boundaries to the exclusion of territorial ones: True Christian belief should be defended as a visible sign of God's sovereignty, regardless of geographical or other borders. Reckoning the demands of justice in these religious terms, Christians have actively intervened in the affairs of various religious and political communities, fighting under the banner of a holy war ideology.

Yet this legacy is not the entire story of Christianity's relation to power, territory, and communal autonomy. Dissident voices of various influence also secured a foothold in the tradition, offering clear counterexamples or direct criticism of intervention and imperialism.

Prominent among the counterexamples are communities that often suffered at the hands of Christian crusaders: members of various Anabaptist groups who sought freedom (and refuge) in southern Germany and, later, in the Netherlands. Not unlike holy warriors, these Christians believe that righteousness should be manifest in this-worldly affairs, that one duty of the Christian is to form a community that witnesses to the Gospel in word and deed. Adult baptism, symbolizing freely chosen faith, marks one's visible entrance to the community, the communion of saints. Discipline is handled not through physical punishment but through the instrument of the ban, the practice of shunning backsliders whose actions merit censure. For these Christians, boundaries are important, but they are cultural and religious, not enforced by the power of the magistrate, whose office Anabaptists are forbidden to assume. Boundaries are marked by a common commitment to cross-bearing, informed by a literal understanding of Jesus's command to love the neighbor and to suffer voluntarily.[59]

In addition to counterexample, Christians developed strong arguments against European imperialism in the sixteenth and seventeenth centuries. Prominent among such critics are Catholic and Protestant writers who self-consciously removed religion as a cause for war. Prompted by religious wars on the continent and in England, as well as the colonial encounter with Amerindians, writers such as Vitoria, Suarez, Gentili, and Grotius appealed to reason and the law of nature as the sole basis for using force.[60] The effect was to reduce war to a political rather than a theological enterprise.

But reducing the justification to natural reason did not eliminate justifications for intervention or elevate territorial borders to a sacrosanct value, for war can be an instrument to secure justice for innocents at risk, regardless of where they reside. Vitoria argues that war could be waged to protect the innocent from human sacrifice or cannibalism,[61] to secure free passage for trade and missionary activity, to protect converts from persecution or repression in their own lands, and to protect populations from tyranny.[62] Such uses of force are viewed within the paradigm of the just war, which assigns natural rights to

individuals irrespective of their other cultural, political, or religious affiliations. Similarly, seventeenth-century Protestant writers provide rationales for
using force to assist outsiders or foreigners. Alberico Gentili (1552–1608)
states that the natural law forbids going to war for purposes of religion, but that
the "union of the human race" places obligations on sovereigns to protect
individuals in other lands from cannibalism, human sacrifice, and other violations of the natural law, and to fight piracy on the seas. Hugo Grotius (1583–
1645) justifies the use of force to protect citizens that one's own sovereign may
have subjugated; and to assist allies, friends, and (where risks are not excessive) strangers in need.[63]

In this regard the writings of sixteenth- and seventeenth-century Christians
provide the seeds for contemporary discussions of humanitarian intervention,
which likewise emphasizes securing justice as a natural right. But in the modern context, considerations of human rights are complicated by the values of
political sovereignty and territorial borders, values that can also be derived
from the natural law.

Political sovereignty is now a core principle in the international security
system, designed to ensure collective autonomy by barring interference from
outside powers. It is meant to enshrine a community's independence from
outside control—the right of a community to determine its own laws and the
means of ordering its own domestic life. In international law and political
theory, regional boundaries imply (at the least) a firm presumption against
intervention, a strong moral barrier to any state that wishes to meddle in
another's jurisdiction.[64]

This right of self-rule is compatible with Christian natural law arguments
regarding humanity's need for community. Individuals cannot flourish without some measure of local control of and participation in a collective existence. Groups thus need autonomy because the individuals that inhabit them
need to be left alone to form a life together. Collective autonomy endeavors
to secure individual autonomy, the experience of freedom, self-determination,
and human dignity.[65]

In this way communities' need for autonomy to protect individual liberty
and human dignity can provide a justification for territorial borders. Yet the
importance of autonomy implies limits to that justification as well, and such
limits have received increasing emphasis in contemporary discussions of international affairs. When borders serve less to protect individual dignity than to
protect leaders or groups who violate human rights, those borders forfeit their
legitimacy. On this view, justifications of borders are connected to more fundamental principles. When those principles are not served, autonomy, borders, and the presumption against intervention become problematic.

The tension in natural law morality between the value of *sovereignty* and
the value of *human rights* has become acute in recent political thought, especially (but not only) in Catholic ethics, requiring social critics to specify the

range and weight of each value.[66] By way of example, consider the recent writings of the U.S. Catholic bishops. Developing a trajectory from the papal encyclical, *Pacem in terris* (1963),[67] and the bishops' pastoral letter, *The Challenge of Peace* (1983),[68] the U.S. Catholic Conference International Policy Committee affirms "the unity of the human family, the interdependence of peoples and the need for solidarity across national and regional boundaries."[69] Advances in technology, worldwide communications, and economic relations have brought people closer together. These changes in transnational dynamics call into doubt the idea of sovereignty and point to the positive moral responsibilities that derive from the values of human dignity and solidarity. The effect is to weaken the value of sovereignty and to connect its legitimacy to the condition that it satisfy natural law tenets.

More specifically, assigning a relative status to the values of sovereignty and political autonomy allows considerations of human rights to trump sovereignty in certain circumstances. According to the bishops, those circumstances include instances in which whole populations are threatened by slaughter, aggression, genocide, or anarchy; when starving children need to be fed; or when it is necessary to strengthen international law and the international community.[70] Summarizing contemporary Catholic social teaching, Kenneth R. Himes writes:

> Catholicism promotes . . . a call to transform, through a prudent strategy, the status quo. The aim is that a true world order be achieved. Such an order would not necessarily mean the withering away of the state, but it will demand that a reciprocal relation of rights and duties be created between states and citizens and between states and other states. If just relations are thereby developed, it may be the case that states will be able to claim sovereignty properly understood, but overbearing claims of absolute sovereignty cannot be admitted. *Stronger than the appeal of sovereignty are the human rights of persons and the obligations of solidarity.* . . . In such a perspective, humanitarian intervention arguably can be part of a sound strategy for achieving international order.[71]

In this way modern Catholic social teaching conceives the value of state sovereignty as derivative from and subordinate to the value of human rights. States that act to undermine the rights of their citizens, or that fail to provide minimum conditions of human well-being, weaken their claims to political legitimacy.

In such circumstances, the cosmopolitan demands of Christianity outweigh the protections normally granted to political autonomy: Nations may intervene on behalf of the innocent who are suffering from oppression or neglect. As the U.S. Catholic bishops remark, "The people of far-off lands are not abstract problems, but sisters and brothers. We are called to protect their lives, to preserve their dignity and to defend their rights."[72] Autonomy and borders are conceived as justified but limited. When dignity is respected only in the breach, outsiders may intervene to secure the protection of distant neighbors—innocent persons whose well-being is at risk.[73]

Conclusion

When considering ethical and political questions pertaining to boundaries, Christianity asserts the priority of the metaphysical over the geographical. This priority has theological and ethical dimensions. Theologically, it implies a hierarchy of being and value according to which God is to receive unconditional loyalty. All lesser loyalties are subordinate to a fundamental love of God, bound as they are by finitude and dependence upon the deity as the author of good. Ethically, this priority assigns at most a provisional and qualified value to regional boundaries, a value that is corrigible when measured against the requirements of universal neighbor-love. Given their instrumental status in a world marked by finitude, sin, and human suffering, boundaries are only a relative good.

In contemporary Christianity, this relativity is evident in recent discussions of property and sovereignty. Within borders, surplus property may be redistributed in dire circumstances of poverty and economic disparity, in which the land of the wealthy may be expropriated for the benefit of the needy. Outsiders are not granted rights of expropriation, but foreign political actors may intervene militarily to secure humanitarian provisions and relief.[74] In the first case borders are sacrosanct when measured against the needs of others; in the second case they are not. In either case regional boundaries are seen as enabling groups to secure a common life together. But when such conventions do more to obstruct than to facilitate well-being, they can give way to demands—pursued by different methods—of universal *agape* and/or human rights.

Notes

I completed a draft of this essay as a fellow in the Program in Ethics and the Professions at Harvard University, and am grateful for the support of its director, Dennis Thompson. I wish to thank Judith Granbois and David H. Smith for their critical comments.

1. For a discussion of this procedure, see Richard B. Miller, *Casuistry and Modern Ethics: A Poetics of Practical Reasoning* (Chicago: University of Chicago Press, 1996), 17–25; James F. Childress, "Moral Norms in Practical Ethical Deliberation," in *Christian Ethics: Problems and Prospects*, ed. Lisa Sowle Cahill and James F. Childress (Cleveland, Ohio: Pilgrim Press, 1996), 196–217.

2. This view is classically set forth in Augustine, *Confessions*, trans., with an intro. by R. S. Pine-Coffin (New York: Penguin Books, 1961).

3. For a discussion, see John M. Rist, *Augustine: Ancient Thought Baptized* (Cambridge: Cambridge University Press, 1994), 214–25.

4. See Thomas Aquinas, *Summa Theologiae* I-II, q. 94. a. 2.

5. This is not to say that the languages of love in Christianity are all the same. There are appreciable differences between, e.g., the eudaimonism of charity in Augustine and the Kantian understanding of *agape* of Kierkegaard. For a discussion of the former, see John Burnaby, *Amor Dei* (London: Hodder and Stoughton, 1938); for a discussion of the latter, and an attempt to craft a normative understanding of Christian love on that basis, see Gene Outka, *Agape: An Ethical Analysis* (New Haven: Yale University Press, 1972).

6. See, e.g., Thomas Aquinas, *Summa Theologiae* II-II, q. 26.

7. In addition to the material cited from Aquinas in the previous note, see, e.g., Karl Barth, *Church Dogmatics*, III/4 (Edinburgh: T. & T. Clark, 1961), 285–323; Soren Kierkegaard, *Works of Love*, trans. Howard and Edna Hong, with a preface by R. Gregor Smith (New York: Harper and Row, 1962).

8. See, e.g., Reinhold Niebuhr, *An Interpretation of Christian Ethics* (New York: Harper and Row, 1935), chap. 4 and passim.

9. See, e.g., Augustine, *Confessions*, bks. 4, 11, and passim; Augustine, *City of God*, trans. Henry Bettenson, with an intro. by David Knowles (New York: Penguin Books, 1972).

10. For a recent expression of this view, see Stanley Hauerwas, *Should War Be Eliminated? Philosophical and Theological Investigations* (Milwaukee, Wis.: Marquette University Press, 1984).

11. See, e.g., H. Richard Niebuhr, *Radical Monotheism and Western Culture, with Supplementary Essays* (New York: Harper and Row, 1943).

12. Clement of Alexandria, "Who Is the Rich Man That Shall Be Saved?" in *The Ante-Nicene Fathers*, ed. Alexander Roberts and James Donaldson (Grand Rapids, Mich.: Wm. B. Eerdmans, 1980), 596.

13. Ibid., 594.

14. Ibid., 595.

15. The differences between the tradition of self-renunciation and the views of Clement of Alexandria exemplify the two-tiered ethic in Christianity, as discussed in Ernst Troeltsch, *The Social Teaching of the Christian Churches*, 2 vols., trans. Olive Wyon, with an intro. by H. Richard Niebuhr (Chicago: University of Chicago Press, 1976).

16. For a discussion, see Justo L. González, *Early Christian Ideas on the Origin, Significance, and Use of Money* (San Francisco: Harper & Row, 1990), 161–66.

17. Ibid., 163.

18. Ibid., 164.

19. Thomas Aquinas, *Summa Theologiae* II-II, q. 66, a. 1.

20. Ibid., a. 2.

21. Thomas Aquinas, *Summa Theologiae* I-II, q. 108, a. 4. The distinction has its origins in Ambrose, *De Officiis Ministrorum*, III, iv.

22. Thomas Aquinas, *Summa Theologiae* II-II, q. 66, a. 5.

23. Ibid., a. 7.

24. Ibid., a. 2.

25. See Bernice Hamilton, *Political Thought in Sixteenth-Century Spain* (Oxford: Clarendon Press, 1963).

26. Francisco de Vitoria, *De Indis*, in *Political Writings*, ed. Anthony Padgen and Jeremy Lawrance (Cambridge: Cambridge University Press, 1991), 250.

27. Ibid., 284.

28. Ibid.

29. Ibid., 286.

30. Ibid., 285.

31. See David J. O'Brien and Thomas A. Shannon, eds., *Catholic Social Thought: The Documentary Heritage* (Maryknoll, N.Y.: Orbis Books, 1992). For an overview of the philosophy of human nature in the papal encyclical tradition, and the various developments within that philosophy, see Charles E. Curran, *Moral Theology: A Continuing Journey* (Notre Dame, Ind.: University of Notre Dame Press, 1982), chap. 8.

32. Paul VI, *Populorum progressio* (1967), in *Renewing the Earth: Catholic Documents on Peace, Justice and Liberation*, ed. David J. O'Brien and Thomas A. Shannon (Garden City, N.J.: Image Books, 1966), par. 23.

33. Ibid.

34. Ibid., par. 24.

35. Ibid., par. 51.

36. Gustavo Gutiérrez, *A Theology of Liberation*, trans. and ed. Caridad Inda and John Eagleson (Maryknoll, N.Y.: Orbis Books, 1973), 27 and passim.

37. Ibid., 36.

38. Ibid., 291–306.

39. For a fuller theological defense of these ideas, and a sustained critique of anthropocentric rather than biocentric approaches to moral value, see James M. Gustafson, *Ethics from a Theocentric Perspective*, 2 vols. (Chicago: University of Chicago Press, 1981–84).

40. See, e.g., Thomas Aquinas on the function of human law in relation to natural law, *Summa Theologiae* I-II, q. 95.

41. Paul Tillich, *The Protestant Era* (Chicago: University of Chicago Press, 1948), 163.

42. See, e.g., Niebuhr, *Radical Monotheism in Western Culture*, 11, 24, 32, and passim.

43. Ibid.

44. H. Richard Niebuhr, *The Meaning of Revelation* (New York: Macmillan, 1941), 57, 59. The problem of religious nationalism was especially acute for German Protestants between the world wars. For a discussion, see Karl Barth, *Church Dogmatics*, III/4, 305–23.

45. H. Richard Niebuhr, *The Social Sources of Denominationalism* (Cleveland: Meridian Books, 1929).

46. H. Richard Niebuhr, "War as the Judgment of God," *Christian Century* 59 (May 3, 1942): 631. I discuss Niebuhr's views in *Interpretations of Conflict: Ethics, Pacifism, and the Just-War Tradition* (Chicago: University of Chicago Press, 1991), chap. 6.

47. Vitoria, *De Indis*, in *Political Writings*, 278.

48. Ibid.

49. Paul VI speaks of the right of immigration, but his remarks are confined to the case of guest workers. See *Populorum progressio*, par. 17.

50. For an instructive discussion, see Michael Walzer, *Spheres of Justice: A Defense of Pluralism and Equality* (New York: Basic Books, 1983), chap. 2.

51. The importance of community might also imply a limited right of exit, although it would be difficult to imagine how any authentic community could coerce membership.

52. Barth, *Church Dogmatics*, III/4, 301.

53. Ibid., 297.

54. Ibid., 301.

55. See, e.g., Augustine, "On the Spirit and the Letter," in *Augustine: Later Works*, trans. with an introduction by John Burnaby (Philadelphia: Westminster Press, 1955), 193–250; Martin Luther, "The Freedom of the Christian," in *Luther's Works*, ed. John Dillenberger (New York: Doubleday, 1961), 42–85; Paul Tillich, *Love, Power, and Justice* (New York: Oxford University Press, 1954).

56. See Bernard of Clairvaux, "Letter 391," excerpted in *War and Christian Ethics*, ed. Arthur Holmes (Grand Rapids, Mich.: Baker Book House, 1975), 88–89.

57. For a discussion, see James Turner Johnson, *Ideology, Reason, and the Limitation of War: Religious and Secular Concepts, 1200–1740* (Princeton: Princeton University Press, 1975), 110–17.

58. Ibid., chap. 2.

59. See, e.g., Menno Simons, *Complete Writings* (Scottdale, Pa.: Herald Press, 1956).

60. For useful discussions of these authors, see Quentin Skinner, *The Foundations of Modern Political Thought*, vol. 2 (Cambridge: Cambridge University Press, 1978); LeRoy Walters, "Five Classic Just-War Theories: A Study in the Thought of Thomas Aquinas, Vitoria, Suarez, Gentili, and Grotius," (Ph.D. diss., Yale University, 1971).

61. See Vitoria, *On Dietary Laws*, in *Political Writings*, 225–26; Hamilton, *Political Thought in Sixteenth-Century Spain*, 127.

62. Vitoria, *De Indis*, 278–90; for a fuller discussion of the Spanish Scholastics and other critics of a crusading mentality, see Hamilton, *Political Thought in Sixteenth-Century Spain*, chap. 6; Johnson, *Ideology, Reason, and the Limitation of War*, chap. 3.

63. See Alberico Gentili, *De Iure Belli Libri Tres*, vol. 2, trans. John C. Rolfe, with an intro. by Coleman Phillipson (Oxford: Clarendon Press, 1933), 41, 74, 123–24; Hugo Grotius, *Rights of War and Peace*, trans. A. C. Campbell, with an intro. by David Hill (Westport, Conn.: Hyperion, 1979), bk. 2, chap. 25.

64. For a discussion of cases in which those presumptions are overridden, see Michael Walzer, *Just and Unjust Wars: A Moral Argument with Historical Illustrations* (New York: Basic Books, 1977), chap. 6.

65. On these and other grounds, Christians have argued for the importance of the liberty of conscience, proceeding in quite the opposite direction of a crusade ideology. Since at least the time of Martin Luther (1483–1546), Christians have crafted a language that emphasizes the freedom of the Christian. This view underscores the fact that an individual's religious well-being is finally her own responsibility. Salvation cannot be left to institutional representatives or other third parties; in matters of faith, the relationship must be uncoerced and direct. Communities need auton-

omy in part to protect the freedom necessary for an individual's sincere relationship with God.

66. See n. 1 above.

67. John XXIII, *Pacem in terris* (1963), in *Renewing the Earth: Catholic Documents on Peace, Justice and Liberation*, 124–70.

68. U.S. Catholic Bishops, *The Challenge of Peace: God's Promise and Our Response* (Washington, D.C.: United States Catholic Conference, 1983).

69. U.S. Catholic Conference International Policy Committee, "American Responsibilities in a Changing World," *Origins* 22 (October 29, 1992): 339. See also J. Bryan Hehir, "Just War Theory in a Post-Cold War Context," *Journal of Religious Ethics* 20 (Fall 1992): 237–57.

70. U.S. Catholic Bishops, "American Responsibilities in a Changing World," 339.

71. Kenneth R. Himes, "Catholic Social Thought and Humanitarian Intervention," in *Peacemaking: Moral and Policy Challenges for a New World*, ed. Gerald F. Powers, Drew Christiansen, S.J., and Robert T. Hennemeyer (Washington, D.C.: United States Catholic Conference, 1994), 223–24 (emphasis mine).

72. U.S. Catholic Bishops, "American Responsibilities in a Changing World," 341.

73. Drawing on the principle of *agape*, Paul Ramsey develops an ethics of the just war that potentially opens the door widely to intervention and the danger that states could use an imperialistic rationale to meddle in the affairs of other states. Ramsey was aware of this problem, and thus sought to include the values of international law and order in the calculus of political practical reasoning. See Paul Ramsey, *The Just War: Force and Political Responsibility* (New York: Charles Scribner's Sons, 1968). For subsequent discussions of humanitarian intervention in Christian ethics, see J. Bryan Hehir, "The Ethics of Intervention: United States Policy in Vietnam (1961–68)," (Ph.D. diss., Harvard University, 1976); U.S. Catholic Bishops, "The Harvest of Justice is Sown in Peace," in *Peacemaking: Moral and Policy Challenges for a New World*, 313–46; Kenneth R. Himes, "The Morality of Humanitarian Intervention," *Theological Studies* 55 (March 1994): 82–105, and "Catholic Social Thought and Humanitarian Intervention," in *Peacemaking*, 215–28; Richard B. Miller, "Casuistry, Pacifism, and the Just-War Tradition in the Post–Cold War Era," in *Peacemaking*, 199–213; John Langan, "Justice or Peace? A Moral Assessment of Humanitarian Intervention in Bosnia," *America* 170 (February 12, 1994): 9–14; James Turner Johnson, "Humanitarian Intervention, Christian Ethical Reasoning, and the Just-War Idea," in *Sovereignty at the Crossroads? Morality and International Politics in the Post-Cold War Era*, ed. Luis E. Lugo (Lanham, Md.: Rowman and Littlefield, 1996), 127–43; Richard B. Miller, "Humanitarian Intervention, Altruism, and the Limits of Casuistry," *Journal of Religious Ethics* 28 (Spring 2000): 3–35.

74. Christian pacifists might find this claim incongruous if they understand humanitarian interventions to be a form of war. But pacifists might consider such interventions comparable to police actions rather than war. Insofar as the paradigm of police action is acceptable to pacifists, actions thus conceived might be justifiable, at least in theory. I discuss this point in "Casuistry, Pacifism, and the Just-War Tradition in the Post–Cold War Era," in *Peacemaking*, 199–213.

Two

The Value of Limited Loyalty

CHRISTIANITY, THE NATION, AND TERRITORIAL BOUNDARIES

NIGEL BIGGAR

SOME OF the more interesting things that Christianity has to say about territorial boundaries come by way of its views on the nation, national identity and loyalty, and nationalism. Historically, of course, Christianity—or, rather, Christians—have said different and sometimes quite contradictory things on these topics. Some have considered each nation to be specially ordained by the eternal God, while others have stressed the mutable historicality of national compositions and boundaries.[1] Some have virtually equated loyalty to the nation with loyalty to God, while others have regarded it as inimical to pacific, universalist Christian faith. As with any historically longstanding and geographically widespread tradition, Christianity is far less a single coherent system of thought than it is a set of debates, sustained over centuries, unified by reference to common authorities, but bringing into play many points of view. Strictly speaking, then, to "represent" what the tradition has to say on any given issue would involve the exhaustive and impartial presentation of a number of rival points of view—and this would certainly have the value of adding grist to the mill of discussion. Nevertheless, if we are actually going to enter a tradition of discussion, and not merely survey it from the vantage point of Olympian neutrality, we must venture judgments, preferring some arguments to others and giving reasons for these preferences; rather than merely represent what the tradition *says*, we must present what we think it *should say*. This is what I have chosen to do here. Therefore, what follows is not a representation of all that Christians have said about nations and national loyalty, and about their implications for territorial boundaries, but rather a presentation of what I think Christians should say about them.

This essay, then, is much narrower in focus than Richard Miller's panorama, and it presupposes most of what he has to say—especially about the limitations of the rights of ownership by obligations to the common good. My main quarrel with him is over his specification of the Christian understanding of love as properly "indiscriminate and unconditional" or "cosmopolitan," and over the view of national loyalty that follows from it. That is the major point of disagreement between us. The argument that gives rise to this disagreement now follows.

The Creatureliness of Human Being: Historicality, National Loyalty, and Diversity

Christians should base their view of the nation on their understanding of human being as creaturely. This involves distinguishing it sharply from the universal and eternal being of God and taking seriously its historicality—that is, its boundedness by time and space. Humans come into being and grow up in a particular time, and if not in one particular place and community then in a limited number of them. Human individuals are normally nurtured, inducted into social life, and encouraged in certain self-understandings by their family and by other institutions—educational, religious, recreational, economic, and political—that mediate the history and ethos of their local and national communities. It is natural, therefore, that individuals should feel special affection for, and loyalty toward, those communities that have cared for them and given them so much that is beneficial; and, since beneficiaries ought to be grateful to benefactors, it is right that they should.[2] We have yet to specify the forms that such affection and loyalty should and should not take; but that they should take some form is clear.

This affirmation of a certain kind of national loyalty in terms of the Christian concept of the creatureliness of human being might seem at first sight surprising. For does not Christianity teach that human beings should love one another indiscriminately and unconditionally; and does not this imply that they should transcend all particular "natural" loyalties to family, ethnic community, and nation? Certainly, this claim is made; but, in my opinion, it is made mistakenly.

I would agree that all humans share the common status of children of God, who are indebted for the gift of secular existence and who stand in need of the gifts of forgiveness and of eternal life. I would also agree that we are all made "in God's image" and are thereby dignified with responsibility to manage the rest of the created world;[3] and that each of us is the subject of a vocation to play a unique part in God's Grand Project of bringing the created world to fulfillment. It is true, then, that each of us owes a certain respect to any fellow human being to whom we are related; and in this age of global communications there are few, if any, humans to whom we are not related somehow. Nevertheless, this is not to say that we owe all other humans equal care. We may be responsible, but ours is a responsibility of creatures, not of gods. We are limited in awareness, in energy, and in time. We are able only to take care of some, not all; and there are some to whom we are more strongly obliged by ties of gratitude, or whom we are better placed to serve on account of shared language and culture or common citizenship.

However, it is often said—and Richard Miller says it[4]—that Christian love for others is properly indiscriminate and unconditional. This claim has two main grounds, one biblical and the other theological. The biblical ground comprises those passages in the New Testament where "natural" loyalty to family is severely downgraded. Among these are Gospel passages where Jesus is reported as saying that only those who hate their mothers and fathers can be his disciples,[5] that those who would follow him must "let the dead bury the dead,"[6] and that his "family" now consists of those who have joined him in his cause;[7] and also, by implication, those passages in the Epistles where St. Paul recommends virginity or celibacy as a higher good than marriage.[8]

The theological ground consists of the typically Protestant concept of God's love as showered graciously on every human regardless of his or her moral status—a concept that was most fully developed earlier this century by the Swedish Lutheran theologian, Anders Nygren. According to Nygren, God's love is utterly spontaneous and gratuitous; it is not attracted to the beloved by any of their qualities (how could it be, since those whom it loves are all sinners?), and it is in no sense beholden to them; it is simply and absolutely gracious.[9] As God loves us, so should we love our neighbors, with a pure altruism that entirely disregards their qualities. It is quite true that Nygren himself was not directly addressing the question of whether or not a certain local or national partiality in our affections and loyalties is justifiable, and that his focus was on the religious relationship between God and sinful creatures. Nevertheless, he made it quite clear that Christians are to mediate to their neighbors the same unconditional and indiscriminate love that God has shown them.[10]

What should we make of these biblical and theological grounds? Do they really imply that Christian love should be oblivious to local and national bonds? I think not. Certainly, the so-called hard sayings of Jesus imply that natural loyalties are subordinate to the requirements of loyalty to God, and that sometimes the latter might enjoin behavior that contradicts normal expressions of the former. But, given that Jesus is also reported as criticizing the Pharisees for proposing a piece of casuistry that effectively permits children to neglect the proper care of their elderly parents;[11] and given that—notwithstanding his affirmation and commendation of Gentiles[12]—he apparently maintained his identity as a Jew;[13] there is good reason not to take these "hard sayings" at face value, and to read them as hyperboles intending to relativize rather than repudiate natural loyalties. As for St. Paul, it is notable that, although he reckoned virginity and celibacy superior, he persisted in regarding marriage as a good. In other words, in spite of his urgent sense of the imminent "ending" or transformation of the world by God, and of how this revolution of the current order of things would severely strain marital and family ties, St. Paul never went as far as to say that investment in society through marriage and children should cease. What he thereby implies is that, although the arrival of the world-to-come will involve the transformation of this world and its natural social bonds, it will not involve their simple abolition.

Upon close inspection, then, the New Testament grounds for supposing Christian love to be properly unconditional and indiscriminate are not at all firm. That is even more so in the case of the theological ground. Certainly, if we take Jesus to be God incarnate, we can infer that the love of God for wayward human beings is gracious—that is, both compassionate and forgiving. It is compassionate in that it sympathizes with wrongdoers in their weakness and confusion and ignorance; and it is forgiving in that it is willing to set past injury aside and enter once again into a relationship of trust. But note how limited is the scope of this love: it operates only between an injured party and the one who has done the injury. It is a mode of love, but not the whole of it. Accordingly, it is unconditional and indiscriminate only in a very restricted sense. As compassion, its being proffered is not conditional upon the demonstration of repentance, and it is therefore made available indiscriminately to all sinners. As forgiveness, however, it is only offered in response to an expression of genuine repentance, and therefore only discriminately to penitent sinners.[14] Therefore, insofar as God's love manifested in Jesus is a model for human love, the specific ways in which it is unconditional and indiscriminate bear on how we should treat those who have wronged us; but they have no bearing at all on how we should distribute our limited emotional, physical, temporal, and material resources in caring for the millions of fellow humans who can now claim to be—more or less closely—our neighbors.

So far I have argued that considered reflection upon the Christian concept of the creatureliness of human being—and, specifically, upon the original dependence of any human individual on an historical community—should lead Christians to acknowledge the validity of natural loyalties to those communities (including the nation) into which one is born and in which one is brought up. Now I want to contend that it should also lead them to regard a diversity of ethnic communities, including nations, as a natural necessity that is also good.[15]

Human communities, being creaturely, can only exist in particular times and places, and different geographical locations and historical experiences are bound to generate diverse communities. Human communities, being human, may well all share some common characteristics, but experience of different places and histories is bound to generate differences in political constitutions, institutions, customs, received wisdom, and outlook. As a natural necessity, such diversity could be regarded simply as an unhappy feature of the human condition, providing as it does the occasion for incomprehension and conflict

between communities, and therefore one to be transcended as soon as possible. But Christians, believing as they traditionally do in the unqualified
goodness and wisdom of the divine Creator, should be disinclined to regard
anything natural—whether created or following necessarily from it—as simply
evil. Further, human experience confirms that diversity among peoples can be
a source of value as well as of conflict. As postmodernists never tire of reminding us, there is beauty in difference. But to restrict this value simply to the
aesthetic dimension would be to trivialize many of the differences that concern us here. For differences between constitutions, institutions, customs, wisdom, or outlook, if taken seriously, should provoke not merely wonder but
reflection. Such differences should move each community to ask itself
whether others do not order their social life better, or whether their received
wisdom should not correct, supplement, or complement its own. The value of
communal (and so national) difference here is not just aesthetic, but intellectual and moral: it can enable human beings to learn from each other better
ways of serving and promoting the human good. In other words, its justification is not just postmodernist, but liberal.

This argument that a Christian vision of things should affirm national diversity is supported by history. For, according to Adrian Hastings, Christianity
has been a vital factor in the historical development of national diversity
through its habit of communicating its message by translating it into vernacular languages.[16] Since "a community . . . is essentially a creation of human
communication,"[17] and since the writing down of a language tends to increase
linguistic uniformity,[18] the movement of a vernacular from oral usage to the
point where it is regularly employed for the production of a literature is a
major cause of the development of national identity.[19] Therefore, by translating the Bible into vernacular languages, by developing vernacular liturgies and
devotional literature, and by mediating these to the populace through an educated parish clergy, the Christian Church played a major part in the development of diverse nationalities.[20]

And there is good reason to suppose that this role has not simply been the
accidental effect of a particular missionary strategy. After all, different missionary strategies are possible; and we must ask why Christianity chose the one
that it did. It could, like Islam, have chosen to spread the Word by assimilation rather than translation. Muslims regard the Qur'an as divine in its Arabic,
linguistic form as well as in its content, and the consequent cultural impact of
Islam has been to Arabize, "to draw peoples into a single world community of
language and government."[21] In contrast, Christians do not ascribe divinity to
any particular language, and they thereby implicitly recognize that the Word
of God is free to find (somewhat different) expression in every language.[22]
Accordingly, in the New Testament story of the birth of the Christian Church
on the day of Pentecost, the disciples of Jesus "were all filled with the Holy
Spirit and began to speak in other tongues," so that the multiethnic crowd

who heard them "were bewildered, because each one heard them speaking in his own language."[23] Whereas the story of the tower of Babel in the Hebrew Scriptures presents linguistic diversity as a degeneration (caused by God's punishment of sin) from an original state when "the whole earth had one language,"[24] here the Spirit of God is presented as graciously accommodating Godself to it. This divine self-accommodation implies a respect for and affirmation of the historicality, and therefore diversity, of creaturely human being. Such affirmation is also implicit in the orthodox Christian doctrine of the divine Incarnation, according to which God Almighty became human in Jesus of Nazareth, and in becoming human became historical—that is, a particular man living in a particular time and place. According to the Christian story, it is characteristic of God to be willing to meet human creatures in the midst of their historicality and diversity. Although transcending time and space, God is not alien to them; in this case what is transcended is not repudiated, and may be inhabited. The Christian theological affirmation of human diversity finds further confirmation in the orthodox doctrine of God as a trinity. In Christian eyes, as in Jewish and Muslim ones, God is certainly one, but the divine unity is not simple. God is more like a community than a monad splendid in isolation. The Origin and Basis of the created world, then, is a unity that contains rather than abolishes difference—a unity in diversity, not instead of it.

Thus far we have argued that, on the ground of its understanding of human being as creaturely, Christianity should affirm the special loyalty that grows naturally out of gratitude to a national community that has sustained and nurtured its members; and it should also affirm a diversity of national communities, partly because human diversity is natural to human (and divine) being, and partly because it is aesthetically, intellectually, and morally enriching. There is, however, another dimension to human creatureliness that should lead Christians to qualify their affirmation of national loyalty and diversity: namely, moral responsibility for the common good.

The Creatureliness of Human Being: Responsibility for the Common Good

As creatures, human beings are bound not only by time and space, but also by the requirements of the good that is proper to their created nature. Roughly speaking, service of the human good is what makes actions right, and failure of such service is what makes them wrong. This good is not just private, but common; the good of the human individual—and of each human community or nation—is bound up with the good of others, both human and nonhuman. Acting rightly is important, then, partly because it respects or promotes the good of others in ways they deserve, and partly because in so doing agents maintain or promote their own good—and thereby help to make themselves fit for eternal life.

So human creatures are bound by an obligation to serve the common human good; but being creatures, their powers of service are limited. No human effort, individual or collective, has the power to secure the maximal good of all human beings (including the dead as well as the living), far less of nonhuman ones as well. Each of us must choose to do what we can, and what we may, to advance *certain* dimensions of the good of *some*, trusting God to coordinate our little contributions and guide their unpredictable effects to the benefit of the common good of all. Among those whom we choose to help, it would be right for us to include our benefactors, for gratitude requires it. Thus the justification for special loyalties to such communities as one's family and nation.

But note: What one owes one's family or nation is not anything or everything, but specifically respect for and promotion of their good. Such loyalty, therefore, does not involve simply doing or giving whatever is demanded, whether by the state, the electoral majority, or even the people as a whole. Indeed, when what is demanded would appear to harm the community—for example, acquiescence in injustice perpetrated by the state against its own people or a foreign one, or by one section of the nation against another—genuine national loyalty requires that it be refused. True patriotism is not uncritical; and in extreme circumstances it might even involve participation in acts of treason—as it did in the case of Dietrich Bonhoeffer, whose love for Germany led him into conspiracy to kill Hitler.[25]

National loyalty, as Christians should conceive it, shows itself basically in reminding the nation that it is accountable to God, at least in the sense of being obliged by the good given or created in human nature. By thus distinguishing between its object and God, such loyalty distances itself from the Romantic nationalism that absolutizes and divinizes the Nation, making its unquestioning service the route to a quasi-immortality.[26]

It is true, of course, that the Christian Bible contains and gives prominence to the concept of a People chosen by God to be the medium of salvation to the world; and it is also true that particular "Christian" nations have periodically identified themselves as the Chosen People, thereby pretending to accrue to themselves and their imperialist, "civilizing" policies an exclusive divine authority. But it is fair to point out that the notion of the Chosen People as referring to a particular nation strictly belongs to the Old Testament, not the New; and that one of the main points on which early Christianity differentiated itself from Judaism was precisely its transnational character. Full participation in the Christian religion was no longer tied to worship in the temple at Jerusalem, and was as open to Gentiles as to Jews; for, as St. Paul famously put it, "there is neither Jew nor Greek, . . . ; for you are all one in Christ Jesus."[27] In early, emergent Christianity, the "People of God" came to refer no longer to a particular nation (Israel), but to the universal Church. Certainly, there have been many times when the Church as an institution has become wedded to a particular ethnic culture or the instrument of a particular nation-state. There have been times when the Church's *relative and conditional* affirmation of a particular culture or nation has lost its vital qualifications. But, in light of what we have said above, we may judge that these are times when the Church has betrayed its identity and failed in its calling. They are times when it has failed to maintain the distinction ironically attested by the Nazi judge, who, before condemning Helmuth von Moltke to death, demanded of him, "From whom do you take your orders? From the Beyond or from Adolf Hitler?"[28] And they are times when it has failed to observe the original priority so succinctly affirmed in Sir Thomas More's declaration, moments before he was beheaded for refusing to endorse Henry VIII's assertion of royal supremacy over the English Church, that he would die "the King's good servant, but God's first."[29]

A properly Christian view, then, insists that every nation is equally ac-countable to God for its service of the human good. No nation may pretend to be God's Chosen People in the strong sense of being the sole and perma-nent representative and agent of His will on earth; no nation may claim such an identity with God. This relativization still permits each nation to consider itself chosen or called by God to contribute in its own peculiar way to the world's salvation; to play a special role—at once unique, essential, and lim-ited—in promoting the universal human good. It allows members of a given nation to celebrate the achievements of the good that grace their own history and to take pride in the peculiar institutions and customs in which they have realized it. At the same time, it forces them to acknowledge that their nation's achievement is but one among many; and so to recognize, appreciate, and even learn from the distinctive contributions of others.

But more than this, each nation must realize not only that other nations too have made valuable contributions to the realization of the common good of all things, but also that the achievement of the good in one nation is actually bound up with its achievement elsewhere. National loyalty, therefore, is prop-erly extrovert. As Karl Barth puts it:

> For when we speak of home, motherland, and people, it is a matter of outlook, background, and origin. We thus refer to the initiation and beginning of a move-ment. It is a matter of being faithful to this beginning. But this is possible only if we execute the movement, and not as we make the place where we begin it a prison and stronghold. The movement leads us relentlessly, however, from the narrower sphere to a wider, from our own people to other human peoples. . . . The one who is really in his own people, among those near to him, is always on the way to those more distant, to other peoples.[30]

The point here is not that we should grow *out of* national identity and loyalty and into a cosmopolitanism that, floating free of all particular attachments, lacks any real ones;[31] but rather that, in and through an ever deepening care for the good of our own nation, we are drawn into caring for the good of foreigners. This point is poignantly captured by Yevgeni Yevtushenko in "Babii Yar," his poem about Russian anti-Semitism:

> Oh my Russian people!
> I know you are internationalists to the core.
> But those with unclean hands
> have often made a jingle of your purest name.
> I know the goodness of my land. . . .
> In my blood there is no Jewish blood.
> In their callous rage all anti-Semites
> must hate me now as a Jew.
> For that reason I am a true Russian.[32]

Notwithstanding the tensions that may arise between national loyalty and loyalties that are more extensive, there is nevertheless an essential connection between them.

Christianity, Nationality, and Borders

Christianity, then, should give qualified affirmation to national loyalty and the nation. Such affirmation means that it refuses to dismiss national identity and loyalty simply as false consciousness. It resists liberal cosmopolitanism and Marxist internationalism on the ground that human beings are not historically transcendent gods, but historically rooted and embedded creatures. Accordingly, it recognizes the need to restrict cross-border mobility. Borders exist primarily to define the territory within which a people is free to develop their own way of life as best they can. Unrestricted mobility would permit uncontrolled immigration that would naturally be experienced by natives as an invasion. Successful, peaceful immigration needs to be negotiated. Immigrants must demonstrate a willingness to respect native cultures and institutions, and to a certain extent abide by them. Natives must be given time to accommodate new residents and their foreignness.

Further, the affirmation of national identity means that the consensus that comprises the unity of a nation needs to be more than merely constitutional; it also needs to be cultural. This is partly because a particular constitution and its institutional components derive their particular meaning from the history of their development; and so to endorse a constitution involves understanding that history and owning its heroes. It is also partly because, while consensus over individual and group rights is necessary to prevent the outbreak of conflict, it cannot be secured or sustained without a cultural *engagement* between groups that goes beyond mere respect and achieves a measure of mutual appreciation.

On the other hand, Christianity's qualification of its affirmation of nations means that it is alert to their historical mutability. Although growing out of an extension of natural loyalties, particular nations are human constructions whose culture and ethnic composition are always changing.[33] National myths of racial or ethnic or cultural purity, therefore, are immediately suspect, in which case foreign ways and immigrants can be regarded not just as challenges or threats, but as resources.

The proper willingness of nations to incorporate foreigners—and elements of their foreignness—is bound to produce cultural diversity; but should this be allowed to include a diversity of religions? There are good Christian grounds for supposing that it should. Even if Christians believe that, in the end, they are more right than others (as others no doubt believe that they are more right than Christians), it does not follow from this that others are absolutely or radically wrong. Christians believe that the Spirit of the Christ-like God is universally present to all creatures; so they should expect that God is somewhat known beyond the reaches of the Christian Church. Add to this the Protestant doctrine of the Church as a body that is still *learning* to be faithful—as at once righteous and sinful—and Christians come to be seen as those who have yet more to learn, and who might conceivably do so from non-Christians. Then, combining these theological considerations with the empirical observation (and Christians should not be averse to learning from experience) that the modern era has demonstrated that religious uniformity is not necessary for there to be sufficient moral consensus to ensure social stability, we arrive at the conclusion that a nation should be willing to tolerate religious diversity within its borders.

There are various ways of doing this. The classic liberal way is to aspire to keep public institutions religiously neutral, and thereby accord each religion equal status in the eyes of the state. Alternatively, there may be a society where most members feel some affinity—whether spiritual or cultural—with the state religion, and where members of other religious communities would prefer a polity in which a religion other than their own had privileged public status, rather than a fully fledged liberal arrangement where religion is systematically relegated to the private world. Here religious diversity would coexist with religious establishment.[34]

Christianity's view of the nation implies that its borders should be patrolled so as to control immigration, but that they should be open to foreign immigrants on certain conditions, and therefore that they should contain cultural and religious diversity. The Christian view also implies that the autonomy a nation enjoys within its borders is not absolute. It does not have the right simply to do with its resources whatever it pleases, but only to manage them responsibly; and where it has resources surplus to its own needs, it has a duty to devote them to the good of others—by welcoming refugees, for example, or by donating aid to foreign countries.[35] This concept of a morally limited right to autonomy over material and social assets contradicts the libertarian view that one has an absolute right of disposal over whatever one has acquired legally; and it does so partly on the ground that all creaturely owners are also dependents and beneficiaries. How much we own is due to benefactions and good fortune as well as to skill and entrepreneurial flair. Even where our property was genuinely virgin when we first possessed it, the fact that we had the power to discover it will have owed something to what we had inherited, and ultimately to what our ancestors had been given and the good fortune that had attended the development of their resources. As we have received, so should we give. National sovereignty, then, is not absolute; its exercise is subject to the moral claims of the common good, and when it fails to acknowledge those claims, other nations might have the moral right to intervene—if the requirements of prudence can be met (for example, if it seems that an intervention is likely to achieve what it intends and to do so without risking an escalating conflagration).

In the Christian view that I am commending here, national borders should be conditionally open and they may be transgressed if national autonomy is being exercised irresponsibly. They may also be changed. Nations, as Christians should see them, are neither divine nor eternal, but human and historical. Investment in a nation is not—with all due respect to Fichte—the route to immortality; for that runs through service of the Creator and Sustainer of all things. As historical, nations are mutable. Therefore, the patriot should be willing to contemplate changes in his or her nation—whether in its constitution or even in its very definition—if that is what justice and prudence together require. It is not written in heaven that the United Kingdom should always encompass Scotland, nor the Canadian confederation Quebec, nor the Yugoslav federation Kosovo. Nor is it written that the United States of America must remain united, any more than it was written that the Soviet Union should. Christianity properly precludes a simply conservative view of a nation's internal or external territorial boundaries, and withholds its support from political movements dedicated to preserving those boundaries at all costs.

On the other hand, Christians should be wary of demands for border changes that issue from nationalist fervor fueled by dishonest myths that idealize one's own nation and demonize or scapegoat another, that picture one's own simply as innocent victim and the other's simply as malicious oppressor. The Christian doctrine of the universal presence of sin means that we may not fondly imagine that the line dividing virtue from vice runs with reassuring neatness between our own people on the virtuous side and another people on the vicious one. The line between virtue and vice runs right down the middle of each human community, as it runs through the heart of every individual. Accordingly, no human may stand to another simply as righteous to unrighteous, and the wronged party always shares enough in common with the wrongdoer to owe him some compassion. Nationalist myths that say otherwise tend to exaggerate the injustice suffered, demand a radical and revolutionary remedy, totally discount any moral claims that the "enemy" might have, and brook no compromise.

For an example, take Northern Ireland. It is true that Catholic nationalists there have been seriously oppressed by Protestant unionists, sometimes systematically; and it is therefore reasonable for Catholics to be less than fully confident in British government and to seek protection under the Irish state. One way of securing this would be for the border between Northern Ireland and the Irish Republic to be completely erased, for the former to be incorporated into a "united" Ireland, and for British jurisdiction in the island of Ireland to be removed once and for all. This is what Irish nationalists have traditionally demanded. The problem with this is that there is a substantial ethnic community in Northern Ireland whose national allegiance is strongly British, and who want to become subject to the Irish state about as much as nationalists want to remain subject to the British one. An alternative solution—and one embodied in the Good Friday Agreement reached between the British and Irish governments and the political parties in Northern Ireland in April 1998—is to "thin" the border without erasing it. This involves setting up certain institutions that transcend the borders between Britain and Ireland, on the one hand compromising the substance of British sovereignty over Northern Ireland, while on the other hand maintaining the province's formal constitutional status as part of the United Kingdom. This reassures nationalists by giving Dublin substantial influence over British government in Northern Ireland; and by creating bodies with specific areas of responsibility (for example, for tourism or agriculture), whose jurisdiction runs through the whole of the island of Ireland and is unhindered by the border. But it also reassures the unionists by maintaining the border, eliciting Dublin's formal recognition of it,[36] limiting the jurisdiction of the cross-border bodies to specific areas of economic activity, and thereby securing Northern Ireland's place in the United Kingdom. One threat to this happy compromise, however, could come from the refusal of nationalists to regard it as a permanent settlement and their insistence on viewing it as merely a step on the road to the ultimate goal of the political unification of the whole of the island of Ireland under an Irish state. Such an insistence would be fueled by a traditional resentment of all things British and unionist, one which is blind to the considerable progress in remedying the injustices suffered by Catholics that British governments are widely acknowledged to have made since the 1970s; and which doggedly refuses to acknowledge the right of unionists to maintain their British allegiance for ever.

A Christian vision of things, then, militates against the idealization of the self and the demonization of the other that stifles sympathy and leads a bitter, dogmatic nationalism to brook no compromise in its determination to erase a national boundary. For the same reasons, it also militates against a nationalism that refuses all compromise in its determination to erect a national boundary sufficient to establish political independence. Certainly, Christians should acknowledge the right of an ethnic group to flourish in its own peculiar way—subject, of course, to the requirements of justice and fairness. They should also acknowledge that such peculiar flourishing might need the protection and support of special laws, perhaps a measure of autonomy, and in extreme circumstances even independence. Why should they contemplate independence only in extreme circumstances? Because its achievement is bound to embody a degree of alienation between two peoples formerly united. It involves political divorce, with all the attendant danger of lingering resentment that divorce risks; so if it can be avoided, it should be. For sure, there may be good reasons why independence should be sought and granted. Maybe an ethnic group in a multi-ethnic state has been maltreated, severely and over a period of time; and maybe either the state shows no sign of remedying the abuse, or the injured people can no longer be reasonably expected to trust the state to do what it says it will. Here the pursuit of independence would be consonant with the pursuit of justice. But Christians, with their sensitivity to the creaturely interdependence of human individuals and communities, and with their conviction that the Origin and Basis of things comprises a unity-in-diversity rather than the isolated and alienated unity of absolute self-sufficiency, should be skeptical of cries for independence; and all the more so when these arise from within a culture where independence is something of a fetish and where its prevalent concept is adolescent rather than adult. They should interrogate the demand, asking whether it will bring real and substantial benefits to the people as a whole—and not just, say, provide the local political class with a bigger stage to strut upon.

Conclusion

This essay has brought Christian thinking to bear upon the nature and purposes of territorial boundaries primarily through the concept of human being as creaturely. According to this concept, each human individual is born into, brought up in, and given a grip on life by a particular set of communities, which nowadays almost invariably includes a national community. As creatures, human individuals and groups are also subject to the moral claims of the good given in human nature. Since one of these claims is that beneficiaries ought to be grateful to benefactors, those who have benefited from a nation's protection and nurture owe it a certain loyalty. But this loyalty does not involve the blind endorsement of whatever policies a nation's leadership deems to be in its interests. More precisely, it does not involve the adoption of a narrowly private understanding of those interests. As the good of the individual is bound up with the good of the community, so the good of any single national community is bound up with the common good of all nations. Foreigners should be regarded, then, not simply as aliens but as distant neighbors; and where one nation has charge of more than enough resources to meet its own needs, it should devote its surplus to the good of others.

This view of national loyalty and of the nation carries the following implications for our understanding of territorial boundaries. First, boundaries perform the legitimate function of defining that area of the earth's surface in which a nation has certain freedoms to build its own way of life—in which it enjoys a certain autonomy. These national borders also rightly serve as barriers, insofar as immigration needs to be controlled in order to prevent the destructive invasion of a nation's way of life. Nevertheless, in that the incorporation of foreigners can enhance and enrich a national community, and in that racial or ethnic or cultural or religious purity is a nationalist myth, the barriers should be opened to immigrants whose admission will not be invasive. It follows that national borders should contain cultural diversity—and, given certain views of the Holy Spirit and of the Christian Church, religious diversity too. Further, borders should not be regarded as immutable; for they are as changeable as national constitutions. But they should not be changed in response to the demands of dogmatic, self-righteous nationalism, or in pursuit of the fetish of independence, but only out of deference to the requirements of justice and prudence combined.

Notes

1. See Karl Barth's discussion of these matters and of the history of Protestant thought about them in *Church Dogmatics*, III/4 (Edinburgh: T. & T. Clark, 1961), 285–323.

2. This is true, notwithstanding the fact that communities sometimes let members down badly, in which case it would be reasonable for those members' loyalty to their community to be diminished in proportion to the gravity of its failure.

3. The seminal notion that humankind is made "in God's image" derives from one verse in the Book of Genesis: "Then God said, 'Let us make man in our image, after our likeness; and let them have dominion . . . over all the earth'" (1:26). In the history of Christian tradition this phrase has been interpreted in many different ways; but the interpretation that is closest to the text understands it in terms of the practice of kings in the ancient world of setting up statues of themselves in outlying provinces or having their image imprinted on coinage, in order to represent the presence of royal authority throughout their empire. To be made in God's image, then, is to be made a representative or vicegerent of God, charged with exercising dominion in God's name over the rest of creation. For a history of the exegesis of Genesis 1:26–27, see Claus

Westermann, *Genesis 1–11: A Commentary*, trans. John J. Scullion, S.J. (London: SPCK, 1984), 147–55.

4. See Richard Miller in chapter 1 above, under "Boundaries": "Christianity requires an indiscriminate, unconditional love of others, irrespective of political, social, or national affiliation. . . . Christian *agape*, exemplified by Jesus's teaching and example, is altruistic and cosmopolitan."

5. Matthew 10:37; Luke 14:26.

6. Matthew 8:22; Luke 9:60.

7. Matthew 12:46–50; Mark 3:31–35; Luke 8:19–21.

8. I Corinthians 7.

9. Anders Nygren, *Agape and Eros*, trans. Philip S. Watson (Chicago: University of Chicago Press, 1982), 75–81. Nygren uses the New Testament word *agape* to designate this radically altruistic kind of love, which he believes to be peculiarly Christian, and to differentiate it from the Greek concept of love as essentially self-serving *eros*. *Agape and Eros* was originally published in Swedish in 1930 (Part I) and 1938 (Part II).

10. Ibid., 733–37.

11. Mark 7:9–13.

12. Matthew 8:5–13; 15:21–28.

13. Matthew 15:24, 26; John 4:22.

14. In brief defense of this understanding of forgiveness, let me make two points, one biblical and one empirical. First, in Jesus's parable of the prodigal son, the heartfelt repentance of the son is already fully established *before* we learn of his father's eager forgiveness (Luke 15:11–32). Second, it is unloving and foolish to forgive those who have shown insufficient awareness of what they have done wrong, both because it forecloses their moral education and growth and because it makes it likely that they will injure again.

15. A nation is an ethnic community that enjoys or aspires to a measure of autonomy in the organization of its public life through institutions of its own—whether religious, educational, legal, or political (see David Miller, *On Nationality* [Oxford: Clarendon Press, 1995], esp. chap. 2, "National Identity"). A nation need not be "independent." Scotland, for example, has its own national church, and educational and legal systems—and since 1999 its own parliament; but so long as it remains an integral part of the United Kingdom, it will not be fully "independent."

16. Adrian Hastings, *The Construction of Nationhood: Ethnicity, Religion, and Nationalism* (Cambridge: Cambridge University Press, 1997).

17. Ibid., 20.

18. Ibid., 19ff.

19. Ibid., 12, 20, 31.

20. Ibid., 22, 24, 191–92.

21. Ibid., 201. This statement needs to be qualified in that the traditional dogma of the untranslatability of the Qur'an has come under question as Islam has established itself in non-Arabic cultures.

22. Protestant fundamentalists, who believe the Bible to be inspired by God in the sense of being divinely dictated, come closest among Christians to the traditional Muslim view of the Qur'an; but not even they insist that the Sacred Scriptures should be read publicly only in Hebrew or Greek.

23. The Acts of the Apostles 2:4, 6.

24. Genesis 11:1–9.

25. For a fuller exploration of these themes in the light of Bonhoeffer's life and work, see Keith Clements, *True Patriotism: Love of Country in Dialogue with the Witness of Dietrich Bonhoeffer* (London: Collins, 1986).

26. One classic expression of this nationalism is Fichte's: "The noble-minded man's belief in the eternal continuance of his influence even on this earth is thus founded on the hope of the eternal continuance of the people from which he has developed, and on the characteristic of that people. . . . This characteristic is the eternal thing to which he entrusts the eternity of himself and of his continuing influence, the eternal order of things in which he places his portion of eternity. . . . In order to save his nation he must be ready even to die that it may live, and that he may live in it the only life for which he has ever wished" (J. G. Fichte, *Addresses to the German Nation* [Chicago: Open Court Press, 1922], 135–36). Benedict Anderson specifies this view of the nation as a modern phenomenon, providing as it does a substitute for declining religious modes of thought (*Imagined Communities: Reflections on the Origin and Spread of Nationalism*, rev. ed. [London and New York: Verso, 1991], 11–12).

27. Galatians 3:28.

28. Helmuth James von Moltke, *Letters to Freya: A Witness against Hitler* (London: Collins Harvill, 1991), 409.

29. According to a contemporary report carried in the *Paris News Letter*. See Nicholas Harpsfield, *The life and death of Sir Thomas Moore, knight, sometymes Lord high Chancellor of England*, ed. E. V. Hitchcock and R. W. Chambers, Early English Text Society, Original Series no. 186 (London: Oxford University Press, 1932), Appendix III, 266: "Apres les exhorta, et supplia tres instamment qu'ils priassent Dieu pour le Roy, affin qu'il luy voulsist donner bon conseil, protestant qu'il mouroit son bon serviteur et de Dieu premierement."

30. Barth, *Church Dogmatics*, III/4, 293–94.

31. Barth is right to suggest that such cosmopolitanism is not only undesirable, but impossible: "The command of God certainly does not require any man to be a cosmopolitan, quite apart from the fact that none of us can really manage to be so" (ibid., 293). Here I differ from Miller (in chapter 1 above, under "Mobility"), who understands Barth's "overall impetus" to be "universalist," and interprets him as granting national identity and loyalty only "provisional" affirmation.

32. Yevgeni Yevtushenko, "Babii Yar," in *The Collected Poems, 1952–90* (Edinburgh: Mainstream Publishing, 1991), 103–4. Babii Yar is the name of a ravine on the outskirts of Kiev where at least 100,000 Jews were massacred in 1941. The massacre was carried out by German troops, but not without the tacit approval of many local Ukrainians, who shared in the long Russian tradition of anti-Semitism.

33. Barth is admirably alert to this (*Church Dogmatics*, III/4, 300–302).

34. Whenever proposals are mooted to end the Church of England's privileged status as the state religion of England, Jewish and Muslim leaders regularly leap to its defense. For a Jewish example, see Jonathan Sacks, *The Persistence of Faith* (London: Weidenfield, 1991), esp. 68; and for a Muslim example, see T. Modood, "Ethno-religious Minorities, Secularism and the British State," *British Political Quarterly* 65 (1994): 53–73.

35. See Miller's discussion of Thomas Aquinas's concept of private property in the preceding chapter, under "Ownership and Distribution."

36. As part of the agreement, the Irish government committed itself to hold a referendum on amending articles 2 and 3 of the Irish constitution, so as to relinquish the Irish state's claim to the territory of Northern Ireland. The referendum was subsequently held and the proposal to drop the articles was approved.

Three _____

Toward a Liberal Theory of National Boundaries

LOREN LOMASKY

FOR EACH THEORY of moral philosophy there is a comfort zone within which its tools function most smoothly and effectively but also areas of embarrassment where the fit between intuitions and theory is uneasy. Some examples follow.

An ethic that is centered on respect for and enhancement of *personal autonomy* is at home with the decisions of unimpaired adults acting in the fullness of their powers. Conversely, it stumbles awkwardly when forced to deal with children, the mentally disabled, and those who are chronically vulnerable. To the extent that they are unable to forge, through their own deliberated choices, lives that they perceive to be meaningful and valuable, concern for their autonomy—a concern which they themselves may altogether lack— seems rather beside the point. When autonomy advocates half-concede the lack of fit between theory and practice in such cases by replacing the requirement of full-fledged consent with hypothetical consent or substituted judgment, what they thereby preserve is a pale simulation, the language of autonomy separated from the allegedly crucial moral commodity itself.[1]

Utilitarianism offers a plausible prescription for distributing the benefits and burdens of repeated interactions among similarly situated individuals. Our intuitions tend to be distinctly less friendly to utilitarian maximization, though, when it is to be achieved by sacrificing the vital interests of minorities so as to serve majority preferences, or when it involves the feeding of "utility monsters" whose capacity for hedonic consumption is heroic. *Socialism* manifests an appealing sympathy for the downtrodden and destitute; it resonates to egalitarian ideals of social justice. But because the central planners and commissars are neither saints nor all-knowing sages, socialism is notoriously susceptible to problems of rational economic planning and shortfalls of altruism[2] on the part of the politically powerful.

Classical liberalism[3] is no exception to this rule of thumb. It flourishes at both the macro and micro levels. Although differing amongst themselves with regard both to foundational issues and questions of application, with virtual unanimity liberals posit the existence of *human rights* that proclaim the essential moral status of persons qua persons. Correlative to these rights are duties of forbearance falling on those who transact with rights-holders. These rights and associated duties are *universal*; they are possessed by everyone and owed to everyone. At the other extreme, *particular rights* (and the duties that are correlative with these) are the product of voluntary, consensual undertakings[4] among particular individuals and are limited in their range of application only to these parties. The whole of humanity on the one hand and self-determining individuals on the other hand: these are the foci of moral forces with which liberalism is most at home. Distinctly less easily assimilated, however, are units intermediate between these. Liberals, like anyone else, realize that people tend to live within family structures, but their theories afford scant moral guidance to households made up of parents, children, and assorted other kin.[5] The clans, confessional groupings, and communities with which people typically identify have also been afforded negligible recognition in liberal theory. Communitarians often have faulted liberalism for its disregard of localized forms of life that confer weight and meaning on people's activities.[6] And then there are nation-states.

The classical theory of liberalism grows to maturity contemporaneously with the emergence of nation-states in their modern form. There is, therefore, some irony in the relative lack of interest liberalism has shown in the moral status of national boundaries. Or perhaps it is precisely this simultaneity that has occasioned the neglect; the existence of countries with hard-edged borders could be taken as a fact of life, as inevitable as scarcity or self-interest or death. Liberal theory would take shape constrained by this parameter but would not itself subject that presupposition to rigorous critical examination.

Like many other generalizations concerning the history of political philosophy, this one admits of greater and lesser exceptions. The classical literature yields, to be sure, a number of remarks concerning how borders are initially established in the process of exit from a hypothesized state of nature. Sometimes these are followed by a perfunctory account as to why those demarcations then remain in force indefinitely. Nonetheless, the rule among liberal theorists is to take states in whatever form and variety they come down to us as the relevant objects for molding in accord with precepts of justice.[7] From Hobbes and Locke through to Rawls, the social contract is assumed to establish, and to operate within, fixed national boundaries. What lends legitimacy to those borders is less diligently examined.

Not surprisingly, this tacit acceptance of the state does not sit easily with liberalism's enshrinement of universal human rights and voluntary individual action. The next section of this chapter, "National Borders: Six Stumbling Blocks," identifies six interrelated difficulties that liberalism encounters in coming to terms with national boundaries. Individually and cumulatively they strongly suggest that liberal complacence with a world of state boundaries that distinguish portentously between that which is inside and that which is outside is misguided. Nonetheless, borders also do some service for liberalism, and four respects in which that is so are developed in the following section, "Why Borders?" The final section, "Boundaries within Limits," attempts to draw some preliminary conclusions concerning how liberals ought to think about state borders as they are and as they might become. To anticipate: Hard boundaries resist harmonization with central liberal commitments, while soft boundaries can reasonably be understood as advancing liberal concerns at acceptable moral cost. By a *hard boundary* is meant a demarcation not easily traversable at will which functions to confer substantial benefits or impose substantial costs on individuals by virtue of which side of the line they happen to find themselves. A boundary is *soft* to the extent it is not hard. Hardness and softness so understood are matters of degree and not precisely specifiable, but the impact of this distinction on the prospects of individual actors is far from obscure.

National Borders: Six Stumbling Blocks

1. Moral Arbitrariness and Borders

A baby born a few miles north of the Rio Grande will, by virtue of this natal location, enjoy prospects substantially different from and very likely much superior to those of someone born a few miles south. She will be the beneficiary of a more commodious arena for economic activity to which she will be permitted easy access because of the citizenship this accident of birth confers. Similarly, the political institutions under which she will live are more democratic and more responsive to her interests than those available to the other child. Should she find herself in conditions of exigency, she will enjoy support from a welfare apparatus which, if not munificent, nonetheless substantially surpasses that available to her southern peer. How eminently shrewd a decision to be born where life prospects are good!

But, of course, it was no decision at all that established the birth location, at least none made by that individual. Nor do we seem able to identify any other morally relevant factor that can justify advantages consequent on mere contingencies of geography. It is not possible retrospectively to undo circumstances of birth. But it is possible to allow individuals subsequently to alter their locations so as to better their lot according to their own conceptions of the good. National boundaries as observed in the contemporary world are substantial hurdles in the way of such activity, rendering it difficult or impossible for many individuals to relocate where prospects are more congenial. As such they fasten onto what is morally arbitrary and transform it into a factor critically significant for determining whether people's lives go well or ill.

Historically, some states have restricted individuals' internal mobility through requiring internal passports and establishing checkpoints through which residents must pass as they attempt to relocate. These regimes resemble feudal orders more closely than they do liberal ones, and it is to the credit of liberals that they have uniformly condemned internal restrictions on personal mobility.[8] However, when the transit in question involves crossing national boundaries, liberals have displayed considerably less consistency in condemning constraints on individual freedom. It is not easy to come up with a plausible principled distinction that would justify such markedly different treatment. Isn't it invidiously arbitrary to countenance travel at will from Arkansas to Texas but not from Mexico to Texas? It is difficult to resist an affirmative answer. (The case for a fundamental moral equivalence between international and intranational travel is set out at greater length in the final section of this chapter.)

2. Equality of Rights among Persons

Liberalism ascribes to all persons equal basic rights. The precise content of those rights is, to be sure, somewhat up for grabs. The more pristine versions of classical liberalism recognize predominantly rights to noninterference. But even classical liberals such as Locke, Smith, and Kant make room for some welfare rights, triggered by non-culpable exigency, that afford strong claims of access to positive provision from others. The "new liberalism" of the past century substantially magnifies the scope of these welfare rights as it concomitantly diminishes the scope of some of the old liberalism's proscriptions of interference, especially those concerning discretion over private property.

Whichever construal of liberalism is adopted, national boundaries are problematic. Is the right to noninterference enjoyed equally when some are at liberty to choose among a multitude of positions within productive, wealth-generating economies while others are free only to choose among modes of life in which even subsistence is not assured? Yet more problematic are entitlements to welfare goods. If these are a matter of basic human rights, then it is palpably evident that their enjoyment is grossly unequal and that the impermeability of national borders is a primary culprit in this divergence from principles of liberal equity. If, on the other hand, the benefactions of the welfare state are not the due of needy individuals as a matter of right, then their wide acceptance among liberals seems insufficiently well-grounded. Perhaps they can be reconceived not as rights in the strict sense but rather as compassionate transfers from those who have much to those who have little. However, since degrees of inequality across national boundaries are much more pronounced than those within national entities, welfare policies that are orders of magnitude more generous to co-nationals than they are to recipients of foreign aid appear to be morally offensive distortions of the impulse to benevolence.

3. Unchosen Particular Obligations

As noted above, states provide various benefits to their citizens (or residents; these two classes may or may not differ markedly with regard to eligibility for state-provided goods). Some of these benefits are available on request; others are provided whether or not one asks for or wants them. These do not, however, come free of attached strings. States that giveth also taketh away by requiring a range of performances from their citizens. The primary mode through which the piper extracts his pay is, of course, taxation. But states also lodge other demands against their citizens. They demand fidelity; only against one's own country can the crime of treason be committed. They practice conscription during time of war and sometimes during peacetime (and countries such as the United States which have abandoned a peacetime draft may pointedly insist on the right to resume it). Individuals can be obligated to serve on juries; they are compelled under threat of legal sanctions to reveal information to census takers; in some countries (e.g., Australia) they are required to vote in elections; and so on.

Performances owed to the state of residence/citizenship are particular duties. Only with considerable stretching can they be understood as having been voluntarily incurred.[9] As noted previously, liberalism is distinctly uncomfortable with nonconsensual particular duties. Indeed, a big part of the case for robust rights to noninterference is that they shield individuals from externally imposed encumbrances so that the moral space within which persons can direct their affairs according to their own conceptions of the good will not be unduly compromised. Yet these involuntarily acquired particular duties seem to be part and parcel of a world of states into which one is born and from which emigration is, at best, difficult and costly. The more they extend beyond the level of imposition required to sustain basic functions of a civil order, the more dubious they are from a liberal perspective.

4. Justice and National Entities

According to some theories of justice, entitlements to holdings ought to be a (primary; partial; sole) function of need. According to other theories, entitlements should be as strictly equal across persons as can feasibly be arranged. A variation on this theme is that inequalities in holdings are justified only to the extent that they are to the advantage of the least well-off class.[10] Other theories identify effort, or mixing one's labor with things, or the level of one's marginal contribution to the productivity pot, as pertinent factors for justice in distribution. There is no need to adjudicate here among these competing/ complementary accounts of justice to observe that nowhere in the lot do contingencies of geography enter. Indeed, for each of these theories, the factors identified as morally compelling would seem entirely or substantially to preclude distribution based on accidents of citizenship.

Classical liberalism, in contrast to welfare liberal, social democratic, or socialist politics, is little given to dalliance with notions of distributive justice. Therefore, the tension between universal egalitarian ideals and the actual practice of redistribution in a world in which national borders figure prominently is an embarrassment that can happily be consigned to other points of view. However, the scant consideration accorded distributive justice concerns can be understood as indirect support for classical liberal unease with hard national boundaries. Against his opponents the classical liberal can respond that even if it be granted for the sake of argument that coercively imposed redistribution is an appropriate means for the pursuit of ideals of distributive justice, the reality of hard borders that artificially confine the class of eligible recipients to compatriots undermines any social justice-based warrant that can be put forward on behalf of the legitimacy of nation-states.[11]

5. States and Ethnicity

It can be said in favor of the claims of the nation-state that it is not merely an arbitrary carving up of the world into discrete and unequal political units. Rather, those states that reflect shared ethnicity, culture, language, or the like afford individuals a context within which they are uniquely empowered to draw on resources that afford them the ability to construct for themselves worthwhile, meaningful lives. That is the positive side, and we shall return to it in the next section's exploration of the case for national boundaries. Here, though, it must be noted that from the perspective of much of the liberal tradition such an invocation of national (or ethnic; or cultural) communities is problematic.

First, it takes as the primary seedbed for individuals' projects and commitments not their own autonomous choices but rather the inherited ethos of the collectivity into which they are born. Externally imposed conceptions of the good labor under much the same liabilities for liberals as do externally imposed obligations.[12] Second, as political entities increasingly are defined by nationality characteristics, the exit option of "voting with one's feet" is yet further diminished, thus exacerbating the various problems surrounding accidents of natal geography by hitching them to ethnic differentiations among persons that are equally arbitrary from the moral point of view.

6. The Internal Exit Option

Exit does not only take the form of leaving. Rather, it can involve withdrawal from one set of relations and the subsequent taking up of some other set. When one abandons the Methodism of one's birth to take up Buddhism, selects a different long distance telephone carrier, drops out of the Republican party to become a Democrat, divorces and remarries, one has exited from *there* so as to enter *here*. (Mergers and divestments are marketplace analogues.) This ability to withdraw from patterns of association no longer desired so as to form new ones that are deemed preferable is cherished by liberals. It is a primary means through which individuals formulate and commit themselves to the furtherance of projects that confer meaning on individual lives.

Liberal states are, of course, zealous to protect the internal exit options of private individuals, illiberal states considerably less so. Both, however, are distinctly unfriendly to such rearrangements as they extend to groups of individuals desirous of establishing for themselves alternative political orderings. With only rare exceptions, they refuse to recognize in geographical sub-entities a right of secession. Attempts to dissociate typically are bloody: the American Civil War; the dismemberment of the former Yugoslavia, and so on. National boundaries, therefore, are problematic not only with regard to those whom they exclude—would-be immigrants and foreign nationals who wish to establish temporary employment arrangement in the host country—but also with regard to members of subnational enclaves who are included against their will.

Why Borders?

If there are states, then there are boundaries that demarcate their extent: that is a matter of definition, a necessary truth. What is not necessary, however, is the degree to which boundaries exclude and include, the degree to which they sustain or stand athwart the projects of individuals. These are not facts of nature or theorems of logic but rather are a function of the decisions of political agents. In order to make headway in assessing the optimal degree of hardness for national boundaries, it is necessary to fill in both sides of the balance sheet, to do an accounting of the assets as well as the liabilities. Which liberal ends do borders serve? Four suggest themselves.

Civility and States

Borders are intrinsic to the establishment of morally secure zones such that individuals are able to pursue their various ends free from incessant predation by others. For this to amount to civility rather than escape or domination it must feature reciprocity: The forbearance that one receives from others is the same forbearance that is extended to them. It is the basic rights of persons that constrain predation. The mere existence of such rights is not, however, sufficient to secure this happy consummation. They must be rendered credible against would-be violators via effective enforcement. But in addition, abstract rights to life, liberty, and property must be filled out with determinate, publicly accessible content if they are to serve as navigational guideposts for individuals seeking to ascertain what is and what is not permissible. For example, individuals might come to know via the exercise of pure philosophical reason that they are at liberty to appropriate unowned property. But which performances constitute valid acts of appropriation is not discernible a priori but rather must be established conventionally as the rule in force for a particular domain. Similarly, it may be a precept of liberal theory that individuals enjoy a right to transfer their assets at death by bequest, but the specific formalities that must be observed in order that a document have the status of a binding last will and testament are the contingent determinations of some particular society. Precisely because basic rights are universal, they are to be construed as malleable normative forms into which determinate content must be poured if they are to be rendered practically efficacious.[13] Such conferral of content need not take place under the aegis of a legislative body; evolving customs or decisions as common law rules can supply the necessary substance. Whatever the process of their emergence, though, rights-in-force, unlike the abstract conceptions of the philosophers, are vivified only within the precincts of a political order.

Theorists' accounts differ concerning their answer to the question of how states give effect to individuals' rights against predation. For Hobbes, prior to the original compact there exist no moral protections. Rather, "every man has a Right to every thing: even to one anothers body."[14] Only with the coming of Leviathan are there duties of forbearance incumbent on individuals, and these are brought into being via the edict of the sovereign.

Locke takes issue with Hobbes's construal of the state of nature. It is not to be identified with the state of war, Locke argues, because it is governed by a rationally accessible law of nature under which men live. The author and ultimate enforcer of that law is God, and among the rights His law confers is an executive right held by all persons to punish transgressors of the natural law. But because God's enforcement, although utterly reliable, is long-delayed and for the most part not of this world, and because ad hoc human enforcements are of markedly irregular quality, the peace individuals enjoy in the state of nature is unsettled and fragile. "I easily grant," says Locke "that *Civil Government* is the proper Remedy for the Inconveniences of the State of Nature, which must certainly be Great, where Men may be Judges in their own

Case."[15] On Locke's account, then, the moral force of human rights is unacceptably feeble until they are enshrined within political societies.

Insofar as Locke's derivation of the state rests on theological premises of a premodern cast, its utility for contemporary liberals is compromised. By abandoning resort to a divine lawgiver as the ground of a cognitively accessible moral order, Kant avoids theological entanglements and simultaneously offers a tighter and more philosophically compelling justification of the state. As is well known, Kant grounds morality on the a priori fundamental principle of practical reason, the categorical imperative. It is therefore tempting to suppose that the existence of the state is irrelevant to individuals' ability to ascertain and fulfill their moral duties. That, however, would be a mistaken inference. For although it is a precept of the logic of practical reason that one must act always to treat persons as ends in themselves and not merely as means, what treating someone as an end entails with regard to specific performances is not similarly knowable a priori. One fails to treat another as an end in himself if one appropriates that person's material goods; no such failure occurs if those goods are unowned. Which of the two is my appropriation of *this*? Unless there exist authoritative, publicly accessible rules governing property appropriation and transfer, the question is unanswerable in principle. An agent may have performed ritualistic acts by which she meant thereby to indicate that she has claimed for herself some desired item, but her wanting this performance to have that significance does not make it so. Just as one cannot engage in linguistic interactions by uttering sounds of one's own verbal coinage, one does not engage in moral transactions with others by privately willing one's own exclusive title to some item of property. Both language and ownership of property presuppose public standards of meaning. The crucial difference between these two human practices is that talking does not as such impose obligations on others, but creation of exclusive title to things does. That is why linguistic adequacy can be achieved without the superintendence of an Académie Française, but morally adequate recognition of property claims does presuppose the existence of an authoritative political order.

For liberals of a classical orientation, property rights enjoy a centrality that has largely been displaced in more recent iterations of the liberal venture. It is worth underscoring, therefore, that the Kantian argument is not confined to the morality of utilizing *things*. Rather, it extends to the life and liberty of *persons*. That one may not use another as a mere means to one's ends implies the impermissibility of launching unprovoked assaults on others. But because one may not permissibly regard oneself as a mere means either, one is entitled, indeed perhaps obligated, to resist incursions on one's own moral personhood. However, in the state of nature there exist no public standards via which one can distinguish between the innocent and culpable. If others threaten to deprive one of items necessary for one's continued subsistence as a self-directing agent—and in the state of nature such threats are constant—then it is not possible significantly to progress in the moral realm beyond Hobbes's right of each to all things, including the person of others. Thus Kant argues:

> A state of peace among men living together is not the same as the state of nature, which is rather the state of war. For even if it does not involve active hostilities, it involves a constant threat of their breaking out. Thus the state of peace must be *formally instituted* . . . which can happen only in a *lawful* state.[16]

Because the practice of morality between individuals requires that they be at peace with one another, and because they cannot genuinely achieve peace, as opposed to a temporary suspension of hostilities, unless their interactions are governed by law, the existence of a juridical order is a necessary condition for moral practice (although not, of course, for its a priori categorical form). Thus according to Kant, unlike Locke, exit from the state of nature into civil society is not an option that individuals may at their discretion elect to employ in order to relieve themselves of the former's inconveniences. Rather, it is strictly mandatory:

> [T]he first decision the individual is obliged to make, if he does not wish to renounce all concepts of right, will be to adopt the principle that *one must abandon the state of nature* in which everyone follows his own desires, and unite with everyone else (with whom he cannot avoid having intercourse) in order to submit to external, public and lawful coercion. . . . In other words, he should at all costs enter into a state of civil society. . . . Anyone may thus use force to impel the others to abandon this state for a state of right.[17]

And also unlike Locke, Kant need not resort to a notion of tacit consent stretched beyond the limits of what is plausibly voluntary to establish the authority of the state, nor need he wrestle with the problem of independents who conscientiously refuse to enter civil society.[18] That is because respect for basic liberal rights is not in tension with the formation of the state but rather demands it.

Although I believe Kant's justification of the state to be the strongest available, this is one of numerous foundational areas in which liberals agree to disagree. But whether via a Kantian or some alternative approach, concern for zones of civility within which individuals can enjoy a decent degree of security from unwarranted interference is the linchpin of the liberal state. The extent of those zones is defined by states' borders. In that sense the liberal rationale for national borders follows forthwith. However, the moral necessity that there be borders does not as such imply anything specific concerning how hard they properly should be as devices for inclusion and exclusion. All that can be said at this point is that they must be functional with regard to the primary purpose of securing the preconditions of civility. So, for example, the most plausible basis for justifiable restrictions on immigration is exclusion of those who can reasonably be believed to threaten rights violations. Similarly, there is a strong onus within liberal orders against the imposition of specific duties of performance, but insofar as these may be necessary for the maintenance of a rights-respecting, rights-protecting regime, that onus can be met. Taxation in support of defense against enemies both foreign and domestic, or even compelled military service in time of war, can thus be understood as consistent with liberal principles. At the risk of stating the obvious, I append a reminder that not every call for the imposition of such duties is reputable. It is likely that more sins against liberal principles have been committed in the name of defense than on any other basis.

Public Goods

It is morally incumbent on states to defend zones of civility. Beyond the domain of what the political order is strictly required to do extends an indefinite range of ends that states are permitted, even well-advised to pursue. Provision of amenities that render the lives of citizens more comfortable and commodious is another legitimate area of state activity. I do not mean thereby to suggest that provision via political means is the primary avenue for their securement. That is what the market is for, and in that capacity it performs wondrously well. Nonetheless, there are certain goods and services with regard to which the engine of capitalist production sputters, those dubbed by economists *public goods*. There are two defining features of a public good: (1) Its consumption by one person does not preclude its like consumption by others; and (2) if the good is made available to one person, then others cannot be excluded from also enjoying it. Distinguished political economists of an impeccably liberal persuasion have conjoined their advocacy of a sharply limited political realm with acknowledgment of the advisability of political provision of public goods. Government, argues Adam Smith, is necessary for

> erecting and maintaining those publick institutions and those publick works, which though they may be in the highest degree advantageous to a great society are, however, of such a nature that the profit could never repay the expence to any individual or small number of individuals, and which it, therefore, cannot be expected that any individual or small number of individuals should erect or maintain.[19]

As with purported necessities of defense, public goods designations can serve as a pretext to disguise plunder of some by others. But although notoriously vulnerable to abuse—not only among liberals of a Jewish persuasion is "pork barrel" not kosher!—provision of public goods via political means is defensible in principle. If the interests of all affected individuals are advanced on balance by coercive taxation to fund goods that would otherwise not be available due to excessive transaction costs or free-riding, then this policy cannot summarily be condemned as impermissibly using some individuals as mere means for the ends of others. Rather, each person has from her own perspective reason to endorse it. Although those of the libertarian wing of classical liberalism tend to reject tax-supported public goods, on principle, they are, I believe, mistaken in doing so.[20]

A further justification for national boundaries is, then, that they demarcate a domain within which public goods are made available to those who are constrained to fund them. That manner of statement conveys the strengths but also the limits of the argument: it is only as good as the extent to which externalities are internalized through political means. That is, the greater the overlap between the class of those who enjoy the benefits and the class of those who pay the tariff (and the closer the proportionality between individuals' subjectively valued benefits and their tax shares), the greater the justifiability. For those goods the enjoyment of which extends throughout but not beyond the polity, national borders can be rationalized on economic as well as political grounds. National defense is the stereotypical public good in this sense, representing as close to an ideal case as one can find. For other public goods provided at a national level the fit is apt to be less close, and as noted above, some can amount to blatant extortions. Goods for which the relevant scope of consumption is either appreciably smaller than or appreciably greater than the national entity ought not be funded from a tax base delimited by those borders. For example, measures to combat global warming by restricting the generation of greenhouse gases are better pursued on an extra-national basis, while provision of rapid transit services within a locality is properly provided on an intra-national basis. But even when the national entity is not of the appropriate dimensions for advantageous direct provision of some public good, it may figure indirectly in ensuring its availability: nations can negotiate treaties amongst themselves to jointly produce a good of international scope; they can provide an overall framework within which regional or local taxing districts fund projects of a commensurate size. Public goods promotion without provision is, then, an additional function that appropriately constructed national boundaries can serve.

National Ideals

A nation's borders determine the perimeter of a unit of political administration. Often its shaping is the product of historical or geographical accident that easily could have been otherwise and which, had events so transpired, would have possessed a coherence and integrity comparable to that of the borders which actually obtain. But boundaries need not be arbitrary in this sense. Rather, they may include a population largely homogeneous with regard to sharing a common language, customs, history, rituals, and aspirations. If so, the country's political borders will be congruent with cultural or national borders.

The reason this matters is not, for liberals, because of some allegedly deep fact about race or blood being destiny. Indeed, that is the sort of conception which liberals are obliged to resist vigorously because it undermines the voluntary self-direction of individuals. However, for many people a substantial component of that self-direction is to orient themselves along the axis that their cultural community has afforded them, and toward this end they take political autonomy to be a crucial component. A Jewish state in Israel, a free Ireland for the Irish, sending the Raj back whence it came: these and similar aspirations have fueled much of the politics of this century; further episodes of the nationalist drama are certain to be prominent features of the next one. Liberalism is a fundamentally individualistic theory, but if the ends to which individuals swear allegiance happen in large measure to be communal, then a liberal order manifests support for the projects in which its citizens have enlisted by supplying a political infrastructure conducive to satisfying, meaningful communal life. Establishing as far as may be feasible national (or, in a federalist system, subnational) boundaries congruent with ethnic lines of cleavage is, under such conditions, not to foist valuations on the reluctant but rather to accept at face value their own valuations.

The politics of identity does, then, offer some support for national boundaries geographically responsive to communal perceptions. For reasons adduced in the previous section's discussion of "2. Equality of Rights among Persons," however, this justification is double-edged. Borders the explicit rationale of which is to advance the communal life of a stipulated group are thereby rendered unfriendly or, at best, less friendly to those inhabitants who are not members of the favored group. Moreover, they can be oppressive to group members who do not recognize in that membership a central component of their own good. Why should their autonomy be compromised by a heavyhanded nationalism?

A not altogether implausible response is to observe that politics is the art of the possible, and with all due credit to ideals of equality and neutrality, it is not possible to engineer regimes to each person's specifications. Those who are dissatisfied are entitled to sympathy, they are entitled to leave for greener pastures, but they are not entitled to veto that which is responsive to the aspirations of the majority. Note, however, that as the world's territory is increasingly carved up politically along nationalistic lines, there becomes less opportunity to find alternative arrangements for those reluctant to be inducted into communal polities. This difficulty is exacerbated by hard borders that exclude desired immigration. Moreover, national communities that have battled valiantly to secure their own independence typically display considerable opposition to secessionist thoughts of enclaves inspired by different communal ideals. Arab Palestine, the northern six counties of Ireland, and

Kashmir are not, needless to say, happy outposts of peaceful communal life. To summarize: Cultural and nationalist aspirations do provide under certain circumstances further legitimation for appropriately drawn national borders, but they are also extremely likely to prove mischievous.

Considerations of Second Best

Liberalism is a theory within politics, anarchism a theory in opposition to politics. Thus, at a deep level they are diametrically opposed. Nonetheless, liberals more than exponents of other political persuasions are apt to lend a sympathetic ear to anarchistic denunciations of the political order. That order is an *imposed* order. Make no mistake about it; states are in the coercion business. Liberals fully share the anarchist's antipathy to coercion, although from it they draw different conclusions. Still, it can be said that the question of whether states can come to be without massively violating people's rights in the process is one concerning which reasonable liberals and anarchists disagree.

Suppose for the sake of argument that the anarchist is right: A world in which states are absent is morally preferable to one with states. Incorporated within this proposition is a supposition that problems of ensuring civility, supplying public goods, and so on can be addressed satisfactorily through purely consensual activity.[21] If so, a world without states might be nobody's idea of paradise, but neither would it be Hobbes's state of nature. If coercion is not strictly necessary for the attainment of compelling moral goals, then it is strictly impermissible. Ergo, nations and the boundaries that define them are illicit.

Even if the premises of this argument are granted, the conclusion does not follow. Or rather, the conclusion is ambiguous, holding under one interpretation but not the one relevant to contemporary political practice. What I mean is this: If the anarchist is correct, then it was a thoroughly bad idea in the first place to establish nation-states. But in a world chock-a-block full of them, it is by no means evident that any state is morally obliged to disestablish itself. Precisely because the special talent of states is coercion, a populace without a political apparatus of its own is a sheep among wolves. It may be intrinsically better to be a sheep than a wolf; a world of sheep may be intrinsically better than a world of wolves; but to be the only animal in the jungle who lacks sharp teeth and claws may be the worst status of all. To switch metaphors to one more common in the professional literature, deployment of a statist apparatus is the dominant strategy in a prisoner's dilemma. The anarchist is arguably correct in maintaining that transcending the interactive circumstances that generate the prisoner's dilemma is the morally optimal solution but, although devoutly to be wished, it is not an outcome open to any of the players to choose.[22] What they can choose is to arm themselves in a dangerous world in which that is what others are doing. Elementary considerations of prudence suggest that they are well-advised to do so.

For those tempted to embrace anarchism, this is the crucial argument for the legitimacy of states possessing defensible borders. For liberals the argument is secondary; what they take it to establish is that the case for boundaries is morally overdetermined. That does not mean that its force is negligible. Rather, the argument from second best is pragmatically powerful. For although the warrant of propositions of foundational philosophical theory may be shrouded in epistemic murkiness, that states are a fact of life now and for the foreseeable future is evident. So long as it remains evident, considerations of second best weigh heavily.

Boundaries within Limits

As states are bounded, so too are the ambitions of this essay. They do not extend to development of a comprehensive listing of conditions necessary and sufficient for liberal optimality of states' contours. The goal has been the far more modest one of identifying the various assets and liabilities attaching to national boundaries. That is not by way of apology; modesty is, after all, a virtue. Yet, as Aristotle observes, the virtuous is a mean between extremes of deficiency and excess, and it would be timorously deficient to take leave of this moral accounting with entries on both sides of the balance sheet but no speculation concerning the bottom line. Without any pretensions of putting myself forward as a philosophical C.P.A., it is to the bottom line I now turn.

Hard or Soft Boundaries?

Boundaries, insofar as they function to define the extent of states, are, from the liberal perspective, justifiable. That liberals reject anarchism is not exactly news. Somewhat more newsworthy is that these boundaries alter the rights and obligations possessed by individuals in the state of nature, and that this alteration occurs irrespective of whether the parties have consented to it. For example, individuals residing within its perimeter are obligated to obey the positive legal enactments of the state. They are obligated to pay taxes levied against their person and property.[23] They come to possess civil rights that individuals in the state of nature lack. Unlike the bylaws of a club, these attach to individuals in virtue of their location vis-à-vis national boundaries rather than—*pace* Locke—as consequences of memberships that they have voluntarily undertaken.

Not all borders are created equal. Fulfillment of their primary function requires that they be constructed so as to facilitate maintenance of civility within and defense against predation from without. If borders are strategically indefensible or subsume perpetually hostile groups unwilling to live at peace with each other, their functionality is compromised, perhaps fatally. The greater the extent to which borders serve to internalize externalities surrounding the provision of public goods via political means, the better. Beyond this, liberal political philosophy has little to contribute to the theory of optimally carving out national boundaries.[24]

It can be a good bit more voluble, though, concerning the optimal permeability of borders. The opening of this chapter introduced the distinction between hard and soft borders, where by a hard border is understood a demarcation not traversable at will which imposes substantial costs and benefits on individuals in virtue of circumstances of their geography. Hardness is prima facie undesirable insofar as it hobbles the projects of individual actors. Therefore, the onus of justification rests squarely on the shoulders of those who promote the hardening of boundaries. That onus can be met only by demonstrating that the recommended degree of hardness is necessary for carrying out some item on the liberal agenda, and that the moral gravity of this item is comparable to the burdens thereby imposed. One addendum: Most policy goals are analog rather than binary; that is, they are advanced to a greater or lesser extent rather than being on/off. To the extent that enhanced hardness furthers such a goal, policy determination will incorporate adjustment at the margin. That is, increased border hardness is acceptable just up to that point at which marginal gains achieved equal marginal costs incurred. (Here as elsewhere, any appearance of precision in the grounding theory will routinely be belied by the messiness of practice.)

To relieve some of the abstractness of the preceding discussion, I now turn to applications of the principle. One area in which the hardness of boundaries notably affects individuals' ability to advance their interests is *immigration policy*. It was suggested in the discussion above on "Civility and States" that states can properly close their borders to those who pose a significant threat to the rights of their inhabitants. Denying entry to those who have demonstrated a disposition for violent predation is a clear-cut application of this idea. Considerably cloudier, although still within the ambit of this rationale, is denial of entry to those whose religious, political, or ideological orientation incorporates hostility to liberal practices. But even if for the sake of argument a very generous interpretation is extended to the goal of maintaining a zone of civility, it cannot be stretched to legitimate a generally exclusionary immigration policy. Those who wish to traverse a country's borders in order to enjoy access to economic and cultural opportunities do not thereby incur suspicion as potential felons or antidemocratic zealots. The presumption runs in the other direction; people who show themselves willing to bear the hardships of uprooting themselves and their families from all that is familiar so as to begin new lives abroad are not the mostly likely candidates for the role of subversive. And even if erection of an array of barriers will keep out a few additional undesirables among the many innocent seekers of a better life who are excluded, basic considerations of proportionality preclude fishing with so wide a net.

Public goods provision is secondary to securing civility, but it too is a legitimate function of the liberal state, and it has some implications for immigration policy. It can be argued that to admit into the class of public goods beneficiaries individuals who are unable to share adequately in the funding of those goods constitutes unfairness to the beneficiaries who are required to write the checks. However, a presumption that immigrants will be long-term feeders but not contributors at the public trough is neither credible in its own right nor capable of sustaining a case for generally hard borders. If concern for fairness in public goods funding is genuine and not merely a cloak to disguise xenophobia, then it can be addressed through substantially less draconian measures. For example, would-be immigrants can be required to give evidence of a capacity for economic productivity. Lacking that, they can secure entry by being sponsored by those willing to post a bond guaranteeing that they will not become a public charge. I do not mean to endorse such measures, only to observe that on liberal grounds they are clearly preferable to blanket denials of entry.[25]

Restrictions on trade that crosses national boundaries are even more dubious from a liberal perspective. Only rarely will it be even remotely plausible to claim that the movement of traded goods poses a threat to maintenance of civility or levels of well-being enjoyed by nationals.[26] Indeed, because trade is mutually beneficial, the expected effect is in the other direction. Of course, even when advocates of mercantilism are clever enough to devise public interest grounds that are not instantly risible, these almost always are ill-disguised surrogates for an interest that extends to a considerably restricted subset of that public. That domestic manufacturers were not unwilling to seek employment of the political apparatus to preclude competition from foreign purveyors was already well-known to Adam Smith more than two centuries ago.[27] Progress since then in the technology of lobbying and (speaking purely hypothetically, of course) in securing invitations to sleep in the Lincoln Bedroom sustains the seeking of governmentally conferred rents as a viable and remunerative activity. That practice enjoys no credibility from a liberal perspective. Nor, for that matter, is it a legitimate function of the state to take heed of the admonitions of inspired visionaries who perceive sucking sounds of jobs crossing national boundaries and demand the damming of that flow. Even if this does not represent thoroughly crackpot economics, the right of a country's citizens to transact on a voluntary basis with those whom they see fit to favor with their custom does not end abruptly at its borders.

The boundaries of virtually all modern nation-states set out an area in which compulsory *transfers from the relatively rich to the relatively poor* are effected through political means. That is, these countries are one or another species of the genus *welfare state*.[28] Defending the largesse of the welfare state provides what is perhaps the single strongest rationale for hard borders. The argument is straightforward: If people who have little are allowed entry into a welfare state that has much and thereby gain entitlements to its largesse, they will constitute a significant drain on the assets of current inhabitants. In order to defend the redistributive agenda against the political equivalent of a corporation's stock being watered down, it is necessary to rein in access. Hard borders secure that end.

The argument may sound more than a little bit tawdry. It hinges on the desire of the haves to shield some of their assets from the claims of the have-nots. From a classical liberal perspective, however, that desire is eminently reputable. For theorists such as Locke, Hume, Smith, and Kant, a central task of the state is to secure individuals in comfortable enjoyment of their property. Morality may encourage people to be generous and compassionate with the overflow from their plenty, but only in extremis are they strictly obligated to comply with transfers to the less well-off. And so while socialists or welfare liberals can afford to look somewhat askance at this mode of defense against demands for redistribution, classical liberals cannot. People have a right to do as they see fit with what is rightfully theirs: this is a fundamental postulate of that liberal creed.

But saying that this is the strongest rationale for hard borders tacitly assumes that the antecedent of the relevant conditional is accepted. That is, *if* it is morally legitimate to act to ensure the sustainability of the welfare state, *then* it is permissible to bar indigent nonresidents from feasting on its overflow. It is precisely the antecedent, however, that will be contested by classical liberals. Indeed, disputation over its acceptability is what defines the separation between the old and new liberalisms.[29] Classical liberalism rejects the credentials of the welfare state not simply as it has become bloated, corrupt, inefficient, and counterproductive,[30] but at its root. So although it is sympathetic to objections against allowing foreigners carte blanche to take a place in the queue of recipients of transfer payments, it is similarly averse to admitting co-nationals into that line. What is a wrenching issue for those situated at most other positions along the political spectrum[31] is a clear case for classical liberals: Exclusion in defense of the welfare state is wrong.

That is not to say that this line of argument is without interest for classical liberals, but its interest is other than as a defense of hard boundaries. Rather, when antecedent and consequent are reversed it becomes a rather charming *reductio ad absurdum* of welfare liberalism. As already indicated in "Considerations of Second Best," welfare liberalism's conception of social justice grounded in a universalistic egalitarianism fits uneasily with principles of distribution that render those situated within the national borders vastly more equal than those on the outside. If the less well-off citizens of an advanced Western capitalist society are, though deprived relative to local standards, situated somewhere in the upper quintile of the world's population with regard to wealth, income, or overall standard of living, then it is exceedingly difficult to devise a persuasive pretext for safeguarding the stability of the system of transfers which they are pleased to enjoy by denying access to those whose absolute level of well-being is markedly lower and who thereby see their single best chance to lead decent lives vanish at the border checkpoint. We can formalize the argument in this way:

P1. Sustaining the welfare state requires erecting hard borders.

P2. Erecting hard borders entails imposing severe harms on and/or withholding major benefits from the less well-off for the sake of the more well-off.

P3. It is morally impermissible to impose severe harms on and/or withhold major benefits from the less well-off for the sake of the more well-off.

Therefore:

C. It is morally impermissible to sustain the welfare state.

The argument is valid. Whether it constitutes a decisive indictment of the welfare state depends on whether all its premises are true. Of them, the most questionable is P3, the normative premise,[32] but it or some very similar claim underlies welfare liberalism as well as other egalitarian theories of justice. Therefore, even if in isolation the argument is inconclusive, it has considerable bite when offered *ad hominem*. I believe that among the several complaints that can cogently be lodged against contemporary welfare states, one of the most telling is the massive injustices that their hard borders perpetrate. This essay is not, however, a foray in the War between the Liberalisms, nor is it even an examination of immigration policy as such. Rather, it is an explication of the classical liberal construal of the moral status of national boundaries. Given the limits of that assignment, it is enough here to conclude that concern for the flourishing of the welfare state fails to justify the hardening of national boundaries.

A Modest Proposal

This brings us close to the aforementioned bottom line. I should now like to advance a prescription for filling it in that is not as tautologous as it sounds: *State boundaries should be very much like the boundaries of states.* It is not tautologous because it blatantly and deliberately equivocates on the two occurrences of "state." Although the literature of political theory usually understands a state to be a sovereign national entity, the term can also mean a component member of a federal structure. So it is within the United *States* of America, Australia, and other federal republics.

In several respects the boundaries of states in the second sense operate much like the boundaries of states in the first sense. They demarcate areas throughout which a particular civil order obtains. As one crosses the border separating Michigan from Ohio, just as with crossing from Michigan into Canada, what is involved in securing a divorce, purchasing a martini on Sunday, creating a public nuisance, or appealing to the parole board for early release undergoes an identity transformation. States of both kinds supply to their inhabitants public goods which are funded by taxes imposed on a class of people more or less congruent with the beneficiaries of the good. And they also effect compulsory wealth redistributions of a welfare-state type.

In one respect, however, states as federated parts differ significantly from nation-states: their boundaries are remarkably softer. When one travels along I-75, no checkpoint is encountered at the Michigan-Ohio border. Change of residence across state borders is equally unimpeded; a person who wishes to move from Detroit to Toledo is free to just go ahead and do so without asking leave of anyone. Flows of commerce also are virtually unobstructed: neither quotas nor tariffs nor outright bans stand in the way of voluntary interactions between willing buyers and sellers. Even with regard to the provision and funding of public goods, boundaries are mostly innocuous. Ohio motorists can drive along Michigan state roads on the same terms as Michiganders despite not having contributed to their funding. Theoretical worries that such (literal!) free-riding constitutes unfairness or will lead to inefficient underprovision of the good in question are thoroughly belied in practice, probably because terms of access are reciprocal. To be sure, a few instances can be cited in which residents enjoy a status different from that of nonresidents: people who reside in Toledo have to pay substantially more than those from Detroit if they wish to matriculate at Michigan State University; conditions of access to state parks differ; and so on. Compared with the hurdles set up by nation-states, however, these are trivial.

Intranational state borders are, from the liberal perspective, notably more benign than international borders. More precisely, they are benign compared with the hard international borders ubiquitous in the contemporary global arena. Need that be the case? That is, could states satisfactorily carry out their essential functions if the boundaries separating them were softened? This is the $64 question, and it is not for philosophers to prescribe concerning delicate matters of *Realpolitik*. Nonetheless, and with all caveats duly inserted and noted, it is at the very least not obvious that proper political functioning demands hard borders. Empirical evidence of a limited sort is supplied by the member states of the European Community who have progressively softened their borders, such softening emphatically redounding to their mutual benefit. The evidentiary weight of the observation is, admittedly, lessened by the fact that the softening has been largely internal to the Community and coexists with considerable residual hardness around its perimeter. Further evidence, also far from conclusive, is provided by the experience of regional trade alliances such as NAFTA and lowering of global trade barriers under GATT auspices.

Reasonable observers will differ with regard to the implications they draw from such political phenomena. The one respect in which something approaching consensus obtains concerning the greater efficacy of hard borders is their ability to erect walls around the welfare state so as to keep the outs firmly out. This, though, is a rationale that enjoys no credibility among liberals of a classical persuasion and ought to be (and, I suspect, is) a source of no little embarrassment to welfare liberals. With regard to the acknowledgedly legitimate functions of government, consensus is apt to prove more elusive. Lack of certainty should not, however, paralyze political reformers. The thesis emerging from these pages is that from a liberal perspective the onus rests squarely on those who would argue for interposing hard boundaries between individuals and their aspirations. Unless there is a clear preponderance of reasons showing that they are in fact necessary, hard boundaries are impermissible. There exists no such clear preponderance of evidence. The bottom line, then, is that the boundaries surrounding nation-states—in contrast to intranational states—are normatively suspect. To the hard question of the conditions under which national borders are justifiable, softness is the indicated answer.

Notes

An ancestor of these remarks was offered at the University of Colorado political theory seminar. Conversation with the seminar participants afforded me considerable assistance in sharpening the arguments of this essay. Thanks also to Uri Henig and Elizabeth Lomasky for their help in its preparation.

1. Hypothetical consent is not some alternate, lesser variety of consent; it is not consent at all. Rather, it is a surrogate for acts of choice and, therefore, although it may safeguard certain aspects of individuals' welfare, it is altogether irrelevant to maintenance of autonomy.

2. E.g., purges, dispossession, terror, genocide.

3. A word about nomenclature: "Classical liberalism," though ponderous, has come to be the term of choice for referring to the political standpoint which, prior to the triumph of the welfare state, went under the more satisfactory rubric "liberalism." Classical liberalism recognizes in individuals robust rights to be let alone both by other individuals and by the state, in order that they may enjoy a wide liberty to lead their lives according to their own lights. The primary function of the political order is to secure individuals in the possession of these rights against potential aggressors, foreign and domestic. Claims against the state for positive provision of moral goods other than noninterference are either absent or distinctly secondary. I deliberately refrain from

supplying a more precise characterization so as not unduly to constrain by definitional fiat the succeeding discussion of national boundaries. For stylistic and other reasons I shall henceforth employ "liberal" rather than "classical liberal" except where to do so would be ambiguous or otherwise misleading.

4. Or at least primarily so; duties of rectification and, arguably, limited redistribution can arise in the absence of choice.

5. Alone among the canonical liberal authors, Locke devotes significant attention to the moral environment within which children are born and nurtured by mothers and fathers who have a central interest in the prospects of their progeny. See *The Second Treatise of Government*, chap. VI, "Of Paternal Power." Even here, though, the family is less an object of concern in its own right than it is an adjunct to Locke's ongoing critique of Sir Robert Filmer's patriarchal justification of political authority. I have attempted to fill in some of these gaps in *Persons, Rights, and the Moral Community* (New York: Oxford University Press, 1987), especially in chap. 7, "Extending the Moral Community: Children," 152–87.

6. See, for example, Michael Sandel's critique of liberalism's "unencumbered selves" in *Liberalism and the Limits of Justice* (Cambridge: Cambridge University Press, 1982) and Alasdair MacIntyre's invocation in *After Virtue* (Notre Dame, Ind.: University of Notre Dame Press, 1981) of the role of communal virtues and associated narratives for the development of persons' identity.

7. A still useful, if somewhat dated, survey of the central issues is offered by Henry Sidgwick, *The Elements of Politics*, 4th ed. (London: Macmillan and Co., 1919; Kraus Reprint Co., 1969), chap. XIV, "The Area of Government—States and Districts," 217–36.

8. See, for example, Adam Smith, *Wealth of Nations* I.x.c., "Inequalities Occasioned by the Policy of Europe," (Indianapolis: Liberty Classics, 1981), 135–59.

9. Locke's doctrine of *tacit consent* is the best-known attempt to construe as voluntary individuals' susceptibility to state exactions: "[E]very Man, that hath any Possession, or Enjoyment, of any part of the Dominions of any Government, doth thereby give his *tacit Consent*, and is as far forth obliged to Obedience to the Laws of that Government, during such Enjoyment, as any one under it; whether this his Possession be of Land; to him and his Heirs for ever, or a Lodging only for a Week; or whether it be barely travelling freely on the Highway; and in Effect, it reaches as far as the very being of any one within the Territories of that Government." *Second Treatise of Government*, sec. 119 (Peter Laslett, ed. [Cambridge: Cambridge University Press, 1960], 348). There exists an extensive literature surrounding the Lockean doctrine of tacit consent. Liberal commentators tend to be uneasy with so open-ended a conception of how one's acts or omissions can be read as voluntary assumptions of obligation despite the absence of any conscious intention to acknowledge and submit to state authority. It is the sophisticated cousin of the "Love it or leave it!" slogan that sprouted on automobile bumpers during the Vietnam War. Note that even if Lockean tacit consent be granted, it is yet a further step to go beyond the duty of residents and visitors alike to obey the civil laws to duties of specific performance.

10. This is the difference principle made famous by John Rawls in *A Theory of Justice* (Cambridge: Harvard University Press, 1971).

11. Rawls characterizes the basic structure of the political order to which principles of justice apply as a closed society: "We are to regard it as self-contained and as having

no relations with other societies. Its members enter it only by birth and leave it only by death." John Rawls, *Political Liberalism* (New York: Columbia University Press, 1993), 12. Rawls does not thereby mean to preclude rights of emigration or immigration; the characterization is meant simply as an analytical simplification. However, the question it conspicuously begs is whether a state's internal redistributive practices can be justified in a world of vast inequalities between rich and poor nations.

12. See, for example, John Stuart Mill's stout defense of individuality: "He who lets the world, or his own portion of it, choose his plan of life for him, has no need of any other faculty than the ape-like one of imitation. . . . It is possible that he might be guided in some good path, and kept out of harm's way . . . [b]ut what will be his comparative worth as a human being? It really is of importance not only what men do, but also what manner of men they are that do it." Stefan Collini, ed., *On Liberty and Other Writings* (Cambridge: Cambridge University Press, 1989), 59.

13. This argument is more fully developed in *Persons, Rights and the Moral Community*, 101–5.

14. *Leviathan*, chap. 14 (Cambridge: Cambridge University Press, 1991), 91. I do not hereby take any position on the much debated issue of whether Hobbes is or is not properly to be classified among the liberal theorists. If not a liberal, he is the quintessential proto-liberal, the one against whom all succeeding theorists have to test their philosophical mettle.

15. *Second Treatise of Government*, 13.

16. Immanuel Kant, "Perpetual Peace," in *Kant: Political Writings*, ed. Hans Reiss (Cambridge: Cambridge University Press, 1970), 98 (emphasis in the original).

17. *Metaphysics of Morals*, in *Kant: Political Writings*, 137–38. Emphasis added.

18. How to address within a Lockean framework the problem of independents is extensively addressed by Robert Nozick in *Anarchy, State, and Utopia* (New York: Basic Books, 1974), chaps. 4 and 5, pp. 54–119. I criticize Nozick's argument in *Persons, Rights and the Moral Community*, 141–46.

19. *Wealth of Nations* V.i.c., p. 723. For an admirably lucid updating of Smith's discussion, see Milton Friedman, *Capitalism and Freedom* (Chicago: University of Chicago Press, 1962).

20. For an argument to that effect, see *Persons, Rights and the Moral Community*, 146–51.

21. "Satisfactorily" does not mean without significant equity or efficiency shortfalls. Rather, it means not conspicuously falling below the level of attainment achieved by governments. The latter, in case reminder is needed, consistently falls somewhere in the range between OK and dismal.

22. A liberal variation on this anarchistic theme is to hold out prospects of egress from the prisoner's dilemma not by abolition of states but through a peaceful federation in which each has membership. That is Kant's conception of the consummation of liberal politics; see "Perpetual Peace," 93–130 in the Reiss edition.

23. The existence of these obligations is, of course, subject to their otherwise satisfying constraints of justice.

24. One area in which additional contributions would be welcome is the *ethics of secession*. From the liberal perspective, issues surrounding secession are nettlesome. On the one hand, secession enhances the internal exit option for national minorities. On the other hand, whatever liberation it affords to these minorities is typically

counterbalanced by increased oppression of subminorities. Celebrating national autonomy can just as easily find expression in practices of repressing others as in developing
one's own cultural distinctiveness. Indeed, if that distinctiveness incorporates hostility
to designated competitive nationalities, the two are indistinguishable. (Recall the discussion above in "6. The Internal Exit Option.") Moreover, if secession is a standing
possibility, the threat of an undoing of the national boundaries can create insecurities
detrimental to maintenance of civility and provision of public goods. It is also worth
observing that the case for secession will be strongest in illiberal and redistributive
regimes; among governments adhering to the classical liberal tenet that their primary
function is protection of individuals' rights to noninterference, grounds for political
divorce will be infrequent. For a more extended examination of these themes see Allen
Buchanan, *Secession* (Boulder, Colo.: Westview Press, 1991). That these issues are
vexingly difficult is one reason why I do not proceed here to extended consideration of
secession. The other reason is my inability to resolve those difficulties to my own
satisfaction. It is my hope eventually to be able to do better.

25. Public goods provision is to be distinguished from programs mandating either
cash or in-kind transfers of private goods from the more well-off to the less well-off.
Rationales for redistribution are considered below.

26. The qualification is by way of acknowledging a case in theory for restrictions on
the export of items that touch on national security concerns. Justification for restrictions on imports is yet more difficult to sustain.

27. "People of the same trade seldom meet together, even for merriment and diver-
sion, but the conversation ends in a conspiracy against the publick, or in some contriv-
ance to raise prices." (*Wealth of Nations* I.x.c., p. 145.)

28. Governments also routinely compel sizable transfers from the relatively poor to
the relatively rich; as an employee of a state university, I recognize this as a fact of life
which is also a fact of my livelihood. These reverse transfers are as difficult to square
with any of the contending contemporary theories of justice as they are ubiquitous in
practice. That, though, is the subject for another essay.

29. The parameters of that debate are set out more fully in *Persons, Rights and the
Moral Community*, chap. 5, "Two Concepts of Liberalism," 84–110.

30. This is the welfare state of George Bush's simpering, strutting "L-word" as fea-
tured in the 1988 presidential campaign debate with Michael Dukakis.

31. For nativists and right-wing populists this is also an easy call, albeit in a direction opposite to that taken by liberals.

32. Classical liberals believe that individuals' rights are predominantly negative,
shields against interference, and for that reason they might object that, insofar as P3
runs together impositions of harms with failures to supply aid, its warrant is dubious.

Four

Hard Borders, Compensation, and Classical Liberalism

HILLEL STEINER

SUPPOSE THAT you are the classical liberal ruler of a sovereign nation-state and that the integrity of standard human rights is therefore your principal concern. It follows pretty directly that you must be vitally exercised by those six stumbling blocks so succinctly identified by Loren Lomasky as the ones with which the existence of national borders confronts liberals.[1] Does it thence follow that you must accept Lomasky's *Modest Proposal*—that your state's boundaries should be very much like the boundaries between the states composing a federal structure, that is, that they should be *soft*? Do you really have no other option, given your classical liberal commitments?

I'm inclined to agree that, in the world as it mostly is today, you don't. Too much illiberal injustice is fostered by the existence of hard international borders. Indeed, it's an insufficiently remarked fact—one on which the first part of this essay is focused—that such injustice is done not only to persons *outside* those borders but also to many *within* them. For the latter are thereby prevented from freely associating with others on the terms jointly preferred by and mutually agreeable to them. And quite apart from the exploitation (of both insiders and outsiders) that can be thereby engendered, this restriction itself is evidently contrary to a long established and quite fundamental human right.

The Rights of Insiders

Inattention to this fact seems to be instanced in Michael Walzer's argument that, although there can be no moral right to control emigration, there can be such a right in respect of immigration, because

> The restraint of entry serves to defend the liberty and welfare, the politics and culture of a group of people committed to one another and to their common life [whereas] the restraint of exit replaces commitment with coercion.[2]

Now there may well be valid arguments for such a moral asymmetry between emigration and immigration controls. But the error in *this* argument for asymmetry lies in its neglect of the fact that restraint of entry, in denying *insiders* the option of (for example) housing or employing outsiders, thereby similarly replaces insiders' commitment with coercion. For it is one thing for insiders to choose to restrict entry into their own private domains, and quite another for the state to compel them to do so. If some of them lack the sort of commitment that entails such a choice—the sort of thick commitment presumed by Walzer—no liberal can underwrite the substitution of state coercion for that (lack of) commitment.[3] On the face of it, then, the borders of a liberal polity can be no harder than those of the softest-bordered private domain within it. This seems, indeed, to be true of *any* kind of polity where coercion is not allowed to replace commitment.

Consideration of Walzer's argument thus serves to illuminate the often overlooked connections between some *inter*national justice issues—such as immigration and trade controls—and some *intra*national justice issues arising in connection with domestic pluralism. For we might plausibly conjecture that, within any society, any differential hardness in the borders of different individuals' private domains can be attributed to differences between their respective commitments—between their cultures, broadly understood. How receptive you are to the entry of certain types of outsider and/or their exports is going to depend on the particular constellation of moral values, ethnic membership, religious affiliation, economic interests, and so forth, that conjunctively characterize the cultural group of which you are a member and which thus embodies those shared commitments.

Contrary to many of its critics, classical liberalism is neither unmindful nor disrespectful of such shared commitments. Its primary concern is that they not be allowed to *dominate* public policy to the point of encroaching on individuals' human rights. There would arguably be little danger of this occurring within a society—a nation-state—which is culturally homogeneous, since whatever restrictions might be imposed on persons' conduct there could be presumed to enjoy their consent: they may each be presumed to have waived some element of whichever of their human rights would otherwise be violated by those restrictions. Such a state's hard borders would be describable as simply the aggregate reflection of the hard borders of its members' respective domains.

But in the world as it is today, few if any societies exhibit the degree of cultural homogeneity that would warrant this description of hard national borders. Accordingly, and in societies composed of a *plurality* of cultural groups, hard national borders justifiably occasion the classical liberal's suspicion that trade and/or immigration policy is being used to advance the interests of only *some* of those groups, and to do so at the expense of the human rights (of free consensual association) of the members of other groups.[4]

Suppose, however, that there are at least some states which exhibit a Walzerian degree of shared thick commitment such that their having hard borders entails no such rights violations. Would not classical liberals have to concede that, at least in those cases, hard national borders are entirely permissible?

Of course, before conceding, they might well be prompted to wonder why hard borders are needed at all in such circumstances. Why, if there is a shared commitment to excluding outsiders and/or their exports, should it be necessary for such exclusion to be enforced as a matter of state policy? Why can't individuals themselves, given their commitment, each be relied upon to exercise their personal rights in such ways as would achieve that same exclusion effect? Why won't they each simply decline to house or employ outsiders or to purchase their products? To this challenge, the defenders of hard borders can indeed offer an answer—though just how compelling answers of that sort can be for classical liberals has, as I'll suggest, long been a matter of some uncertainty.

The answer I have in mind is one which invokes the standard notion of *public goods*, and I'll sketch its relevance here in very general terms.[5] It's obviously true that the things which are constitutive of a particular culture often include such items as the use of a particular language, the (non)production and/or (non)consumption of particular kinds of material and intellectual artifact, and the observance of particular rites and rituals which are to be kept free from commercial activity. These are or involve social practices which can be sustained only if all (or at least most) members of that cultural group participate in them. Now, it's not difficult to imagine situations in which members find themselves so placed that it is advantageous for each of them, occasionally or frequently, to defect from such participation—or very costly not to do so—as long as the rest do not and continue to sustain that culture.

Salient among the factors making for such situations is the entry into a society of persons or goods of a different cultural provenance: ones that afford personally advantageous opportunities to members of that group—opportunities of which they can avail themselves only by defecting from the group's practices. In these circumstances, it can be argued, hard borders seem to be the only (or best) instrument for protecting that culture's existence, to which all its members are *ex hypothesi* strongly committed. And the conclusion is that hard national borders can thus be said to be a public good and, hence, to enjoy their hypothetical consent and, hence, to entail no violations of their rights.

As I suggested above, classical liberals have, historically, offered a mixed reception to such arguments. Some would simply say that, since it is not the (legitimate) business of the state to maximize social utility, the provision of public goods falls entirely outside the scope of its authority and involves measures which violate individuals' rights. But this is, I think, too simple a response. A more reflective version of it might dispute the inference from hard-borders-as-instrumentally-valuable to hard-borders-as-public-goods. For it might be claimed that cultural group members who engage in defecting conduct *ipso facto* indicate that, however strong their commitment to their culture's existence is, it lacks the sort of priority—relative to the values subserved by defection—that is necessary to characterize a hard border as delivering what, in this context, counts as the on-balance superior good *for them*. An alternative objection might be aimed at the inference from hypothetical consent to "no rights violations," arguing that

> Hypothetical consent is not some alternate, lesser variety of consent; it is not consent at all.[6]

However, some classical liberals, while fully cognizant of these difficulties in identifying genuine public goods and in thence justifying their state provision on grounds of genuine general consent, are prepared to accept that such exercises are certainly not foredoomed to failure.[7] Accordingly, for them and in the circumstances just described, hard borders might appear to be entirely permissible.

The Rights of Outsiders

That appearance, I want now to argue, is illusory. More is needed before classical liberalism can consistently embrace hard borders, even when the public goods and genuine consent conditions are satisfied. For the concern with human rights violations that, for classical liberals, constitutes the acid-test of policy permissibility, has thus far figured in our discussion only with reference to the rights of *insiders*. It is only insiders' rights that can be presumed to be unviolated by hard borders which enjoy general domestic support. *But outsiders, too, have human rights.* And although those rights certainly don't extend to associating with insiders who don't wish to associate with them, classical liberal theory can be shown to assign them (other) rights which have a direct bearing on the permissibility of their exclusion by hard borders. Why? How?

Consider what it is that empowers one insider to exclude another *insider* from his/her own private domain. That is, consider what is implied by deeming some piece of conduct to be an act of *trespass*. Obviously such judgments presuppose some exclusive entitlement on the part of one person to the location entered into by another. What gives the former that entitlement? Again, it is reasonably evident that such entitlements ultimately presuppose some rule for the appropriation of thitherto unowned land: some rule which states the conditions under which a particular individual may acquire the powers permissibly to exclude other persons from a particular site—a site from which those other persons are not otherwise permissibly excludable.

What could the content of that rule be? Lomasky strongly insists that it is ineluctably *conventional*:

> [I]ndividuals might come to know via the exercise of pure philosophical reason that they are at liberty to appropriate unowned property. But which performances consti-

tute valid acts of appropriation is not discernible a priori but rather must be established conventionally as the rule in force for a particular domain.[8]

Several points are worth noting about the bearing of this conventional "conferral of content" claim on the matter of national borders. One is that its reference to "a particular domain" itself presupposes precisely what is at issue here: namely, the existence of an *already legitimately bounded* locality whose occupants are subject to that conventional appropriation rule. This presupposition introduces damaging circularity into the argument since, *ex hypothesi*, that local appropriation rule cannot serve as a reason for *outsiders* to regard sites within that locality as appropriated and themselves as thereby permissibly excludable from them. Outsiders, we might say, have no reason to regard themselves as outsiders.

A more general point pertains to the ambivalence of the concept of "conventional" itself. For to describe a rule as conventional is to imply that it is either nonrational (not discernible a priori) or nonuniversal (local, not global) or both. Lomasky evidently believes that rules of appropriation are, indeed, both. Unlike not only Locke but also Kant, he is thereby disabled from offering an account of how members of groups with respectively different appropriative conventions can be *permissibly* excluded from one another's localities. On his account, they remain entirely at liberty to venture on to, use, and even appropriate what are *for them* these unowned sites. In that sense, Lomasky's is an argument for soft borders—private, as well as national—with a vengeance!

More generally still, this does, perhaps, illustrate the difficulties besetting attempts to derive classical liberal tenets from essentially Hobbesian foundations.[9] Such arguments, it's true, do broadly succeed in showing that predatory (unproductive, non-beneficial) behavior is reduced by the existence of local legal systems, including systems of private property rights nested within them.[10] But they nonetheless leave the boundaries of *both* of these two types of domain seriously under-determined. Convention is left to generate the demarcating rules not only locally for individual private appropriations but also globally for the territorial scope of respective sovereign legal jurisdictions.

Nor is it clear that this under-determination could be remedied by foundationally invoking the value of enhanced personal autonomy.[11] For the aim of enhancing personal autonomy appears to be essentially *aggregative*, rather than *distributive*, in character. The conditions required to enhance, let alone maximize, my (or my fellow group members') autonomy can entail a reduction in those needed to sustain, let alone enhance, yours; and the net result of installing those conditions may be an overall (global) gain in autonomy. So, as with utilitarian maximizers, it's essentially unclear why someone strongly committed to enhancing autonomy would rationally accept any particular boundaries as constraints on the pursuit of that commitment.

Be that as it may, what is clear is that the conjunction of the precepts of reducing predatory behavior and enhancing personal autonomy either *will* deliver a determinate rule for appropriation or it *will not*. If it does, then Lomasky errs in claiming that this rule is conventional and not discernible a priori. If it does not, then we are back with the problem of how outsiders can be permissibly excluded at all.

As the phrase itself indicates, *in rem* rights (rights "against the world")— which property, and especially real estate, titles paradigmatically are—impose correlative duties of forbearance not only on all fellow insiders but on all outsiders as well. Whether those titles are ones held individually by persons or collectively by groups, it's difficult to see how others can be said to bear those correlative duties unless there is some rule which applies to all of them and which generates those duties. To say this is not, implausibly, to deny the possibility of valid local variations. But it is to deny the possibility of such variations in the absence of a valid *global* rule which operates parametrically to determine where one locality ends and another begins. *For it is a necessary truth that local conventions cannot determine their own domains.* And such determinations are certainly *not* the deliverances of brute topographical facts.

In the face of these difficulties, prominent classical liberals have advisedly sought to integrate their accounts of individual rights, appropriation rules, and national borders—to unify them—by exhibiting the second and third of these as being successively *derived* from the first. Both Locke and, less perspicuously, Kant supply accounts of these connections. In Locke's case, the familiar derivation proceeds from each person's foundational right of self-ownership, through the "mixing" of their self-owned labor with particular unowned sites, to the agreement of several site owners to form a common jurisdictional unit, a nation-state. However, recognizing that the aggregate effect of unconstrained unilateral appropriations can be such as to deprive many persons of their thitherto permissible use of any sites whatsoever, Locke imposes the proviso that no one may appropriate more than would leave "enough and as good" for others.[12] This proviso itself entails a foundational right, vesting each person with an entitlement to (be left) an equivalent portion of land.

Kant too, though more obscurely, bases both private appropriation and, thence, territorial sovereignty on the equal entitlements of individual persons. And this derivation proceeds from a very similar pair of foundational premises. The first of these is that each person's sole innate right, being one to freedom, vests him with the "quality of being *his own master*."[13] And the second is that private property presupposes an ahistorically original community of land (*communio fundi originaria*) which Kant regards as an a priori deliverance of practical reason, as is the ahistorical "general will of humanity" which, he insists, is what underwrites particular appropriations. Put simply, all persons are ultimately equal shareholders in the land.[14]

How should we understand these equal individual entitlements in a world like our own, where most land has been privatized and *all* of it has been absorbed into one sovereign legal jurisdiction or another—a world where states and individuals claim powers to exclude others from what would otherwise be permissibly available for their use? The obvious commonsensical answer here invokes the idea of *compensation*. Persons are to be compensated, by their deprivers, for what they have been deprived of. What appropriators and their successors—whether groups or individuals—each deprive others of is the liberty to use the particular sites they claim to own. Accordingly, the aggregate owed compensation is equivalent to the net benefits that would accrue from such use. And broadly speaking, what this amounts to is the *value* of those sites *per se*: that is, the gross value of those sites *minus* the value of any improvements made to them by their owners. Each person's entitlement is thus one to an equal share of that value.[15]

A plausible concrete construal of these entitlements is that they jointly constitute a *Global Fund*, in which each person, regardless of location, is an equal shareholder.[16] And one intuitively attractive interpretation of such shareholders' claims on the Fund is that they amount to equal entitlements to an *unconditional basic income*—or, perhaps, to an *unconditional basic initial endowment* which, being less paternalistic, would be a more Kantian or liberal instantiation of them.[17]

Nor should this entitlement be assimilated to the sorts of foundational *positive* right which, as Lomasky correctly suggests, are centrally characteristic of "new liberal" and social-democratic conceptions of distributive justice and which classical liberals traditionally reject as entailing unjust encroachments on individuals' property rights and, more generally, their negative rights to others' forbearance. For as an entitlement to *compensation*, it no more signifies a foundational positive right than does any standard restitutional claim against perpetrators of theft, personal injury, or contractual default—claims of a kind which classical liberalism strongly underwrites. It is compensation for failures to respect individuals' foundational *negative* rights to others' forbearance from engrossing more land than would leave "enough and as good" for them.

Borders and International Justice

The global reach of this compensatory entitlement yields important implications for international distributive justice in general, as well as the permissible hardness of national borders in particular. With regard to the latter, it implies that persons who have *not* been compensated for the deprivation of their liberty to use a particular owned site retain that liberty and may not be permissibly excluded from it. Accordingly, for them, that site's boundaries must be soft. And as was noted previously, the national borders of a classical liberal polity can be no harder than those of the softest-bordered private domain within it. The fact (if it is a fact) that all the members of that polity prefer it to have hard borders—that hard borders are a genuine public good for them—is insufficient to justify their exclusion of those outsiders. Conversely, of course, those who *have* been compensated may legitimately be denied entry in these circumstances.

Beyond these implications for national borders, there are good grounds to suppose that even many of those who are *not* classical liberals may find considerable merit in a Global Fund regime. For its effects seem likely to include the creation or reinforcement of several benign incentive structures informing relations both within and between nations.[18] A principal reason for this is that the Fund's impact is bound to be strongly redistributive, inasmuch as its revenues reflect the vastly unequal values of sites as diverse as an acre in the Sahara Desert and an acre in downtown Manhattan. So the correspondingly differential incidence of the Fund's levies, in conjunction with the *per capita* parity of its disbursements, pretty much guarantee a substantial reduction in international (as well as national) economic inequalities.

It is an undisputed fact that these international inequalities have always played a major role in generating high levels of demand for emigration. Under the regime of the Global Fund, poorer nations, being its net beneficiaries, would find fewer of their members leaving to seek their fortunes in wealthier societies. Hence persons exercised about lagging rates of development in Third World economies—rates which are not enhanced by the departure of many of the more skilled members of their labor forces—thereby have reason to regard the Fund's operation in a positive light. And the same would be true of those with a Walzerian concern that local norms and cultures not be swamped by influxes of outsiders.

A second arena in which the Fund's operation can be expected to generate benign effects is that of the perennial problem posed by international boundary disputes, over land whose legitimate titleholders are difficult to identify. Such disputes have long been fertile sources of international tension and flash points for military conflict. The Global Fund can be seen to address this problem by fostering a greater willingness on the part of the disputants to compromise in their demands, inasmuch as it attaches a price tag to any instance of territorial acquisition or retention. Accordingly, those interested in extending the domain of peaceful resolution of international conflicts ought to endorse it.

Finally, and especially in today's world of pluralistic nation-states, there is the moral problem posed by such odious practices as ethnic cleansing and forced expatriation. It is obviously true that the motivations for engaging in such practices are often diverse, deeply felt, and rooted in longstanding grievances. However this may be, the existence of the Global Fund would give nations stronger *dis*incentives to continue to permit these practices. It would do so because their aggregate receipts from the Fund would decline with their loss of those members, while their payment liabilities to it would remain the same. Indeed, and insofar as national prosperity is a function of total personal income, nations might well come to cherish each of their members all the more—to accept their cultural diversity—for being sources of guaranteed income!

In short, you don't have to be a classical liberal to see the economic development of poorer societies and the peaceful resolution of international and domestic conflicts as Good Things. But, in the quest for a just means of bringing them about, it may help.[19]

Notes

1. See Loren Lomasky's discussion under "National Borders: Six Stumbling Blocks," in chapter 3 above.

2. Michael Walzer, *Spheres of Justice* (Oxford: Martin Robertson, 1983), 39.

3. The same applies, *mutatis mutandis*, with regard to restrictions on international trade and investment; see my "Trading with the Enemy," in *Legal and Moral Aspects of International Trade*, ed. Geraint Parry, Asif Qureshi, and Hillel Steiner (London: Routledge, 1998).

4. See my "Trading with the Enemy," 203–4, and "Libertarianism and Transnational Migration," in *Free Movement*, ed. Brian Barry and Robert Goodin (Hemel Hempstead: Harvester Wheatsheaf, 1992), 91. Note that the classical liberal's objection to hard borders in these circumstances is *not* that some cultural groups are coercively advancing their own interests at the cost of other groups' *interests*. For the classical liberal lacks any independent standard for the appropriate balance to be struck between different groups' interests: that is, any standard which is not derivative from the demands of respecting *individuals'* human rights.

5. See David Miller, *On Nationality* (Oxford: Oxford University Press, 1995), 87–88, 102, 147.

6. Lomasky, chap. 3 above, n. 1.

7. Even these classical liberals might, however, balk at accepting restrictions on *exit* (on emigration and the export of investment capital)—restrictions traditionally abhorred by classical liberalism—even if such restrictions could be shown to be public goods. Lomasky, *Persons, Rights and the Moral Community* (Oxford: Oxford University Press, 1987), 146–51, offers a well-balanced assessment of the difficulties in identifying genuine public goods and justifying their provision by the state.

8. Lomasky, chap. 3 above, section on "Why Borders?"

9. Lomasky himself (ibid., n. 14) raises the question of "whether Hobbes is or is not properly to be classified among the liberal theorists," and answers that "if not a liberal, he is the quintessential proto-liberal, the one against whom all succeeding theorists have to test their philosophical mettle." Constructing taxonomies is, of course, always

difficult. But this one strikes me as misleading. For there is surely a world of difference between political theories that begin from axioms about individuals' *motivation* and those that take axioms about individuals' *rights* as their starting points. The latter may well need to test their mettle against the former in regard to the prospects for persons *complying* with their correlative duties—especially in relation to public goods; but that is no reason for placing the former in the same classification.

10. Such local legal systems are construed as public goods. Parity of reasoning here would suggest, moreover, that a *global* legal system, within which these local systems are in turn nested, is itself a public good.

11. Cf. Lomasky, chap. 3 above, intro. and passim.

12. John Locke, *Two Treatises of Government*, ed. Peter Laslett (Cambridge: Cambridge University Press, 1967), Second Treatise, chap. V.

13. Immanuel Kant, *The Metaphysics of Morals*, ed. Mary Gregor (Cambridge: Cambridge University Press, 1991), 63.

14. Ibid., 71–74; cf. my "Kant, Property and the General Will," in *The Enlightenment and Modernity*, ed. Robert Wokler and Norman Geras (London: Macmillan, forthcoming).

15. For a more detailed derivation of this entitlement, see my *An Essay on Rights* (Oxford: Blackwell, 1994), chaps. 7, 8; and "Choice and Circumstance," *Ratio*, 10 (1997): 296–312, reprinted in *Ideals of Equality*, ed. Andrew Mason (Oxford: Blackwell, 1998).

16. Cf. my *Essay on Rights*, chap. 8, and "Just Taxation and International Redistribution," in *Nomos XXXIX: Global Justice*, ed. Ian Shapiro (New York: New York University Press, 1999).

17. See Philippe Van Parijs, *Real Freedom for All* (Oxford: Oxford University Press, 1995), for an extended account of one justice-based argument for unconditional basic income.

18. See Nicolaus Tideman, "Commons and Commonwealths," in *Commons without Tragedy*, ed. Robert Andelson (London: Shepheard-Walwyn, 1991), for a more extended discussion of some of these incentive structures.

19. Cf. my "Territorial Justice," in *National Rights, International Obligations*, ed. Simon Caney, David George, and Peter Jones (Boulder: Westview Press, 1996); reprinted in *Globalization and Public Policy*, ed. Philip Gummett (Cheltenham: Edward Elgar, 1996), and in *Theories of Secession*, ed. Percy Lehning (London: Routledge, 1997).

Five

Territorial Boundaries and Confucianism

JOSEPH CHAN

TERRITORY is a political concept. It does not simply refer to a geographical space, but to "the land or district lying around a city or town and under its jurisdiction," as the *Oxford English Dictionary* defines it. The concept thus designates a relationship between a community of politically organized people and their space. In more exact terms, a territory is a geographical space that is under some kind of jurisdiction or control of certain people organized in the form of a political community. Similarly, the concept of territorial boundary does not simply refer to geographical boundaries; it denotes, rather, the limit of jurisdiction of a certain political community with regard to a certain geographical space. Territorial boundaries signify a separation of a political community from adjacent territories that are under different jurisdictions.

"Territory" in the Chinese language also carries this connotation of the jurisdiction of a political community. The Chinese word for territory is *jiang tu*: *jiang* means frontier or boundary, and *tu* means land. The two words together refer to the territory of a political unit. *Jiang* is itself a word about frontier or boundary. If emphasis is to be put on the concept of territorial *boundary*, *jiang yu* or *jiang jie* will be used. *Jiang* can be found in many ancient classical texts. It has, for example, appeared in *Mencius* six times.[1] Each time when the word appears in *Mencius*, it refers to the boundary of a state. For example, *chu jiang* means "out of a state,"[2] *ru jiang* means "enter into a state."[3] Like "territory," then, *jiang* and *jiang tu* are political concepts, and they refer to the territory or territorial boundaries of a political community.

It should be noted that the *concept* of territory or territorial boundary defined here is neutral with respect to the question of what form a political community takes. There are, of course, *conceptions* of territory and territorial boundary. Because of the close connection between territory and political community, different types of political community—and different theorizing of them—may generate different conceptions of the significance and functions of territory and territorial boundary. The territory and territorial boundaries of a modern, sovereign European nation-state, of the ancient Chinese empire, and of an ancient Greek *polis* may carry different significance and perform different functions. Questions about these conceptions, therefore, inevitably raise a series of questions about political communities—about their nature and purposes, their stage of development, the basis of political authority, their scope of jurisdiction, and their relations with other political communities.

Territorial boundary has become a significant issue primarily with the rise of the modern nation-state. The modern concept of nation-state comprises several elements: sovereignty, territory, and an equal status in the international system. The modern nation-state is at once both sovereign and territorial, in the sense that it has the impersonal, supreme legal authority to give and enforce the law within a demarcated territorial area. However, as Jean Gottmann notes, in ancient and medieval times, the authority of rulers rested primarily on the allegiance of individuals or organized bodies, rather than on the possession of land areas. From the late fifteenth century, the essence of political authority was gradually transferred to the control of well-defined territory. "The sixteenth century, however, was the decisive time in European affairs, when politics and legal doctrines began claiming territorial sovereignty as a prime attribute of kingdoms or states. By the end of the eighteenth century the notion of national sovereignty over well-delimited territory had come to the fore in political practice as well as in the theory of jurisprudence."[4]

Before the nation-state era, territorial boundaries were not clearly defined. They were dependent on the ability of the central government to control and administer the outer areas of the state rather than on the demarcation of territorial jurisdiction between states.[5] Border territories functioned primarily as buffer areas providing security for the state and facilitating trade with the outside world. Most of the time, however, emperors were more concerned with maintaining their administration in the inner areas than in the frontiers, unless the empire was engaged in self-defense or aggressive wars. Given this political reality, territorial boundaries did not seem to perform many functions other than being a buffer zone for security and trading, nor did they receive much theoretical reflection by political thinkers of ancient times. Thus it would not be a surprise to find that in Confucianism, as probably also in other premodern ethical traditions such as the ancient Greek, there was not much direct discussion on the question of territorial boundaries or on such related questions as ownership, distribution, diversity, or mobility. In fact, the latter set of questions have become significant only in the present world order, where globalization of technology, production and distribution of goods, and mass media have seriously constrained and challenged the sovereignty of modern territorial states. In a more or less globalized world order, the questions about the functions of territorial boundaries, the limits of state sovereignty, and the relations between political and territorial boundaries become significant practical issues.

Premodern ethical traditions may all lack systematic, direct discussions on issues of territory and territorial boundaries. But among them, different premodern traditions may also have different *internal* reasons for lacking those discussions. In this chapter, I shall try to explore some such internal reasons in Confucianism. I shall first briefly introduce the basic ideas in the Confucian ethical tradition, and then discuss the traditional Chinese conception of political community and the world. In order to bring out its uniqueness, I shall also compare it with the classical Greek conception. Then I shall try to show how Confucianism can be seen as having some bearing on the question of territory and territorial boundaries, despite the fact that these questions did not receive systematic theorizing in the tradition.

The Confucian Ethical Tradition

The Confucian tradition began before Confucius (551–479 B.C.), although it is difficult to date its birth.[6] If "Confucianism" means a tradition of thought wholly created by Confucius, then it is a misleading translation of the original Chinese *Ru jia*. Confucius regarded himself as a person who transmitted the old tradition rather than creating a new one. The Chinese term *Ru jia* means a school of *Ru*, "a type of man who is cultural, moral, and responsible for religious rites, and hence religious."[7] Nevertheless, it was Confucius who most creatively interpreted the rich tradition that he had inherited, gave it a new meaning, and expounded it so effectively that his views have influenced a great number of generations of *Ru* to come. *The Analects*, which is a record of the teachings of Confucius written by his students, is the most fundamental text in the Confucian tradition. The other two major exponents of Confucian thought in classical times were Mencius (c. 379–289 B.C.) and Xunzi (c. 340–245 B.C.). Their works, *Mencius* and *Xunzi*, are also important texts in the tradition.

Since the classical period, Confucianism has continued to evolve over more than two thousand years, and it has developed into a complex tradition with many different strands and variants. This makes any interpretation of Confucianism inevitably controversial, and any proposal to give an essentialist interpretation of the true nature of the tradition must be received with great caution and suspicion. What follows, therefore, is only one interpretation of Confucian ethics and political thought as developed primarily in the classical tradition. But this interpretation also takes account of the works of influential modern Chinese intellectuals, especially Confucian scholars. In this chapter, "the Confucian tradition" should be understood in this highly qualified sense.

The Confucian ethical tradition is a system of human relationships based on the virtue of *ren*. The moral ideal for each individual is the attainment of *ren*, the highest and most perfect virtue. *Ren* is a human quality, an expression of humanity. One way to understand *ren*, as Confucius himself does, is to say that *ren* is to "love your fellow men" (*ai ren*).[8] *Ren* is primarily expressed through human relationships, although later Confucians suggest that *ren* can be expressed also through a harmonious relationship between human beings and nature. For Confucians, the most natural and important site for the expression of *ren* is the family. Mencius says that young children naturally know to love their parents, and when they grow they will naturally respect their elders.[9] *Ren* manifested in the parent-child relationship is filial piety (*xiao*), and in the sibling relationship, brotherhood (*ti*). The Analects says that these two virtues form the root of *ren*.[10]

The familial virtues are not only the root of *ren* but also the basis of a stable social and political order. It is rare for a person who has the virtues of filial piety (*xiao*) and brotherhood (*ti*) to have the inclination to be rebellious against his or her superiors.[11] D. C. Lau, a translator of *The Analects*, comments that "if being a good son makes a good subject, being a good father will also make a good ruler. Love for people outside one's family is looked upon as an extension of the love for members of one's own family."[12] Confucianism gives a high priority to five basic relationships: father-son, husband-wife, elder brother-younger brother, ruler-ruled, and friend-friend. Among these five, the first three are familial relationships. Although the last two are nonfamilial, they are conceived analogously in familial terms. The ruler-ruled relationship is analogous to that of father-son, and friend-friend to elder brother-younger brother. The principles of conduct as required by benevolence for the two nonfamilial relationships, loyalty and friendship, have to be understood in light of their analogous familial principles, filial piety (*xiao*) and brotherhood (*ti*). Generally speaking, society is the family writ large. This is why some scholars have termed China a "familistic society, one in which the family, and the kinship system deriving from it, has an unusually strategic place in the society as a whole."[13]

While Confucianism takes the family to be the most fundamental social unit in Chinese society, it does not preach a petty-minded, close-knit society, for the Confucian family is also a highly elastic entity, and its spirit and care can be extended to places far away from home. Ambrose King has pointed out that the term "family" (*jia*) is conceptually unclear; and, theoretically, the family can be extended to cover the whole world (*tian xia*).

> Sometimes it includes only members of a nuclear family, but it may also include all members of a lineage or a clan. Moreover, the common expression *ji jia ren* ("our family people") can refer to any person one wants to include; the concept of *ji jia ren* can be contracted or expanded depending upon the circumstances. It can theoretically be extended to an unlimited number of people and thereby becomes what is called *tian xia yi jia* ("all the world belongs to one family").[14]

Part of the reason for the elasticity of the family is that the family is often used as a model to understand other social relationships, and hence its language and virtues are often stretched to cover nonfamilial spheres. But the more important reason lies in an important aspect of the Confucian conception of *ren*, an aspect that we have not discussed so far. While *ren* finds its most immediate and natural expression in the family, it never stops at the gateway of the home. Confucius says that when a young man is away from home, he should extend brotherhood (*ti*) to others and "love the multitude at large" (*fan ai zhong*).[15] *Ren* can transcend the natural bonds among family members because *ren* is also the ability of a person to "infer" another's needs and wants from one's own.

> Now the man of [*ren*], wishing to be established himself, seeks also to establish others; wishing to be enlarged himself, he seeks also to enlarge others. To be able to judge *of others* by what is nigh *in ourselves*;—this may be called the [method of *ren*].[16]

Confucius sometimes calls this method of *ren* the art of *shu*, which can be expressed positively or negatively. Positively, a man of *ren* seeks to establish and enlarge others insofar as he seeks also to establish and enlarge himself.[17] Negatively, *shu* tells us not to impose on others what we ourselves do not desire.[18] This art of *shu*, when applied to the familial virtues, becomes what Confucius and Mencius say respectively:

> All within the Four Seas are one's brother.[19]

> Treat the aged of your family in a manner befitting their venerable age and extend this treatment to the aged of other families; treat your own young in a manner befitting their tender age and extend this to the young of other families.[20]

Contemporary Chinese historian Qian Mu (1895–1990) has suggested that the Chinese family can branch out vertically and horizontally to all mankind and integrate them into a whole. Filial piety (*xiao*) connects people vertically: it refers to a deep respect for the parents and all ancestors of a family, and by extension, to other people's parents and ancestors as well. Brotherhood (*ti*) connects people horizontally, which can be extended to anyone in the world, for as Confucius says, all within the Four Seas are one's brother. This elastic conception of the family has enabled the Chinese to slide easily from "familism" to "cosmopolitanism," back and forth.[21]

To summarize the points thus far: there are two features of the Confucian conception of human relationships and moral order that are particularly relevant to the present purpose of this chapter. The first is the *potentially unbounded* nature of human relationships and the scope of *ren*. Even though *ren* always begins in familial relationships, and one's attention and care should naturally be directly more to one's close partners such as family members than to strangers, Confucianism insists that the practice of *ren* has no outer limits, and its principles like *shu*, filial piety, and brotherhood have no outer limits as well. *Ren* implies the cultivation of oneself in relation to others, beginning with the family and friends, and ultimately, to the whole world. The second feature is the *elastic* nature of human relationship. It is not only that familial relationships (such as father-son) are often the basis for understanding the nature of other relationships (such as ruler-ruled); sometimes one's friends can be regarded as the very members of one's family. Familism in practice may mean closed-mindedness and exclusion, but in Confucian theory at least, it is elastic and has a strong degree of openness and inclusiveness.

This Confucian conception of the elastic and potentially unbounded nature of human relationships and moral order fits naturally with the traditional Chinese conception of the ideal political order. The highest political order for the Chinese is the order of *tian xia* (the world under Heaven), which has no territorial limit; and it provides the broadest site one could imagine for the practice of *ren* and for the actualization of one's self. I shall now articulate this traditional Chinese conception of political order.

The Chinese Conception of *Tian Xia*

In the classical Chinese ethical tradition, unlike in the modern conception, territory and territorial boundaries are relatively unimportant issues. This may be partly due to the fact, commonly acknowledged by all classical ethical and political theories alike, that these issues were not of any fundamental importance in premodern times. But there seems an internal, theoretical reason for the absence of discussion in the Chinese case. The Chinese conception of the ideal political order admits of no territorial boundaries. The Chinese notion of "the world under Heaven" (*tian xia*) represents the ultimate stage of the development of political order, whereas states are seen as an incomplete realization of the Chinese ideal. Liang Qichao (1873–1929) was probably the first modern Chinese intellectual who stressed the importance of the notion of *tian xia* in understanding the traditional Chinese conception of the political order, and used such terms as "transnationalism" or "cosmopolitanism" to characterize it. His view influenced a few generations of modern Chinese scholars in interpreting the nature of Chinese politics and political culture. Liang writes,

> Since civilization began, the Chinese people have never considered national government as the highest form of social organization. Their political thinking has always been in terms of all mankind, with world peace as the final goal, and family and nation as transitional stages in the perfecting of the World Order [*tian xia*]. China has contended, moreover, that politics exists for all mankind, and for not the interests of any one group or section of mankind.[22]

In the following discussion, I shall basically follow this tradition of interpretation first developed by Liang. But I must first add two important qualifications about this tradition of interpretation. First, the traditional Chinese perspective of a world political order transcending states was developed before

Confucius and Mencius. It was shared by different schools of thought, including Confucianism, and in itself this perspective is not uniquely Confucian. The Confucians simply inherited the basic political vocabulary of the day and accepted what was the generally shared vision of the world order. But, as we shall see later, Confucianism played an important role in shaping later understandings of what ought to be the proper nature and basis of the order of *tian xia*.

Second, it is important to note that the terminology used by Liang to describe the order of *tian xia* may be misleading. His terms "transnationalism" and "cosmopolitanism" seem to suggest that there is equality between nations and national cultures in the world order, and that the cosmopolitan political order should be neutral toward different nations and cultures. Understood in this way, these terms do not properly describe the traditional Chinese conception of world order. As will be explained later, the classical Chinese political tradition never held the view of equality between the cultures and ethical systems of different nations. On the contrary, the culture of the people in the central regions of China, the *zhu xia*, was, according to the traditional Chinese view, superior to those of the barbarians living on the four quarters of the continent and the rest of the world. It was thought that the superior culture should be transmitted to the world, and that the world should be under one rule, the rule of the most wise and ethical man. Looking from the outside, then, this view could perhaps be better termed as "imperialism" than "cosmopolitanism." But imperialism is not entirely accurate either, because it carries the connotation of a mighty nation using force to conquer or dominate other nations and cultures. The major scholars in the Confucian tradition, such as Mencius, opposed the use of force (although it was advocated by some other thinkers, and indeed it occurred). While Confucians adhered to the idea of *tian xia* being ruled by one culture and by one wise and ethical man, they typically favored peaceful persuasion and the setting of example by members of the culturally superior group. This point will be further developed below. Suffice it to say here that while Liang rightly pointed out that the notion of *tian xia* is useful to understand the traditional Chinese conception of political order, "transnationalism" and "cosmopolitanism" as coined by him to describe that conception can easily create misunderstandings.

The concept of *tian xia* is central to the Chinese conception of political order and territorial boundaries. From the West Zhou dynasty (1075–771 B.C.) through the Qin dynasty (221–206 B.C.), *tian xia* (literally translated, it means "all under Heaven") had appeared as a concept referring to a universal political order over and above the order of individual "states" (*guo*). But *tian xia* is a rich concept, and it can be used with varying degrees of abstractness. In its most concrete, institutional sense, it refers to universal kingship, or a kingdom or empire with universal jurisdiction. States (*guo*) are political units governed by feudal lords (*hou*), whereas the universal empire is founded and maintained by the Son of Heaven (*tian zi*), who possesses the mandate of Heaven. The distinction between the two kinds of political order emerged in the West Zhou dynasty, when the Zhou king was regarded not only as one feudal lord among others but as the Son of Heaven ruling over all states governed by feudal lords.

The disintegration of the Zhou dynasty led to the Spring Autumn and Warring States periods (770–221 B.C.), which scholars call the "pre-Qin age." In this period, there were many states coexisting and fighting each other for a few hundred years. Although there was no corresponding political reality that matched the order of universal empire, *tian xia* was still frequently used in political and philosophical discourses, and the dominant political ideology was unificationism—the hope of merging all states into one giant empire with unlimited territorial boundary. Instead of being just a historical notion describing the political reality of the Zhou empire, the order of *tian xia* gradually became an ethical and political ideal guiding and judging the politics of the real world. The Confucian school of thought, as represented by Confucius, Mencius, and Xunzi, was particularly instrumental in idealizing the order of *tian xia*, and endowing it with much critical, ethical import. Mencius says that the great man practices the great way (*da dao*) of the world (*tian xia*).[23] Xunzi says that while individual states may be an object of seizure, *tian xia* is so grand and important that only a real sage is morally entitled to rule over it, and there are important moral principles governing the order of *tian xia*.[24] Even hereditary monarchy may not be legitimate if the monarch fails to conduct politics according to the moral principles grounding the order of *tian xia*. In this more abstract sense, then, the Confucian conception of *tian xia* refers to an ideal moral and political order admitting of no territorial boundary—the whole world to be governed by a sage according to principles of rites (*li*) and virtues (*de*). This ideal transcends the narrowness of states. As Benjamin Schwartz has observed,

> Although the notion of universal kingship itself was pre-Confucian and was indeed taken for granted by most of the "hundred schools" of thought during the late Zhou period, it does seem to become linked almost indissolubly over the course of time with an absolutization of the Confucian moral order.[25]

All these interrelated senses of *tian xia* can be found in classical Chinese historical and philosophical texts. And this makes translation of the concept into English difficult. Sometimes it means "the empire" or "the kingdom," sometimes it means, in a simple geographical sense, the whole world, and sometimes it points to a substantive conception of an ideal political and ethical order covering the entire world under the Heaven.[26]

Before proceeding to discuss in greater detail what a Confucian perspective would say on questions of territorial boundaries, I want to further emphasize the uniqueness of the Confucian perspective by comparing it to the classical Greek perspective. As I noted earlier in this chapter, unlike the modern conception of the state and territorial boundaries, both classical Greek and Chinese conceptions lack systematic discussions on territorial boundaries, because such boundaries play no important theoretical role in their political theories. But the two traditions may have different internal reasons for not giving an important role to territorial boundaries. Let me first briefly outline the classical Greek tradition, taking Aristotle and the Athenian tradition as representatives, and then compare it with the Chinese one. For Aristotle, although territory is one important *material* condition for a polis,[27] it is never an *essential* part of a polis. Territory is not part of the Aristotelian definition of the *polis*. For Aristotle, a *polis* is a community of citizens (*politai*) in a constitution (*politeia*).[28] Mogens H. Hansen, a historian of ancient Greece, argues that:

> Aristotle only picks up two of the three elements that comprise the modern juristic idea of a state—the people and the constitution: the territory is left out altogether, and that is not by chance. . . . We nowadays tend to equate a state with its territory—a state is a country; whereas the Greeks identified the state primarily with its people—a state is a people. Of course, the Greeks knew all about the territory of a state. But territory was not nearly as important for them as it is for us: in all the sources, from documents and historical accounts to poetry and legend, it is the people who are stressed and not the territory, a habit of thought that can be traced back to the poet Alkaios round about 600 B.C. It was never Athens and Sparta that went to war but always "the Athenians and the Lakedaimonians."[29]

For Aristotle, the essence, or characteristic activity, of a *polis* is the deliberation and administration of public affairs by citizens sharing in a constitution, citizens who are capable of ruling and being ruled in turn.[30] A territory at most makes possible the activity of ruling and being ruled, since human activities need to take place somewhere. In itself, however, a territory is no part of the activity of ruling and being ruled as such. Here we can see why Aristotle insists that a *polis* must be strictly limited in terms of the size of its population and territory. A population and territory too large cannot be easily surveyed, and as a result citizens would find it difficult to "know each other and know that kind of people they are."[31] And this is detrimental to the activities of the *polis*, since such activities (electing officials, deliberating and making decisions on collective affairs, etc.) require knowledge of the people involved—their abilities, character, and political views.[32]

As in the classical Greek conception, territory and territorial boundaries are relatively unimportant issues in the classical Chinese tradition. However, unlike the Greek emphasis on the limited size of population and territory of a *polis*, the Chinese conception of the ideal political order admits of no territorial boundaries. Why did the Greeks and the Chinese have different views on the size of the territory of a political community? The answer lies, I think, in their different conceptions of political community and the essence of politics. As pointed out before, for the Athenians, politics is essentially public and collective, and the *polis* is the community of citizens as a whole taking part in the making of collective affairs. Citizens develop their virtues and obtain honor through collective activities in the face-to-face *polis*. It is this reason that explains why a political community must be limited in size. If the Greek conception of political community is *political* or *collective*, then the Chinese conception can be called *ethical*. In the Chinese conception, the importance of politics lies not in collective participation in collective decisions, but in its promotion of the highest moral good in individual lives (*ren*), and its accompanying moral order, a harmonious order of social relationships. As explained earlier, there are two features of the Confucian conception of human relationships and moral order that are important to the issue of a universal political order envisaged by the Chinese. The first is the potentially unbounded nature of human relationships and the scope of *ren*. The practice of *ren* begins from the individual self but can be enlarged through a series of concentric circles to include the family, the state, and ultimately the world (*tian xia*). Although the ideal of virtues and human relationships should first be cultivated in one's home, they can be practiced everywhere and are applicable to everyone irrespective of his or her place of residence or ethnicity. The second feature of the Confucian conception is the notion that the ideal social relationships are elastic enough to encompass many people. Because the Confucians see the moral order as having universal applicability and as being elastic enough to encompass many people, the political order, being an instrument to promote the moral order, is naturally seen as also universal, having no boundary of territory or of ethnicity.

I have described the traditional Chinese theory of *tian xia* and its relationship with the Confucian ethical theory. I have also briefly contrasted the Greek with the Chinese conceptions. In the next section, I shall try to relate this theory of *tian xia* to a number of issues concerning territorial boundaries. Classical Confucianism does not explicitly address these issues, and so I can only draw out implications both from the theory itself and from various major classical Confucian texts such as *The Analects*, *Mencius*, and *Xunzi*. The emphasis of the next three sections, on ownership, distribution, and diversity, is on describing how classical Confucianism would look at issues concerning territorial boundaries, given the nature of states and politics in the premodern period of Chinese history. In the last section of this chapter, I shall try to describe how the traditional picture was seriously challenged and rejected in modern times, how contemporary Confucian scholars have wrestled with the question of the nation-state within the constraints of Confucianism, and whether contemporary Confucianism could have anything further to say on the contemporary issues of territorial boundaries.

Ownership

According to the traditional Chinese perspective, the entire world, starting from the central regions of the continent and reaching beyond to the outer boundaries of the four seas, in principle belongs to the king, the Son of Heaven. According to the common saying: "There is no territory under Heaven which is not the king's; there is no man on the borders of the land who is not his subject."[33] This view is mentioned in *Mencius*[34] and *Xunzi*,[35] and the latter especially quotes it with approval. There are two features of the nature of this world empire that are worth mentioning. The first concerns the *unity* of the political order, the second concerns the *moral foundation* of this order.

The multi-states system had persisted for more than five hundred years in the Spring Autumn and Warring States periods. It would not be inaccurate to compare this situation to that of the multi-states/empires system in early modern Europe. But instead of taking the European path of developing an international system of equal sovereign territorial states, the Chinese were always attracted to the ideal of universal kingship as first exemplified by the Zhou dynasty. The dominant ideology was grand unificationism (*tian xia da yi tong*). In this view, even when *tian xia* is disintegrated, sooner or later a ruler will rise as the Son of Heaven, unifying all states into one universal empire. Mencius was once asked how the Empire (*tian xia*) could be stabilized, and his reply was, "through unity" (*ding yu yi*).[36]

Given this ideological background, states and their territories were regarded as only transient entities. Ultimately they would have to be merged into the universal empire that reaches to the four seas. In fact, in the Spring Autumn period, scholars like Confucius and his disciples did not think that they owed allegiance to any one particular state. They rather traveled among the states to persuade and help the rulers to adopt and implement the principles of *ren* and *li* (or the Way). Confucius, Mencius, and Xunzi all regarded themselves as people whose ultimate goal was to help unify the world and develop a moral and political order according to the Way.[37]

The second point to make concerns the moral foundation of the universal political order. The Confucians have always stressed the importance of morality. They have never been willing to take politics as just a phenomenon of sheer power or a set of institutional arrangements. They believe that power and institutions can be effective only when they are set up, regulated, and used by benevolent leaders (leaders of *ren*). This can be seen from the following discussions relating to the ownership of territory and territorial boundaries.

The Confucians of Mencius's time had a consensus on the basis of the empire or the cosmopolitan order. They all believed that the possession and maintenance of the empire was based on practicing benevolent rule. For example, Mencius said,

> The Three Dynasties won the Empire (*tian xia*) through benevolence (*ren*), and lost it through cruelty. . . . An Emperor (*tian zi*) cannot keep the Empire within the Four Seas unless he is benevolent; a feudal lord cannot preserve the altars to the gods of earth and grain unless he is benevolent.[38]

> There are cases of a ruthless man gaining possession of a state, but it has never happened that such a man gained possession of the Empire.[39]

Xunzi has a similar passage stressing the importance of benevolence as the basis of possessing the empire:

> I say that a state, being a small thing, can be possessed by a petty man. . . . The empire is the greatest of all, and only a sage can possess it.[40]

> [T]he worthiest of men could embrace all within the four seas.[41]

It also follows from this theory that the mandate of the Son of Heaven is conditional upon his benevolent rule. If he fails to practice *ren*, he will lose his kingdom.[42]

Furthermore, Xunzi relates the proper way of acquiring the empire to the issue of territory. He holds the view that to gain the empire is above all to gain the hearts of the people, rather than to compel them to submit their lands and territories to the king. This view again indicates that in the Confucian conception of the political order, territory is only a derivative issue. The true basis of the political order lies in the voluntary submission of the people, and only a benevolent king could command such a voluntary submission. If a king, however small his state and territory may be, can win the hearts of the people of other lands, he can also naturally win their lands and territories. No doubt, territory can be an expression of the state's right or jurisdiction. But the right of the state depends not upon the sheer size or power of the state but upon whether it practices the Way. Here is an important passage from *Xunzi*:

> "Gaining the empire" does not mean that other men bring their own lands and territories and follow after him, but refers rather to no more than that his Way is sufficient to unify the people. If the people of other lands are indeed one with me, then why would their lands and territories abandon me and attach themselves to another? . . . "[A] territory of a hundred square *li* is sufficient to encompass every gradation of authority," and "the perfection of loyalty and trustworthiness and the

evident manifestation of the principle of humanity and morality are ample enough to encompass all mankind." When these two principles are united, the empire can be gained and the feudal lords who are the last to make common cause are the first to be imperiled. An Ode says:

From the east, from the west,
From the north, from the south,
There were none who thought of not submitting.

This refers to the unification of mankind.[43]

Mencius has a strikingly similar passage. In ancient times, the main purpose of territorial boundaries was for the security of a state. But Mencius insists that the advantageous terrain and solid walls of boundaries are much less important than the human factor in securing the safety of a state. Like Xunzi, Mencius believes that the key to success is the practice of the Way.

Heaven's favorable weather is less important than Earth's advantageous terrain, and Earth's advantageous terrain is less important that human unity. . . . It is not by boundaries that the people are confined, it is not by difficult terrain that a state is rendered secure, and it is not by superiority of arms that the Empire is kept in awe. One who has the Way will have many to support him; one who has not the Way will have few to support him.[44]

In Confucianism, the effect of moralizing politics is indeed deep and pervasive.

Distribution

Which goods (living space, natural resources, or products and services) do territorial boundaries properly reserve to some people and deny to others? Theoretically, territorial boundaries serve to distribute nothing, since strictly speaking there is no such thing as territorial boundary under the Confucian ideal theory of the cosmopolitan political order. But when that condition does not obtain, when there are states and political communities ruling over people in different territories, what would Confucianism say? It is difficult to be confident of an answer. Classical Confucianism has said virtually nothing on this subject. But one might perhaps argue that in Confucianism there seems no reason why one's moral duties to others must stop at the borders of one's political community. While it is true that *ren* is primarily relational and personal, there is practically no limit for extending *ren*: it can even be extended to strangers and people all over the world. Mencius's famous example of a child on the verge of falling into a well serves to illustrate this. For Mencius, a man with *ren* would be moved by compassion to save the child, not because he had personal acquaintance with the child's parents, nor because he wanted to win the praise of his fellow villagers or friends, but simply because of his concern for the suffering of a human person.[45] At the end of the same passage, Mencius says that if a man's heart is fully developed, "he can take under his protection the whole realm with the Four Seas, but if he fails to develop them [qualities of *ren*], he will not be able even to serve his parents." We have reason to believe that, for Confucianism, the practice of *ren*, whether it is by a state or an individual person, should transcend territorial boundaries. Mencius teaches his disciples:

> Treat the aged of your family in a manner befitting their venerable age and extend this treatment to the aged of other families; treat your own young in a manner befitting their tender age and extend this to the young of other families.

The practice of *ren* does not stop at the gateway of one's home. Nor does it stop at the border of one's political community. This brings us to the Confucian ideal theory of social order, the ideal of the Grand Union. Confucius says:

> When the grand course was pursued, a public and common spirit ruled all under the sky, they chose men of talents, virtue, and ability. . . . Thus men did not love their parents only, nor treat as children only their own sons. A competent provision was secured for the aged . . . . They showed kindness and compassion to widows, orphans, childless men, and those who were disabled by disease, so that they were all sufficiently maintained. . . . [They accumulated] articles [of value], disliking that they should be thrown away upon the ground, but not wishing to keep them for their own gratification. . . . In this way [selfish] schemings were repressed and found no development. Robbers, filchers, and rebellious traitors did not show themselves, and hence the outer doors remained open, and were not shut. Thus was [the period of] when we call the Grand Union.[46]

Diversity

According to the Chinese conception, the political order is based on neither ethnic nor territorial premises. The Chinese answer to the question of "Who should rule?" is this: the most virtuous sage. The sagely qualities have nothing to do with one's ethnic background. Mencius says that the early sage kings like Shun and Wen (prior to 2000 B.C.) were born in different times and in different "barbaric" regions hundreds of miles apart, yet both practiced the same way of the sage in the Central Kingdoms and became kings.

> Shun was an Eastern barbarian; he was born in Chu Feng, moved to Fu Hsia, and died in Ming Tiao. King Wen was a Western barbarian; he was born in Chi Chou and died in Pi Ying. Their native places were over a thousand *li* apart, and there were a thousand years between them. Yet when they had their way in the Central King-

doms, their actions matched like the two halves of a tally. The standards of the two sages, one earlier and one later, were identical.[47]

How would Confucians look at ethnic minorities? There are, I believe, four central elements in their attitudes toward ethnic minorities. First, Confucians in the classical period believed that people in the central regions of China, the *zhu xia*, were ethically and culturally superior to the barbarians living on the four quarters (*man, yi, rong, di*). Confucius says,

Barbarian tribes with their rulers are inferior to Chinese states (*zhu xia*) without them.[48]

Mencius also held the view that the barbarians were inferior to, and hence susceptible to be influenced by the Chinese:

I have heard of the Chinese converting barbarians to their ways, but not of their being converted to barbarian ways.[49]

Second, Confucians held the view that these barbarians were also human beings capable of understanding, respecting, and developing human virtues (*de*) and practicing rites (*li*).[50] The Chinese should treat them with benevolence (*ren*), that is, in the same way as they treat their fellow Chinese.

Fan Chih asked about benevolence. The Master said, "While at home hold yourself in a respectful attitude; when serving in an official capacity be reverent; when dealing with others do your best. These are qualities that cannot be put aside, even if you go and live among the barbarians."[51]

The Master said, "If in word you are conscientious and trustworthy and in deed single-minded and reverent, then even in the lands of the barbarians you will go forward without obstruction."[52]

Third, and related to the second point, those who have successfully acquired virtues and practiced rituals would be regarded as people of *zhu xia* and members of the Central Kingdoms. In modern terms, they would become Chinese. The quality of being "Chinese" was thus defined more in ethical or cultural than in ethnic terms, and the Chinese empire was multiethnic. Han Yu (A.D. 768–824), a famous Confucian scholar of the Tang dynasty (A.D. 618–907), said that Confucius's *Spring and Autumn Annals* holds the following: For those feudal lords [in the Chinese regions] who adopt the rites (*li*) of the barbarians, we should regard them as barbarians; but for those barbarian states which are advanced enough to adopt the Chinese rites, we should regard them as Chinese states.[53]

Fourth, peaceful edification and persuasion rather than violent or military domination should be the strategy to deal with the barbarians. The Chinese should practice benevolent rule to attract people from the four quarters to reside in the Central Kingdoms. This view is consistent with the Confucian general emphasis on voluntary submission as the basis of political rule. "When distant subjects are unsubmissive, one cultivates one's moral quality in order to attract them, and once they have come one makes them content."[54]

To conclude, while Confucianism has a strong element of cultural elitism, it has no advocacy of brutal suppression or forceful domination of the "inferior" by the "superior" cultural group.

Confucianism, Nation-States, and the New World Order

Thus far we have focused on the classical Chinese theory of world order and classical Confucian moral and political theory. One might ask, however, to what degree these theories correspond to what has actually happened in the history of Chinese politics before the modern age, and to what extent they still survive in contemporary Chinese politics. Benjamin Schwartz has argued that the Confucian ethical-political cosmopolitanism generally accords with what is found in pre-twentieth-century Chinese history as the Chinese "perception" of the world order. The phrase "Chinese perception" is used advisedly by Schwartz, for he allows the possibility that the Sinocentric world order may not be an "objective" political fact accepted by all who became involved in it. Yet, as many historians (including Schwartz himself) have argued, many "barbarian" states, including those tributary states outside China and those foreign dynasties ruling over China, have in the end come to accept the Chinese perception of the world order.[55] This perception adopts "the concept of universal kingship and *tian xia* with concretely Confucian criteria of higher culture."[56] In this world order, China occupies the center and treats all foreign countries as alike and inferior to China.[57]

It should be noted, however, that the "Sinocentric" world order—the Chinese empire and its tributary system—was not like European imperialism by conquest and colonization. As some historians have argued, the tributary system had evolved primarily as a response to deal with foreigners who wished to have trading or diplomatic relations with China. The tributary system was also not exploitative in economic terms. Strictly speaking, there was no Chinese empire outside Chinese lands.[58] On the treatment of ethnic minorities, it was mentioned above that the classical Confucian attitudes toward ethnic minorities have two elements: superiority of the Chinese culture and peaceful transformation of the barbarian ones. While the superiority element was adopted by many Chinese (until the twentieth century), the peaceful strategy was not adhered to all the time. Generally speaking, throughout Chinese history the policy on ethnic minorities has oscillated from peaceful indifference or accommodation at one extreme to aggressive suppression and discrimination at the other.

A more "positive" and interesting case of toleration followed by syncretism was the gradual assimilation of the Jews who settled in China after the twelfth century. According to a recent study, the Jews were never discriminated against for being Jewish, and many of them successfully passed the civil service exams. Their success in these exams brought them government employment outside of their Jewish communities, resulting in a great number of intermarriages, and the "Confucianization" of Jewish intellectuals and sometimes entire communities.[59]

The Chinese perception of the world order was completely shaken up by Western invasions in the twentieth century. Prominent intellectuals such as Liang Qichao quickly accepted the Western multi-state system, and came to the judgement that traditional Chinese "cosmopolitanism" led to the failure to develop a strong nation-state. Given the weak position of China in the world, both nationalist and communist governments in China have found that an order based on the notion of equal sovereignties would be advantageous to them. Cultural superiority has turned into a culture of despair; culturalism of the old days has now become nationalism.[60]

Since China has entered "the family of nations" in the modern era, territorial boundaries have become a more significant issue. Before this, as Wang Gungwu, a contemporary Chinese historian, notes, the Chinese borders in the northern and western regions had never been clearly defined. For many "kingdoms and tribal groups that accepted the Chinese tributary system, boundaries were either unclear or not contiguous with China, and their tributary missions arrived by sea."[61] But following her defeat in the Second World War, China eagerly reasserted control over territories lost to Western states and over her frontier areas with neighboring ones.[62] The model of a territorial sovereign state has often been used as a weapon to protect her territory, security, and internal affairs from Western interference. "Whatever happens in the Chinese territories is the internal affair of the sovereign state of China," the communist government regularly asserts.

One feature of the traditional Chinese conception of political order has, however, persisted stubbornly for more than two thousand years. Justifiably or not, the Chinese seem to have faithfully accepted the belief that political unity yields stability and strength in a country. Thus, despite the fact that China has been divided for lengthy periods in the past, "the driving force behind all governments has always been to reunify the empire."[63] The strong stand of the People's Republic of China on the question of unification with Taiwan, Hong Kong, and Macau has much to do with this long-lived ideology of unificationism. But even this traditional ideology is now couched in terms of the language of sovereignty and nation-state. The Chinese government claims that Taiwan, Hong Kong, and Macau belong to the same big Chinese family, and as such they are inseparable parts of the territory of

China. Any movement for independence or separation in these regions would be seen as aggression against the sovereignty of China, which would never be tolerated.

So there are clear political and practical reasons that forced the Chinese to give up the traditional Chinese theory of world order, and to accept the modern world order of equal nation-states. But how did those Chinese who are still inclined toward Confucianism or who identify themselves as Confucians—many of them scholars and intellectuals—face these fundamental changes? Most of them embraced the new world order of equal nation-states and the language of state sovereignty, but how could they justify this change of attitude in terms of Confucian theory?

Answers to these questions may be found in the response of a Confucian philosopher, Mou Zongsan (or Mou Tsung-san) (1909–95), who was one of the most original and influential contemporary Confucian philosophers. Other contemporary philosophers include Tang Junyi (1909–78), who worked closely with Mou, and Xu Fuguan (1903–82). These philosophers' main contribution was twofold: they offered systematic and original expositions of Chinese philosophy, especially Confucianism, trying to show that it still offers a profound understanding of humanity and can give valuable spiritual insights to modern people; and they revised and further developed Confucianism to incorporate modern liberal political values such as freedom and democracy. Among these philosophers, Mou went a little further than others in trying to wrestle with the questions of the nation-state, sovereignty, and the world order within the constraints of Confucianism. Mou injected new meanings into the traditional Confucian distinction between the superior (Chinese) and inferior cultures (yi xia zhi bian) and the notion of tian xia, and he developed a view of culture and morality that suits the existence of different cultures having equal standing in the new world order.

Traditional Confucianism has a hierarchical conception of cultural and ethical systems, which themselves are closely interwoven. The people in the central regions of China, the people of zhu xia, were thought to be ethically and culturally superior to the barbarians living around those regions. Confucius himself helped to link culture and morality by arguing that rituals, music, poetry, and literature are all closely connected to the development of one's humanity and morality, and all these elements of a culture can be judged as more or less ethically superior or inferior. Because the Confucians thought they had grasped the nature of human virtues and vices better than others, and because their ethical views were developed within, and intermingled with, their own cultural and political contexts, it seems natural that they also came to believe that the culture of the central regions of China was superior to others. This belief, together with the view that the ethically and culturally superior people or individual person should rule the world, gave rise to the traditional Chinese theory of world order.

Thus, one way to reject this traditional picture is to reject the superiority of Chinese culture and to affirm a diversity of cultures that are worthy of equal respect. This is exactly what Mou does.[64] He argues that even if the Way of Heaven, or the *logos*, or humanity, is the same for all human beings in the world, it admits of different concrete expressions in different cultures. The four basic ethical instincts of human beings—the heart of compassion, of shame, of courtesy and modesty, and of right and wrong, as identified by Mencius[65]—are the same for everyone, but their concrete norms and modes of expression may vary from culture to culture. Similarly, the principle of benevolence, of righteousness, of rites, and of wisdom can be realized in different ways. Why is the diversity of expressions of the *logos* possible and inevitable? Mou gives two reasons. First, the *logos* is abstract in itself and has to be fleshed out in human bodies and in human psyches, dispositions, and actions. But human psyches and temperaments (*qi zhi*) vary a great deal from individual to individual, and similarly a culture, which is a complex pattern of human values, attitudes, and norms of conduct developed over time, has its own "psyche and temperament" (*qi zhi*), which may be different from those of other cultures. There is no necessity for a particular culture to develop its psyche and temperament in a particular way; it is a result of all kinds of contingent factors. But just as different human psyches and temperaments may be complementary and make human life interesting, different cultural orientations and modes of expressions of the *logos* are something to be welcome rather than regretted. This is especially so if we also consider the second reason given by Mou. He argues that the *logos* or humanity is only known and grasped by human beings slowly in a piecemeal way. It will not be grasped in its entirety in one single act of human understanding. A culture begins life when it grasps partially the meaning of humanity. It grows by exposing itself to new experiences and adventures, and by learning from those of other cultures. So we ought to respect cultures, for they all make their own contributions to the development and expression of humanity.

But how does respect for cultures lead to an endorsement of the nation-state? Here Mou asserts, without much elaboration, that a culture evolves over time and develops into a tradition only with the support of social and political institutions. A nation-state, by giving priority to the culture of the national group in a political community, seems the best form of government that can help promote and further develop a national culture. I believe many standard arguments made in the West to support the idea of nation-state can fill the gaps left by Mou, but we have no space to rehearse them here.[66] My main concern here is to show how Mou tried to create room for a pluralistic view of cultures and hence a practical reason for the nation-state within Confucianism.

While rejecting the rigid hierarchical view of cultures in traditional Confucianism, Mou does not abandon the traditional notions of *tian xia* and *yi xia zhi bian* (the distinction of the superior and the barbarian); rather, he gives them a new meaning. For him, even though many different cultures are worthy of equal respect, there may be some ideologies or political powers that despise and destroy cultural traditions, and repress humanity. Mou sees communist states and ideologies as an example of this kind, and labels them as "barbaric." Any true Confucian must oppose the barbaric communist ideology and power because it demeans and represses humanity. Mou also retains the notion of *tian xia* and holds the traditional view that the greatest extension of human order must cover the entire world. The order of *tian xia* in modern times, however, can only mean harmonious peaceful coexistence of nation-states. This order does not replace smaller units such as families and states, but only supplements them and coordinates them in a way that facilitates the development of all states. Mou has in mind the role and nature of the United Nations as the coordinating body of the order of *tian xia*.

Mou expressed these thoughts in the 1950s, when the nation-state was regarded as the most appropriate form of government domestically and internationally, and when the United Nations was only recently established. Since the 1980s, however, we have seen important changes in the international economic and political order. Globalization of information technology and of the production and distribution of goods, the vast flow of immigration from developing countries to developed ones, and the emergence of supranational regimes such as the European Union—all these have markedly shaped the global order and the politics of nation-states. Scholars and writers of Confucianism have not yet responded to this new situation. In fact they are still grappling with basic issues like human rights and liberal democracy, trying to ascertain the extent to which Confucianism can embrace them without uprooting its central values.[67] Does Confucianism in its present state have anything useful to say on the issues of territorial boundaries in the present global order? In my view, it has something to say, but not much. Traditional Confucianism does say that the state has a responsibility to ensure a decent living for all, and that it is important to extend one's care to strangers as well as close friends and family members. So the Confucian emphasis on the unlimited scope of *ren* might be enough to reject "hard" territorial boundaries as defined by Loren Lomasky, which "confer substantial benefits or impose substantial costs on individuals in virtue of which side of the line they happen to find themselves."[68] But the Confucian view that it is natural and right for a person to show more concern for people close to him or her than to strangers would lead one to accept at least some kind of territorial boundary that distributes more resources to citizens of a community than to outsiders. Beyond this, however, Confucianism is not able to deal with complex questions about the distribution of entitlements and resources arising from territorial boundaries. In fact, it has not yet developed a theory of distributive justice within the context of a modern political community, let alone a theory of justice between states or a theory of entitlements of the citizens of a political community versus outsiders. Confucianism still has a long way to go before it can come to terms with these issues.

Notes

The author wishes to thank Michael Nylan and Daniel A. Bell for their helpful comments on an early draft of this chapter.

1. References to Mencius and Xunzi are to the works of these two philosophers as preserved by later scholars. The authorship of *Mencius* is a controversial issue. Some argue that the main bulk of the work was written by Mencius himself. Others suggest it was compiled by an editor from notes taken by Mencius's disciples.

2. *Mencius*, bk. III, pt. B, 3; bk. IV, pt. B, 3. Unless otherwise stated, all translations of *Mencius* and *The Analects* are taken from *Mencius*, trans. D. C. Lau (London: Penguin Books, 1970) and *Confucius: The Analects*, trans. D. C. Lau (London: Penguin Books, 1979) respectively.

3. *Mencius*, bk. VI, pt. B, 7.

4. Jean Gottmann, *The Significance of Territory* (Charlottesville: University Press of Virginia, 1973), 17.

5. See Ishwer C. Ojha, *Chinese Foreign Policy in an Age of Transition: The Diplomacy of Cultural Despair* (Boston: Beacon Press, 1971), 146–47; and Wang Gung-Wu, *The Chinese Way: China's Position in International Relations* (Oslo: Scandinavian University Press, 1995), 53.

6. For more detailed discussion, see Liu Shu-Hsien, *Understanding Confucian Philosophy: Classical and Sung-Ming* (Westport, Conn.: Greenwood Press, 1998), chap. 1.

7. Tang Chun-I, *Essays on Chinese Philosophy and Culture* (Tapei: Students Book Co., Ltd., 1988), 362.

8. *The Analects*, bk. XII, 22.

9. *Mencius*, bk. VII, pt. A, 15.

10. *The Analects*, bk. I, 2.

11. Ibid., bk. I, 2.

12. Ibid., translator's introduction, 18.

13. This is Talcott Parsons's view, as cited in Ambrose Y. C. King, "The Status of the Individual in Chinese Ethics," in *Individualism and Holism: Studies in Confucian and Taoist Values*, ed. Donald J. Munro (Ann Arbor: Center of Chinese Studies, University of Michigan, 1985), 58.

14. Ibid., 61.

15. *The Analects*, bk. I, 6.

16. Ibid., bk. VI, 30. This translation is taken from "Confucian Analects," trans. James Legge, in his *The Chinese Classics*, vol. I (Hong Kong: Hong Kong University Press, 1960), 194.

17. *The Analects*, bk. VI, 30.

18. Ibid., bk. XII, 2; bk. XV, 24.

19. Ibid., bk. VII, 5.

20. *Mencius*, bk. I, pt. A, 7.

21. Qian Mu, *Zhongguo wen hua shi dao lun* (Taipei: Shang Wu, 1993), 50–53.

22. Liang Qichao, *History of Chinese Political Thought during the Early Tsin Period*, trans. L. T. Chan (Taipei: Cheng-Wen Publishing Company, 1968), 2.

23. *Mencius*, bk. III, pt. B, 2.

24. *Xunzi: A Translation and Study of the Complete Works*, vols. 1–3, ed. and trans. John Knoblock (Stanford: Stanford University Press, 1988), bk. 18. Hereafter cited as *Xunzi*.

25. Benjanmin I. Schwartz, "The Chinese Perception of World Order, Past and Present," in *The Chinese World Order: Traditional China's Foreign Relations*, ed. John King Fairbank (Cambridge: Harvard University Press, 1968), 278.

26. Mencius's usage of "All under Heaven" was standard: it starts from the continent but reaches to the Four Seas beyond the continent; it admits of no territorial boundary. Mencius was also explicit in following the established distinction between "All under Heaven" and states. Mencius says, "There is a common expression, 'The Empire (tian xia), the state (guo), and the family (jia).' The empire has its basis in the state, the state in the family, and the family in one's own self." See *Mencius*, bk. IV, pt. A, 5.

27. Aristotle, *The Politics*, trans. T. A. Sinclair (London: Penguin Books, 1981), 1325b33ff.

28. Ibid., 1276b1.

29. Mogens Herman Hansen, *The Athenian Democracy in the Age of Demosthenes* (Oxford: Blackwell Publishers, 1991), 58.

30. Aristotle, *The Politics*, 1326b11ff.

31. Ibid., 1326b11ff, 1326b39ff.

32. Ibid., 1326b11ff.

33. *Shi*, Lesser Odes, "Beishan."

34. *Mencius*, bk. V, pt. A, 4.

35. *Xunzi*, bk. 24. 1.

36. *Mencius*, bk. I, pt. A, 6.

37. Ibid., bk. III, pt. B, 3; see also Liang Qichao, *Xian Qin zheng zhi si xiang shi* (Shanghai: Zhong Hua Shu Ju, 1988[1936]), 194.

38. *Mencius*, bk. IV, pt. A, 3.

39. Ibid., bk. VII, pt. B, 13.

40. *Xunzi*, bk. 18. 2.

41. Ibid.

42. In *Mencius*, there are many passages carrying this message. See, for example, bk. IV, pt. A, 9.

43. *Xunzi*, bk. 11. 6.

44. *Mencius*, bk. II, pt. B, 1.

45. Ibid., bk. II, pt. A, 6.

46. "The Li Ki," trans. James Legge, in *The Sacred Books of the East*, ed. F. Max Muller (Oxford: Clarendon Press, 1885), vol. 27, bk. 7, pp. 364–66.

47. *Mencius*, bk. IV, pt. B, 1.

48. *The Analects*, bk. III, 5.

49. *Mencius*, bk. III, pt. A, 4.

50. See *Xunzi*, bk. 1.

51. *The Analects*, bk. XIII, 19.

52. Ibid., bk. XV, 6.

53. Han Yu, "Yuan Dao," in *Han Yu San Wen Xuan*, eds. Gu Yisheng and Xu Cuiyu (Hong Kong: Joint Publishing [H. K.] Co., Ltd., 1992), 1–20.

54. *The Analects*, bk. XVI, 1. See also bk. XIII, 4, and *Mencius*, bk. XIV, 4.

55. Schwartz, "The Chinese Perception of World Order, Past and Present," 276–77. See also Wang Gung-Wu, "Early Ming Relations with Southeast Asia: A Background Essay," in *The Chinese World Order: Traditional China's Foreign Relations*, ed. John King Fairbank (Cambridge: Harvard University Press, 1968), 34–62; and Wang, *The Chinese Way*, 51–59.

56. Schwartz, "The Chinese Perception of World Order, Past and Present," 277.

57. Wang, "Early Ming Relations with Southeast Asia: A Background Essay," 61.

58. See Wang, *The Chinese Way*, 57–58; Ojha, *Chinese Foreign Policy in an Age of Transition*, 16.

59. See Wendy Robin Abraham, "The Role of Confucian and Jewish Educational Values in the Assimilation of the Chinese Jews of Kaifeng, Supplemented by Western Observer Accounts, 1605–1985" (Ed.D. diss., Columbia University Teachers College, 1989).

60. Ohja, *Chinese Foreign Policy in an Age of Transition*, chap. 2.

61. Wang, *The Chinese Way*, 53.

62. Ohja, *Chinese Foreign Policy in an Age of Transition*, 148.

63. Wang, *The Chinese Way*, 53.

64. The following discussion of Mou's ideas is based on Mou Zongsan, *Dao de de li xiang zhu yi*, 6th ed. (Taipei: Xue Sheng Shu Ju, 1985[1959]), esp. 39–67, 135–50, 245–62.

65. *Mencius*, bk. II, pt. A, 6.

66. See David Miller, *On Nationality* (Oxford: Clarendon Press, 1995).

67. For some recent efforts, see *Confucianism and Human Rights*, eds. Wm. Theodore de Bary and Tu Wei-Ming (New York: Columbia University Press, 1998). See also Joseph Chan, "A Confucian Perspective on Human Rights for Contemporary China," in *The East Asian Challenge for Human Rights*, eds. Joanne Bauer and Daniel A. Bell (New York: Cambridge University Press, 1999), 212–37.

68. See Loren Lomasky in chapter 3 of this book.

Six

Boundaries of the Body and Body Politic in Early Confucian Thought

MICHAEL NYLAN

NEITHER the concept nor the term "Confucianism" existed until Jesuit missionaries in China felt the need to invent a Chinese counterpart for Christianity in Europe. Summaries of early "Confucian" teachings on a given issue, then, necessarily overlook one distinction important to early thinkers in China, while foisting on readers a second distinction anachronistic for the period: The term *Ru*, now employed to translate "Confucianism," originally referred simply to "classicists," and early thinkers were quite careful to distinguish between the set of professional "classicists" (*Ru*), many of whom employed the body of teachings they had mastered to further their own ambitions or those of their state, and the much smaller subset of self-identified ethical followers of Confucius (551–479 B.C.). In addition, the books that we now dub the Five "Confucian" Classics (the *Wu jing*) constituted a common store of knowledge for all literate Chinese in imperial China; as authoritative texts thought to encapsulate the Way of Antiquity, they were read on multiple levels besides the moral. This chapter, in order to focus on the complex issue of boundaries, inevitably downplays the still more complex conceptual problems that have arisen from the regular conflation of "Confucian," "classicist," and "Chinese."[1] For the purposes of this essay, I will adopt "Confucian" as a convenient category under which to group the materials found either in the Five Classics or in the writings of Confucius's most prominent early ethical followers.

Using this somewhat contrived definition, we can say that Confucian thought at its inception represented a series of loose teachings in support of moral action, rather than a unitary creed enjoining a discrete set of beliefs; in other words, it was an orthopraxy, not an orthodoxy.[2] To the degree that specific teachings were devised to guide the individual to the Confucian Way, they enjoined the would-be Confucian to weigh the relative claims of incommensurate goods in order to find the single most humane solution to problems posed by social interaction. This solution was then identified in Confucian literature as the "Middle Way." To take a single example, strict loyalty to one's superiors in the sociopolitical hierarchy was to be balanced by the subordinate's duty to reprimand his superior when necessary; likewise, the injustice inherent in any hereditary system of rank was to be offset by the social mobility inevitably fostered by the startling redefinition of "nobility" promoted by Confucius (wherein commitment to classical ideals replaced aristocratic birth).[3] As Confucius distinguished himself from contemporary leaders on the basis of his consistent refusal to offer a set of rules about right and wrong,[4] sweeping generalizations about "Confucian" positions on any given topic can at best serve as vague "guideposts" to the Way, indicating proximate sites of ethical concern rather than the exact locations of ethical solutions.

If the model of the Sage-Master Confucius resists reductionist attempts, the subsequent history of Confucianism makes it even less amenable to easy characterizations. As an approach to rule and self-rule, a self-conscious "Confucian" movement emerged in the late Warring States period (475–222 B.C.), centuries after the death of the Master, Confucius, so that considerable controversy always existed as to the core content of the Supreme Sage's teachings. And though early Confucian classicism advocated certain archaic and archaizing practices in the hopes of curbing current social ills, it took *Ru* teachings in the long imperial period (221 B.C.–A.D. 1911) some time to acquire some semblance of a coherent belief system; it did this in response to four main stimuli: (1) the concurrent articulation and widespread acceptance of Yin/yang and Five Phases cosmological conceptions; (2) the perceived need of the Chinese imperial state after unification in 221 B.C. to have classicists on its payroll devise suitable criteria to evaluate candidates for public office; (3) the impact of Buddhism from the third century A.D. on; and (4) the introduction of Christianity more than a millennium later.[5] Still, because the Confucian Way was never an exclusive religion, but rather a series of precepts and practices designed to increase the adherent's capacity to feel and express sympathy for others, self-identified Confucians who came into contact with local cultures with their alternate structures were apt to readily absorb and accommodate other beliefs and practices. Some of these adaptations necessitated conscious reformulations of the basic Confucian teachings, of course, but many transformations seem to have occurred without attracting much notice, then or now. Meanwhile, to the utter consternation of late purists and the endless confusion of modern scholars, many of the most famous proponents of Confucian values down through the ages (e.g., Mencius and Han Yu) have sought to "prove" the value of Confucius's Middle Way by linking it with the preservation of a distinctive "Central States" identity, though entirely separate "Chinese" ethnic and national identities were themselves relatively late and loose inventions, fleshed out in response to major "barbarian incursions," including those of the Western powers in the late nineteenth and early twentieth centuries.[6]

For the foregoing reasons, it is best to think of "Confucian" learning as a cluster of problems and themes evolving over time and place, as particular thinkers trained in classical texts chose to focus on a set of key concepts over others while integrating outside influences.[7] This chapter traces early Confucian notions of boundaries, where "early Confucian" refers to the Warring States and Han writings of self-identified Confucian thinkers. Such a focus fulfills two useful functions: First, the period under consideration was the formative stage in the development of Confucian teachings, a stage that is frequently ignored or misunderstood.[8] Second, my paper then complements Joseph Chan's submission to this volume, whose argument builds upon early twentieth-century readings of the early writers, not only in its easy conflation of the "Confucian" and Chinese traditions but also in its propensity to read into early texts what one historian calls "compensatory universalism."[9] Hence, the decision to have this essay draw most of its evidence from the rather small corpus of texts that early on—if erroneously—came to be most closely associated with the figure of Confucius: the Five "Confucian" Classics[10] and their attached traditions.

Eight Tenets

The authors of these texts seem relatively unconcerned about some of the questions that interest modern theorists on the topic of territorial boundaries. For example, on diversity, the authors in this volume consider the question: "Do differences in ethnicity-culture, language, religion, or moral practices constitute an appropriate basis for the division of living space between communities?" Confucian teachers had good reasons for ignoring certain problems attending such divisions of living space. First of all, for most of the long history of Confucianism, Chinese and "barbarian" lived cheek-by-jowl in many areas, with "empire" as much a habit of mind as an actualized reality;[11] occasional enforced separations into different locales were most often mandated not by a "Confucianized" ruling elite, but by successive "barbarian" conquerors of China who feared that their own peoples would become overly sinicized. Given the admirable material culture, ritual elegance, and political stability that they associated with the Confucian way of life, early Confucians little feared that Chinese would be tempted to adopt barbarian ways wholesale.[12] Second, Confucius left his disciples in no doubt that "barbarians" and Chinese are "very much alike in nature, though they come to differ by custom";[13] thus, the "barbarians," no less than the Central States inhabitants, could master the techniques of self-cultivation so as to realize their human potential. Since "all within the Four Seas are brothers," the early Confucians fervently hoped that the not-yet-civilized would eventually embrace their cultural patterns (wen), adopting their rites and their written language.[14] Third, as noted above, because the Confucian Way was a behavioral Way, not a religion, adherents in good conscience could profess equal devotion to the gods of the "native" Chinese religion, Taoism, and to the "foreign" gods of Buddhism, Manicheanism, or Christianity. "All roads lead to the Tao," as one Confucian classic put it.[15] Fourth, throughout China and all the East Asian countries that came under Confucian influence (Korea, Japan, and Vietnam), people spoke mutually incomprehensible languages though they shared a single writing system.[16] In short, a great diversity of languages, religions, moralities, and cultures coexisted as the norm within the Confucian cultural horizon, where neither cultural and linguistic boundaries nor ethical responsibilities ever neatly coincided with political borders.[17] Not surprisingly, then, Confucians made no strong practical or theoretical moves to erect fixed boundaries between communities or to restrict mobility across territorial boundaries—the popular myth of the Great Wall notwithstanding.[18] Perhaps the simplest way to categorize the disparate concerns expressed by self-identified followers of Confucius is to focus on the elaborate analogies framed between the physical body and the body politic. On the questions of ownership, autonomy, and the distribution of scarce resources, those analogies, then, underlie the following observations on the subject of "Confucian" boundaries.

In early Confucian theory, geographic boundaries are emphatically (a) permeable and (b) expandable, because the health of the body and body politic is thought to depend always on flow and change, rather than on fixedness. In addition, (c) neither the body nor the state is ever seen as the "possession of one man." Instead, both are conceived as entities held in trust, in effect "works in progress" extending over space and time.[19] To the Confucian, these obvious "facts" attesting to the blurry boundaries of the body and body politic by no means precluded order, for (d) order in the Confucian tradition emanates from a stable—precisely because it is not rigidly placed—center attuned to social and cosmic patterns. In the body, the center was defined as the heart/mind, locus of the proper motivations for social interaction; in the body politic, as the ruler or, in the absence of a good and wise ruler, the sage. (There was far less emphasis in early Confucian thought on an interior or distinctly "spiritual" life than we might expect, either from later Chinese traditions or from Western stereotypes of the "mysterious East.") However, (e) early Confucian writings insist on unambiguous territorial and social boundaries when boundaries are established for specific ritual purposes; such boundaries are to be promptly deconstructed once their ultimate ritual aims have been achieved. Thus (f) strictly physical demarcations, like contemporary social hierarchies, played a limited role as auxiliary "supports" to the twin centers of the heart/mind and ruler as the centers set about their all-important task of insuring proper relations, but the physical props for morality were thought to play a lesser role in moral cultivation than the suasive examples conveyed through family and scholastic affiliations, or sagely teachings. It was always the logic of moral situations and relational space, in other words—not the precise location of any thing, person, or event—that most attracted the "true" Confucians, those devoted to notions of ritual efficacy.[20] This was so in part because (g) the secure acquisition of true power depended upon the steady buildup of moral charisma, not upon the land, persons, or things at one's disposal. After all, a strain of Chinese folk wisdom preserved in the "Confucian" Classics and their associated traditions, most prominently in commentaries to the *Changes* (*Yi jing*), argued that (h) no possession—even land—is intrinsically good or lucky, since the relative benefits accruing from possession depend upon timing and location, as well as the owner's present rank and situation in life.[21]

Charismatic Power as a Function of Sharing Space

To support this series of eight hypotheses, some of which may strike readers as counterintuitive or just plain wrong, let me begin with a legend that many Confucians thought encapsulated much of the sacred Way of the Ancients. The story purports to relate events in the life of the pre-dynastic "founder" of the Zhou dynasty (c. 1050–256 B.C.), the very dynasty that set the pattern for all subsequent notions of cultivated society, according to Confucius.[22] Once upon a time a petty local ruler of the small state of Bin, named Danfu, found his fertile lands to be the envy of all his neighbors in the Central Plain of the area now known as China. Foreseeing the continual invasions to which his state would be subjected, Danfu reasoned, "The people enthrone a ruler in order to benefit from him. The people would fight back for my sake, but I cannot bear to kill fathers and sons in order to remain as their ruler!" In response to advisors who urged him to stay and fight to preserve the sacred ancestral temple, he replied that his duty to the ancestors was essentially a "private" obligation that must give way to his public duty to the people. So Danfu forsook his ancestral homelands, moving his home some 60 miles to the northwest, to a significantly less fertile district nestled in the foothills of Mount Qi. Then, to his astonishment, "the entire populace of Bin, bearing their old on their backs and carrying their children in their arms," followed him there on foot, at which demonstration of loyalty many neighboring states sought alliances with Danfu.[23]

This legend touches upon a number of the values that I have mentioned above: the (real) inconsequence of set boundaries; the potential for expansion (in this case, of authority and power) beyond the original boundaries; the state as shared possession; and the ruler as stable center of community life. And this legend is hardly an isolated one. Confucian compendia regularly associate the acquisition of charismatic power with similar acts of "yielding" space.[24]

To understand why this was so, we must put early Confucian beliefs within their proper historical context, taking into account the profoundly religious underpinnings of this humanistic world view, and then calculating the effects on its teachings of two contemporary debates on political ethics, along with early Chinese medical theories about the body. Regarding the religious background, as far back as the first written script in China (1300 B.C.), the entire area of the proto-Chinese polity was thought to enjoy the explicit protection of the ruler's ancestors who resided in heaven.[25] Back then, too, the very life of the ruler, let alone the possibility for his continuing physical health and good fortune, came as gift from these same ancestral spirits. In part because of the teachings of Confucius himself, eventually other persons of sufficient moral stature were thought to merit heaven's equal consideration, by virtue of their faithful conformity with what was widely perceived as the old aristocratic Way of the Ancients. In any case, because the earliest discourses in China could not envision a body or body politic surviving long without the active intervention of the beneficent gods, all the Confucian virtues in some sense boiled down to a willingness to express one's recognition of the heavy debts owed to others, both living and dead, for one's own life and property, a recognition that supposedly spurred the person to develop the imaginative and emotional capacities required to treat inferiors in rank, property, age, or understanding with genuine consideration (shu).

No doubt, the Confucians were even more aware of the moral obligation to requite ethical debts and exemplify personal generosity because their sense of group identity had been forged in the course of voicing their vehement opposition to two sorts of influential political theory in the late Warring States period: that of the Realpoliticians and that of Yang Zhu. The backers of Realpolitik argued that the state was in effect the possession of one man, the ruler, to do with as he chose. Then Yang Zhu—in the manner somewhat reminiscent of John Locke—stated that the physical body constituted the individual's most basic private possession, from which evolved rights to autonomy. Thinking that both doctrines, in propounding absolutism and autonomy, undermined the will to seek the kind of delicate balance required for humane social orders, early Confucian teachers argued instead that the apparent owners of bodies and of states—the individual persons and the titled rulers—held these assets only temporarily in trust for all members of the community. Therefore, benefits associated with possession of the body or the state should be spread as widely as possible within the bounds of the respective communities (i.e., in the case of the family, shared with its members living and dead; in the case of the state, shared with all subjects in the state).[26] Apparent—even legal—possession of a body or a state, then, had little real standing in moral terms; blessings offered and requited through ritual were made to join communities across time and space.

Chinese medical theory underlined this Confucian emphasis on fluidity, since it posited the regular circulation of blood and qi (configured energy) as the primary definition of physical and moral health.[27] Accordingly, the health of the body politic was thought to depend upon the smooth flow of communication between ruler and people and the circulation of goods, on a strict analogy with the physical body:

> When the ruler's virtue does not flow freely, and the wishes of his people do not reach him, there is stasis in the state. When stasis lasts for a long time, a hundred pathologies arise in concert, and a myriad catastrophes swarm in. . . . The reason that the sage-kings valued heroic retainers and faithful ministers is that they dared to speak directly, breaking through such stases.[28]

Because, as one early classicist put it, "The Way of [true] humanity lies in making contact,"[29] the Confucians labored to devise suitable methods to optimize this flow of wealth and services: wealth would be regularly dispersed through ritual gift exchanges[30] and through the enforcement (under social pressure, under political and legal sanctions) of the ruling elite's duty to distribute grain and other basic necessities to the poor.[31] Moral learning would circulate throughout the realm from the true king and his ministers to commoners and then back from "those below" to the court, "exactly as vital qi circulates through the human body."[32] The state would facilitate this "appropriate" movement of persons and information within the realm.[33] Social mobility, for instance, would be encouraged through largely meritocratic educational and bureaucratic systems—a revolutionary idea attributed directly to Confucius.[34] And persons engaged in ritual would assume a variety of shifting roles, each identified with specific physical sites. Basically, "goods and grains [in company with people and ideas] shall be allowed to circulate freely, so that there is no hindrance or stagnation in distribution."[35]

Once these discrete strands of Confucian theorizing had been woven together, there resulted a remarkably coherent picture of the ideal state and the ideal person (the sage, who in the best of all possible worlds was also the king): these were robust circulatory systems producing a surplus of energy, which in turn boosted the moral and physical health of weaker things nearby, until "Moral influence irresistibly filled to overflowing the whole of All-under-Heaven within the Four Seas."[36] In theory, this moral power knew no bounds, since it resonated with all things that were in sympathy with it, however distant in time and space, operating like a tuning fork that magically sets to humming stringed instruments across the room.[37]

Consequently, the dividing lines between heaven and earth, between past and present, were to collapse, at least when the cosmos was lucky enough to be ruled by a sage-king: the Confucian exemplar "in contemplating Heaven, becomes Heaven; in contemplating Earth, becomes Earth; in contemplating Time, becomes timely."[38] After all, "the sage is teacher to a hundred generations,"[39] because "all the ten thousand things were there within" him.[40] This was how "Confucian" classicists subtly reinterpreted the explicit claim of older elite traditions that "All land is the king's land / All humans within the borders are his subjects."[41] Hence, my preliminary characterization of territorial boundaries in Confucian discourse as eminently "permeable" and infinitely "expandable." (Lands with fixed borders and kings without the requisite moral capacities to extend generosity to others through a process of "likening to oneself"—like the sorriest of "skin-bound" persons—were considered woefully limited and so remarkably unappealing to the early Chinese.)[42]

To be realized, this ideal capacity to transcend ordinary boundaries (dubbed the "Great Peace" in the state and "sagehood" predicated on psychic equilibrium in the person)—a crossing-over not to be confused with a breakdown of order—depended fundamentally on the vibrant potency of the center (the ruler, in the case of the state). Confucian texts identify the ruler as "ultimate" locus or "center," even as "vibrating dipole"[43] of his state, not because rulers per se are an intrinsically more "valuable" breed of human beings than the rest of us; not even because rulers have been anointed by Heaven.[44] No, the king is "center" because he, by virtue of his influential position, has the potential to generate the greatest number of effective moral acts in all directions. Also, according to Confucian assumptions of "proximity" (a kind of geomorality), humans are more likely to attain moral enlightenment the closer their proximity to his suasive example. In consequence, the ruler functions as potential hub of all action.[45] Not surprisingly, then, the character for "king" (three parallel horizontal lines joined by a vertical) shows the king to be one who joins, symbolizes, and stabilizes the parallel moral realms of Heaven, Earth, and Man.[46]

"One starts with unity and proceeds to plurality," as one Confucian master wrote.[47] For him, as for all early Confucians, what mattered most was seeing that this vital center held firm. Then and only then would all the other things, people, and events lapse "naturally" into their correct places (zheng), with the result that each—human or nonhuman—would be free to develop spontaneously in its own distinctive pattern.[48] The moral center, the Confucians asserted, would hold so long as the heart/mind persists in choosing the right, so long as the emperor scrupulously "conforms to Heaven" (by watching the celestial patterns) and "orders things" on earth (by setting an exemplary pattern for morality, communicated through regular ritual performances).[49] One of the chief—if not the chief—way that the good ruler (or, in his absence, the sage) sets a compelling example of perfect virtue is by acknowledging the most elementary truth: that his most fortunate possession of a body, territory, and portable property represents the cumulative achievements of successive generations over time, and so the primary benefits of possession—economic wealth and moral insight—are to be shared with others in the community, particularly those who are noble-minded (out of admiration) or less fortunate (out of pity).[50]

Obviously, not a few rulers in real life were reluctant to exert the full measure of their charismatic influence, when such exertion would entail significant "sharing" of their persons, their goods, and their lands with others. Then the Confucians hastened to point out the practical advantages that would invariably accrue from acts of generosity: Sharing, they said, leaves the person secure from the threat that others will steal his things out of envy or need.[51] Sharing promises to yield aesthetic pleasures also, because "only the good and wise man is able to [i.e., fully knows how to] enjoy his possessions."[52] Sharing even binds the gods, ghosts, and men to the donor, thereby vastly increasing his power. "It was by sharing . . . that the [ideal] men of antiquity were able to enjoy," maintain, and pass on their physical patrimony (the body, the land, the possessions).[53] Supreme power, after all, rests in the person's ability to confidently call upon the aid of a unified community in a crisis: that "the people are prepared to die" for a person is what it means to be truly powerful.

Conversely, "One can never [truly] 'gain' the empire without the heart-felt admiration of the people in it."[54] Kings whose subjects are disloyal are rightly said to have "no men" in their service.[55] As a rule, to have insecure or disreputable possessions is tantamount to having no possessions at all, since such possessions bring no certain blessings. Those who do not acknowledge their obligations to others by sharing their blessings will doubtless find "their persons in danger and their territories reduced."[56] Nevertheless, the more cautious of the early Confucian masters were quick to remind followers that they had promised only that the steady accumulation of moral acts would yield unmistakable, if intangible influence; after all, *de* (charismatic virtue) operated on others just like the unseen wind. It was simply that intangible moral influence so often coincidentally brought tangible powers and possessions in its wake, as men came willingly to offer their goods and their persons to charismatic leaders.[57]

Organizing Space Appropriately

This early Confucian stress on the real if sometimes immaterial advantages of virtuous conduct coexisted with a strong and abiding interest in drawing lines and limits for material things in space. We see this in the many passages where the overwhelming moral influence of the Confucian exemplar is expressed in spatial terms, as when the ruler is compared to "the compass in motion describing a complete circle through the sites," or the carpenter's square, which "secures things [in their proper place]."[58] The unknown authors of the Confucian classics continually—some would say *ad nauseam*—listed among the paramount arts of ruling, reserved to sages and true kings, the art of organizing space appropriately. Certainly, the construction of temporary physical boundaries in space for ritual purposes—boundaries increasing in number and size in direct proportion to the importance of the ritual activities conducted within—was perceived as absolutely crucial, insofar as set boundaries helped focus the attention of less cultivated heart-minds upon that distillation of the truly holy (via communication and other reciprocal exchanges) that was the goal of ritual acts performed within the extra-sacred space. On the model of the "natural" or "spontaneous" Tao's ordering of large blocks of space and time in the universe, humans could partake of divinity whenever they managed to order, through ritual, their infinitely smaller spheres of human interaction.[59]

Hence, the strict spatial segregation by hierarchies of gender, rank, and age: "Men took the right side and women the left; men stayed behind another of a father's years."[60] The goal was not only to forestall overfamiliarity, lest that breed contempt between the groups, but also to grant each person his or her due allotment of private space. (The few rituals that worked to upset commonplace perceptions of the physical boundaries demarcating rank, gender, age, or social status, as when a young boy impersonating an ancestor took precedence over his father, somehow worked as exceptions that proved the rule; they merely served to underscore the profound moral utility of the normative space units that usually structured everyday life.) In any case, multiple references to ordering space pepper multiple chapters of the *Rites, Documents, Odes,* and *Mencius* classics, as well as the Han dynasty neoclassics. According to these accounts, the legendary sages of antiquity divided All-under-Heaven into five concentric regions; into four, nine, or twelve major provinces; and into innumerable well-field plots of 900 Chinese acres each. In each case, the sages had discerned an underlying order, which they sought to respond to and strengthen by further replication.[61] Spatial schemas, even spatial fantasies, were therefore one means by which early Confucian culture declared its faith in the inherently orderly processes of the cosmos, on the one hand, and in the vast human potential for constructed order on the other. Another was the Confucian—or was it merely Chinese?—preoccupation with place-naming, a skill by which unremarkable space was transformed symbolically into monumental "place" (i.e., space with a specific, memorable history).[62]

Confucians, too, were inclined to wax eloquent on the subject of halting "inappropriate" flows in physical space. That much flow was indeed appropriate and that this appropriate flow should be encouraged, all Confucian thinkers agreed upon. At the same time, flows must never be allowed to run on in a chaotic and uncontrolled fashion. (Once again, the analogy with the body worked, for the flow of blood and *qi* in the body must be contained within appropriate channels, lest there occur disastrous leakages of the vital substances.) In company with other thinkers of their time,[63] the Confucians firmly believed that the vast majority of people fared best—both in moral and in economic terms—when they stayed put in relatively small communities (in "natural" units of about "100 *li* [square]"), where shared histories and a uniform code of morality kept members alive to their obligations to care for one another humanely.[64] Most people who had left their ancestral graves far behind could be expected to feel a sense of what we today might call "alienation." Physically adrift, once they had lost their "rightful" place in the world, they were more likely to be beset with economic difficulties and psychic insecurities, which could then lead to the commission of serious crimes against properties and persons. (Of course, the Confucian theorists realized that most migrants had been driven from their lands by unjust wars, unwise policies, or natural disasters, in mass migrations that typically threatened the security of the state and its remaining inhabitants.) In further explanation of this, the Confucians were wont to explain that different types of location, each with its own characteristic climate, topography, and *qi* ("cold or hot, dry or moist"), were apt to engender varying aptitudes and habits in those born in different regions, making it all the more vital that a sage "at center" reveal to each separate group its own distinct Middle Path, which could then be harmonized with the others.[65]

Nonetheless, as the legend of good king Danfu suggests, the early Confucians thought the specific site of ritually demarcated space, let alone territorial possessions, to be comparatively unimportant, so long as the sage held forth "at center." (Could it be that the locations of land units mattered so little because they tended not to correspond exactly with the main units of organized society in China: the clan lineages and the professional affiliations?) For example, when the early Confucians discussed the Five Sacred Mountains, they glanced over questions about the precise location at which these Mountains were situated; they were intent upon seeing the right number of mountains grandly honored in ritual.[66] And once again, it was the ritual "center" among the Mountains, Mount Tai, that was deemed most important, though Mount Tai at no time corresponded to the actual geographical center of a Chinese or proto-Chinese state. Similarly, Chinese capitals were moved repeatedly over the course of Chinese history, sometimes several times within the course of a single dynasty, to suit the convenience of the emperor or to adapt to changing socioeconomic and political realities. The Confucians offered no vociferous protests; one chapter in the "Confucian" *Documents* instead celebrated the model king who moved his capital repeatedly.[67] For Confucians, what made a site holy over time was the quality and quantity of sacred acts enacted at the site (for example, the continuation of special sacrifices to the gods), where the sacred tended to include the mundane and the secular, as well as the overtly religious.[68] What made any city a king's capital, in particular, was the erection of ritual halls and educational institutions, where the classical Way of the Ancients—both the practice and theory of it—would be sponsored by the state and transmitted to successive generations.[69] The focus, in other words, remained on the accumulation of humane deeds fostering community, in the serene confidence that such accumulations ultimately would spawn signs of supramundane power in time or space.

Ultimately, this approach allowed Confucians remarkable play when imagining space in ethical terms. While no early Confucian ever exhibited a romantic love for wilderness terrain, as "the wastes" lay beyond the cycle of ritual obligations constructed by sages,[70] these same Confucians felt entirely comfortable adopting the shifting perspectives found in classic Chinese landscape art when faced with the need to formulate complex moral judgments. A famous passage from the *Gongyang* commentary to the *Spring and Autumn Annals* (a work ascribed to Confucius) will demonstrate my point. The commentary states: "When it [the sacred *Annals* text] takes the point of view of the capital, then the Central States' culture surrounding it [near the Yellow River] is considered 'outside' [and so meriting a different treatment]; and when it takes the point of view of the Central States, then the Yi and Di barbarians are considered 'outside.'"[71] Similarly, the Confucian thinker Mencius, in trying to persuade others that virtue is really the "natural" course for humans, weighed a series of possible implications of analogies constructed between "inside" vs. "outside" and "nature" vs. "nurture"; meanwhile, the *Rites* chapters tried to apportion mourning duties within the family circle, a most delicate ritual matter, through language that calculates degrees of kinship more or less "inside" or "outside."[72] Space had acquired this ethical character, for each and every aspect of the cosmos in its appropriate location revealed, to the enlightened heart-mind, the moral connections threading through the universe. Humans who yearned for true greatness had only to study and emulate the patterns of location to discern fundamental truths, as the *Book of Rites* attested in the following passage:

The courses of the heavenly bodies supply the most perfect lessons, and the sages possessed the highest degree of virtue. Above, in the hall of the ancestral temple, there was a jar of wine, with clouds and hills represented on it on the east and with sacrificial victims represented on it in the west. Below the hall, the larger drums were suspended in the west, and the smaller drums that answer them on the east. The ruler appeared at the top of the steps on the east; his wife, in the apartment on the west. The sun makes its appearance in the east; the moon makes her appearance in the west. Such are the different ways in which the processes of dark and light are distributed in nature, and such are the arrangements for the [corresponding] positions of husband and wife.[73]

Conclusion

While the Confucian Way is all too often mischaracterized as a sort of slavish devotion to a monolithic tradition, it arose in reaction against prevailing conventions, out of successive attempts to selectively appropriate, reconfigure, and promote the most "nonregressive" (i.e., humanizing) tendencies within pre-Confucian traditions.[74] In the spirit of Confucian accommodation, we might consider borrowing certain messages drawn from Confucian history, the better to reconfigure our own moral priorities—all the more so as the Confucians have long been in the habit of contemplating a world in which a very many people are crowded into exceedingly tight spaces.[75] I myself applaud the clarity of the Confucian vision that requires vast empires to be balanced by sharp "turns toward the local," so that small communities, admittedly with the informed support of exemplary leaders at the pinnacle of power, are expected to define appropriate responsibilities and reasonable expectations for their own members.[76] Our society would surely profit as well from a consideration of the fundamental Confucian proposition that we "share" our bodies and our properties with others, for as long as we careen between belief in ourselves as fully autonomous, "self-made" beings and as pathetic creatures entrapped by our preconscious pasts while maintaining our nationalistic and global allegiances, we will tend to ignore the all-important roles of middle-level social groupings (the extended family, the immediate neighborhood) in fostering ethical action. The Confucian preference for "soft boundaries" for the body and body politic satisfies both moral and practical considerations.[77] Equally sound are related beliefs that Confucians have shared with thinkers of many other religious or philosophical traditions: first, that levels of self-cultivation, rather than quantities of material commodities, mark the fully mature adult; and second, that good states by definition find ways to single out moral adults for public recognition and rewards, so that their examples will be easily identified, closely studied, and widely emulated by society. According to the Confucian view, any society that celebrates mere freedom from intervention as its highest goal will inevitably pay a heavy price in terms of the physical, mental, and moral health of its members. Concomitantly, the just state, properly constituted, notwithstanding its extendable borders, owes to all its own people provisions for a secure economic livelihood (famine relief in times of natural disaster, the supervision of granaries and markets, and so on), no less than a fine education in moral thinking.

I end with an observation: We who tend—certainly in our more uncritical moments—to view ourselves as inheritors of a "Western tradition" must acknowledge that, thanks to our particular history, the knowledge of geography and indeed, the focus on boundaries, are intimately related to capitalism's expanding role in the nineteenth and early twentieth centuries. Hence, our propensity to see "space, as a social fact, as a social factor and as an instance of society, [as] . . . always political and strategic."[78] By contrast, early Chinese thinkers developed a distinct discipline of learning called *di li* ("Earth's patterns"; their closest counterpart to our "geography") which looked to ethnographic and historical knowledge, not iconic knowledge (the need for better maps and diagrams to aid expansion).[79] The Chinese interest in human history and human customs operated on three related assumptions: first, that the past was indeed relevant to the present and changing world; second, that space—like time—could be configured in such a way as to direct our attention productively to the very human need for frequent ethical interaction; and third, that this elusive yet desirable Way was itself reducible neither to objective knowledge nor to multiple acquisitions; rather, it was to be equated with the kind of learning that informs conscious, ethical action. Let us hope that our future endeavors more closely enter into the Chinese spirit of di li than that of the "Western" explorer-geographers, insofar as we take up the larger task of seeking ethical solutions to guide the cultivation of "All-under-Heaven."

Notes

1. For the confusion between "Confucianism" and "classicism" (both are *Ru*), see Michael Nylan, "Rethinking the Han Confucian Synthesis," *Imagining Boundaries: Changing Confucian Doctrines, Texts, and Hermeneutics*, ed. Kai-wing Chow, On-cho Ng, and John B. Henderson (Albany: State University of New York Press, 1999). Concerted efforts by responsible scholars to separate "Confucianism" from "Chinese" have repeatedly foundered. See, e.g., *A Confucian World Observed: A Contemporary Discussion of Confucian Humanism in East Asia*, ed. Tu Wei-ming, Milan Hejtmanek, and Alan Wachman (Honolulu: University of Hawaii Press, 1992).

2. For the very useful distinction between orthopraxy vs. orthodoxy, see William Watson, *Death Ritual in Late Imperial China*, ed. James L. Watson and Evelyn S. Rawski (Berkeley: University of California Press, 1988), chap. 1. For the Confucian concern with motivations and with practice, rather than with doctrines, see David Nivison, *The Ways of Confucianism* (Chicago: University of Chicago Press, 1996), 119. Probably, the Chinese conception of civilization (*wen*, literally "cultural patterns") became more "bookish" and more "historical" under later neo-Confucianism.

3. Confucius defined *zhong* ("loyalty") and *shu* ("consideration," "reciprocity," or "likening [others to oneself]") as the core of his teaching. See *Analects* 4/15.

4. *Analects* 18/8: "As for me, I am different from any of these. I have no 'thou shalt' or 'thou shalt not'." Cf. Arthur Waley, *The Analects of Confucius* (London: Vintage, 1938), 222.

5. Lionel Jensen, "The Invention of 'Confucius' and His Chinese Other, 'Kong Fuzi,'" *Positions* 1:2 (Fall 1993): 414–49; William W. Appleton, *The City of Cathay: The Chinese Vogue in England during the Seventeenth and Eighteenth Centuries* (New York: Columbia University Press, 1951). For "unified empire" as a late concept, probably postdating Confucius, see Gu Jiegang, "Qin Han tong yi de you lai he zhan guo ren dui yu shi jie de xiang xiang," *Gushi bian* 2 (1927): 1–10; Wang Yong, *Zhongguo di li xue shi* (Taipei: Student Bookstore rpt. of Shanghai, 1938 ed.), 12.

6. The term "Central States" was apparently coined in the Warring States period (475–222 B.C.) in the area that corresponds roughly to present-day northeast and central China, an area dominated by the Yellow River and long considered (erroneously)

the single "wellspring" of civilization. As each of the ruling houses of the Central States traced its roots back to either Shang or early Zhou rule, elites in the Central States emphasized the great continuities among their cultures once they were confronted with the rise of two new superpowers from outside the region: Qin far to the northwest, and Chu to the south. The Central States identity was based primarily on cultural identity.

"Chinese identity," by contrast, arose very gradually in response to a succession of "barbarian" conquests, e.g., that in A.D. 417, when the whole of northern China was conquered by the Toba nomads. It was not fully formed until after 1840, when the old culturalist arguments yielded to new arguments about race, which pitted Manchus against the Chinese, and the Chinese against the Euro-American imperialists.

7. See Nivison, Ways of Confucianism, 5.

8. Because later neo-Confucianism, influenced by Buddhism (itself influenced by the Greco-Roman world) shares more presumptions with Christianity, it requires less effort to appreciate it than the "stranger," pre-Buddhist classicism. Hence, the comment made by the scholar Jacques Gernet to a student specializing in Han classicism, "You have to admit that your Han people were a rather odd bunch, and that the Chinese of the 16th–19th centuries were quite different!" (reported in Anne Cheng, "Intellectual Self-Awareness in Han Times," paper given at the Association for Asian Studies annual conference, 1996).

9. The so-called "universalism" of Ru thought is undoubtedly the product of the Jesuit construction of "Confucianism" as "bearer of China's significance" in debates over truth, God, and representation. See Lionel M. Jensen, Manufacturing Confucianism: Chinese Traditions and Universal Civilization (Durham: Duke University Press, 1997), esp. 4, 260; Jensen, "Invention of Confucius," 415–49; D. R. Howland, Borders of Chinese Civilization (Durham, N.C.: Duke University Press, 1996), 7, 31, 199. Classical notions could easily be made to accommodate foreign notions of universal kingship, since the semantic fields of Chinese characters can be radically expanded to express new concepts. Magoshi Yasushi, for example, notes in a recent article one major shift in the meaning of fundamental vocabulary: that of ren (from "king's relatives" to "common people") in connection with the Mandate of Heaven theory. See "Kōkotsubun ni mieru hito" ("Men" in the Oracle Bone Script), Tōhōgaku 92:2: 17–29.

Early conceptions of kingship hardly correspond with the idea of "universal kingship," which presupposes a number of preexisting borders. Rather, the early Chinese are concerned with that portion of the known world under the direct protection of the ancestors (tian xia), a portion of territory that expanded over time, but had no precise theoretical limits until the late nineteenth century, when the modern notion of the nation-state imposed the necessity for precisely demarcated territorial boundaries. (Often tian xia now, by contrast, is translated not only as "the whole empire" but even as "the whole world.") Nonetheless, in early China, the legitimacy of political rule was quite closely tied to the possession of land. When, for example, the early Chinese were faced with the conundrum, "Why did the Supreme Sage not rule as Son of Heaven (i.e., emperor), given his obvious qualifications?" the classicists' answer was that Confucius lacked a territorial base from which to become ruler. See, e.g., Yang Xiong, Fa yan, in [Xin bian] Zhuzi ji cheng (Taipei: World Books, 1974), II, 10:30. Note finally that the early Ru school went on record opposing the notion that "moral good and the moral order are universal" (contra Chan, chap. 5 above, section on "The Confucian

Ethical Tradition"); that was the Mohist position, which Confucius, Mencius, and Xunzi vehemently opposed.

10. None of the Five Classics are reliably linked with Confucius before 100 B.C., nearly four hundred years after the Master's death in 479 B.C. To date, early traditions have only one of the "Confucian" Classics figuring largely in Confucius's teaching: the *Odes*, some version of which—oral or written—the Master reportedly urged his disciples to study. See Michael Nylan, *The Five "Confucian" Classics* (New Haven: Yale University Press, 2001), chap. 1; Steven Van Zoeren, *Poetry and Personality: Reading, Exegesis, and Hermeneutics in Traditional China* (Stanford: Stanford University Press, 1991). Note that the *Analects*, which purports to transcribe the conversations of Confucius with his disciples, was regarded as a secondary or supplemental "Classic" in Han times, since it did not record traditions handed down from high antiquity.

11. *Li ji*, "Wang zhi," 5/40 (Legge, I, 229–30) accepts this, for example. For more information, see Xing Yitian, "Tian xia yi jia: chuan tong Zhongguo tian xia guan de xing cheng" (The one family "under Heaven": the formulation of the traditional concepts of China and "All-under-Heaven"), *Qin Han shi lun kao* (Taipei: Dongda, 1987), 3–42, esp. 22ff. Cf. Zhao Diehan, "Chun qiu shi qi de Rong Di de li fen bu ji qi yuan liu," *Da lu za zhi* 11:2 (July 31, 1956): 6–13; 11:3 (Aug. 15, 1956): 21–25. The early ethical followers of Confucius were certainly aware of differences in ethnicity and language, but they regarded such distinctions as fundamentally less significant than a person's commitment to the Moral Way. See, e.g., *Analects* 3/5, which says, "The barbarians of the East and North who have retained their princes are not in such a state of decay as we inheritors of xia" (note Joseph Chan's completely different rendering of this passage in chap. 5 of this volume, section on "Diversity"); and *Mencius* 3A/4, which refers to "the shrike-tongued barbarians of the South." Certainly, the *Gongyang Traditions* uses "barbarian" loosely to describe anyone of any ethnicity who fails to adopt the fine old Zhou system celebrated by Confucius. See Pu Weizhong, *Chun qiu San zhuan zong he yan jiu* (Taipei: Wenjin, 1995), 138–50.

12. *Mencius* 3A/4: "I have heard of the Chinese converting barbarians to their ways, but not of their being converted to barbarian ways." Note that the gap in the material standards of "barbarian" and "Central States" peoples was not so large under Eastern Zhou rule (771–256 B.C.) as it would become later.

13. *Analects* 17/2. The consensus in early China was that the Central States had adopted the models and institutions of the Odes, Documents, Rites, and Music for (their) government, while the Rong and Yi (barbarians) continued to lack these models. See, e.g., *Zuo zhuan*, Duke Ch'eng 2, *fu* 3. Such notions are the subject of Michael Loewe, "China's Sense of Unity as Seen in the Early Empires," *T'oung Pao* 80 (1994): 6–25, esp. 17ff.

14. *Analects* 9/13; 12/5; 17/2. Cf. *Analects* 3/5, trans. in note 11 above. This accounts for the popular legend, recorded in many places, including the "Tang wen" chap. of the *Liezi*, that Yu traversed the whole world, which he "mistook to be one state." The *Da Dai Li ji*, "Xiao xian," chap. states that all the distant lands submitted to the sage-ruler Shun. The importance of ritual practice lay in its capacity to "facilitate passages and/or to authorize encounters between opposed orders." See Pierre Bourdieu, *Outline of a Theory of Practice*, trans. Richard Nice (Cambridge: Cambridge University Press, 1977), 120.

15. *Han shu* (Beijing: Zhonghua, 1970), 22:1027, where the "roads" belong to the

Six Classics, later (e.g., in *Han shu* 30:1746) equated with all learning. Note that there have been no specifically religious persecutions in China, though state persecutions of religious groups have occurred when the groups threatened the hegemony of the Chinese state in economic and political matters (as when, for example, the tax-free lands attached to major monasteries threatened the economic health of the imperial budget). This chapter does not specifically address the question of slavery, which played a small role in early China, with most slaves being either war captives or criminals. See Clarence Martin Wilbur, *Slavery in China during the Former Han Dynasty* (Chicago: University of Chicago, 1943).

16. Linguists, such as Dr. Mary Erbaugh (City University, Hong Kong), are wont to say that the only difference between a "dialect" and a "language" is that a language has a standing army behind it. On the sage-king's provisions for linguistic incomprehensibility, see *Li ji*, "Wang zhi" 5/40 (Legge, I, 229–30). Of course, one question that immediately arises in connection with language is, why the persistence of the Chinese worldview in Japan, Korea, Vietnam, and other of China's neighbors into the mid-nineteenth century? A good start has been made in Howland, *Borders*, which notes that countries sharing the use of the special Chinese literary language (*wen yan wen*) were often dubbed "countries sharing Civilization" (*wen ming*), a term that obviated reference to political borders (p. 7).

17. Here I am reminded of the remark recorded of the Emperor Sui Yangdi when he crossed the Yangtze river during a campaign: "I am father and mother of the people. How can I be constrained by this mere belt of water, and so fail to assist those in trouble?" See *Nan shi, zhuan* 10, "Chen benji" (Basic annals of Chen) (Beijing: Zhonghua, 1975), 1:307.

18. *Mencius* 1B/5 explicitly states that under the true kings, there was to be "inspection but not levies at border stations." *Mencius* 2A/5 tells the ruler to make conditions such that "travellers . . . [from other states] will be only too pleased to go by way of your roads." For the myth of the Great Wall as territorial boundary, see Arthur Waldron, *The Great Wall of China* (Cambridge: Cambridge University Press, 1990).

19. Even in the case of the dead ancestor, ritual-time and shrine-space continued to define the person, as is clear from the early stelae accounts and the performative formulas of the liturgies for the deceased. See Kenneth E. Brashier, "Evoking the Ancestor: The Stele Hymn of the Eastern Han Dynasty (25–220 c.e.)" (Ph.D. thesis, Cambridge University, 1997).

20. This probably explains the well-known propensity of Chinese to regard as truly "ancient" a pagoda entirely rebuilt in 1912 on a Tang dynasty site. It is not so much the bricks or even the site that matters, but the moral acts that occurred there over time.

21. Cf. the famous Chinese proverb about "the old frontiersman's horse." For the *Changes*, see Kikuchi Kiyokatsu, "Chūgoku ni okeru chūō no kenkyū: Ekikyō o chūshin to shite" (Research on the "center" in China: with the *Changes* as center), *Risshō Daigaku kyōyōbu Kiyō* 24 (1991): 25–40; Willard J. Peterson, "Making Connections: 'Commentary on the Attached Verbalizations' of the *Book of Change*," *Harvard Journal of Asiatic Studies* 42:1 (1982): 67–116; and Michael Nylan, ed. and trans., *T'ai hsüan ching, or The Canon of Supreme Mystery by Yang Hsiung* (Albany: State University of New York Press, 1993; hereafter THC). A useful overview of some of these issues is provided by Robin D. S. Yates, "Body, Space, Time, and Bureaucracy: Boundary Creation and Control Mechanisms in Early China," *Boundaries in China*, ed. John Hay

(London: Reaktion Books, 1994), 62. By sites (i.e., Space), the early Chinese meant "locations favorable or unfavorable for a given action."

22. *Analects* 3/14, wherein Confucius says, "I follow Chou."

23. *Shi ji* (Beijing: Zhonghua, 1959), 4:113–14. Cf. *Shang shu da zhuan*, attributed to Fu Sheng, *ICS Ancient Chinese Text Concordance Series No. 5* (Hong Kong: Commercial Press, 1994), 27.

24. For example, Mencius insists that the virtuous founders of the Shang and Zhou dynasties were willing to submit to smaller powers. *Mencius* 1B/3 repeats legends of virtuous heirs who yielded territory and rank, including Taibo, Bo Yi, and Shu Qi. See Nylan, "Confucian Piety and Individualism," *Journal of the American Oriental Society* 116 (Jan.–March, 1996): 1–27.

25. One later manifestation of this tight connection between the ancestors or Heaven and their people below can be found in the presumed correlations between Earthly markings (the works of man) and Heavenly doings (the works of the gods: the demarcation of time zones, calendrical practices, the production of climate and distinctive things); these are formulated in the *fen ye* theory, which enjoyed great popularity in China from at least Han times. Still, one must note that neither the word *Zhongguo* (originally "Central States," rather than the "Middle Kingdom" of the Orientalists) nor the word *tian xia* ("All-under-Heaven") is found on the bronze and bone inscriptions. It is also hard to accept the "Shang" dynasty as fully "Chinese," despite accounts of the later systematizing texts in the Han. See Robert W. Bagley, "Shang: China's First Historical Dynasty," in *The Cambridge History of Ancient China: From the Origins of Civilization to 221 B.C.*, ed. Michael Loewe and Edward L. Shaughnessy (Cambridge: Cambridge University Press, 1999). William G. Boltz, "Inscriptions, Monumentality and Literacy in Ancient China: The Role of Writing in the Shang and Early Western Zhou" (unpublished ms.), makes the useful distinction between "early civilization in China" (where China is only a geographic designation) and "early Chinese civilization."

26. *Mencius* 1A. Cf. Yang Xiong, "The Plume Hunt": "[The emperor] shares with the common folk, and by this means he has attained his present success" (trans. after David Knechtges, trans., *Wenxuan, or Selections of Refined Literature*, vol. 2 (Princeton: Princeton University Press, 1987), 135.

27. For the relation of moral health to the flow of *qi*, see *Mencius* 2A/2. Nathan Sivin, "State, Cosmos, and Body in the Last Three Centuries B.C.," *Harvard Journal of Asiatic Studies* 55:1 (1995): 5, states: "In China, ideas of Nature, state, and the body were so interdependent that they are best considered a single complex." Cf. G. E. R. Lloyd, *Adversaries and Authorities* (Cambridge: Cambridge University Press, 1996), chap. 9.

28. *Lü shi chun qiu* 12/10a-b, trans. modified from Lloyd, *Adversaries*, 191. A number of classical and Confucian texts, such as Lu Jia's *Xinyu*, make similar arguments, though the point is more concisely stated here.

29. Yang Xiong, *Fa yan* 3:7. Cf. *Han shu* 56:2507, where the bad state is described as one in which the *qi* is completely blocked.

30. See Nylan, "Confucian Piety"; Mayfair Mei-hui Yang, *Gifts, Favors, and Banquets: The Art of Social Relationships in China* (Ithaca: Cornell University Press, 1994).

31. See, e.g., *Mencius* 1A/3. The ruler's duty to redistribute wealth is also the subject of the "Great Plan" chap. of the *Documents*. *Mencius* 1B/4 makes it the ruling elites'

business to distribute aid to the needy. *Mencius* 2A/8 justifies the states' taxation by its periodic redistribution to the poor. For the practical ramifications of the failure to redistribute wealth, see *Mencius* 1B/6, 8 on the Mencian right to rebel, an expanded version of the Mandate of Heaven theory.

32. Sivin, "State, Cosmos," 22.

33. *Li ji*, "Wang zhi" 5/22 (Legge, I, 216), where audiences and sacrifices are conducted by the king in each and every outlying domain, bringing the royal presence there; meanwhile, lists of local market prices, descriptions of local peoples, and such are compiled, in the hopes that local conditions will "come alive" to the throne at the center. With state expenditures also, provisions were to be made for adjusting the "outgoing by the incoming."

34. The slogan "Employ the Worthy" began with the Mohists, a group that aimed to "reform" the *Ru*. However, the germ of the idea may be traced to Confucius's insistence on teaching the aristocratic Way of the Ancients to persons of low rank, so long as they were sufficiently motivated; also to Confucius's insistence that he, along with other followers of the Way, was fit to advise kings, despite his low rank. Mencius (late fourth century B.C.) urged rulers to found schools at the village, prefectural, and county levels, so as to maximize the contributions to the state of local talents. In practice, the educational institutions of imperial China (including the examination systems) were not as meritocratic as usually assumed, since wealth, social position, and official rank gave distinct advantages to certain candidates hoping for advancement.

35. *Xunzi*, chap. 9; trans. follows Burton Watson, *Basic Writings* (New York: Columbia University Press, 1963), 43.

36. *Mencius* 4A/6; trans. follows D. C. Lau, *Mencius* (New York: Penguin, 1970), 120. For claims that a man of virtue can start with a small state, and within 5–7 years come to rule the empire, see ibid., 4A/7; for "moving towards goodness" as related to "expansiveness," see *Mencius* 7A/13.

37. Kenneth J. DeWoskin, *A Song for One or Two: Music and the Concept of Art in Early China* (Ann Arbor: University of Michigan Press, 1982), 73ff.

38. *THC*, "Xuan wen," 453. In some sense, Confucians put potentially dangerous exchanges between Heaven and Earth (as in the legend of Zhongli) on a new footing.

39. *Mencius* 7B/15.

40. *Mencius* 7A/4. Wang Yangming (1472–1529) took this to mean that for the perfected person, "all things are one body" (so that he feels as deeply for all things as for himself).

41. Ode 205. For the idea that "there is nothing 'outside' [or 'foreign'] to the [true] king," see *Gongyang Traditions* (hereafter *Gongyang*), Duke Cheng 15. For the claim that "A son does not consider that he has his own self, nor does an official," see *Shi ji* 47:1909.

42. The phrase "skin-bound" person comes from John Emerson, "Yang Chu's Discovery of the Body," *Philosophy East and West* 46:4 (1996): 536, which cites, among others, Marriot, Takeo Doi's *The Anatomy of Dependence* (1973), and Louis Dumont's *Essays on Individualism* (1986). Notions of "individual autonomy" and states' rights would have mystified most early Chinese and disgusted the Confucians. Thus, some have described the "traditional self" in China as "plural," "diffuse," "empty," and "divided." I dispute the last two characterizations, since the ideal person in such societies is full (of potential interactions with others) and strongly centered, in a word, "inte-

grated" and "integrating" (*cheng*). Hence, the early *Ru* emphasis on the *rong* ("capacity to encompass") of the sage or sage-king: see the "Hong fan" chap. of the *Documents*; also Liu Xiang, *Shuo yuan*, chap. 1. Moral men like Confucius are to be *bo* ("wide-ranging"); by legend, some sages even sport four eyes and four ears, signifying their concern for all things in all directions.

43. The phrase is that of Ezra Pound's, used in his translation of the Confucian classic, the "Zhong yong."

44. The oldest beliefs in China presumed that the king was "center" by virtue of genealogy; as the direct descendant of the Supreme Ancestor in heaven, the Lord on High, the king had the capacity to apply for favors from the ancestors, though he acted on behalf of his family members. Late in the Warring States period, theorists argued that any man who was a sage had the right to achieve political power. Such beliefs seemed to be confirmed when a commoner, Liu Bang, ascended to the throne in 206 B.C. For the king as center, see, e.g., *Shi ji* 99:2716.

45. This would explain why Confucius, the "uncrowned king," never ascended the throne nor transformed the world: he had no throne from which to affect ever-expanding circles of subjects. Enthroned kings, when good, have the people "acknowledge their virtue" and "return to their virtuous example" (both *gui de*), as explained in *Hou Han shu* (Beijing: Zhonghua, 1965), 79A:2561. Note that while theorists associated with other "schools" were intent upon establishing a physical place (Kunlun) as *axis mundi*, the Confucians worked to establish the human ruler as *axis mundi*. See Gu Jiegang, "Yu gong zhong de Kunlun," *Li shi di li* 1 (1981): 3–8. The Legalists also acknowledged the ruler as center, but on a very different ethical basis: that the ruler had "fixed" (i.e., pacified) and therefore owned all the land in all directions. See the inscription on the Qin stele at Langya, as recorded in *Shi ji* 6:244–45. For the term "proximity," see Howland, *Borders*, 14, 40.

46. Dong Zhongshu: "Occupying the center of Heaven, Earth, and Man, passing through and joining all three—if it not be the king, who can do this?" See *Chun qiu fan lu*, sec. 43 (11:5a–5b).

47. *Xunzi*, chap. 9. Xunzi in chap. 32 promises that the final result of "holding fast to unity" and "behaving like Heaven and Earth, . . . sun and moon" will be that "the empire is but a single corner" of the area under the ruler's influence.

48. A favorite Confucian phrase was *ge de qi suo* ("May each attain its proper place"). See, e.g., *Xunzi*, chap. 9; Dong Zhongshu, cited in *Han shu* 56:2503. That the particular form of each and every creature was devised for the common good is the assumption of Dong, cited in *Han shu* 56:2520. Cf. the discussion in Yang Xiong's THC, Tetragram 2, Appraisal 2. Note finally that "center-ultimate," as elaborated in the *Changes*, *Rites*, and *Documents* canons, nonetheless is associated invariably with flexibility and responsiveness to changes over time and place.

49. *Han shu* 56:3509.

50. For the Confucian insistence that there are no self-made men, but only sage-king inheritors of accumulated achievements, see Pan Piao, "On the Destiny of Kings," as translated in *Sources of Chinese Tradition*, vol. 1, ed. Wm. Theodore de Bary, Wing-Tsit Chan, and Burton Watson (New York: Columbia University Press, 1960), 176–80. For the king's duty to share blessings with others, see *Mencius* 1A/1–4.

51. Therefore, even in the relatively modernized "south" China of the early twentieth century, collective possession, rather than private possession, was the norm, as

noted by Fei Hsiao-t'ung, *Peasant Life in China* (New York: Oxford University Press, 1946), chap. 4 ("Property and Inheritance") and chap. 11 ("Land Tenure"). Items of clothing, esp. undergarments and hair ornaments, were the sole exceptions to the general rule of collective possession; they alone were considered "personal" or "private"—rather than family, village, or state—property.

52. *Mencius* 1A/1. Secure enjoyment of pleasures in the company of others is said to be always greater than any enjoyment of secret or personal pleasures (*Mencius* 2A/1). "Sharing enjoyment with the people" is, in fact, Mencius's definition of "true kingship" (*ibid.*, 1B/1). Cf. Xunzi's famous dictum (chap. 4): "The man of Yue feels at home in Yue, the man of Chu feels at home in Chu. However, a [true] gentleman feels at home in elegant culture [wherever it is found]."

53. *Mencius* 1A/1. The "Ru xing" chapter of the *Li ji* states that the good *Ru* will consider the territory he has acquired to be the "accomplishment of just deeds." Xunzi's chapter, "On Ritual," offers two related arguments: (1) that sacrificial offerings are important because they habituate the person to sharing with the unseen, thereby refining her powers of imagination; (2) that the true king ensures that selfish acts by officials are severely punished. Both these Confucian thinkers may have derived their emphasis on sharing from the "Hong fan" chap. of the *Documents*, whose argumentation begins with the paradoxical premise that to give away power is to gain it. See Michael Nylan, *The Shifting Center: The Original "Great Plan" and Later Readings*, Monumenta Serica Monograph Series, no. 24 (May 1992).

54. *Mencius* 4B/16. As *Mencius* 1A/7 argues: "Now if you would practice benevolence in the government of your state, then all those in the Empire who seek office would wish to find a place at your court, then all farmers would wish to till the land in your outlying regions, and all merchants to enjoy the refuge of your market-places."

55. See *Mencius* 1A/2; *Mencius* 1B/12: "Practice benevolent government and the people will be sure to love their superiors and die for them." For the expression, "no men," see, e.g., Ode 258.

56. *Mencius* 4A/2. Mencius writes, to seek to "to extend one's territory by such means [that are typically employed] is like looking for a fish by climbing a tree" (*Mencius* 1A/7). The analogy is made to hitting the target in archery; it requires a kind of focus, not strength (*Mencius* 5B/1; cf. 4A/3; 5A/1). Xunzi puts the case succinctly: It is the dictator, not the true king, who is intent upon "opening up lands" and waging war against his neighbors (chap. 9).

57. See for example *Analects* 2/18. One translation of this passage evokes this idea well, that by Waley, *Analects of Confucius*, 92.

58. THC, "Xuan tu." Cf. Tetragram 2/App. 2: "A pivot set directly center/ Sweeps full circle, not in angles." Similarly, the heart-mind, so long as it is "unbiased" and "upright," seeking only the common good, is said to be like the balance and plumb line.

59. The Confucians believed that each aspect of Heaven and Earth, as well as time, reveals the innate capacity within all living beings for order and harmony. Accordingly, they "divided space up into distinct units, each with its own peculiar concrete characteristics and each coordinated with time: the east was spring, the south summer and so on." See Robin Yates, "Body, Space," 61ff. Cf. Sekiguchi Jun, "Keishokan keisei katei no ichi kōsatsu" (An investigation into the process of canon formation), *Saitama Daigaku kiyō* 28 (1993), on Yi Feng. For ritual "wrapping" of space to enhance certain

human relations, see Joy Hendry, *Wrapping Culture* (Oxford: Oxford University Press, 1993), 98–137.

60. *Li ji*, "Wang zhi" 5/46 (Legge, I, 245).

61. It is therefore the sage-king who "correctly positions the month [or moon]" (i.e., even controls time and space), since he emulates Heaven's brilliant order and thereby brings it to perfection. This is the explicit premise of the entire *Gongyang Traditions*, which purport to elucidate the *Chun qiu* ascribed to Confucius himself.

62. Early Confucians certainly knew the Mohist canon, which argued: "Spatial positions are names for that which is already past."

63. Thinkers we would now, on the basis of anachronistic criteria, call the Real-politicians (or Legalists), the Agriculturalists, and the proto-Taoists, among others (e.g., Shang Yang, Zhuangzi, Laozi).

64. Ikeda Yuichi, "Chūgoku kodai no seikatsuken to hō hyakuri: toshi no nōson o megutte" (The sphere of life and its ambience in ancient China: towns and villages), *Chūgoku no toshi to nōson* (Tokyo: Kyūkoshoin, 1992), 29–59. This article shows that the 100 *li* territorial unit was considered the largest, stable moral unit outside the family. Sages, of course, were notable exceptions to this general rule. Yu, the primeval flood-queller, supposedly traversed the entire length and breadth of "All-under-Heaven," without ever stopping at his home to take rest and comfort.

65. Confucians were agreed that the location of one's birth affects one's "natural" predispositions (good and bad). The *Li ji*, "Jing jie" chapter, gives this as the reason for having more than one "Confucian" classic, as the different classics together provide a range of tools to use in ruling peoples with different dispositions. Confucians debated whether these "natural" dispositions were to be fostered or restrained. Confucians, in any case, were not surprised to find that laws and customs varied over time, as the *qi* that informs human nature varies over time and place.

66. See James Robson, "Moving Mountains and Competing Yüeh: The History and Historiography of the Southern Marchmount" (unpublished ms.). Following Miyazaki Ichisada's work, Robson shows that the identity of the Five Sacred Mountains changes over time, though Mount Tai, considered the ritual "center" for the group (but not the geographic center), is always included. Cf. Tong Shuye, *Zhongguo gu dai di li kao lun wen ji* (Hong Kong, n.p., 1987), 7ff., 18–19.

67. *Documents*, "Pan geng." Regarding the early imperial moves of the capital, the dynastic histories (e.g., the *Shi ji* biography of Lou Jing) clearly show that there was no perceived need to place the capital at the geographic center of the land; see *Xi Han hui yao*, chap. 64. For the earliest notions of the "King's City" in China, see Nancy Shatzman Steinhardt, *Chinese Imperial City Planning* (Honolulu: University of Hawaii Press, 1990), chap. 1; and Li Min, *Shang shu yu gu dai shi yan jiu* (Henan: Zhongzhou shuhuashe, 1983), chap. 13.

68. Paul Wheatley, *Pivot of the Four Quarters: A Preliminary Enquiry into the Origins and Character of the Ancient Chinese City* (Edinburgh: Edinburgh University Press, 1971), chap. 5, suggests that the central point could be moved or duplicated in a new site, as geometrical space was less important than existential space. "The sacred space delimited in this manner within the continuum of profane space provided the framework within which could be conducted the rituals necessary to ensure that intimate harmony between the macrocosm and microcosm without which there could be no prosperity in the world of men" (p. 418). By contrast, in communities that accept

monotheistic religions based on revelation, only certain geometrical locations can become sacred because that is where God has chosen to reveal his message. For the secular as the sacred, see Herbert Fingarette, *Confucius: The Secular as Sacred* (New York: Harper & Row, 1972).

69. For example, during the Han dynasty (206 B.C–A.D. 220), four institutions defined the capital: the Biyong (Circular Moat); Mingtang (Sacred Hall); Lingtai (Numinous Terrace); and Taixue (Imperial Academy). Palaces could be built anywhere, so many "traveling palaces" were built far from the capital.

70. Hence, my jaundiced view of the many scholars who have tried to claim that the Chinese, including the Confucians, have a finer appreciation for the merits of preserving the natural environment than people from "the West." Probably, a certain reverence for the land is to be found more often among farmers than among the urban population, especially farmers whose ancestral shrines are situated near their farmlands, and 80 percent of the Chinese population until quite recently were farmers. Still, the Chinese have been no less loathe to destroy their natural environment than we. On this, see He Bochuan, *China on the Edge* (San Francisco: China Books and Periodicals, 1991), chaps. 2, 4, and Vaclav Smil's many publications.

71. See *Gongyang*, Duke Ch'eng 15. Cf. the story that is told of Confucius: "When Confucius ascended an eastern hill, he thought [his home state of] Lu small; when he ascended Mount Tai [the sacred peak in the east], he thought the empire small" (cited in Tong Shuye, "Han dai yi qian Zhongguo ren de shi jie quan nian yu yu wai jiao tong de qu shi," *Zhongguo gu dai di li kao zheng lun wen ji* (Shanghai: Zhonghua, 1962), 3. Note that Confucian definitions of community do not generate a fixed distinction between "inside" and "outside" persons. In the nineteenth century, this question would reoccur in a new form: Are countries sharing the Chinese written literary language to be considered "insiders" or "outsiders" in the new era of nationalism?

72. A late example of this tendency to examine complex questions from shifting perspectives can be found in Wang Fuzhi's (early seventeenth century) *Shangshu yin yi* (Eliciting the meaning of the documents), which bases its analysis on the difference between the "heaven seen from the point of view of men" and the "heaven seen from the point of view of the myriad things." See Yamaguchi Hisakazu, "Sonzai kara ronri," *Tōhōgaku* 57 (1979): 48–61.

73. *Li ji* 10/29 ("Li yun" chap.), trans. modified from Legge, *Li ki*, I, 410–11.

74. The phrase "nonregressive" comes from Heiner Roetz, *Confucian Ethics of the Axial Age* (Albany: State University of New York Press, 1993), 5.

75. E. N. Anderson, Jr., "Some Chinese Methods of Dealing with Crowding," *Urban Anthropology* 1:2 (1972): 141–50.

76. *The Case Against the Global Economy, and for a Turn toward the Local*, ed. Jerry Mander and Edward Goldsmith (San Francisco: Sierra Club, 1996), esp. Part II. See Fox Butterfield, "Study Links Violence Rate to Cohesion in Community," *New York Times*, 17 Aug. 1997, p. 27.

77. Adopting the terminology of Loren Lomasky in chap. 3 above.

78. James Hevia, "Guest Ritual and Interdomainal Relations in the Late Qing" (Ph.D. thesis, University of Chicago, 1986), 246. Those who did not participate in the classical cultural patterns were not so much "uncivilized" or "barbarian" as undifferentiated—without a place in the hierarchy of the moral universe understood as Civilization.

79. To possess a map of a certain territory implied the right to rule that area, so maps were generally given at the ceremonies of investiture for local princes. Otherwise, the production of maps was tied to a desire for military conquest. Thus, the production of maps lagged far behind many other forms of cultural production in imperial China. There were, for example, no maps of Japan readily available before the sixteenth century, when Japanese pirates began to raid the southeast China coast in large numbers. See Cordell D. K. Yee, "Chinese Maps in Political Culture," in *The History of Cartography*, vol. 2, bk. 2, ed. J. B. Harley and David Woodward (Chicago: University of Chicago, 1994), 71–95; Joseph Needham, "Geography and Cartography," *Science and Civilisation in China*, vol. 3 (Cambridge: Cambridge University Press, 1959), 543–56.

Seven

International Law, Boundaries, and Imagination

ROBERT McCORQUODALE

BOUNDARIES are integral to international law. They are a cause of conflict and a reason for peace. They establish order and lead to disorder. They provide a protection and a weapon. They include and exclude. They define and divide. They are real and imagined.

The primary components of the international legal system are states, and territorial boundaries are a key element in how states are defined by that system. Because there are so many disputes over boundaries—both land and maritime—the international legal system has designed rules to define and maintain boundaries and to deal with situations where boundaries are violated. These rules themselves constitute a system of boundaries, for international law—like any legal system—is a process by which legal rules (or boundaries) are created in order to structure and organize societies and relationships.[1] And while the territorial boundaries determined by the international legal system are often artificial and contested, they are necessary to the operation of the system.[2]

Historically, the international legal system has been considered to be a system for states alone, where international law is the law between states and regulates the interaction of states through their consent—express or implied. The primary sources of international law—as set out in article 38 of the Statute of the International Court of Justice—arise from the actions of states.[3] The legal rules generated by this system are generally complied with because states "recognize that the observance of law is in their interest, and that every violation may also bring particular undesirable consequences."[4] This view of international law—which will be assumed here to be the prevailing or "traditional" view—is based on a positivist theory of international law in which the autonomy and freedom of the individual (to which the state is equated) is upheld, and where law-making is seen as being dependent on the consent of states.[5] Thus international law, as traditionally conceived, is a law for and by states.

This view of international law is widely challenged today. It is argued that the concept of international law as a state-based process "is incapable of serving as the normative framework for present or future political realities. . . .

[N]ew times call for a fresh conceptual and ethical language."[6] The fresh concepts and ethics that have been suggested include the inclusion of non-states, such as indigenous peoples and international organizations, within the international legal system;[7] the application of feminist theory to the international legal system;[8] and the movement away from a subjective system reliant on binary oppositions.[9] Thus the ethical and conceptual foundations of international law are being substantially reimagined.

In the light of these challenges to the international legal system, what is attempted in this chapter is to indicate how the international legal system establishes and deals with a particular type of boundary: the territorial boundary. The main issues that will be dealt with are the definitions of territorial boundaries and the purposes they serve, and how ownership relates to territorial boundaries. Briefer consideration will be given to four other issues: which goods territorial boundaries reserve to some and deny to others; how cultural diversity is accommodated; the extent to which there is freedom of movement across boundaries; and the relationship between territory and political autonomy. For each issue the prevailing international legal view will be explained, followed by some critiques of that view. It will be argued that international law in relation to territorial boundaries must be reconceived so that it is regulated in terms of an international society that is inclusive of all, allows all to find and use their voices, is creative of identity opportunities, and recognizes diversity within the universality of international society.

Definitions of Territorial Boundaries

Boundaries and States

Throughout the twentieth century, every edition of *Oppenheim's International Law* has maintained the same definition of territorial boundaries:

> Boundaries of State territory are the imaginary lines on the surface of the earth which separate the territory of one State from that of another, or from unappropriated territory, or from the Open Sea.[10]

These lines are not only imaginary; they are invented and created by the international legal system. After all, "the distinction sometimes made between artificial and natural boundaries is geographic rather than legal, for so-called natural boundaries, making use of natural features such as rivers or mountains, usually need further definition in order to produce a precise boundary line."[11] Thus a large number of the disputes between states that are litigated before the International Court of Justice involve a clarification of the precise boundary line (land and maritime) between states and require the Court to apply international law to determine that boundary.[12]

At the same time, having a defined territory is one of the essential international legal criteria for determining if an entity is a state.[13] Attaining the category of a "state" is vital in international law, because if an entity is a "state," then it has the capacity to avail itself of all the rights and be subject to all the duties within the international legal system. Therefore, if an entity can show that it has control over a defined territory, it can become the most powerful player in the international community: a state. In fact, it need not have complete control over its territory or definite boundaries, as

> uncertainty as to boundaries [cannot] affect territorial rights. There is for instance no rule that the land frontiers of a state must be fully delimited and defined, and often in various places and for long periods, they are not.[14]

In light of this position, "even a substantial boundary or territorial dispute with a new state is not enough to bring statehood into question."[15]

From the perspective of the international legal system, the purpose of territorial boundaries is to clarify which entities are states and to separate states from each other, in order to structure that system. As states largely determine the development of international legal rules, they are in a position to establish the rules concerning territorial boundaries. The International Court of Justice confirmed this when it stated that

> the fixing of a frontier depends on the will of the sovereign states directly concerned. There is nothing to prevent the parties from deciding by mutual agreement to consider a certain line as a frontier, whatever the previous status of that line. . . . [A] boundary established by treaty . . . achieves a permanence which the treaty itself does not necessarily enjoy. The treaty can cease to be in force without in any way affecting the continuance of the boundary.[16]

An example of the central role of states in determining territorial boundaries is seen in the rule of *uti possidetis juris*. This rule provides that states emerging from colonial administrative control must accept the preexisting colonial boundaries. It was first propounded in Latin America at the beginning of the nineteenth century, then formally adopted by the Organization of African Unity in 1964.[17] It has also been applied (incorrectly) to the European mainland during the breakup of the former Yugoslavia.[18] Indeed, *uti possidetis juris* is now considered "a firmly established principle of international law where decolonization [is] concerned."[19] The aim of this rule is to achieve stability of territorial boundaries and to maintain international peace and security. This was made clear by the International Court of Justice when it said that

> The maintenance of the territorial *status quo* in Africa is often seen as the wisest course, to preserve what has been achieved by peoples who have struggled for their independence, and to avoid a disruption which would deprive the continent of

the gains achieved by much sacrifice. The essential requirement of stability in order to survive, to develop and gradually to consolidate their independence in all
fields, induced African states judiciously to consent to the respecting of colonial
frontiers.[20]

In aiming to achieve stability, peace, and security, the power of the new
state is affirmed. The new state, as agreed by all states, cannot be undermined
by challenges to its boundaries. So the rules developed by the international
legal system to deal with boundaries are affirming of the state structure of that
system.

Inequities

The major problem with accepting this "traditional" position is that this
definition and purpose of territorial boundaries is fundamentally inequitable.
By ignoring natural boundaries and by ensuring that new states, and the
boundaries of new states, are decided in the interests of the existing states, the
international legal system recreates and affirms the dispositions by colonial
powers. For example,

> One of the remarkable features of independent Africa today is the legacy of ill-
> defined boundaries. . . . [T]he European expansion in Africa produced a territorial
> division which bore little relation to the character and distribution of the popula-
> tions of the former colonies and protectorates. Thus, the international boundaries
> now inherited by the newly independent African states were arbitrarily imposed by
> ex-colonial European powers.[21]

The territorial boundaries in Africa and Asia, many of which are straight
lines, were drawn up by colonial powers to preserve "spheres of influence,"
with little respect for natural or cultural boundaries. As one of the architects
of this arbitrary division said at the time:

> We have been engaged . . . in drawing lines upon maps where no white man's feet
> have ever trod; we have been giving away mountains and rivers and lakes to each
> other, but we have only been hindered by the small impediment that we never knew
> exactly where those mountains and rivers and lakes were.[22]

One example of this ignorance is the Caprivi Strip in Namibia—a finger of
land only 20 miles wide stretching to Zambia and Zimbabwe. This was included in the 1890s as part of then German South West Africa "due to poor
geographical knowledge, since the intention had been to secure access to the
Zambezi for the German colony, in the [mistaken] belief that an important
communications route was involved."[23]

The inequities of these colonial boundaries are fixed forever by the rule of *uti possidetis juris.* Indeed, in the *Land, Island and Maritime Dispute* case it was noted that *"uti possidetis juris* is essentially a retrospective principle, investing as international boundaries administrative limits intended originally for quite other purposes."[24] So this rule gives legitimacy to unlawful acts purely on the basis that those unlawful acts occurred during the colonial era. Interestingly, it is the new states that have emerged from colonial domination that have sought most strongly to confirm this position and so to assert their own power. Further,

> not only were the legal instruments inherited, the institutions, personnel and the mode for dealing with the subject of boundaries have remained basically the same as their European antecedents or their derivatives. Little wonder that border relations in Africa have continued to feature the same kind of mutual jealousy, conflict and tension, and have continued to be managed within the framework of the same kind of diplomacy and laws that govern such relations in Europe.[25]

Even in boundary disputes today, which still occur despite the claim that *uti possidetis* ensures stability, peace, and security, reliance is often placed on colonial dispositions.[26]

Thus the imaginary lines created by international law to form territorial boundaries between states serve the purpose of preserving the status quo in the international legal system. They preserve the power of existing states as these international legal rules

> allocate power across time by entrenching the categories and generalizations of the past and thus dissipating the power of the present . . . [and reflect] the extent of decisional conservatism within the system.[27]

Despite its stated aim to preserve the freedom of states and to provide "stability and finality,"[28] the traditional approach taken to territorial boundaries in international law offers neither liberty nor flexibility. It is inequitable and with limited imagination as it reasserts closed minds rather than open possibilities. The rules that define territorial boundaries thus establish nearly impermeable boundaries within the international legal system.

Ownership

State Sovereignty

The connection between the definition of territorial boundaries and the definition of statehood was shown in the previous section. The reason questions of precise boundary lines are so important to states and can become a matter of dispute—including armed conflict on occasion—is because of the link between territorial boundaries and an important aspect of statehood: state sovereignty. State sovereignty is one of the fundamental concepts in international law.[29] As was held in the *Island of Palmas* case:

> Sovereignty in the relations between states signifies independence. Independence in regard to a portion of the globe is the right to exercise therein, to the exclusion of any other state, the functions of a state. The development of the national organisation of states during the last few centuries and, as a corollary, the development of international law, have established this principle of the exclusive competence of the state in regard to its own territory in such a way as to make it the point of departure in settling most questions that concern international relations.[30]

Indeed, the direct connection between territorial boundaries and sovereignty was made in 1910 when the Permanent Court of Arbitration held that "one of the essential elements of sovereignty is that it is to be exercised within territorial limits, and that, failing proof to the contrary, the territory is co-terminous with sovereignty."[31] In international law, ownership of territory is the concept used to determine sovereignty.[32]

One way in which the international legal system has clarified ownership of territory is through its rules on the acquisition of territory. While these rules have changed over time,[33] at the beginning of the twentieth century there were five means to acquire territory. These were: occupation over previously unclaimed territory (such as by discovery); prescription, being the exercise of sovereignty for a long period without objection by another state; conquest by use of force; cession, being the transfer of territory by agreement between states; and accretion, where new territory is added by natural means. Gaining ownership of territory by these means may not of itself establish sovereignty over that territory. International legal rules have developed to require a state to establish the necessary evidence to prove continued ownership of territory. Thus discovery and symbolic annexation are said to give only inchoate title,[34] but long-term displays of sovereignty (such as passing legislation over, or trying criminal acts committed in, the territory concerned) could give good title.[35] The most important element is for a state to show "effective occupation." This is because

> Just as before the rise of international law, the boundaries of lands were necessarily determined by the fact that the power of a state was exercised within them, so too, under the reign of international law, the fact of peaceful and continuous display is still one of the most important considerations in establishing boundaries between states.[36]

It is also pertinent that ownership of territory is recognized to be entirely relative to other claims by states to that territory, as

> it is impossible to read the records of decisions in cases as to territorial sovereignty without observing that in many cases the tribunal has been satisfied with very little

in the way of actual exercise of sovereign rights, provided that the other state could not make out a superior claim.[37]

Once a state has established its ownership of a territory, it is very unusual for it to be challenged by the international community, unless all states agree that certain means of obtaining ownership are not in the best interests of all states. Thus, at least since the United Nations was established, the acquisition of territory by force has been considered unlawful. This rule is consistent with one of the purposes of the United Nations: to protect the territorial integrity and political independence of states.[38] The action of the Security Council when Iraq invaded Kuwait is an example of this rule in action.[39]

One other aspect of ownership of territory by a state is that it carries with it "ownership" of the people in that territory. Territorial boundaries are not just delimitations of the territory of a state and of state sovereignty but also define the inhabitants. While "peoples have attachments to several levels of territorialism . . . the actual dominant structure is the state and so, as a generalization, all the peoples on earth are defined by state levels within their boundaries."[40] Further, states are perceived in international law as being the representatives of the inhabitants of the territory within each state's sovereignty, as in order to meet the definition of being a state, there must be a "permanent population."[41] As one writer put it: "most acts of administration commonly relied on to establish sovereignty require the voluntary cooperation of the inhabitants, and, in frontier areas, involve the choice by the inhabitants between the facilities offered by each of the claimant states."[42] Related to this, international law has developed intricate rules regarding the nationality of people in terms of their relationship to states, as determined by the degree of connection people (meaning men, as will be shown) have to the territory of a state.[43]

Therefore, the way in which the international legal system has developed rules regarding ownership of territory has been in relation to accepted exercises of state sovereignty. Ownership is conferred by the actions of states and by the consent of other states. In this respect, sovereignty is seen as a power exercised by states over territory and over the people within the territorial boundaries decided by states. From this perspective, international law is seen as operating as a distributive mechanism for determining which state can exercise sovereignty over certain territory and people.

Privileging and Silencing

This operation of international law confirms the power of the state and the acceptance that sovereignty is in the hands of states alone. It results in privileging certain voices and silencing others. It allows the elites in a territory to gain and exercise power, particularly political and economic power, at the expense of most of the people living in that territory. The state in international law is also a male construct that reinforces a particular view of boundaries. As Hilary Charlesworth makes clear,

> the state constituted by international law is a bounded, self-contained, closed, separate entity that is entitled to ward off any unwanted contact or interference. . . . Like a heterosexual male body, the state has no "natural" points of entry, and its very boundedness makes forced entry the clearest possible breach of international law.[44]

In addition, the acceptance of the state and how it acts within the international legal system largely ignores the fact that the existence of states is itself imagined, as it is an "artificial entity [with all] its decisions, policies and strategies [being] those of the individuals and groups that make up its government."[45]

Not only does the concept of ownership inherent in the traditional approach of international law to territorial boundaries reinforce and privilege a certain view of the state; it is unable to deal sufficiently with alternative conceptions of sovereignty. The development of the right of self-determination is an example of how the international legal system is not prepared to accept a concept once the sovereignty of the state is threatened. The right of self-determination is premised on the idea that peoples can "freely determine their political status and freely pursue their economic, social and cultural development."[46] The international legal system has accepted that the right of self-determination applies to all colonies on the basis that the new state is seen as emerging from the existing colony and hence there is merely a transfer of preexisting sovereignty.[47] However, once self-determination was sought to be applied beyond the colonial context, the international legal system resisted its operation. States claim that the right cannot be exercised where territorial boundaries are in issue, as the right cannot "be construed as authorizing or encouraging any action which would dismember or impair, totally or in part, the territorial integrity or political unity of sovereign and independent states."[48] This resistance by states is clearly seen in the statement by a former United Nations Secretary-General:

> [I]f every ethnic, religious or linguistic group claimed statehood, there would be no limit to fragmentation, and peace, security and economic well-being for all would become ever more difficult to achieve.[49]

This approach upholds the perpetual power of a state at the expense of the rights of the inhabitants, which is contrary to the clear development of the right of self-determination.[50]

There is thus a struggle between the concept of sovereignty as being in the domain of states and a concept of sovereignty as being in the control of the people. The traditional international legal system has insisted—often with appalling consequences—on deeming states as being the same as "nations"—hence the term "nation-state" and the "United Nations." It also assumes that people have a choice about which state they "belong" to.[51] But where the people do not identify themselves solely—or at all—with the state, then the current international legal system tends to legitimate an oppressive government operating within unjust state boundaries and so prevent the people asserting any alternative sovereignty. For example, the Tibetans are not assisted in their dispute with China, and the Kurds are largely left to fend for themselves.[52] The system also assumes that all within the system must aspire to being a state, and indirectly encourages the leaders of peoples claiming self-determination to believe that statehood is the only possibility, even if this may not be in the best interests of those people or of peace and security. Even on the borderlands between states, any institutional integration is strongly resisted by the states involved

> because of the fear [by those states] that the sovereignty of the nation-state would be compromised . . . [especially as] the only institutionalised means of communication across borders was [meant to be] international law and diplomacy.[53]

The position of indigenous peoples is even more precarious, as their relationship with territory does not easily fit within the ownership of territory as defined by international law.[54] For example, in the *Western Sahara Opinion* the International Court of Justice noted that the indigenous peoples had pastures and water holes that they used, during their frequent nomadic movements, on both sides of the alleged border. The court considered that this cross-border migration gave rise to some rights in regard to the territory, which were sufficient to constitute legal ties of allegiance between the territory of Western Sahara and the "Mauritanian entity." Despite this finding, the court was unable to treat these ties in international law as ties of territorial sovereignty between the territories of Western Sahara and either of the two competing states: Morocco or Mauritania.[55]

The traditional approach to ownership of territory is unable to deal effectively with globalization. The process of globalization is part of an "ever more interdependent world,"[56] where political, economic, social, and cultural relationships are not restricted to territorial boundaries and no state or entity is unaffected by activities outside its direct control. The economic process of globalization

> transforms the international economy from one made up of holistic national economies interacting on the basis of national "comparative advantage" into one in which a variety of "competitive advantages" are created in ways which are not dependent on the nation-state as social, economic and/or political unit.[57]

In the light of these globalized changes, territorial boundaries may become of considerably less importance. The World Bank, the International Monetary

Fund, regional development banks such as the European Bank for Reconstruction and Development, and multilateral trade institutions such as the World Trade Organization, have developed in the context of a trend away from the dominance of the state as the exclusive unit of analysis in the international legal system. Globalization has thus been transformative in terms of a reconceptualization of state sovereignty within international law.[58] As the World Bank has noted:

> The state still defines the policies and rules for those within its jurisdiction, but global events and international agreements are increasingly affecting its choices. People are now more mobile, more educated, and better informed about conditions elsewhere. And involvement in the global economy tightens constraints on arbitrary state action, reduces the state's ability to tax capital, and brings much closer financial market scrutiny of monetary and fiscal policies.[59]

It is still too early yet to be certain of the effect of globalization on the ownership of territory by states. States do still control, even if only by self-preserving agreements between them, the territory on which transnational corporations and others operate. But, as the World Bank report indicates, the exclusive territorial sovereign power of the state is being diminished and states are increasingly being shown to be unable to control the activities of transnational corporations.[60] It is important that the international legal system begin to reflect this situation.

International law can countenance some shared sovereignty between states, as seen in shared ownership of parts of the sea and in special territory such as the Antarctic.[61] Even the International Court of Justice in the *East Timor* case seemed prepared to countenance the possibility that there was more than one form of sovereignty over a territory.[62] Within Europe, there have been significant developments in sharing sovereignty. The creation and extension of the European Union establishes a legal institutional framework above states and fosters institutional organization at levels below national governments.[63] The result is that the control of activities on its territory is no longer in the hands of national governments alone. It is a "Europe without frontiers." However, while shared state sovereignty may be occurring within the international legal system, this sharing is still both state- and territory-dependent. States resist any notions of shared (non-state-based) sovereignty not dependent on territory.

The present approach to the determination of ownership of territory by the international legal system is exclusive, partial, and silencing. Territorial boundaries have become barriers. They determine and identify those within and those without the boundary, based on a particular concept of sovereignty. Indeed, many of the claims for self-determination arose because the unjust, state-based, international legal order failed to respond to legitimate aspirations by peoples. It is therefore necessary that territorial boundaries be reconsidered

so that a more flexible system is devised. This flexibility will become imperative as the process of globalization gathers pace.

Distribution

With ownership of territory comes the power of distribution, particularly the
distribution of natural resources. All natural resources, whether located under
the soil or under the sea, whether living or nonrenewable, are deemed to be in
the control of the owner of the territory, that is, the state.[64] There is a much-
proclaimed right of permanent sovereignty over natural resources, which is
based on sovereignty over the adjacent land territory.[65] The economic interests of states, deepened by advances in technology, mean that the determination of maritime boundaries is crucial, and conflict over access to natural
resources will increase.[66] Certain territory is considered not to be in the ownership of any one state, such as the High Seas—which is diminishing considerably in size with each successive treaty—and outer space; while some territory,
such as Antarctica, is subject to special treaty arrangements.[67] However, even
these types of territory are brought within international legal rules in the sense
that it is considered appropriate for states to deal with them as they decide.

In relation to natural resources, the international legal system has largely
followed the approach of the national law of developed states.

> International law has tended to ape the individualistic manners of municipal
> law. . . . [I]nternational law depends to a great extent on "voluntarist" devices, in
> the form of concessions by private law methods, treaties, and various types of inter-
> national agencies and organizations, in order to provide access to resources outside
> national territory. Indeed, the use of "voluntarist" devices in the political conditions
> of the past has led to a situation where law, as applied by some states, had prevented
> a weak or ex-colonial state from having a reasonable level of command over its own
> resources and general economy.[68]

These comments highlight some of the main concerns about the traditional
approach to natural resources: the control of those resources is in the hands of
a few, and the market is by no means free. Certain powerful states are privileged and other states, and most peoples, are silenced.

An example of this can be seen in the negotiations in the United Nations
Convention on the Law of the Sea (1982) concerning the deep seabed. Part
XI of the convention sets up a regime to regulate development and exploitation of the deep seabed. This part declares that no state has, or can claim,
sovereignty over the deep seabed. Rather, the deep seabed "and its resources
are the common heritage of mankind . . . [and] all rights in the resources . . .
are vested in mankind as a whole."[69] Article 140 requires that any development activities on the deep seabed take into account the needs of developing

states, and that there be an equitable sharing of financial and other economic benefits from this development, no matter which state or corporation undertakes the development.[70] Part XI was an attempt to address long-term inequities in the international legal system.

However, the consequence of the adoption of this part of the convention was that most of the developed states, such as the United States and the United Kingdom, refused to ratify the convention at all. They threatened to upset the whole process of clarification of the rules regarding maritime territory that had been developed by the convention. After more than ten years of dispute about this issue, an "Agreement" was reached to deal with the deep seabed.[71] This agreement, which is meant to be merely an interpretation of how Part XI is to be implemented, is significantly different from the terms in Part XI of the convention and is designed to override that part. For example, issues such as transfer of technology and providing financial benefits to developing states have been dispensed with or put in economic rationalist terms, so that technology can now only be obtained on "fair and reasonable commercial terms and conditions on the open market."[72] As a consequence, far from operating as a common heritage of humankind, the "deep sea-bed mining industry is now being offered a stable, market-orientated legal regime. . . . The ideology of the 1970s has given way to sound commercial principles."[73] An attempt at an alternative international image with a utopian vision has been roughly reshaped into a realist mask. The difficulty with this reshaping is that

> [i]t is questionable how sound it is for a legal theory to accept the absolute ownership by a state of the "natural resources" within its sphere of jurisdiction, given that territorial boundaries are not coextensive with the scope of international economic relations and so, logically, do not mark the limits of an international obligation to co-operate.[74]

There is one area of the international legal system where state sovereignty and the territorial integrity of states have been diminished in the interests of preserving natural resources. This is in the development of international environmental law. The sheer scale of the environmental issues has meant that significant international cooperation has been necessary irrespective of the limits of territorial boundaries. But these developments have still occurred largely within the framework of a state-based international legal system in which states define their own responsibility and their own territorial obligations. This limits the potential scope of their obligations, as states do not tend to take action against each other due to fear of reciprocity.[75]

So the international legal system is capable of alternative visions as to how to deal with natural resources freed from restrictive territorial boundaries. But those visions are too often blocked by powerful economic forces. Even the crucial role of indigenous peoples in ensuring sustainable development can be considered irrelevant in economic terms. They simply do not have sufficient

state-like sovereignty to be able to negotiate for a more equitable role in dealing with natural resources.[76] The irrelevance of non-states in the distribution
of resources is seen starkly in a decision of the International Court of Justice
in a case about a maritime delimitation between Denmark and Norway. As
part of its claim for a larger maritime territory, Denmark raised the issue of the
attachment of the people of Greenland to the sea, and their economic dependence on fishing. The Court dismissed these issues by saying:

> the attribution of maritime areas to the territory of a state, which, by its nature, is
> destined to be permanent, is a legal process based solely on the possession by the
> territory concerned of a coastline.[77]

Thus any socioeconomic factors were dismissed as being irrelevant. In the end,
territorial boundaries alone determine how resources are distributed.

Diversity

The international legal system celebrates the universal. Its existence is premised on the idea that there are legal rules that are universal, irrespective of culture, ethnicity, religion, or social practices. Law is a culture.[78] While
parts of the international legal system, such as international human rights law,
raise concerns about universality, the system reinforces that universality.
For example, in the Vienna Declaration on Human Rights (1993) it was
proclaimed:

> All human rights are universal, indivisible and interdependent and interrelated.
> The international community must treat human rights globally in a fair and equal
> manner, on the same footing, and with the same emphasis. While the significance
> of national and regional particularities and various historical, cultural and religious
> backgrounds must be borne in mind, it is the duty of states, regardless of their polit-
> ical, economic and cultural systems, to promote and protect all human rights and
> fundamental freedoms.[79]

Thus, cultural and religious backgrounds may influence the application of the
international human rights law, but the concepts are deemed to be universal.

In relation to territorial boundaries, culture, ethnicity, religion, or social
practices are largely irrelevant, as living space is determined by the state territorial boundary. After all, one intention of territorial boundaries is that they
enhance "group cohesion by psychologically sharpening the different identification of community members from others across the boundary."[80]
The state is meant to be the only relevant identity for the inhabitants of a
territory. This causes significant problems in a multiethnic state (and all states
are to some degree). The consequence, at least for most states that emerged
from colonial administrations, was that the new governments sought to assert

powerfully the state identity above all other identities. These governments argue

> against the maintenance of the traditional indigenous institutions, which they con-
> sider to be dangerous and anachronistic and [accuse] the tribalism, the regionalism,
> and the racism as being the bitter enemies of national-state building.[81]

For example, in Indonesia, an archipelagic state of many cultures, religions, and practices, once the Dutch colonizers left, successive governments have propounded a national language (Bahasa Indonesia) and an ideology (pancasila) that promote a pretended national unity.[82] One possible consequence of this "national-state building" is that "State power wielded by the State's functionaries might also be used to serve the particularistic interests of the rulers, that it might be used against the interests of the people and that it might take the form of repression."[83] Indeed, the history of internal conflicts is replete with examples of repression by the state against a group within the state seeking to assert its separate identity from that of the state.[84] This is one reason why there is so much resistance by states to allowing the right of self-determination to include secession of a group within the state.[85]

Occasionally, a territorial boundary can disappear partly due to perceptions of, or a desire to create, common cultures. An example is the unification of Germany. In the Preamble to the Treaty on the Final Settlement with Respect to Germany (1990), it was expressly mentioned that the "German people, freely exercising their right of self-determination, have expressed their will to bring about the unity of Germany as a state." However, it needs to be recognized that "nations and peoples, like genetic populations, are recent, contingent and have been formed and reformed constantly throughout history."[86] At the same time, there is a significant development within the European continent of subsidiarity and regional autonomy, as will be discussed below, that creates a multilevel identity. Yet many identities—gender, religious, or linguistic identities, to name a few—transcend territorial boundaries. Peoples such as the Kurds may have an identity that transcends those boundaries wholesale, but these are only tolerated by the international legal system as long as they do not seek to challenge the sovereignty of the state.[87] Indeed, the international legal system may itself define which identities warrant protection. For example, in the Convention on the Prevention and Punishment of the Crime of Genocide (1948), genocide is defined in relation to "national, ethnical, racial or religious groups."[88] Important though this convention is, it does not include other groups, such as those defined by their language, their gender, or their sexuality. Thus states, which draft treaties, still control the definition of groups.

While jurisdictional divisions within a state—such as a federal system—may allow for differences in culture, language, religion, or social practices, these divisions are largely irrelevant to the international legal system.[89] States are one uniform unit from this perspective. The traditional international legal system imagines that one voice speaks for all the people in the state. National unity triumphs over cultural diversity. Territorial boundaries are thus meant to determine identity and living space at the cost of diversity, multilevel sovereignties, and real identities. Alternatives are within the imagination of this system but have not yet been applied frequently enough to become an acknowledged international possibility.

Mobility

The ability to move within and across territorial boundaries is determined by states. A state determines who are its "nationals":

> It is . . . for every sovereign State to settle by its own legislation the rules relating to the acquisition of its nationality, and to confer that nationality by . . . its own organs. . . . It is not necessary to determine whether international law imposes any limitations on its freedom of decision in this domain. . . . Nationality serves above all to determine that the person upon whom it is conferred enjoys the rights and is bound by the obligations which the law of the State in question grants to or imposes on its nationals.[90]

By determining who are its nationals, a state also determines who are nonnationals: who is the "other." Others do not have the same rights and obligations with regard to that state. Indeed, despite the apparent clear wording of international human rights law that human rights apply to all persons within a state irrespective of nationality, national courts continue to deny rights to nonnationals.[91] There are also particular problems of stateless individuals.[92]

The main area where territorial boundaries and mobility are opposed is in relation to refugees. Refugees are individuals and groups who flee the state of which they are nationals due to a fear of persecution. The international legal system tried to deal with refugees by drafting the Convention Relating to the Status of Refugees (1951) and the Protocol Relating to the Status of Refugees (1967). These establish criteria for defining "refugees," the grounds for seeking asylum in other states, and the international legal obligations of all states towards "refugees."[93] However, these obligations are very narrow[94] and open to interpretation, so that governments have generally found ways of further limiting the number of people they consider to be refugees entitled to asylum within the terms of the convention.[95]

In addition, these international legal obligations are gender-biased, in that the definition of a refugee able to activate the obligations of states under the convention is premised on the refugee being male. A key aspect of the definition relates to political persecution, which "is much more relevant to the fact of a man in a male-oriented society (as all societies basically are, in the twentieth century) than to that of a woman."[96] There is no understanding or scope for inclusion of gender-based persecution in the convention, with no account taken of the reality that almost eighty percent of refugees are women and children.[97] Where gender-based violence occurs, it is only "persecution" for the purposes of the convention's definition of a refugee if the state is clearly the persecutor. Yet

> much of the violence committed against women on a global scale—rape, physical abuse, and murder—occurs in the so-called "private" sphere. It is perpetuated by husbands, boy-friends, in-laws, and, in the case of genital mutilation, women in the local community.[98]

The international legal system has therefore recreated many of the boundaries found in national legal systems, such as the division between public and private areas of law. Not only are women and children the vast majority of refugees, they are the ones least likely to be able to invoke the international legal obligations of states to care for refugees. The convention also does not deal with displaced persons within their own state's territorial boundaries who may be equal in number with the estimated 20 million refugees worldwide.[99] The international legal system is so concerned to protect the (public) territorial boundaries of the state that the women and children who are suffering because of state or private actions are forgotten. They have become invisible in their millions.

The existence of refugees has been considered to be a threat to international peace and security.[100] This is because refugees cross territorial boundaries without a state's consent (particularly without the "receiving" state's consent), contrary to traditional expectations of the international legal system. The focus of attention is on the "receiving" state. International action is usually taken to try to feed and house the refugees until another state can be persuaded to accept them. Refugees are often just "left to rot" at great cost to the United Nations or to humanitarian organizations.[101] Thus, once the refugees cross their state's territorial boundary, it is an issue for the receiving state. The role and obligations of the state of origin (the "exiling" state) are largely ignored. As a consequence, "being a disaster response regime focused almost exclusively on post-flow [of refugees] relief and humanitarian protection, the current framework underwrites mass movement, thereby facilitating its occurrence."[102]

An example of how receiving states may react is found in Europe. While freedom of movement within Europe is guaranteed to European Union nationals,[103] there is also a recognition "that manifestations of racism and xenophobia are steadily growing in Europe."[104] The two issues, together with economic considerations, combine to show that

> [t]he successful elimination of internal frontiers [in Europe] will of course accentuate in a symbolic [way] (and in a very real sense too) the external frontiers of the Community. . . . In one way, the more that these external boundaries are

accentuated, the greater the sense of internal solidarity. . . . But in the very concept of [European] citizenship a distinction is created between the insider and outsider that tugs at their common humanity.[105]

So the "Europe without frontiers" is a Europe where the internal frontiers have been lowered but the external frontiers—being the new European bound-aries—have been raised very high. Refugees may not easily enter.

The territorial boundary as conceived by the international legal system, whether a state boundary or a regional boundary, limits the mobility of both nationals and nonnationals. The present international legal system is so deter-mined to protect the interests of states and their territorial boundaries that any people who seek to move across those boundaries are seen as intruders. If they can enter at all, they enter at their own risk.

Autonomy

The international legal system has traditionally linked political autonomy (often called "state sovereignty") and territorial boundaries, as was shown above. This is because the international legal system has traditionally been premised on the notion that states have autonomy within that system, and that autonomy, which is exercised by national governments, arises from the determination of territorial boundaries between states.[106] In other words: "states are said to be sovereign, thus able to determine for themselves what they must or may do. . . . Consequently, many writers use the language of autonomy when they declare that international law requires the consent of the states that are governed by it."[107]

However, this traditional approach is unsustainable today. As former United Nations Secretary-General Boutros Boutros-Ghali said:

> The time of absolute and exclusive sovereignty . . . has passed; its theory was never matched by reality. It is the task of leaders of states today to understand this and to find a balance between the needs of good internal governance and the requirements of an ever more interdependent world. Commerce, communications and environ-mental matters transcend administrative borders; but inside those borders is where individuals carry out the first order of their economic, political and social lives.[108]

The impact is even deeper than this, as:

> [c]omplete autonomy may have been acceptable in the past when no state could take actions that would threaten the international community as a whole. Today, the enormous destructive potential of some activities and the precarious condition of some objects of international concern make full autonomy undesirable, if not potentially catastrophic.[109]

These words are relevant not only to the state's autonomy within the interna-tional legal system, but, as Boutros-Ghali makes clear, to the state's political autonomy within its internal legal system so that there is good internal governance. These two systems are inextricably linked.

An area where the two systems are most obviously linked is that of human rights. How a state treats the people within its territorial boundaries is no longer a matter for that state alone; as the Vienna Declaration of the 1993 World Conference on Human Rights put it: "[t]he promotion and protection of all human rights is a legitimate concern of the international community."[110] One human right that has been of particular relevance to the issue of political autonomy and territorial boundaries is the right of self-determination, discussed above. This is because the right of self-determination does not only protect peoples when they seek to change the relationship between themselves and other states, as occurred when colonies became independent states. It also concerns the right of peoples within a state to choose their political status, the extent of their political participation, and the form of their government.[111] The right of self-determination thus has an internal aspect, [112] one which allows a range of options other than outright secession.[113] Peoples may exercise their internal self-determination by such methods as the creation of a federation; guarantees of political power to defend or promote certain group interests; control over certain aspects of policy, such as educational, social, or cultural matters; or by providing for a specific, recognized status to a group. The type of self-determination claimed will usually depend on the constitutional order of the state concerned, and may challenge the present centralized structure of most states. This variety of possible exercises of the right occurs because

> the concept of self-determination is capable of embracing much more nuanced interpretations and applications [than just that of independent statehood], particularly in an increasingly interdependent world in which the formal attributes of statehood mean less and less.[114]

Indeed, a state that does not protect the right of internal self-determination not only is in breach of international law but, because "the possession of territory has been the precondition for the exercise of legitimate political authority on the international level,"[115] such actions could result in the denial of a state's legitimacy within the international legal system.[116]

The obligations on a state to comply with internal self-determination are increased by global economic pressure. Many of the developed states and the globalized economic institutions, such as the World Bank and the International Monetary Fund, as well as transnational corporations, are demanding that "good governance" be a condition of their investment in developing states.[117] Good governance could be seen to mean the extent to which a state allows different political autonomies within itself, including the exercise of internal self-determination. However, these conditions may result in harm to the human rights of the inhabitants of the state if not carefully monitored.[118]

It is vital that the tightly woven connection between territorial boundaries of states and political autonomy be untangled. This would enable much more diverse possibilities where the political linkages between peoples and states are not dependent on territory, such as by allowing Serbian nationality to a person born and resident in the state of Bosnia-Herzegovina, or by the use of inter-state, intrastate, and cross-regional structures similar to those established in 1998 in Northern Ireland.[119] Within Europe, there are now a series of different levels of political power—albeit still largely dependent on the boundaries of the states within the European Union—from local or regional areas (offering political autonomy to some peoples—such as the Scots—as an exercise in internal self-determination) to national governments (with state power), to the European Union decision-making bodies that are able to respond to re-gional, national, and European voices. The consequence is that the sover-eignty or political autonomy of each state within the European Union is not absolute. This multilevel, shared sovereignty is not strictly limited to a state's boundaries, and could be a means to reduce the potential for conflict over territory. For example,

> [a] combination of local autonomy or federalism with a regional system of political and economic integration, coupled with an effective international supervision of individual and minority rights, can take much of the pressure out of territorial ques-tions. A curtailment of the predominant role of the state will also make the question of which national government has control over a particular province or locality appear less important.[120]

Such separation of the connection between political autonomy and territorial boundaries would also assist in dealing with the concerns of peoples who live on the borders between states. These people often feel a greater affinity with each other than with the distant national governments.[121] Above all, it would foster an alternative to the concept "of human beings that envisions their freedom and security in terms of bounded spheres."[122]

To untangle this connection between territorial boundaries and political autonomy, defined as being the power of the state, would also indicate a significant shift in the nature of the international legal system. The system could no longer be seen as one based on the consent of states alone. It would enable an understanding that "the autonomy of the individual state [is] dependent on, rather than automatically antithetical to, the inter-national community."[123] It would be a system in which the role of the people in determining the status of the state in international law is recog-nized. It would make the opening words of the United Nations Charter— "We, the Peoples"—be of true international legal significance. Above all, it would remind the international community that "it is for the people to de-termine the destiny of the territory and not the territory the destiny of the people."[124]

Conclusion

The prevailing concept of the international legal system is that territorial boundaries establish statehood and that territorial boundaries are the basis for state sovereignty (ownership).[125] Accordingly, the distribution of natural resources, concepts of diversity, and the mobility of people are considered within this state-based framework, and the political autonomy of the state and territorial boundaries are completely entwined. The current international legal system recreates and affirms the dispositions by colonial powers, it privileges certain voices and silences others, and it restricts the identities of individuals to those defined by state boundaries. The effect of this is to reinforce the state-based framework of the international legal system and to limit the influence of other factors. This is because this system, as traditionally conceived "naturalises and legitimises the subjugating and disciplinary effects of European, masculinist, heterosexual and capitalist regimes of power."[126]

While territorial boundaries are artificially created by the international legal system, they tend to arise only from the imagination of these regimes of power. There is little room for the imagination of the developing states, of non-state actors, of women, or of alternative concepts of the international legal system. Occasionally, these different imaginations do have some expression, such as in the development of internal self-determination and of the common heritage of mankind, but they are quickly limited by the prevailing international legal system. Law, in determining rules (and hence legal boundaries), is self-limiting because "law purports to preserve institutional stability and continuity [and] reform must build from existing legal precedents and doctrines,"[127] and so law allows change incrementally from the status quo position. However, as the "intrusive, intersubjective, and symbolic qualities of modern law continually interact with social practices and relationships, making legal change is an integral, necessary component of social change."[128] It does leave open the possibilities for new imaginations of international law to emerge.

There are new ways to imagine the international legal role of territorial boundaries. Some of these ways are institutional, as seen in the multilevel sovereignties in Europe, and some are structural, as in the diminished importance of territorial boundaries due to the process of globalization. Above all, the new imaginations are conceptual. They have to be able "to convert those borders from their prevailing postures as ramparts into a new veritable function as bridges,"[129] and to focus on relationships and not on imaginary constructs.[130]

This language of international law in relation to territorial boundaries must be in terms of an international society that is inclusive of all, allows all to find and use their voices, is creative of identity opportunities, and recognizes diver-

sity within the universality of international society. There are some indications that the international legal system can reimagine itself, even to the point
where:

> [s]overeignty over territory will disappear as a category from the theory of interna-
> tional society and from its international law. . . . With the exclusion of the concept
> of sovereignty over territory, international society will find itself liberated at last to
> contemplate the possibility of delegating powers of governance not solely by refer-
> ence to an area of the earth's surface.[131]

This liberation would enable a new imagination of the role of territorial
boundaries in international law.

Notes

1. See Frederick Schauer, *Playing by the Rules: A Philosophical Examination of Rule-
Based Decision-Making in Law and Life* (Oxford: Oxford University Press, 1991), 1: "We
think ourselves free, yet we are surrounded by rules. As we negotiate the maze of life,
rules are recurring obstacles, foreclosing otherwise attractive paths and requiring otherwise unappealing ones." See also Jennifer Nedelsky, "Law, Boundaries, and the
Bounded Self," *Representations* 30 (1990): 162.

2. Humphrey Waldock, *Brierly's The Law of Nations*, 6th ed. (Oxford: Oxford University Press, 1963), 41, states that "law can only exist in a society, and there can be no
society without a system of law to regulate the relations of its members with one another. If then we speak of the 'law of nations' we are assuming that a 'society' of nations
exists."

3. Article 2(1), United Nations Charter, provides that all states are juridically
equal.

4. Louis Henkin, *How Nations Behave*, 2nd ed. (New York: Columbia University
Press, 1979), 320.

5. See Jonathan Charney, "Universal International Law," *American Journal of International Law* 87 (1993): 532.

6. Fernando Tesón, "The Kantian Theory of International Law," *Columbia Law
Review* 92 (1992): 53–54.

7. See, for example, Philip Allott, *Eunomia: New Order for a New World* (Oxford:
Oxford University Press, 1990).

8. See, for example, Hilary Charlesworth, Christine Chinkin, and Shelley Wright,
"Feminist Approaches to International Law," *American Journal of International Law* 85
(1991): 631.

9. See, for example, Martti Koskenniemi, *From Apology to Utopia: The Structure of
International Legal Argument* (Helsinki: Finnish Lawyers Publishing Cooperative,
1989).

10. See Lassa Oppenheim, *International Law*, 1st ed. (London: Longman, 1905),
253; and see also, for example, 8th ed. (by Hersh Lauterpacht, 1955), 531; and 9th ed.
(by Robert Jennings and Arthur Watts, 1992), 661.

11. Ibid., 9th ed., 662. In the first edition it is stated (at p. 256) that "the term 'natural boundaries' [is] of no importance whatever to the Law of Nations, whatever value [it] may have politically." For a lengthy discussion of types of territorial boundaries in international law, see A. Cukwurah, *The Settlement of Boundary Disputes in International Law* (Manchester: Manchester University Press, 1967), 9–26.

12. See, for example, *North Sea Continental Shelf Cases (Germany v. Denmark and The Netherlands)*, International Court of Justice (I.C.J.) Reports (1969), 3; *Frontier Dispute Case (Burkino Faso v. Mali)*, I.C.J. Reports (1986), 554; and *Land, Island and Maritime Frontier Dispute Case (El Salvador v. Honduras)*, I.C.J. Reports (1992), 35. There are also many boundary disputes litigated through arbitration, such as *Island of Palmas (The Netherlands v. United States)*, Reports of International Arbitral Awards (hereafter R.I.A.A.) 2 (1928): 829.

13. The Montevideo Convention on the Rights and Duties of States (1933), article 1, provides: "The State as a person of international law should possess the following qualifications: (a) a permanent population; (b) a defined territory; (c) government; and (d) capacity to enter into relations with other States."

14. *North Sea Continental Shelf Cases*, 32.

15. James Crawford, *The Creation of States in International Law* (Oxford: Oxford University Press, 1979), 40.

16. *The Territorial Dispute (Libya v. Chad)*, I.C.J. Reports (1994), 37.

17. The principle of *uti possidetis* was expressly adopted by the Organization of African Unity in 1964 (AGH/Res. 16[1]). See Surya Sharma, *Territorial Acquisition, Disputes and International Law* (The Hague: Martinus Nijhoff, 1997), 119–29; Tomas Bartos, "Uti Possidetis. Quo Vadis?" *Australian Yearbook of International Law* 18 (1997): 37; and Malcolm Shaw, "Peoples, Territorialism and Boundaries," *European Journal of International Law* 8 (1997): 478.

18. In the opinion of the committee established by the European Community to consider legal questions arising from the conflict in the former Yugoslavia (the Badinter Commission): "former boundaries became frontiers protected by international law" due to *uti possidetis*, unless there was contrary agreement (*European Journal of International Law* 3 [1992]: 185). However, the former Yugoslavia was never a colony, and the relevant boundaries in issue were internal federal boundaries, not preexisting colonial boundaries.

19. *Frontier Dispute Case (Burkina Faso v. Mali)*, par. 20. The principle has been upheld in *Land, Island and Maritime Dispute Case (El Salvador v. Honduras)*.

20. *Frontier Dispute Case (Burkina Faso v. Mali)*, par. 25.

21. A. Cukwurah, "The Organisation of African Unity and African Territorial and Boundary Problems, 1963–1973," *Indian Journal of International Law* 13 (1973): 178. See Anthony Angie, "Finding the Peripheries: Sovereignty and Colonialism in Nineteenth-Century International Law," *Harvard Journal of International Law* 40 (1999): 1; and, generally, Mohammed Bedjaoui, *Towards a New International Economic Order* (Paris: Holmes & Meier, 1979).

22. Lord Salisbury, speaking in 1890, as quoted in the Separate Opinion of Judge Ajibola, in *The Territorial Dispute (Libya v. Chad)*, 53.

23. Malcolm Shaw, *Title to Territory in Africa* (Oxford: Clarendon Press, 1986), 51. See also Edward Hertslet, *The Map of Africa by Treaty*, 3rd ed. (London: Frank Cass, 1910), vol 3., 899–906.

24. *Land, Island and Maritime Dispute Case (El Salvador v. Honduras)*, 388.

25. Anthony Asiwaju, "Borders and Borderlands as Linchpins for Regional Integration in Africa," in *Global Boundaries*, ed. Clive Schofield (London: Routledge, 1994), 57, 60–61.

26. For example, in a case currently before the International Court of Justice between Namibia and Botswana, the key document is a treaty between the United Kingdom and Germany, signed in Berlin in 1890 concerning a division of "spheres of influence" between those colonial powers: *International Court of Justice, Communiqué No. 99/2*, 10 February 1999.

27. Schauer, *Playing by the Rules*, 173. This criticism is developed by the New Stream of critical legal scholars in international law, such as David Kennedy, "A New Stream of International Law Scholarship," *Wisconsin International Law Journal* 7 (1988): 1; and Koskenniemi, *From Apology to Utopia*.

28. *Temple of Preah Vihear Case (Cambodia v. Thailand)*, I.C.J. *Reports* (1962), 34.

29. See, for example, Oscar Schachter, "Sovereignty—Then and Now," in *Essays in Honour of Wang Tieya*, ed. Ronald Macdonald (Dordrecht: Martinus Nijhoff, 1993), 671.

30. *Island of Palmas (The Netherlands v. United States)*.

31. *North Atlantic Coast Fisheries Case (United Kingdom v. United States)*, Permanent Court of Arbitration, R.I.A.A. 11 (1910), 180.

32. Philip Allott, *Eunomia*, 246, notes that "sovereignty in the interstatal world came to be conceived simply as authority deriving from land-holding, a concept reminiscent of the so-called feudal systems of pre-modern societies."

33. See Donald Greig, "Sovereignty, Territory and the International Lawyers' Dilemma," *Osgoode Hall Law Journal* 26 (1988): 127.

34. *Island of Palmas*, 846.

35. See, for example, *Minquiers and Ecrehos Case (France v. United Kingdom)*, I.C.J. *Reports* (1953), 47.

36. *Island of Palmas*, 839.

37. *Legal Status of Eastern Greenland Case (Norway v. Denmark)*, *Permanent Court of International Justice Reports, Series A/B* (1933), No. 53.

38. Article 2(4), United Nations Charter.

39. See, for example, Security Council Resolutions 660, 661, and 662 (1990).

40. Ilidio do Amaral, "New Reflections on the Theme of International Boundaries," in *Global Boundaries*, 16.

41. Article 1 of the Montevideo Convention on the Rights and Duties of States (1933).

42. Athene Munkman, "Adjudication and Adjustment—International Judicial Decision and the Settlement of Territorial and Boundary Disputes," *British Yearbook of International Law* 46 (1972–73): 107.

43. See *Nottebohm Case (Liechtenstein v. Guatemala)*, I.C.J. *Reports* (1955), 4; and *Iran-United States Case No.A/18, Iran-United States Claims Tribunal Reports* 5 (1984): 251.

44. Hilary Charlesworth, "The Sex of the State in International Law," in *Sexing the Subject of Law*, ed. Ngaire Naffine and Rosemary Owens (Sydney: LBC, 1997), 259.

45. Ibid., 252.

46. Common article 1 of the International Covenant on Economic, Social and

Cultural Rights (1966) and the International Covenant on Civil and Political Rights (1966).

47. In the *Namibia Opinion, I.C.J. Reports* (1971), 31, it was held that the "development of international law in regard to [colonies] . . . made the principle of self-determination applicable to all of them."

48. The Declaration on Principles of International Law concerning Friendly Relations and Co-operation among States in accordance with the Charter of the United Nations, annex to General Assembly Resolution 2625 (XXV), 24 October 1970.

49. Boutros Boutros-Ghali, *Agenda for Peace*, United Nations Document A/47/277-S/24111 (1992), par. 17.

50. For further discussion, see Robert McCorquodale, "Self-Determination: A Human Rights Approach," *International and Comparative Law Quarterly* 43 (1994): 857.

51. See text at note 42. See also Benedict Anderson, *Imagined Communities: Reflections on the Origin and Spread of Nationalism*, 2nd ed. (London: Verso Publications, 1991).

52. See Robert McCorquodale and Nicholas Orosz, eds., *Tibet: The Position in International Law* (London: Serindia, 1994); Oscar Schachter, "United Nations Law in the Gulf Conflict," *American Journal of International Law* 85 (1991): 468–69; M. Woollacott, "Turks and Kurds Must Rethink Their Politics," *Guardian Weekly*, 28 February 1998, 12; and "Denying Kurdish Rights," *Le Monde*, 18 February 1998.

53. Niles Hansen, "European Transboundary Cooperation and Its Relevance to the United States-Mexico Border," *Journal of the American Institute of Planners* 49 (1983): 336.

54. See James Anaya, *Indigenous Peoples in International Law* (New York: Oxford University Press, 1996).

55. *Western Sahara Opinion, I.C.J. Reports* (1975), 64.

56. Boutros-Ghali, *Agenda for Peace*, par. 17.

57. Philip Cerny, "Globalisation and Other Stories: The Search for a New Paradigm of International Relations," *International Journal* 51 (1996): 626.

58. Ibid., 624.

59. World Bank, *World Development Report 1997* (Oxford: Oxford University Press, 1997), 12.

60. See further, Robert McCorquodale with Richard Fairbrother, "Globalization and Human Rights," *Human Rights Quarterly* 21 (1999): 735.

61. See, for example, Donald Rothwell, *The Polar Regions and the Development of International Law* (Cambridge: Cambridge University Press, 1996).

62. *East Timor Case (Portugal v. Australia), I.C.J. Reports* (1995), par. 32, and Judge Vereshchetin (Separate Opinion), 137–38.

63. This is fostered in particular by the principle of "subsidiarity" and the development of the idea of "a Europe of the Regions." See A. Scott, J. Peterson, and D. Millar, "Subsidiarity: A 'Europe of the Regions' v. the British Constitution," *Journal of Common Market Studies* 32 (1994): 47.

64. See, for example, articles 1 and 2 of the Convention on the Territorial Sea and the Contiguous Zone (1958), and article 2 of the United Nations Convention on the Law of the Sea (1982).

65. See General Assembly Resolution 1803 (XVII) and the Charter of Economic Rights and Duties of States (General Assembly Resolution 3281 (XXIX)). Economic

self-determination has been used in the context of sovereignty over natural resources: see common article 1(2) of the International Covenant on Economic, Social and Cultural Rights and the International Covenant on Civil and Political Rights.

66. Many of the territorial boundary disputes decided by the International Court of Justice are about maritime boundaries. In regard to other conflicts over natural resources, there is, for example, a dispute between Israel and Jordan over access to water from the Sea of Galilee. See "Israel Holds Back Water for Jordan," *The Guardian Weekly*, 21 March 1999, 4.

67. See note 64 above.

68. Ian Brownlie, *Principles of International Law*, 4th ed. (Oxford: Oxford University Press, 1990), 258.

69. Articles 136 and 137.

70. There was also to be a transfer of technology to developing states—article 144.

71. Agreement to the Implementation of Part XI of the United Nations Convention on the Law of the Sea (1994), *International Legal Materials* 33 (1994): 1099.

72. Ibid., sec. 5 of the Annex to the Agreement.

73. David Anderson, "Legal Implications of the Entry into Force of the UN Convention on the Law of the Sea," *International and Comparative Quarterly* 44 (1995): 318–19.

74. Anthony Carty, *The Decay of International Law* (Manchester: Manchester University Press, 1986), 6.

75. An example of this is in the lack of any claims by states in relation to the Chernobyl nuclear accident in 1986. See Philippe Sands, "The Environment, Community and International Law," *Harvard International Law Journal* 30 (1989): 393.

76. See James Anaya, *Indigenous Peoples in International Law*, esp. 104–7.

77. *Maritime Delimitation in the Area between Greenland and Jan Mayen (Denmark v. Norway)*, I.C.J. Reports (1993), 38, par. 80. Also in *The Territorial Dispute (Libya v. Chad)*, the court held that as the treaty between Libya and France settled the boundary, any issues relating to the indigenous people were irrelevant (par. 75).

78. See Kathy Laster, *Law as Culture* (Sydney: Federation Press, 1997).

79. Par. 5, Vienna Declaration and Programme of Action arising from the 1993 United Nations World Conference on Human Rights.

80. Eisuke Suzuki, "Self-Determination and the World Public Order: Community Response to Territorial Separation," *Virginia Journal of International Law* 16 (1976): 792–93. Boundaries are a psychological phenomenon with a social function. See Friedrich Kratochwil, Paul Rohrlich, and Harpreet Mahajan, *Peace and Disputed Sovereignty: Reflections on Conflict over Territory* (Lanham, Md.: University of America Press, 1985), 117.

81. Ilidio do Amaral, "New Reflections on the Theme of International Boundaries," 20.

82. Adam Schwarz, *A Nation in Waiting: Indonesia in the 1990s* (Boulder, Colo.: Westview Press, 1994).

83. Ibid., 8.

84. Patrick Brogan, *World Conflicts: Why and Where They Are Happening* (London: Bungay, 1987), vii.

85. "Many peoples today are deprived of their right of self-determination, by elites of their own countrymen and women: through the concentration of power in a partic-

ular political party, in a particular ethnic or religious group, or in a certain social class"—statement by United Kingdom representative to Third Committee of the General Assembly on 12 October 1984 (*British Yearbook of International Law* 55 [1984], 432).

86. Eugene Kamenka, "Human Rights, Peoples' Rights" in *The Rights of Peoples*, ed. James Crawford (Oxford: Oxford University Press, 1988), 133. See also Philip Allott, "The Nation as Mind Politic," *New York University Journal of International Law and Politics* 24 (1992): 1361; Nathaniel Berman, "Sovereignty in Abeyance: Self-Determination in International Law," *Wisconsin International Law Journal* 7 (1988): 51; and Anderson, *Imagined Communities*.

87. See Christine Chinkin and Shelley Wright, "The Hunger Trap: Women, Food and Self-Determination," *Michigan Journal of International Law* 14 (1993): 262.

88. Article 2.

89. Though the Badinter Committee did give international legal significance to the internal federal boundaries of the former Yugoslavia (see note 18).

90. *Nottebohm Case (Liechtenstein v. Guatemala)*. The court made clear that international law only checks to see if a state may exercise its protection over a national when there are competing claims of nationality between two or more states.

91. See, for example, *Reno v. American-Arab Anti-Discrimination Committee*, 525 U.S. 471 (1999), pt. III, in which the court held that "an alien unlawfully in this country has no constitutional right to assert selective enforcement as a defense against his deportation." There are some human rights that allow the possibility that they may not be exercised by nonnationals, as long as a state can justify this; see, for example, article 2(3) International Covenant on Economic, Social and Cultural Rights (1966).

92. In *Dickson Car Wheel Company Case (U.S. v. Mexico)*, R.I.A.A. 4 (1931): 678, it was stated: "A State . . . does not commit an international delinquency in inflicting an injury upon an individual lacking nationality." See further, Peter Mutharika, *The Regulation of Statelessness under International and National Law* (Dobbs Ferry, N.Y.: Oceana Publications, 1977).

93. There are also regional treaties dealing with refugees, e.g., Organization of African Unity Convention Governing the Specific Aspects of Refugee Problems in Africa (1969).

94. See Isabelle Gunning, "Expanding the International Definition of Refugee: A Multicultural View," *Fordham International Law Journal* 13 (1989–90): 35; Lawyers Committee for Human Rights, *The UNHCR at 40: Refugee Protection at the Crossroads* (New York: Lawyers Committee for Human Rights, 1991); and Guy Goodwin-Gill, *The Refugee in International Law*, 2nd ed. (Oxford: Clarendon Press, 1996).

95. See, for example, *Applicant A v. Minister for Immigration and Ethnic Affairs*, Australian Law Reports 142 (1997): 331; and comment by Christopher Ward, "Principles of Interpretation Applicable to Legislation Adopting Treaties," *Federal Law Review* 26 (1998): 207.

96. Anders Johnsson, "The International Protection of Women Refugees: A Summary of Principal Problems and Issues," *International Journal of Refugee Law* 1 (1989): 222.

97. Deborah Anker, "Women Refugees: Forgotten No Longer?" *San Diego Law Review* 32 (1995): 772.

98. Audrey Macklin, "Refugee Women and the Imperative of Categories," *Human*

Rights Quarterly 17 (1995): 213, as quoted in Burns Weston, Richard Falk, and Hilary Charlesworth, *International Law and World Order*, 3rd ed. (St. Paul, Minn.: West, 1997), 647.

99. United Nations High Commissioner for Refugees, *Handbook on Procedures and Criteria for Determining Refugee Status* (Geneva: United Nations, 1995).

100. This was one justification for Security Council Resolution 929 (1994).

101. Gervase Coles, *Conflict and Humanitarian Action: An Overview* (Geneva: United Nations High Commissioner for Refugees, 1993), 31.

102. Jack Garvey, "The New Asylum Seekers: Addressing Their Origin," in *The New Asylum Seekers: Refugee Law in the 1980s*, ed. David Martin (Dordrecht: Martinus Nijhoff, 1986), 181.

103. See, for example, articles 48–50 of the Treaty Establishing the European Community (1957), which provide for freedom of movement for all workers in the European Community.

104. European Declaration on Racism and Xenophobia (1991).

105. Joseph Weiler, "Thou Shall Not Oppress a Stranger: On the Judicial Protection of the Human Rights of Non-EC Nationals—A Critique" *European Journal of International Law* 3 (1992): 65, 68.

106. For example, "territory is co-terminous with sovereignty": *North Atlantic Coast Fisheries Case (United Kingdom v. United States)*.

107. Charney, "Universal Law," 530.

108. Boutros-Ghali, *Agenda for Peace*, par. 17.

109. Charney, "Universal Law," 530.

110. Vienna Declaration and Programme of Action on Human Rights, article 4. See also Michael Reisman, "Sovereignty and Human Rights in Contemporary International Law," *American Journal of International Law* 82 (1990): 866.

111. The right of self-determination also has economic, social, and cultural aspects: see note 65 above.

112. State practice shows the application of an internal right of self-determination as seen in the international community's response to denials of this right to blacks in Southern Rhodesia and in South Africa. Security Council Resolutions 216 and 217 (1965) and 232 (1966) with respect to Southern Rhodesia and Security Council Resolutions 282 (1970), 392 (1976), 417 (1977) and 473 (1980) with respect to South Africa.

113. Circumstances where secession may be legally justified will still occur, such as "where the majority [in a State] refuses to even recognize a substantial minority or ethnically distinct nation, and prevents it from sharing in the life of the State, external self-determination or secession may seem like the last hope for those who feel like they are treated as aliens in their own country": Hurst Hannum, *Autonomy, Sovereignty and Self-Determination: The Accommodation of Conflicting Rights* (Philadelphia: University of Pennsylvania Press, 1990), 64.

114. James Anaya, "The Capacity of International Law to Advance Ethnic or Nationality Rights Claims," *Iowa Law Review* 75 (1990): 842.

115. Kratochwil, Rohrlich, and Mahajan, *Peace and Disputed Sovereignty*, 3.

116. See Thomas Franck, *The Power of Legitimacy among Nations* (New York: Oxford University Press, 1990), 236–37. Also in the European Community Declaration on the Guidelines on the Recognition of New States in Eastern Europe and in the

Soviet Union, *European Journal of International Law* 4 (1993): 72, there is the requirement that a potential new state has constitutional guarantees of democracy and of "the rights of ethnic and national groups and minorities" before recognition by the European Community states would be granted.

117. See David Forsythe, "The United Nations, Human Rights, and Development" *Human Rights Quarterly* 19 (1997): 334.

118. See Anne Orford, "Locating the International: Military and Monetary Interventions after the Cold War," *Harvard Journal of International Law* 38 (1997): 443; and McCorquodale and Fairbrother, "Globalization and Human Rights."

119. United Kingdom, Northern Ireland and Ireland Agreement (10 April 1998), *International Legal Materials* 37 (1998): 751.

120. Christoph Schreuer, "The Waning of the Sovereign State: Towards a New Paradigm for International Law?" *European Journal of International Law* 4 (1993): 447, 469.

121. See Oscar Martinez, "The Dynamics of Border Interaction," in *Global Boundaries*, 1.

122. Nedelsky, "Law, Boundaries, and the Bounded Self," 163.

123. Charlesworth, "Sex of the State in International Law," 260. See also Anne Orford, "The Politics of Collective Security," *Michigan Journal of International Law* 17 (1996): 373.

124. Judge Dillard, Separate Opinion in *Western Sahara Opinion*, 122.

125. *Island of Palmas Case*, 838.

126. Dianne Otto, "Rethinking Universals: Opening Transformative Possibilities in International Human Rights Law," *Australian Yearbook of International Law* 18 (1998): 35.

127. Katharine Bartlett and Rosanne Kennedy, introduction to *Feminist Legal Theory*, ed. Katharine Bartlett and Rosanne Kennedy (Boulder: Westview Press, 1991), 2.

128. Kathryn Powers, "Sex Segregation and the Ambivalent Directions of Sex Discrimination Law," *Wisconsin Law Review* 31 (1979): 63.

129. Asiwaju, "Borders and Borderlands as Linchpins for Regional Integration in Africa," 58.

130. Nedelsky, "Law, Boundaries, and the Bounded Self," 163.

131. Allott, *Eunomia*, 329.

Eight

Territorial Sovereignty

COMMAND, TITLE, AND THE EXPANDING CLAIMS
OF THE COMMONS

RAUL C. PANGALANGAN

I SHARE much of Robert McCorquodale's approach to the way in which international law deals with issues of boundaries and similarly will begin my analysis by looking at territory as conceptually bound up with the idea of state sovereignty. I will likewise challenge international law's fixation on the state as the preeminent actor, stifling collectivities within states (e.g., minorities claiming self-determination), and likewise deterring people from reaching out and finding common cause (e.g., human rights) with others beyond national borders.

I find, however, that the emerging decline of the state as the chief international actor is just one element in a larger shift, which occurs in the very notion of sovereignty itself, away from its *territorial* aspect and toward greater reliance on its *decisional* aspect. That shift, I propose, is conditioned by state interests as much as by inherited concepts and embedded norms that continue to shape the debate on national territory. The problem therefore is as much political as it is intellectual. The primacy of the state may be explained by power politics, but the rise of decisional over territorial notions can be explained only by the deeper politics of how and why old ideas persist.

I will therefore trace the norms underlying the notion of boundaries through the "conceptual provenance" of key doctrines. "Modern" international law actually emerged from an earlier shift in the concept of sovereignty, from the decisional to the territorial, from command over people's allegiances, to title over land. Today we are completing that cycle, as we recognize that control over *territory* has served merely as the doctrinal proxy for control over *resources*—natural, economic, or strategic—and correspondingly, that while territorial lines are drawn and kept through geo-military power, resources are susceptible of more sophisticated modes of control, generally decisional in character, and thus more easily subject to overlapping claims by non-state groups and to communal regulation by a putative international community.

These shifts have obscured the emphasis on the spatial dimension of sovereignty, disaggregated the competencies bundled up in the erstwhile monolithic concept of sovereignty, allowed new actors to claim these newly spun-off competencies, and recast territorial sovereignty from a source of power to a basis of responsibility (specifically as regards the environment). This chapter will document these shifts by examining the authoritative norms recognized in international law in the following contexts: the conceptual provenance of sovereignty—the conflation of *imperium* (rule) and *dominium* (title) in the modern state—in the rule of princes over their realm; the age of imperialism, when inhabited parts of the globe were deemed to be *res nullius* (property of none) and colonized; decolonization, self-determination, and the ironies of *uti possidetis* (preserving borders inherited from the colonizer); and the expansion of the global commons, Roman law's *res communis* (property of all) now extended to cover the ocean floor and "the Moon and other celestial bodies" as part of the "common heritage of mankind."[1]

I conclude here by asking this question: If new technologies have slowly obsolesced the role of place, why then does the spatial aspect of sovereignty persist? Why the persistence of territory, the primacy of place over decisional competence? The principal reason is that the post-World War II legal order was built on the need to preserve peace and that absent more accurate, less contested indicators of sovereignty, borders remained the simplest mode of ensuring compliance. A second reason is that "new" natural resources, though they call for new regimes of owning and use, are accessed in places fixed at least at the outset by nature and not by people. Finally, norms of human dignity, whose enforcement hitherto was locked into state jurisdiction, have seen states yielding jurisdiction but not territory, which remains doctrinally entrenched.

In this context, the traditionally exclusivistic notions of statehood, sovereignty, and territory remain principally as devices for managing the permissible use of force—international law's *peace-maintaining* aspect; but the preeminently normative claims of human dignity prevail when merely jurisdictional exclusivity, not territory itself, is at stake. Territoriality itself is slowly giving way to regimes of sharing which place certain territorial resources beyond appropriation by states and reserve these as the "common heritage of mankind"—international law's *resource distribution* aspect.

A brief note on method is warranted here. In international law, the threshold issue is whether a norm is authoritative, for example, whether it gives rise to a legal obligation, whether it is binding on states merely on the basis of their consent given through treaties, or through some form of communal consensus which has "crystallized" into custom. This is a separate subject in itself, the term of art being "sources of international law,"[2] which begins international law inquiries, academic and judicial.

For the purposes of this chapter, and in order to spare the reader the burden of the protracted debate on "sources," I will rely on the unassailable statement of these sources set forth in the charter of the International Court of Justice, the judicial organ of the United Nations, which derives international law from multilateral treaties, judicial decisions, and academic writing, all of which I cite in this essay not just as independent sources of law in themselves, but also, where indicated, as articulations of international custom.[3]

Territorial Sovereignty: Operative Mechanism for the Idea of Peace among States

The Foundational Norms of the Postwar International Legal Order: The Duty to Refrain from the Use of Force and from Intervening in Domestic Jurisdiction

"Modern" international law is marked by the emergence of the "secular, national, territorial"[4] state. "At the basis of international law lies the notion that a State occupies a definite part of the surface of the earth, within which it normally exercises . . . jurisdiction over persons and things to the exclusion of the jurisdiction of other States."[5] Boundaries or frontiers are "imaginary lines on the surface of the earth which separate the territory of one State from that of another, or from unappropriated territory or from the open sea."[6] In a frontier dispute between two former colonies in Africa, the parties asked the World Court "not to give indications [of equity, for instance] to guide them in determining their common frontier, but to draw a line, and a precise line."[7]

The international legal order that emerged after the Second World War was built on the inviolability of national territory as a function of its central concern for international peace. The core of this legal order is the prohibition on the "use of force . . . against the territorial integrity or political independence" of a state,[8] which protects both the spatial and decisional aspects of sovereignty. Corollary is the prohibition against intervention in "matters belonging to the domestic jurisdiction of States," traditionally called the "reserve domain" of states, though it pertains not to space but to autonomous decision making.[9] Both these principles have been recognized as fundamental "purposes" in the Charter of the United Nations, which two decades later were reaffirmed in the authoritative Declaration of Principles of International Law[10] adopted by the UN General Assembly and whose legal significance lay in the fact that it provides "evidence of the consensus among Member States . . . on the meaning and elaboration of the principles of the Charter."[11] That Declaration included "the duty to refrain from the threat or use of force to violate the existing international boundaries of any State or as a means of solving . . . territorial disputes and problems concerning frontiers of States," while restating the duty of nonintervention.[12]

The World Court affirmed these principles as rules of customary law binding independent of treaties in *Military and Paramilitary Activities (Nicaragua v. United States)*,[13] a case involving attempts by the United States to subvert the Sandinista government in Nicaragua, wherein the court expressly linked territorial sovereignty with the principle of nonuse of force. "The effects of the principle of respect for territorial sovereignty inevitably overlap with those of the principles of the prohibition of the use of force and of non-intervention."[14] American assistance to the Contras, a military group opposed to the Sandinistas, as well as the direct U.S. attacks on Nicaragua's oil installations, the mining of its ports, and unauthorized overflight "not only amount to an unlawful use of force, but also constitute infringements of the territorial sovereignty of Nicaragua, and incursions into its territorial and internal waters" and airspace.[15] The court emphasized that sovereignty extended to a state's territorial sea and airspace.[16]

The court also affirmed the nonspatial aspects of sovereignty in addressing the U.S. argument that the Sandinistas had established a totalitarian government. The court held that the rule of nonintervention emanated from sovereignty, which entailed "the freedom of choice of the political, social, economic and cultural system of a State. . . . The Court cannot contemplate the creation of a new rule opening up a right of intervention by one State against another on the ground that the latter has opted for some particular ideology or political system."[17]

Decolonization and the Test of Effective Sovereignty

Decolonization emerged after the Second World War as the principal idea that shaped and indeed transformed international law, discarding some established doctrines and reinforcing others. During the age of empire, colonies were acquired on the basis of the doctrine of res nullius. Native peoples then rebelled, throwing off the colonizer, and claiming the right to self-determination. At the moment of triumph, they ironically insisted on maintaining the very borders created often artificially by past colonial masters; and after independence, they denied to subnational minorities that same right to self-determination.

Territory can be classified into sovereign territory, non-self-governing trusts and mandates ("territory not subject to the sovereignty of another State but possessing a status of its own," non-sovereign though non-colonial), res nullius ("legally susceptible to acquisition by States but not yet placed under territorial sovereignty"), and res communis ("not capable of being placed under State sovereignty," e.g., high seas, outer space).[18]

When European powers acquired lands in Asia, Africa, and the Americas, there were several ways by which the acquisition could be characterized under international law. The first was to consider the land res nullius, the classic case of "discovering" new territory, uninhabited, abandoned, or inhabited by relatively few persons totally bereft of social organization. The second, to the extent that these lands were actually inhabited by organized communities accordingly vested with sovereignty, was via conquest; thus the "just wars" debate that dominated international law during that era. And third, that unless these communities had organized themselves in the form of states resembling those of the European powers, the inhabitants "were merely factually and not legally in occupation of the territory," which therefore could be treated as *res nullius*.[19] This has been rejected, in modern times, by the World Court, which found in the *Western Sahara* case that this region's inhabitants, though merely nomadic tribes, had some forms of legal ties with neighboring nations and that the territory was not *res nullius* at the time of Spanish colonization.[20]

Today, the principal requisite for territorial sovereignty is "effective sovereignty." It is drawn from the famous case *Island of Las Palmas v. Miangas*[21] between two colonial powers, the United States and the Netherlands, over an island between what is now the Philippines and Indonesia. The United States claimed the island by virtue of transfer ("cession") from Spain, effected in the Treaty of Peace after Spain's defeat during the Spanish-American War. The arbitrator in that case found that Spain indeed discovered the island during the sixteenth century but that the Netherlands, and not Spain, had since exercised sovereignty. He then established what is now referred to as the doctrine of "inter-temporal law," that even if international law at the time of discovery recognized mere discovery as basis of title, international law at the time of the dispute required effective occupation. Discovery gave rise merely to inchoate title, and becomes actual title only through the actual and durable taking of possession.

Uti Possidetis *and* Self-Determination: Peace vs. the Rhetoric of Entitlement

While this discourse is conducted in the language of entitlement,[22] the underlying concern in international law remains the avoidance of inter-state recourse to aggression, and the rhetoric of self-determination repeatedly yields to the primacy of the claims of inter-state peace. Decolonization advances national claims of self-determination as regards "political independence," but yields to the prior claims of peace as regards "territorial integrity." That irony manifests itself in the principle of *uti possidetis juris*, "the preservation of the demarcation under the colonial regimes corresponding to each of the colonial entities that was constituted as a State."[23] Post-independence territorial disputes have been decided on this basis.

While *uti possidetis* is conceptually derived from the principle that a change of sovereignty does not affect boundaries,[24] Latin American countries, upon becoming independent, were among the first postcolonial states to adopt it also for the sake of stability.[25] The borders of the new states were based on a "rule of presumed possession by previous Spanish administrations"[26] until the moment of independence. *Uti possidetis* did not freeze borders, but merely assumed that the change of sovereignty by itself did not change the status of the border. But it was "indispensably necessary" in order that the dissolution of the Spanish empire did not leave any land *res nullius*, fair game to a fresh round of territorial disputes, and avoiding the difficulties of establishing precise locations in poorly mapped areas.[27]

When *uti possidetis* collides with self-determination, or stated otherwise, when the claims of peace among nations clashes with the claims of justice by peoples, consistently, the claims of peace have prevailed. The Declaration of Principles of International Law earlier cited, which affirmed in grand terms the right of peoples "freely to determine, without external interference, their political status and to pursue their economic, social and cultural development,"[28] nonetheless concludes with the standard qualifier: "Nothing in the foregoing paragraphs shall be construed as authorizing or encouraging any action which would dismember or impair, totally or in part, the territorial integrity or political unity of sovereign and independent States. . . ."[29]

In a relatively recent territorial dispute in Africa, the World Court affirmed this preference. In *Frontier Dispute (Burkina Faso v. Mali)*, the court recognized that decolonization would otherwise lead to the disintegration of boundaries in former colonies, "especially in the African context," and that—however unsatisfactory "from the ethnic, geographical or administrative standpoint"[30]—these inherited boundaries may not be altered on the considerations of equity or fairness. A separate opinion expressly recognized that inherited frontiers may indeed be altered as a result of "deliberate or implicit decisions" taken by virtue of the right of self-determination.[31]

> At first sight [*uti possidetis*] conflicts outright with . . . the right of peoples to self-determination. In fact, however, the maintenance of the territorial *status quo* in Africa is often seen as the wisest course, to preserve what has been achieved by peoples who have struggled for their independence, and to avoid a disruption which would deprive the continent of the gains achieved by much sacrifice. The essential requirement of stability in order to survive, to develop and gradually to consolidate their independence in all fields, has induced African States judiciously to consent to the respecting of colonial frontiers, and to take account of it in the interpretation of the principle of self-determination of peoples.[32]

The court's function was merely to "indicate the line of the frontier inherited by both States from the colonizers on their accession to independence, . . . not to give indications to guide them in determining their common frontier, but to draw a line, and a precise line."

Uti possidetis therefore exemplifies the disjuncture between two aspects of sovereignty. Its peace-keeping aspect maintains the stability of territorial boundaries, while its decisional aspect upholds the right to self-determination of its occupants. When lines of territory do not match lines of community, under *uti possidetis*, peace trumps justice, and the national community's claim to decide for itself yields to international law's insistence on fixed boundaries as the guarantor of peace. This disjuncture is not wholly undesirable considering the rise of ethnic violence—in the former Yugoslavia, Rwanda, and Indonesia—wherein decisional claims of ethnic identity (and of the ethnic group as a unit for exercising self-determination) translate into claims over land. Indeed, a fresh approach by the World Court opens the door to a less mechanical application of *uti possidetis* which looks instead at the acquiescence of other states and the claimant's vigilance over the territory. Where the *"uti possidetis juris* position [at the time of independence] cannot be satisfactorily ascertained on the basis of colonial titles and *effectivités*," the World Court has instead relied instead on effective possession,[33] which, as explained in a separate opinion, was but a proxy to the real test, namely, the acquiescence of other states and their acceptance of the adverse claim.[34] Significantly, the judgment underscores the law's usual abhorrence of a vacuum and the need to identify a state responsible for territory.

> Territorial sovereignty also connotes obligations and, in the first place, the obligation to maintain and protect it by observing a vigilant conduct towards possible inroads by other States. International law is particularly inimical to prolonged situations of "abstract territorial sovereignty" or of "territorial sovereignty by mere title" when a competing territorial sovereignty claim of another State, accompanied by *effectivités* of that State on the ground, is not challenged as it should be at the relevant times.[35]

Decolonization, at the moment of triumph, has thus turned its back on decisional self-determination, and has embraced the primacy of inter-state peace, and through *uti possidetis* has affirmed inherited borders, however artificial and inconsistent with the way people had actually organized their communal lives. At the same time, *uti possidetis*, hitherto based almost exclusively on the peace-maintaining function of inherited borders, has been recast to recognize that claims to territory give rise not just to power but to international responsibility as well.

"Owning": Its Prerogatives and Burdens

The Secular and Territorial Modern State

In international law, the "modern state" is contrasted to systems of governance associated with feudal rule or religious belief elaborated in what an author has referred to as "primitive legal scholarship."[36] In international law, this modern view is traced to the "venerated" Hugo Grotius and his classic *De Jure Belli ac Pacis Libri Tres* (On the Law of War and Peace) first published in 1625.[37] Accounts vary on the credit to be given to Grotius as the founder of modern international law,[38] but his modernizing influence lay in his secularizing the claims of morality and justice,[39] the then radical view that the sovereign is subject to the rule of law,[40] and in recognizing that *ius gentium* derived as much from the overriding claims of justice as it did from the volition of states.[41]

This contrast is maintained today as regards the territory of newly independent states, where native notions view the ruler as "king of his people, not of his people's lands"[42] and as engaged in the "governance of people rather than place."[43] In Africa, for instance, the precolonial concept of society which persists today is based on personal allegiance to tribe rather than territory, reinforced by the existence of "natural separation zones" like deserts and forests which defined "frontier zones" but not strict territorial boundaries.[44] In former colonies in Asia, the indigenous sense of territory was porous and permeable, especially since fealty was between persons and not on the "unambiguous mapping out of space."[45] In the current dispute over certain islands in the South China Sea, several countries have opposed China's claims based on ancient imperial edicts, contending that the emperor during those days reigned over subjects, not territory, and even then by virtue of suzerain power to collect tribute from vassals, and not by sovereign command.[46]

Significantly, while the modern state is contrasted to feudal rule, its governing concepts are traceable to these feudal origins. The "impermeability of statehood" and the "territorial inviolability" of the state as a "monolithic entity"[47] derive from conceptual baggage which originated from the age of princedoms:[48]

> The excesses and excrescences of "sovereignty" are due in part [to] the provenance of the term and its entry into the international political and legal vocabulary. . . . The law of inter-prince relations, with its roots in religious law, natural law, Roman law and morality, was later subsumed and assimilated into the modern law of nations, but it did not shed its origins and its princely paraphernalia.[49]

Thus, it is explained, the duty of personal loyalty of vassal to lord that lay at the heart of feudalism became the duty of allegiance to states, and likewise, the feudal bond to the land became the territorial scope of state power,[50] translating respectively to *imperium* or authority (general power of government and administration[51]) as well as *dominium* or title (public ownership of property within the state[52]).

"New Natural Resources" and the Global Commons

Grotius, writing "Of Things Which Belong to Men in Common" in the *Law of War and Peace*, comments that "certain things, such as the sea both as a whole and in its principal divisions, cannot become subject to private ownership" for the following reasons: The oceans are so vast that "it suffices for any possible use on the part of all peoples, for drawing water, for fishing, for sailing." Only "a thing which has definite limits" can be occupied, and not "liquids, which cannot be limited or restrained, except they be contained within some other substance" (citing Aristotle). Lakes, ponds, and rivers can therefore be acquired—as well as bays, because they are "shut in by lands" on both sides—but not the open sea, which Grotius held free and open to navigation.[53] International law today, for reasons discussed below, no longer holds these views.

The first set of factors is the emergence of "new natural resources,"[54] examples of which are the geo-stationary orbits of satellites, the seabed and ocean floor, and outer space, which requires new approaches that posit a "trans-spatial mankind . . . beyond flags, colours and banners" and a "trans-temporal mankind" where the present generation is but the manager of the common heritage, accountable to future generations.[55] It was emphasized that these "new" resources emerged not solely due to technological progress, but as much from the rearrangement of social relations.

Earlier, in 1959, the Antarctica Treaty[56] effectively suspended the respective territorial claims of its signatories, who thereby accepted the "limited assertion of full sovereign rights"[57] and subjected themselves to a new regime of joint development. This system of "suspended claims"[58] responded to the inadequacy of the regime of title available under international law, because it was difficult to apply the traditional modes of acquiring territory, especially due to the harshness of Antarctic conditions, the remoteness of areas claimed, the fragility of its ecosystem, and the fact that the contested areas had no indigenous population.[59]

By 1967, this regime was rejected as oligarchic and inadequate for regulating outer space. The Treaty on the Outer Space, the Moon and Other Celestial Bodies,[60] the culmination of a series of UN General Assembly resolutions and thereby "cogent evidence" of rules of international custom, provides that "outer space, including the Moon and other celestial bodies, is not subject to national appropriation by claim of sovereignty"[61] and shall be "the province of all mankind."[62] By virtue of these principles, their exploration and use shall, on one hand, be free to all states without discrimination and on the basis of equality, and on the other, be solely for "the benefit and in the interests of all countries, irrespective of their degree of economic or scientific development."[63]

The 1982 Convention on the Law of the Sea,[64] again uniquely authoritative due to its history of protracted codification and its many signatories, regards the seabed and ocean floor as "the common heritage of mankind,"[65] and thus inalienable,[66] immune from claims of sovereignty by any state,[67] and the rights to which are "vested in mankind as a whole, on whose behalf the Authority [thereby created] shall act."[68]

The convention likewise "unbundles" the resources of the sea that, until a few decades earlier, had been classified either as the territorial sea—that band of waters adjacent to the land mass—or as the high seas, wherein the only principal stakes were, as in Grotius's time, navigation and fishing. These old stakes were broken down to their different aspects, and new stakes were created. As regards the waters, innocent passage is contrasted to military use, surface passage to submarine passage. As regards the airspace, varying rights of overflight are recognized. As regards the resources of the sea, varying degrees of sovereignty are recognized: a territorial sea subject to full sovereignty no different from land; a "contiguous zone" immediately outside territorial waters but not part of the high seas, lying outside sovereign waters but subject to extended jurisdiction for customs, fiscal, immigration, and sanitation law; and a newly recognized "exclusive economic zone" extending a maximum of 200 nautical miles beyond land-based "baselines" but subject to sovereign rights solely for economic purposes. These economic purposes pertain to the "living and non-living" natural resources of the sea, the seabed and its subsoil. New stakes were recognized: civil jurisdiction measures in a "contiguous zone." New stakes in the sea were found. The continental shelf, or the seabed and subsoil extending from the land mass, was not claimed by any state until the 1945 Truman Declaration by the United States.[69] A new use of the seabed was regulated: the laying of submarine cables and pipelines. And entirely new interests were recognized, namely, scientific research and the protection of the environment.[70]

The implications of the "global commons" were developed in a dissenting opinion in the World Court relating to the recent attempt by New Zealand to stop French nuclear tests in the Pacific. In the *1995 Nuclear Tests* case,[71] New Zealand cited a 1974 judgment of the court, wherein the court bound France to its unilateral undertaking to stop the tests, and thus found the case mooted. However, the court majority now declined jurisdiction on the ground that the 1974 judgment dealt with *atmospheric* nuclear tests, and could not be invoked to stop the *underground* tests being conducted by France. While the majority nonetheless recognized the "obligations of States to respect and protect the natural environment," a dissenting opinion emphasized that this obligation entails a broader reading of the court's powers:

> This Court . . . necessarily enjoys a position of special trust and responsibility in relation to the principles of environmental law, especially those relating to what is described in environmental law as the Global Commons. When a matter is brought before it which raises serious environmental issues of global importance, and a *prima facie* case is made out of the possibility of environmental damage, the Court is entitled to take into account the Environmental Impact Assessment principle in determining its preliminary approach.[72]

The court is also entitled to take account of a state's territorial concern about the environment:

> The marine environment belongs to all, and any introduction of radioactive waste into one's territorial waters must necessarily raise the danger of its spread into the

wider ocean spaces that belong to all. . . . If such danger can be shown *prima facie* to exist or be within the bounds of reasonable possibility, the burden shifts on those who claim such action is safe to establish that this is indeed so.[73]

Another dissent traced international instruments which aim to prevent radioactive contamination of the environment, establishing what he saw as the trend toward recognizing a "duty not to cause . . . serious damage which can reasonably be avoided."[74]

Place: Its Relevance and Irrelevance to Human Dignity

The Right to Self-Determination

The right to self-determination has been formulated as a decisional claim ("the right freely to determine," as earlier described in *Nicaragua*[75]), and not as a territorial claim. The Declaration of Principles of International Law, in recognizing the right of self-determination, specified that the right cannot be cited to "dismember or impair the territorial integrity or political unity" of states.[76] Both international human rights covenants recognize the right to self-determination of "peoples" but protect "ethnic, religious or linguistic minorities" only in non-territorial terms, in terms of a right to enjoy a culture, practice a religion, or use a language.[77]

International law, however, has only with resistance recognized the territorial implications of self-determination. One step in that direction is the emerging consensus that self-determination applies, not only to colonized nations, but to minorities within states as well.[78] The above-cited Declaration of Principles itself opens the possibility for secession by oppressed minorities, but in cryptic language, when it describes the states thus protected from dismemberment: "States conducting themselves in compliance with the principle of equal rights and self-determination of peoples as described above and thus possessed of a government representing the whole people belonging to the territory without distinction as to race, creed or colour."[79] Significantly, when the 1949 Geneva Conventions were amended in 1977, their protection was extended to wars of national liberation, "armed conflicts which peoples are fighting against colonial domination and alien occupation and against racist regimes in the exercise of their right of self-determination."[80]

In the *Timor Gap* case, the World Court affirmed that the right to self-determination, being a right *erga omnes* ("against the world"), may be asserted by third parties, thus creating another mode by which self-determination is de-localized. At the time, the territory of East Timor was a non-self-governing territory under the occupation of Indonesia. Portugal challenged before the World Court an agreement allocating maritime claims between Australia and Indonesia as inconsistent with the right of the people of East Timor to self-determination. (These dicta notwithstanding, the court threw out the case just the same, on the ground that it raised issues against a party, Indonesia, over which the court had not acquired jurisdiction.)[81]

Crimes against Humanity: Primacy of Norms, Irrelevance of Place

Territorial sovereignty has been described as having also a particular, procedural aspect, sovereignty "writ small" so to speak, comprising specific legislative and administrative competencies.[82] In this sense, it further serves the functions of "separati[ng] the physical operations of police and security forces" and "separati[ng] jurisdiction," for example, the application and enforcement of its laws.[83] The World Court, for instance, in a case involving the mining of Albanian waters, rejected a state's claim of a right of intervention in order to secure evidence in the territory of another state, the court observing that "[b]etween independent States, respect for territorial sovereignty is an essential foundation of international relations."[84] The leading case on this point is the SS Lotus case,[85] which arose from the collision in the high seas between two vessels, one French, the other Turkish, resulting in the death of Turkish nationals. An officer in the French vessel was arrested for homicide upon reaching port in Turkey. France objected to the application of Turkish jurisdiction for deaths occurring outside its territory. The court affirmed the classic view that "jurisdiction is certainly territorial [and] cannot be exercised by a state outside its territory." (This dictum notwithstanding, the court proceeded to uphold Turkish jurisdiction, holding that since the incident happened on a vessel of Turkish registry, the vessel assimilated to Turkish territory.)

With regard to human rights, however, territoriality has impeded enforcement, because the state where the offense was committed usually possesses the exclusive power to prosecute offenses. Nevertheless, local courts have asserted their power to try human rights abuses committed in foreign countries. The most prominent case is Filartiga v. Peña-Irala,[86] wherein a U.S. federal court held liable a former Paraguayan police chief—detained while visiting the United States—for the torture and murder of a Paraguayan national in Paraguay. The U.S. court assumed jurisdiction under the Alien Tort Statute, which vested jurisdiction where a right protected under international law has been violated, provided the court acquires personal jurisdiction over the defendant. This precedent has since been applied by U.S. courts, including in the series of human rights cases against Ferdinand Marcos and his daughter.[87] More recently, a Spanish court asked the United Kingdom to extradite to Spain, Augusto Pinochet, for human rights violations in Chile, including the murder of Spanish citizens. The British government chose instead to send Pinochet back to Chile, where legal action against the former dictator continues.[88]

In all these cases, courts created under the municipal law of a state exercise extraterritorial jurisdiction over acts committed outside that state and apply human rights norms originating from international law. Place is increasingly made irrelevant to the enforcement of international norms of human dignity.

International Jurisdiction over War Crimes and Crimes against Humanity

International humanitarian law is that branch of law which protects human dignity in situations of armed conflict. Since the Second World War, these rules have been applied by *ad hoc* international tribunals, like the International Military Tribunal at Nuremberg established in 1945,[89] the Tokyo War Crimes Tribunal established in 1948,[90] the International Criminal Tribunal for Former Yugoslavia established in 1993,[91] and the Rwanda War Crimes Tribunal established in 1994,[92] and by domestic courts (as in the United States[93]) as well. These tribunals have considered many of these humanitarian concerns as having the authority of customary law,[94] and to have been largely codified in the 1949 Geneva Conventions[95] and the 1978 Protocols.[96] In July 1998, however, the International Criminal Court, or ICC, was created, a standing tribunal to prosecute "the most serious crimes of concern to the international community as a whole," namely, genocide, crimes against humanity, war crimes, and the crime of aggression.[97] The ICC thus fully de-localizes the prosecution of acts that offend communally held values.

Conclusion

Advances in military, industrial, and informational technology may have obsolesced the vital role of place in contests of power, which have become far too complex for the comparatively primitive game of stealing land. Yet the operational guarantees of peace are still spelled out in the legal language of the territorial state, law-making for international security being too guarded and too stubborn. Between war and peace, between displacing and merely influencing the sovereign, is a continuum too subtle to be regulated by law, which in the end is called upon merely to "draw a line, and a precise line." Ironically, therefore, place—in default of other possibly more accurate elements—now serves as one of the most telling legal indicators of breaches of the rule of nonuse of force and nonintervention.

Two notable exceptions exist. The first pertains to territory as a resource, where the law has been equal to the richness of new inter- and intra-state relationships, and new notions of what is owned, who owns, what it means "to own" in the first place, have been codified into treaties. Vast resources are being taken beyond reach of sovereign claims, and reserved for a vaguely formed international community. The second pertains to international human rights, wherein, on one hand, the sense of home is inseparable from certain group identities and, on the other, constraints of place have long impeded the prosecution of offenders and the protection of victims, and special regimes have been crafted that erode the exclusivity of states' territorial jurisdiction. In this respect, states have yielded territorial jurisdiction but not territory itself.

Peace, resource-sharing, and justice have long been separate agenda in international law, the first assigned primarily to the realm of politics; the second, the realm of economics; and the third, the realm of domestic law. Today the paths converge in the international law discourse on territorial sovereignty, because place is the most rudimentary yet most categorical of markers in the law regulating the use of force; place determines access to resources; and the struggle for dignity is not tied down to place, but is fought and won in the hearts of people.

Notes

1. As declared in the preamble of the UN Convention on the Law of the Sea (1982) and the Agreement Governing the Activities of States on the Moon and Other Celestial Bodies (1979), art. 11.

2. See Robert Jennings and Arthur Watts, eds., *Oppenheim's International Law*, 9th ed. (Harlow, Essex, England: Longman, 1992), vol. 1, 22–52; Louis Henkin, *International Law: Politics and Values* (Dordrecht and Boston: Martinus Nijhoff, 1991), 26–44; Oscar Schachter, *International Law in Theory and Practice* (Dordrecht and Boston: Martinus Nijhoff, 1991), 34–48; Rosalyn Higgins, "International Law and Avoidance, Conflict and Resolution of Rights—General Course on Public International Law," *Recueil des cours* 230 (1991): 9, 42–67; Ian Brownlie, *Principles of Public International Law*, 4th ed. (Oxford: Clarendon Press, 1990), 1–31; James Brierly, *The Law of Nations: An Introduction to the International Law of Peace*, 6th ed. (Oxford: Clarendon Press, 1963), 56–68.

3. Statute of the International Court of Justice, art. 38, par. 1. These sources are:

"(a) international conventions establishing rules expressly recognized by the contesting States;
"(b) international custom, as evidence of a general practice accepted as law;
"(c) the general principles of law recognized by civilized nations; and
"(d) judicial decisions and the teachings of the most highly qualified publicists of various nations."

4. Brierly, *Law of Nations*, 7.

5. Ibid. See also *Oppenheim's International Law*, vol. 2, 563 ("definite portion of the globe which is subject to the sovereignty of a state").

6. *Oppenheim's International Law*, 2:661.

7. *Frontier Dispute (Burkina Faso v. Republic of Mali)*, Judgment, *I.C.J. Reports* (1986), 554; see also *International Legal Materials* (hereafter *I.L.M.*) 25 (1986): 146.

8. UN Charter, art. 2(4) ("All Members shall refrain in their international relations from the threat or use of force against the territorial integrity or political independence of any State. . . .").

9. UN Charter, art. 2(7) (prohibiting the UN from "interven[ing] in matters which are essentially within the domestic jurisdiction of states").

10. Declaration on Principles of International Law Concerning Friendly Relations and Co-operation among States in Accordance with the Charter of the United Nations, UN General Assembly Resolution 2625 (XXV), 24 October 1970, in Ian Brownlie, ed., *Basic Documents in International Law* (Oxford: Clarendon Press, 1995), 36.

11. Ibid.

12. Ibid.

13. Merits, Judgment, 27 June 1986, *I.C.J. Reports* (1986); *I.L.M.* 24 (1985): 59 (hereafter, *Nicaragua*).

14. *Nicaragua*, p. 128.

15. Ibid.

16. Ibid., 111.

17. Ibid., 133.

18. Brownlie, *Principles*, 10.

19. Malcom Shaw, *Title to Territory in Africa: International Legal Issues* (Oxford: Clarendon Press, 1986), 31–32.

20. *Western Sahara*, I.C.J. Advisory Opinion; *I.L.M.* 14 (1975): 1355.

21. R.I.A.A. 2 (1928): 841. See also *Minquiers and Ecrehos (France v. United Kingdom)*, *I.C.J. Reports* (1953), 47.

22. Ian Brownlie, *Boundary Problems and the Formation of New States* (Hull, U.K.: Hull University Press, 1996), 3 (sovereignty "implement[s] the notion of entitlement").

23. Ibid., 5.

24. *Temple of Preah Vihear Case (Cambodia v. Thailand)*, *I.C.J. Reports* (1962), 6.

25. *Land, Island and Maritime Frontier Dispute (El Salvador v. Honduras: Nicaragua Intervening)* (hereafter *El Salvador v. Honduras*), Judgment of 11 September 1992, *I.C.J. Reports* (1992), 351; *I.L.M.* 29 (1990): 1345. See also *Oppenheim's International Law*, 669.

26. Brownlie, *Boundary Problems*, 5.

27. Ibid., 6. See also *Burkina Faso v. Mali*, Judgment, *I.C.J. Reports* (1986), Separate Opinion by Judge Luchaire, 652–54.

28. See also common article 1 to the International Covenant on Economic, Social, and Cultural Rights, No. 14531, 993 *United Nations Treaty Series* (hereafter *U.N.T.S.*) 3 (1976), and the International Covenant on Civil and Political Rights, No. 14668, 999 *U.N.T.S.* 171 (1976).

29. Declaration of Principles of International Law, in Brownlie, *Basic Documents*, 36. Subsequent text is reproduced below in section on "Place: Its Relevance and Irrelevance to Human Dignity."

30. *Frontier Dispute (Burkina Faso v. Republic of Mali)*, Judgment, *I.C.J. Reports* (1986), 554.

31. Ibid., 652–54.

32. Ibid., 566–67.

33. *El Salvador v. Honduras*, I.C.J. *Reports* (1992), 351.

34. Ibid., 579.

35. Ibid. In the *Case Concerning the Territorial Dispute (Libyan Arab Jamahiriya v. Chad)*, I.L.M. 33 (1994): 571, Libya based its claim on the coalescence of rights and titles originally held by the indigenous inhabitants and successive rulers, whereas Chad invoked a 1955 treaty between France and Libya, relying on French *effectivités*. The World Court held that the treaty was controlling.

36. David Kennedy, "Primitive Legal Scholarship," *Harvard International Law Journal* 27:1 (Winter 1986): 1.

37. James Brown Scott, intro. to Hugo Grotius, *Law of War and Peace*, trans. Francis Kelsey (Washington, D.C.: Carnegie Endowment for International Peace, 1925).

38. See John Dunn and Ian Harris, eds., *Grotius*, 2 vols. (hereafter Grotius Collection) (Washington: Carnegie Endowment for International Peace, 1997). But see Brierly, *Law of Nations*, citing the work of earlier authors, possible precursors to ideas today attributed to Grotius; and Kennedy, "Primitive Legal Scholarship," who includes Grotius in his list of "primitive legal scholars" but recognizes the modern ideas Grotius presented in "primitive" language.

39. Roscoe Pound, "Grotius in the Science of Law," in Grotius Collection, vol. 1, p. 1 (originally published in the *American Journal of International Law* 19 [1925]: 685).

40. Hersch Lauterpacht, "The Grotian Tradition in International Law," in Grotius Collection, vol. 1, p. 396 (originally published in the *British Yearbook of International Law* [1946]).

41. Kennedy, "Primitive Legal Scholarship," 27.

42. L. Ali Khan, *The Extinction of Nation-States: A World without Borders* (The Hague and Boston: Kluwer Law International, 1996), 62. See also Connie McNeely, *Constructing the Nation-State: International Organizations and Prescriptive Action* (Westport, Conn.: Greenwood, 1995), 4.

43. Carston, "Borders, Boundaries, Tradition and States in the Malaysian Periphery," in *Border Identities: Nation and State at International Frontiers*, ed. Thomas Wilson and Hastings Donnan (Cambridge: Cambridge University Press, 1998), 8–9.

44. Shaw, *Title to Territory in Africa*, 1–2, 27.

45. Carston, "Borders, Boundaries," 218.

46. Peter Kien-hong Yu, *A Study of the Pratas, Macclesfield Bank, Paracels, and Spratlys in the South China Sea* (Taipei: Tzeng Brothers, 1988); Daniel Dzurek, *The Spratly Islands Dispute: Who's On First?* (Durham, U.K.: International Borders Research, 1996); Mark Valencia, *China and South China Sea Disputes: Conflicting Claims and Potential Solutions in the South China Sea* (Oxford: Oxford University Press, 1995).

47. Brierly, *Law of Nations*, 1–2.

48. Henkin, *Politics and Values*, 12.

49. Ibid., 9.

50. Ibid., 1–2.

51. Brownlie, *Principles*, 109.

52. Ibid., 109.

53. Grotius, *Law of War and Peace*, 186–91, 210–11.

54. Rene-Jean Dupuy, ed., *The Settlement of Disputes on the New Natural Resources* (The Hague: The Hague Academy of International Law, 1982).

55. Ibid., 479.

56. The Antarctic Treaty (1 December 1959); Christopher Joyner and Sudhir Chopra, eds., *The Antarctica Legal Regime* (Dordrecht and Boston: Martinus Nijhoff, 1988), esp. Christopher Joyner, "The Antarctica Legal Regime: An Introduction," p. 6, and Howard Taubenfeld, "The Antarctica and Outer Space: An Analogy in Retrospect," p. 269; Donald Rothwell, *The Polar Regions and the Development of International Law* (Cambridge: Cambridge University Press, 1996); Emilio Sahurie, *The International Law of Antarctica* (Dordrecht and Boston: Martinus Nijhoff, 1992); Peter Beck, *Who Owns Antarctica? Governing and Managing the Last Continent* (Durham, U.K.: International Borders Research Unit, 1994).

57. Rothwell, *Polar Regions*, 445, citing article IV of the treaty.

58. Gerard Mangone, "Unrecognized Boundaries in the Antarctica Case," in *National and International Boundaries* (Thessaloniki: Institute of International Public Law and International Relations of Thessaloniki, 1985), 145.

59. Rothwell, *Polar Regions*, 1–9.

60. Treaty on Principles Governing the Activities of States in the Exploration and Use of Outer Space, including the Moon and Other Celestial Bodies, *I.L.M.* 6 (1967): 386; Brownlie, *Basic Documents*, 209–10.

61. Outer Space Treaty, art. 2.

62. Ibid., art. 1.

63. Ibid.

64. UN Convention on the Law of the Sea, in Brownlie, *Basic Documents*, 129.

65. Ibid., art. 136.

66. Ibid., art. 137(2).

67. Ibid., arts. 1 and 137(1).

68. Ibid., art. 137(2).

69. Truman Declaration, Proclamation on the Continental Shelf of 1945, 10 Fed. Reg. 12,303, 12,304 (1945).

70. UN Convention on the Law of the Sea, in Brownlie, *Basic Documents*, 129–239.

71. *Request for an Examination of the Situation in Accordance with Paragraph 63 of the Court's Judgment of 20 December 1974 in the Nuclear Tests Case (New Zealand v. France)*, *I.C.J. Reports* (1995) (hereafter *1995 Nuclear Tests*), 288, in relation to *Nuclear Tests Case (Australia v. France; New Zealand v. France)*, *I.C.J. Reports* (1974), 457.

72. Dissenting Opinion of Judge Weeramantry, *1995 Nuclear Tests*.

73. Ibid.

74. Dissenting Opinion of Judge Koroma, *1995 Nuclear Tests*.

75. *Nicaragua*, p. 133.

76. Declaration of Principles of International Law, in Brownlie, *Basic Documents*, 36.

77. International Covenant on Civil and Political Rights, art. 27 ("In those States in which ethnic, religious or linguistic minorities exist, persons belonging to such minorities shall [have] the right . . . to enjoy their own culture, to profess and practise

their own religion, or to use their own language."). Cf. International Covenant on Economic, Social, and Cultural Rights, art. 1.

78. Brownlie, *Boundary Problems*, 10–11.

79. Declaration of Principles of International Law, in Brownlie, *Basic Documents*, 36.

80. Protocol Additional to the Geneva Conventions of 12 August 1949, and relating to the Protection of Victims of International Armed Conflicts (Protocol I), No. 17512, 1125 *U.N.T.S.* 3, art. 1(4).

81. *Case Concerning East Timor (Portugal v. Australia)*, Judgment, *I.C.J. Reports* (1995), 90; *I.L.M.* 34 (1995): 1581.

82. Brownlie, *Principles*, 108.

83. Brownlie, *Boundary Problems*.

84. *Corfu Channel Case (United Kingdom v. Albania)*, Merits, Judgment, *I.C.J. Reports* (1949), 34.

85. *SS Lotus Case (France v. Turkey)*, Permanent Court of International Justice, Series A, No. 10 (1927).

86. 630 F.2d 876 (2d Cir. 1980) (Kaufman, J.). See also Anne-Marie Burley, "The Alien Tort Statute and the Judiciary Act of 1789: A Badge of Honor," *American Journal of International Law* 83 (July 1989): 461–93.

87. *Trajano v. Imee Marcos-Manotoc*, Nos. 86-2448, 86-15039, 1989 WL 76894, at 1 (9th Cir. July 10, 1989); *In re Estate of Ferdinand E. Marcos*, United States: Court of Appeals for the Ninth Circuit Opinion (Alien Tort Statute; extraterritorial jurisdiction over torture), *I.L.M.* 32 (1993): 106. See also Ralph Steinhardt, "Fulfilling the Promise of Filartiga: Litigating Human Rights Claims against the Estate of Ferdinand Marcos," *Yale Journal of International Law* 20 (Winter 1995): 65–103.

88. Bartle and the Commissioner of Police for the Metropolis and Others (Appellants), *Ex Parte* Pinochet (Respondent) (On Appeal From a Divisional Court of the Queen's Bench Division); Evans and another and the Commissioner of Police for the Metropolis and Others (Appellants), *Ex Parte* Pinochet (Respondent) (On Appeal from a Divisional Court of the Queen's Bench Division); Decision of 25 November 1998, denying Pinochet's claim of immunity; Decision of 15 January 1999 (setting aside the decision of 25 November 1998); Decision of 24 March 1999 (affirming the 25 November 1998 decision, but only for torture and conspiracy to torture committed after 8 December 1988, when the Convention against Torture took effect in the United Kingdom, and thereby allowing the extradition proceedings to proceed), at *http://www.publications.parliament.uk/pa/ld199899/ldjudgmt/jd990324/pino1.htm*; *The Kingdom of Spain v. Augusto Pinochet Ugarte*, Magistrates' Court, Judgment of 8 October 1999 (allowing the secretary of state to extradite Pinochet), at *http://www.open.gov.uk/lcd/magist/pinochet.htm*.

89. Charter of the International Military Tribunal (6 October 1945), annexed to the Agreement for the Prosecution and Punishment of Major War Criminals of the European Axis (8 August 1945), 82 *U.N.T.S.* 279 (London Agreement).

90. International Military Tribunal for the Far East, Judgment (1 November 1948), implementing the Cairo Declaration (1 December 1943), the Declaration of Potsdam (26 July 1945), the Instrument of Surrender (2 September 1945), and the Moscow Conference (26 December 1945).

91. Statute of the International Tribunal for the Prosecution of Persons Responsible for Serious Violations of International Humanitarian Law Committed in the Territory of the Former Yugoslavia since 1991, annexed to the Report of the Secretary-General Pursuant to Paragraph 2 of Security Council Resolution 808 (1993).

92. UN Security Council Resolution 955, UN Doc. S/RES/955 (1994), Statute of the International Tribunal for Rwanda, establishing the International Criminal Tribunal for the Prosecution of Persons Responsible for Genocide and Other Serious Violations of International Humanitarian Law Committed in the Territory of Rwanda and Rwandan citizens responsible for genocide and other such violations committed in the territory of neighbouring States, between 1 January 1994 and 31 December 1994.

93. *Yamashita v. Styer*, 327 U.S. 757 (4 February 1946); see also *Hirota v. MacArthur*, 338 U.S. 197 (20 December 1948).

94. See, respectively, the following: Judgment, The Trial of Major War Criminals: Proceedings of the International Military Tribunal-Nuremberg (London: His Majesty's Stationery Office, 1950), pt. 22; Judgment, International Military Tribunal for the Far East, Judgment (1 November 1948), in *The Tokyo War Crimes Tribunal*, vol. 20, ed. R. John Pritchard and Sonia Zaide (New York: Garland Publishing, 1981), 48; and *The Prosecutor v. Tadic*, IT-94-1-AR72 (2 October 1995).

95. No. 970, 75 *U.N.T.S.* 31 (1950).

96. Protocol I, *supra*, n. 79; and Protocol Additional to the Geneva Conventions of 12 August 1949, and relating to the protection of victims of non-international armed conflict (Protocol II), No. 17513, 1125 *U.N.T.S.* 609 (1977).

97. Rome Statute of the International Criminal Court, UN Doc. A/CONF.83.9 (17 July 1998).

Nine

Islamic Perspectives on Territorial Boundaries and Autonomy

M . R A Q U I B U Z   Z A M A N

AT THIS TIME in history, when the world is divided into nation-states with too few virgin tracts of land to be claimed, it seems the task of defining territorial boundaries should be quite an easy one. However, the task becomes somewhat arduous when we try to approach it in terms of ethical perspectives that have religious sanctions. After all, if ethics is "the study of the right and the good, i.e., right conduct in the affairs of human life and the pursuit of the good life,"[1] then the question arises whether or not the current territorial boundaries that determine the position of the nation-states are all ethical. This chapter will attempt to define territorial boundaries and their ethical implications from Islamic points of view. Since the principal focus of the exposition in this chapter is on Islamic legal traditions, a brief introduction to the various schools of jurisprudence in Islam is imperative.

The two basic sources of Islamic thought and legal system are the divine revelation, the Qur'an, and the *sunna* (or the way of life) of the prophet Muhammad consisting of what he said, did, advised, and agreed to,[2] as documented by later generations in the *hadith* literature. From these two sources, jurists deduced rules and injunctions through various interpretive processes, including *qiyas* (analogical reasoning based on Qur'an and *hadith*), *ijtihad* (systematic original thinking),[3] *ijma'* (consensus among jurists), and *ra'y* (reasoning based on equity or public welfare).[4] The fruit of these early jurists' efforts was the emergence by the end of the ninth century of four schools of jurisprudence within the majority Sunni tradition, the Hanafi, Maliki, Shafi'i, and Hanbali.

Beyond the ninth century, no other school of law was able to gain a wide following within Sunni Islam. The Shi'i legal tradition evolved independently of developments in Sunni Islam, but this school—which itself was divided into several schools—always remained a distinctly minority tradition. We will, therefore, focus on Sunni thought in this chapter, although it should be mentioned that the differences between Sunni and Shi'i lawyers on most topics are not great.

Why the focus on law—and medieval law at that—in a chapter discussing Islamic ethical approaches to questions of boundaries? The reason is that the fruits of the early lawyers' labors, the body of Islamic law (*fiqh*), is synonymous in the view of many contemporary Muslims with *shari'a*, which represents the divine will revealed to the Prophet as guidance for all dimensions of human life. Thus, "Law in the Islamic sense is a set of value-oriented guidelines directed toward the divine purpose of Allah. Islamic law, therefore, is primarily normative rather than prescriptive and is designed for moral education as well as for legal enforcement."[5]

Of course, various reformist movements have arisen throughout Islamic history, and beginning in the nineteenth century, modernist intellectuals sought to separate *fiqh* from *shari'a*, and thus open the door to legal innovation based upon fresh readings of the ethical imperatives of the Qur'an and *sunna*. Yet, as the continuing controversies in Muslim states on the meaning and status of *shari'a* in public life demonstrate, *fiqh* still remains for many Muslims intrinsically related to the *shari'a* and thus provides a normative standard for what constitutes "genuine" Islam. We will examine these issues further as we proceed with our interpretation of Islamic perspectives on autonomy and territorial boundaries.

Defining Boundaries

The term *boundary* refers to any or all of the following: "border," "limit," "bound," "confine," "end," and "frontier." Territorial boundary, therefore, defines the limit of the area in which individuals, groups, or societies exercise rights and/or controls. The "boundary" demarcates one property from another and, thus, makes it possible for the owner or the renter (in some cases, manager or operator) to enjoy the fruits of the products and services, or the sanctity the boundary provides.

Human beings need order and structure to nurture fully all of their potentials. The search for order is the reason we enact laws, set boundaries, and seek religion. In the absence of territorial boundaries we would have chaos and injustice. The struggle for mere survival would take all of our energies and resources. It is difficult to imagine what the nature of human civilization would have been were there no order or structure in socioeconomic relations between various groups of people. The need for redemarcation of agricultural plots washed away by the frequent floods in the Nile delta apparently prompted the Egyptians, as early as 2000 B.C., to develop what came to be known later (at around 550 B.C.) as Pythagorean geometry.[6] From the records of history we find that not only economic growth but also cultural and intellectual development flourishes where there exists a healthy respect for law and order and where there is an atmosphere that is conducive to the pursuit of

personal growth and fulfillment. The existence of territorial boundaries provides the security that is needed to promote economic and social progress by
making it possible for individuals to reap the benefits of their personal efforts
and initiatives.

Islam emphasizes the sanctity of personal property. Prophet Muhammad, in
his farewell pilgrimage, declared to the gathering: "O men, your lives and your
property shall be as inviolate as this holy day and holy month. Remember that
you will indeed meet your Lord, and that He will indeed reckon your deeds."[7]
At the same time, Islam reminds its adherents that with the right to own
personal property comes the responsibility to see that this right is not misused.
The Qur'an (17:26–27) implores on all, "Squander not thy wealth in wanton-
ness and extravagance. Lo! The squanderers were ever brothers of the devil,
and the devil was ever an ingrate to the Lord."[8] The Qur'an further emphasizes
that those who live around the property—the deserving kinsmen, the needy,
the wayfarer, and the orphan—all have rights to be assisted by the property
holder, since it is God who provides sustenance in abundance for whom He
pleases, and He provides in a just manner (17:28–30).

Islam puts responsibility not only on individuals to utilize their resources
prudently, but also on communities to assure that the needs of all are attended
to in a balanced manner.[9] Communal property rights, as manifested by territorial boundaries, allow communities free choice as to the disposal of their property, but societies also bear responsibilities to the needy similar to those indicated by the above Qur'anic verses.

Ownership

Islam emphasizes individual initiative in property ownership and manage-
ment, but with clear reminders, as found in numerous Qur'anic verses, that:
"To God belongs all that is in the heavens and on earth" (2:284; see also
3:180, 4:126, 48:7, 53:25, 63:7).[10]

Human beings, as God's vicegerent on earth, are entitled to own and use
God-given resources for their legitimate needs. The uniqueness and individuality of man is such that inequality in the accumulation of wealth and resources is inevitable.[11] "And it is He who hath made you His representatives
on the Earth, and hath raised some of you above others by various grades, that
He may test you by His gifts" (6:165). Whatever degree of wealth individuals
possess, God reminds them: "And know you that your possessions and your
progeny are but a trial; and that it is God with whom lies your highest reward"
(8:28). Further, "And do not eat up your property among yourselves for vani-
ties, nor use it as bait for the judges, with intent that you may eat up wrong-
fully and knowingly a little of (other) people's property" (2:188).

While encouraging Muslims to own and operate properties to meet their earthly needs, Islam urges them to share the fruits of their labor and wealth with the poor and the needy and for the common good.[12] Muslims who have *nisab* (income adequate for an acceptable standard of living) must pay the obligatory charitable levy, called *zakat*, to purify their wealth. They are also advised repeatedly to give to charities voluntarily.[13]

Ownership rights imply the presence of territorial boundaries. The question is, how does one acquire ownership of landed property?

At the outset of the Islamic state in Medina, Prophet Muhammad set the principles of property ownership and rights on the following basic principles: (1) All land belongs to God, and as such, all humans, as creatures of God, have a right to use it for their personal and societal benefit; (2) already occupied and tilled land belongs to its rightful owner, and the owner's rights to sell or transfer or give it in trust are to be recognized and protected by the state. Any fraudulent transaction or forced occupation is to be rendered null and void by the authority.[14]

As the Islamic state expanded over the following centuries beyond Medina to distant lands, the rules were expanded and sometimes adjusted, but with the same underlying principle of protecting property rights. According to the schools of Islamic jurisprudence, ownership can be achieved in a number of ways:[15]

> On *payment of land tax*, kharaj, *to the* imam, *the Islamic state's ruler*. The laws of *kharaj* were formulated in response to the conquest of large amounts of territory by the early Muslim armies. At the time of the conquest, a payment of *kharaj* levy confirmed the right of the tiller to the land. The Islamic laws prevented the development of serfs by transforming land into a commodity and the payment of *kharaj* tax by the peasant cultivators as the proof of their land ownership. Although it originated as a tax on non-Muslim landholders, *kharaj* continued to be assessed even after the landholder converted to Islam or the property was sold to a Muslim. In addition, Muslims were assessed the *'ushr*, a levy of one-tenth the value of the produce on the land.
>
> *Through the allocation or assignment* (iqta') *of wasteland* (mawat) *by the leader*.[16] Lands assigned in this way then become subject to the *kharaj* and/or *'ushr* levies. Uninhabited and unoccupied land is open to reclamation by any person. Whatever a person can till or build on, within certain reasonable limits, would be deemed as that person's property. Previously occupied but now abandoned (*'adi*) land can be taken or allotted to anyone who wants to resettle there. If resettled land is not used for three years or more by the present owner/occupier, it is deemed "abandoned" and can be reclaimed by another settler. When the state has granted land from its holdings (land that fell into the state coffers as a result of conquest or through bequests, etc.) on certain conditions or for a limited period, the ownership reverts back to the state, in case the conditions have not been met or at the expiration of the term.

On the other hand, the caliphs as well as local governors could permanently allocate public lands to those who desired to cultivate or settle on them. Once properly occupied or granted by the authority, the property would legally belong to the owner, and could not be reclaimed by the administration. Land designated for "public" use (such as a prairie, pond, or salt mine) could never become "personal" property, but must be preserved for unrestricted public use.

Through various types of gifts, such as (a) donation, (b) bequest, or (c) inheritance. Ownership of landed property can be transformed into a trust, or *waqf*, for charitable purposes.[17] All legal experts agree that the condition for such an endowment is that it be established in perpetuity, so long as the original intent or benefit of the endowment remains. For example, if a piece of land is dedicated to the construction of a mosque, it cannot be claimed as the property of the original owner or his/her heirs, or sold or transferred to other owners, so long as the mosque continues to function as a place of worship. The jurists are divided, however, on what happens to the *waqf* once the property falls into disuse. Some maintain that in this event it should revert to the original owner or his/her heirs. Others argue that the establishment of a *waqf* alienates the property rights of the original owner forever, and therefore unused endowments revert to the possession of the state. These rulings generally applied to both Muslims and non-Muslims.

Through various channels of exchange for a commodity, such as (a) sale or (b) preemption (shuf'a). Because of the sanctity of personal territorial boundaries guaranteed by Islam, there are some limitations on transfers of properties that have common borders and shareholders. The principle of *shuf'a*, or preemption, needs to be addressed here briefly to demonstrate how the sanctity of territorial boundaries puts some limit on the owner's right to dispose of property as he or she pleases. Under the law of preemption it is the right of a third party, the preemptor, to step in when a contract is made between the seller of the property (a Muslim) and the purchaser (a Muslim or a non-Muslim), and to claim the place of the buyer and take possession of the property according to the terms and conditions of the sales contract.[18] Since it is the Islamic laws of inheritance which tend to create fragmentation of landed property by requiring distribution of property among all heirs, the laws of preemption tend to mitigate the situation by allowing the joint owners (co-sharers) to claim property being sold to outsiders. The preemptory rights can be used to prevent inconveniences that an outsider might cause to the co-sharer or to keep away a disagreeable neighbor.[19]

In the majority of the Sunni schools of law, the right of preemption can be claimed by: (1) a co-owner, or a partner of the property sold; (2) "a participator in the immunities and appendages of the property, such as the right to water and roads or a common access";[20] (3) a neighbor or owner of the adjoining property (confined to adjoining houses, gardens, and small tracts of land, but not large landholdings). According to the Shafi'i school and in Shi'i law, however, the preemptory right is limited to co-sharers when their number is only two. "It does not recognize the right on the ground of vicinage or on the ground of participation in appendages."[21] In all schools the right of preemption exists only for immovable property such as land, buildings, or trees. [22]

To summarize, ownership of landed property is confirmed by the payment of tax (*kharaj* and/or '*ushr*), which entitles the owner to dispose of his/her property through various channels of transfer discussed above, including setting up of *awqaf* (plural of *waqf*). Ownership entails the creation of territorial boundaries that makes it possible to transform landed property into a commodity and subject it to the various methods of exchange. The state in a Muslim country does not own all the land; it only owns the land that does not belong to anyone else. The state, however, may assert its rights to own and control land and other natural resources deemed necessary for the welfare and progress of the general public. Finally, it is important to emphasize that under Islamic law, state property is not the property of the *imam*. His personal property is distinct and must be acquired in the same manner as that of any other person.

For more than a millennium, Muslim rulers in various parts of the world essentially followed these basic principles, as evinced in the elaborate revenue records they maintained. When the countries were colonized during the eighteenth and nineteenth centuries, the colonial authorities sometimes modified these laws according to European codes, but in general they allowed traditional Islamic patterns of land ownership to remain in place under new administration. Modern Muslim states by and large maintained this colonial legacy while in some cases attempting various redistribution schemes for the sake of economic development and social welfare.

Distribution

In an Islamic state, not all resources can be owned individually. The society collectively (i.e., states in modern times) is responsible for maintaining and managing environmental (natural) resources such as water, minerals, and forests for the collective good of all.[23] All members of the society who are living in peace in a Muslim state are entitled to the benefits to be derived from these natural resources. The state is responsible for ensuring the distribution of resources by developing infrastructure to promote economic activities. Creation and distribution of public goods are part of the obligatory duties of the state (*furud kifaya*). It is also incumbent upon the state to ensure adequate living spaces with defined boundaries for all of its citizens, irrespective of their diversity in faith and social characteristics. While the Muslims are prohibited from certain products and services (alcohol, pork, intoxicants, gambling, etc.), the non-Muslims may be permitted to use them under stipulated conditions. As the representative of the society, the state has the right and obligation to promote welfare for all.

Certain aspects of the Islamic penal code which appear overly harsh may in fact be understood only in the context of the full social welfare system that the religion enjoins. The Qur'an states on the subject of stealing, for example: "Now as for the man who steals and the woman who steals, cut off the hand of either of them in requital for what they have wrought, as a deterrent ordained by God" (5:38). Yet this punishment is grounded in "the fundamental principle of Islamic law that no duty (*taklif*) is ever imposed on man without his being granted a corresponding right (*haqq*); and the term 'duty' also comprises in this context, liability to punishment."[24] Thus, before anyone's hand can be cut off, the Islamic state must ensure that every citizen, Muslim as well as non-Muslim, has economic, social, and political protection and security. Thus, the nation's economic resources must be shared in such a way that everyone is able to meet his or her basic needs. If, after a basic minimum standard of living is met, someone steals to accumulate wealth, only then may the prescribed punishment even be considered, after due attention is given to mitigating circumstances. Thus, we see that the second caliph, 'Umar b. al-Khattab, waived the punishment during a period of famine.

From the opinions of jurists it is clear that "the cutting-off of a hand in punishment for theft is applicable only within the context of an already existing, fully functioning social security scheme, and in no other circumstances."[25] Establishment of a functional social security system for all citizens is an obligatory duty of the Islamic state. This can be done only when there is distributive justice in the state. Islam provides specific means for this in a number of ways. First, the role of the state in the creation and distribution of public goods has already been mentioned above. Second, the state is responsible for the collection of *zakat* from the Muslims who possess wealth above a standard minimum and for distribution of the proceeds to specific categories of people—the first two of which are the indigent and the needy—Muslims as well as non-Muslims. It is true that the various schools of Islamic *fiqh* interpret differently what exactly is to be collected and distributed by the state (e.g., how to differentiate between apparent and non-apparent wealth, *amwal zahira* and *amwal batina*). But there is no doubt that the Muslims must pay *zakat* on their wealth as part of the five pillars of Islam. The non-Muslims do not pay *zakat* because it is a religious duty for the Muslims only. Yet the indigent and the needy among them are entitled to share the benefits.

Ironically, many governments in Muslim states today, especially the oil-rich countries of the Middle East, do not make serious attempts to collect *zakat* because they either feel *zakat* proceeds are not needed to carry out some rudimentary charitable work for the benefit of the disadvantaged, or do not think it is worth the bother for them. It took a concerted effort over a number of years in the early 1980s to convince the Kingdom of Saudi Arabia not to burn the hundreds of thousands of cattle slaughtered during the annual pilgrimage (*hajj*), but to process them and distribute the meat among the poor outside Saudi Arabia. Similarly, such an oil-rich country could collect *zakat* from its citizens for distribution of proceeds to the poor Muslim countries if it had the desire to do so.[26] But Saudi officials have resisted acknowledging any international distributive justice claims on their vast oil wealth, preferring to operate within the framework of "foreign aid," rather than Islamic *zakat*. The Saudi state is one of the largest foreign aid donors in the world, as determined by percentage of GNP. Yet whether such aid serves the poorest and neediest Muslims is open to question, because under the foreign aid regime, most of the wealth goes into the hands of corrupt government officials in recipient states. The average wealthy citizen, motivated by a sense of pious obligation to the disadvantaged, is often more effective in promoting social welfare in poorer countries.

The Islamic system contains a number of other distributive measures aimed at maximizing the circulation of wealth. Apart from collecting *zakat*, the Muslim state is entitled to assess other types of taxes for social welfare purposes. *Zakat* is not strictly speaking a government "tax"—it is a religious levy to bring distributive justice only.[27] The Qur'an exhorts Muslims repeatedly to give as much as feasible in voluntary charities (*sadaqa*) above the *zakat* due in order to attain piety. Kind words or deeds to benefit others are also considered as charities. The goal is to make the life of the members of the society in general a fair and pleasant one, because in the absence of that, human beings cannot achieve spiritual well being.

The state is also obligated to undertake other measures aimed at promoting distributive justice. Prevention of fraud and illegal transactions are major responsibilities of the state, since only in their absence can economic justice and fair play be realized. For this, medieval Islamic civilization introduced the institution of *hisba* and made it the responsibility of a government functionary, the *muhtasib*, to ensure ethical and spiritual conduct by the citizens. One of the *muhtasib's* most important duties was to prevent usurious transactions (*riba*) in the marketplace. Usury brings undue economic hardships to the poorest borrower, and justice requires its absence from the economic scene.

Finally, Islamic laws of inheritance—one of the most complicated aspects of the *shari'a*—have the purpose of widely disseminating wealth among the deceased's heirs. All heirs, male and female, have a stake in the inheritance according to formulae intended to meet the various needs and responsibilities of family members.

Diversity and Autonomy

Islam emphasizes the unity of human origin, as can be seen from the following Qur'anic verse: "O mankind! We created you from a single (pair) of a male and a female, and made you into nations and tribes, that you may know each other (not that you may despise each other). Verily the most honored of you in the sight of God is he who is the most righteous of you. And God has full knowledge and is well acquainted with all things" (49:13).

Islam refers to *umma*, the Muslim community, in all deliberations about political entities. All Muslims, regardless of their place of origin or abode, language, and ethnicity, are part of the same *umma*. National boundaries, unlike personal territorial boundaries, are anathema to Islam. "Territorial nationalism, with its emphasis on what is called national characteristics,"[28] is of Christian-European origin and, as I discuss below, still enjoys only limited support among Muslim thinkers.

The maintenance of the unity of the *umma* has been a moral concern of Muslim thinkers throughout Islamic history, even after in reality the Islamic world fragmented into many separate political units. When Abu Bakr, the first caliph, declared war against rebel bedouin tribes in Arabia, the Muslim elites all sided with him so that the central authority of *khalifa* (caliph) could be enforced. The internal strife following the murder of the third caliph 'Uthman and the succession of 'Ali produced the most serious divisions within the early Islamic community. These conflicts brought the Umayyad dynasty to power, which then managed to maintain the unity and central authority of the Muslim state, keeping the *umma* together for another century.[29]

The perceived necessity to maintain the unity of the *umma*, as enjoined by the Qur'an (see esp. 3:103–5), prompted the majority of Muslim jurists to support the office of the *khalifa*, despite the character and disposition of its incumbent, so long as he proclaimed in public loyalty and submission to the *shari'a*. To classical political theorists like Abu Yusuf (d. 798), al-Baghdadi (d. 1037), al-Mawardi (d. 1058), and Abu Ya'la (d. 1065), the communal unity of the *umma* could only be possible under political and legal unity. In order to preserve this unity, they were willing to compromise with the political realities of their time, which often included giving allegiance to less than ideal rulers.[30] Nevertheless, many of the jurists played the role of the loyal opposition to corrupt caliphs.

The Abbasid revolt against the Umayyads in the middle of the eighth century ushered in a new period of increasing political fragmentation of the Islamic empire. The jurists were forced to reconcile the power struggle between the center and the breakaway areas on the periphery of the Islamic empire with the ideal of the unified caliphate. Grudgingly, some approved "the existence of more than one legitimate independent political unit and authority. Some jurists approved of this when the units were far apart geographically and thus difficult to run under a single administration. The jurists no longer paid much attention to the question of the office of the *khalifah* when it could no longer be preserved."[31]

The tension between the political authority to govern and the legal authority to legislate that evolved from the dynastic periods of Islam (from the Umayyad period onward) continued throughout the medieval period. Further development of the *shari'a* was seriously limited when Abbasid jurists curtailed legal innovation in order to prevent political meddling from the rulers. As a result, the *shari'a* became less and less relevant to Muslim practice, especially in administrative or constitutional matters. Medieval works dating back to the eleventh century were still read as representative of the Islamic ideal even though Muslim realities had long since diverged from it. Al-Mawardi's theory of the state, for example, dominated Islamic political thinking for centuries, up to the time of the gradual encroachment of Western colonial powers in Muslim lands during the eighteenth and nineteenth centuries.

It fell upon Jamal al-Din al-Afghani (d. 1897) to issue clarion calls to all Muslims to wake up and face the dangers of Western expansionism. He urged Muslims to go back to the study of science and reasoning and adapt medieval Islamic concepts to meet the needs of modern times. His call for the political unification of the Muslim world, known as pan-Islamism, revived the concept of one *umma*. While he understood the importance of constitutional governments as the bulwark against Western power and intrigues and, hence, the necessary growth of national states, he abhorred nationalism that was narrowly based on race, language, or culture, and consequently, transformed into secular states. While he realized that modern political developments would lead to nation-states, he wanted to keep the door open for the eventual and progressive unity of the Muslim *umma*. His ideas were mirrored in the works of other contemporary Muslim intellectuals, such as Sayyid Ahmad Khan of India (d. 1898) and Muhammad 'Abduh of Egypt (d. 1905). The political thought of these modernists still reverberates throughout the Muslim world. Support for purely secular national states among Muslim thinkers is wanting. They are still reeling from the secularization of Turkey by Mustafa Kemal Ataturk.[32]

As in previous centuries, some contemporary Muslim scholars have attempted to reconcile Islamic ideals with prevailing political realities. The modern Muslim states can still pursue the concept of one *umma*, these intellectuals suggest, by following the basic precepts of the *shari'a* to enforce equal treatment of their subjects—Muslims as well as non-Muslims—and through treaties and agreements (in modern times, diplomatic relations) with other nation-states following the footsteps of the Prophet and the covenant that the second caliph, 'Umar b. al-Khattab, enacted with non-Muslims after the conquest of Egypt.[33] James Piscatori suggests that "over time authoritative Muslim writers have come to elaborate a new 'consensus of speech' (*imja' al-qawl*), which argues that the territorial state is a natural and even worthy institution."[34] With the diffusion of the nation-state model throughout the world during the twentieth century, the function of the state is now to enforce and promote the "reformatory program which Islam has given for the betterment of mankind."[35]

From its very origins, the Islamic worldview acknowledged and embraced the existence of non-Muslim communities, some living within *dar al-Islam* (the area in which Islamic sovereignty prevailed and where the *shari'a* was enforced), others outside of it. The classical Islamic theory provided recognition for the autonomy of non-Muslims living within *dar al-Islam*. The non-Muslims were "protected minorities," such as were the Jews under the so-called Constitution of Medina contracted by the Prophet shortly after his arrival in the town. Similarly, Christians and other Jewish tribes living in the Arabian peninsula were recognized as autonomous communities during the lifetime of Prophet Muhammad. These "protected minorities" were collectively called *ahl al-dhimma* (people receiving protection), and an individual living in such a community was known as a *dhimmi*. Protected minorities under the Ottoman Turks were known as *millet*.[36] Millet or *milla* (the original word in Arabic) may be defined as a religious society, and Islamic society, or *dar al-Islam*, is composed of not only the Muslims, but also Christian, Jewish, Magian (Zoroastrian), Sabaean, Buddhist, and even Hindu religious communities, because all of them identify themselves by their religious affiliations. Isma'il al-Faruqi writes, "Islamic jurisprudence equally recognizes those people who opt for non-religious identification provided they have a legacy of laws (even if secular) by which they wish to order their lives. The only group which may be barred from membership is that whose law is anti-peace. . . . Islamic jurisprudence thus enables one to affirm today that any group claiming itself to be a *millah* on whatever grounds is entitled to membership."[37]

The Arab tradition (dating back to the pre-Islamic period) of a strong tribe protecting a weaker tribe in return for certain consideration seems to underlie the concept of *ahl al-dhimma*. W. Montgomery Watt asserts that Islamic states on the whole had an excellent record of tolerance and treatment of non-Muslim minorities.[38] The *dhimmis*, in return for taxes and tributes agreed to by treaties, were accorded protection from external enemies, and the same protection internally as was guaranteed to the Muslims.

The most significant special tax imposed upon *dhimmis*, according to the *shari'a*, was the *jizya*, or poll tax. The payment of *jizya* guaranteed non-Muslims protection by the Islamic state without having to give their lives defending the state against its enemies. If the state proved unable to defend the non-Muslims, the *jizya* was returned. If the non-Muslims chose to fight alongside the Muslims against a common enemy, the *jizya* was not collected. Likewise, in modern times, when Muslims and non-Muslims coexist peacefully within a Muslim state, there is no reason why non-Muslims could not opt to join hands with the Muslims in defense of the country and in maintaining internal law and order. The rationale for levying *jizya* would therefore no longer exist.

According to the classical theory, protected minorities enjoyed a large sphere of autonomy in their own affairs, with the Muslim rulers serving as arbiters when disputes needed to be settled between various parties. The religious head of each minority community was responsible for collecting tributes and taxes, and for administering law courts dealing with its religious matters. While the status of "protected minority" originated during the Prophet's lifetime as a way of dealing with the people of the Book (*ahl al-kitab*, principally Jews and Christians), it was eventually extended to people of other religions, including Hinduism. Of course, the preceding discussion does not mean that intolerance towards *dhimmis* was unknown in Islamic history. But most of the cases of widespread intolerance and discrimination can be ascribed to political weakness or strife within the Islamic state, when Muslims and non-Muslims suffered for their lives and property.

To summarize the main points of the Islamic view toward communal autonomy: Ethnicity, culture, language, and even religion do not provide grounds for the division of living space between communities under Islam. Once a non-Muslim community accepts the sovereignty of the Islamic state and becomes *ahl al-dhimma*, it acquires defined rights and duties vis-à-vis the state, the Muslims, and other non-Muslims living within *dar al-Islam*. While some Muslim cities have contained "quarters" for one religious community or another, this pattern of urban settlement was largely a voluntary development rather than a policy of segregation by the state. By and large, Muslims and non-Muslims have mixed freely in the public spaces of Muslim cities.

The Islamic state cannot regulate the moral practices of non-Muslims until they conflict with those of the Muslims. Unless the non-Muslims themselves choose to practice their different lifestyle away from the personal living spaces of the Muslims, or their moral practices are a threat to the way of life and beliefs of the Muslims, the state has no right to herd them together within any designated territorial boundaries.

The classical Islamic approach to questions of diversity and political autonomy beyond *dar al-Islam* must be studied with reference to the Islamic theory of international relations, known as *siyar*. This worldview was the product of persistent persecution of Muslims, first by the Meccan idolators, principally by the rich tribe of Quraysh and its allies; then by the frequent betrayals of non-Muslim tribes of Medina; followed in the final years of the Prophet's life by conflict with the Byzantine empire to the north. The unceasing hostility towards the Muslims by their non-Muslim neighbors forced the early Muslims to struggle for survival and, thus, war and fighting became an integral part of the relationships with non-Muslims. As a by-product of the struggle, Muslim jurists took excessive recourse of the concept of *naskh* (abrogation) in formulating their views on external relations with non-Muslim enemies, and ignored some of the very basic Qur'anic verses dealing with persuasion (*husna*), patience (*sabr*), tolerance (*la ikrah*), and the right to self-determination (*lasta 'alayhim bi-musaytir*), in favor of an aggressive conception of *jihad*.[39]

Since *fiqh* is the interpretation of the Qur'an and *sunna*, there has not been unanimity of opinion among the various schools of thought on all issues, especially regarding *siyar* and *jihad*. *Siyar* describes the rules of conduct for Muslims in dealing with the unbelievers of enemy territory or those with whom they have established treaties of nonaggression. The Qur'anic verses and the Prophetic traditions on *jihad* address how Muslims should respond to the hostilities of the enemies of Islam. The principles of *siyar* follow from them.

The conditions for and conduct of *jihad* are issues that have historically created controversy among Muslim jurists. Islamic legal precedents that were set during the time of the Prophet and his immediate successors, the first four "rightly guided" caliphs (*al-khulafa' al-rashidun*), served the Muslim community well until the advent of the Umayyad dynasty in A.D. 661. The people of the newly conquered territories could not shed entirely their pre-Islamic customs and culture and acted, in some cases, contrary to the standards set forth by the jurists and the government.[40] For all practical purposes, from the rise of the Umayyads through the rest of the dynasties of Muslim history, *fiqh* more often than not ceased to represent actual policies or regulations of the Muslim state. *Fiqh* essentially has been nothing more than legal opinions of various scholars of divergent schools of jurisprudence, and they differ on the nature of *jihad* and the conduct of international relations generally.

A few additional related concepts need to be defined here before we investigate the principles of *jihad* and *siyar*. Beyond the frontiers of *dar al-Islam*, medieval jurists conceived the existence of other territories or realms, including *dar al-harb* (world of war, i.e., non-Muslim territory hostile to Muslims)[41]; *dar al-aman* (non-Muslim territory which is at peace with Muslims)[42]; and *dar al-'ahd*, otherwise referred to as *dar ul-sulh*[43] (non-Muslim territory which pledges through treaty to acknowledge Muslim sovereignty, but maintains local autonomy by paying some land taxes in lieu of *jizya*, or poll tax).

The *harbis*, or inhabitants of *dar al-harb*, are enemies of Islam and, as such, have no right to enter into Muslim territories without express permission. However, a *harbi* who receives a guarantee of safe passage (*aman*) from even the poorest and the weakest Muslim is secure from harm for at least one year. At the expiry of that date, the *harbi* is bound to depart—unless, of course, he or she converts to Islam and becomes a part of the Muslim *umma* (community or society). The inhabitants of *dar al-aman*, the *musta'mins*, are treated according to the conditions of treaty between them and the Muslim state. The *musta'mins* are governed by their own laws, are exempt from taxes, and enjoy other privileges.[44]

Historically, the question of whether or not the Islamic state (*dar al-Islam*) is obligated to wage *jihad* against *dar al-harb* raised contradictory opinions from the various Sunni schools of jurisprudence. Abu Hanifa (d. 767), the founder of the Hanafi school, and Sufyan al-Thawri (d. 778) state that fighting against non-Muslims is not obligatory unless they themselves initiate it, in which case it becomes obligatory on Muslims to fight back.[45] Al-Sarakhsi (d. 1097), a Hanafi jurist, on the other hand, asserts that the commands for fighting the nonbelievers were revealed in the Qur'an by stages. At the final stage it was made mandatory to subdue the Arab polytheists, as well as other non-Muslims, and previous verses permitting peaceful coexistence were abrogated. Al-Shafi'i is of a similar opinion.[46]

The jurists are also divided on the issue of whether or not a *harbi* who is granted *aman* (safe conduct or protection) to enter *dar al-Islam* but who commits a crime while in Islamic territory is subject to Islamic legal punishment; Abu Hanifa asserts that such *harbis* are not subject to Muslim legal punishments, al-Shafi'i says that they are. Similarly, contradictory views are expressed on whether or not a Muslim who kills a non-Muslim subject is liable to be executed or required to pay the blood money to the victim's family. Juristic opinions also vary on who may be legitimately fought and killed during *jihad*, and on the treatment of enemy populations after their defeat.[47] In fact, if all the legal opinions of Muslim jurists are compared, it would not be surprising to find many contradictory assertions. To quote Abu Sulayman, a contemporary scholar of Islamic approaches to international relations: "The parts of *fiqh* manuals dealing with the question of international relations—the chapters on *al-jihad* and related matters such as *al-jizyah* and *al-siyar*—actually deal with matters that are highly political and can hardly be looked upon as simply enforcements or the carrying out of opinions of the *'ulama* (religious scholars), who had become more and more removed from the center of power and decision making."[48]

The early Muslim political thinkers, whether Abu Yusuf, deriving his political theories based on the practices of the Abbasid caliphs, or al-Mawardi, basing his on those of the Buwayhids and Abbasids,[49] paid more attention to the political realities of their times than to the *fiqh* of their respective schools of thought.[50] Some modern writers like Majid Khadduri have selectively chosen to emphasize one school of thought (Shafi'i) while ignoring others. In his *Islamic Law of Nations*, Khadduri asserts that *jihad* is made incumbent by God upon all Muslims to slay all polytheists wherever they are found, and that the "law of Islam" allows granting a treaty with the *harbis* for no more than ten years.[51] Khadduri presents the extreme views of al-Shafi'i and ignores the equally authoritative views of Abu Hanifa, who asserts that peace treaties, initially contracted for ten years, can be renewed as any other contract, as long as it serves the interest of the Muslims. Ibu Rushd (d. 1198) is of the opinion that not only Abu Hanifa, but also Malik ibn Anas (d. 795) and Ibn Hanbal (d. 855), the founders of the Maliki and Hanbali schools of *fiqh*, supported the notion of an indefinite peace treaty as long as it served the interest of the Muslim state.[52] Undoubtedly, as these jurists realized, everyone's interest is served in peace rather than war. Thus, we see that the majority of the founders of the Sunni schools of jurisprudence did not agree with the idea that *jihad* against *dar al-harb* was necessary or inevitable.

As regards Khadduri's point about polytheists, jurists like Abu Hanifa and Malik believe that the injunctions in the Qur'an and *sunna* referred only to the Arab polytheists such as Quraysh, who worshipped idols without believing in a supreme deity. Many of the jurists argue that the *jizya* could be collected from all polytheists except the Arab pagans, especially the Quraysh, who had repeatedly incited war against the Muslims in the lifetime of the Prophet.

It appears that the injunction about *jihad* against idolaters is not an obligation unless they initiate fighting, and only then does it become the duty of the Muslims to fight back in fulfillment of God's decree. Let us examine the Qur'anic verses that explain the position of Islam with respect to *jihad*:

> And so when the sacred months are over, slay those who ascribe divinity to any being but God [i.e., slay the pagans] wherever you may find them, and seize them, beleaguer them, and lie in wait for them in every conceivable place. But if they repent, and take to prayers, and render the purifying dues, let them go their way: for behold, God is much-forgiving, a dispenser of grace. [9:5]

This verse is sometimes referred to as the "verse of the sword" by those who want to project Islam as a belligerent religion. They add another Qur'anic verse to strengthen their position: "O you who believe! Fight those of the disbelievers who are near to you, and let them find harshness in you" (9:123). But these verses are only two among scores that deal with the subject of Muslim treatment of non-Muslims. They must be read in conjunction with such other Qur'anic verses as the following: "Let there be no coercion in matters of faith" (2:256); and "Fight in God's cause against those who wage war against you; but do not commit aggression, for verily God does not love aggressors" (2:190).

Taken in its entirety, the Qur'an makes clear that war (*jihad*) is permissible only in self-defense: "If they do not let you be, and do not offer you peace, and do not stay their hands, seize them and slay them whenever you come upon them. It is against these that We have clearly empowered you [to make war]" (4:91). But, "If they desist—behold God is much-forgiving, a dispenser of grace; and if they desist, all hostility shall cease" (2:192–93).

Verses must be read in context; that is, the time and circumstances for the revelation of various Qur'anic verses have to be considered before any given verse can be generalized as the "Islamic" view. Verses like 2:190 and 2:256 are general ethical injunctions, applicable to all times, whereas verses 9:5 and 9:123 specifically refer to the Quraysh and other pagan Arab tribes who were bent upon destroying Islam and the Muslims at the time of the Prophet.[53]

With reference to *dar al-'ahd*, a non-Muslim territory may acknowledge by treaty or other agreement (*'ahd*) the sovereignty of the Islamic state, thereby maintaining its local autonomy. The *'ahd* defines the rights and obligations of both parties. There have been disagreements among the jurists whether or not the Islamic state may renounce such treaties if conditions are in their favor. Since the *'ahd* can be a major diplomatic tool to regulate foreign affairs, such as peace agreements with non-Muslim states, it is an important issue in modern times, where nation-states establish diplomatic relations and live, more or less, in peace with each other. The Shafi'i school invalidates any treaty with a duration of more than ten years, while the other Sunni schools place no such restrictions. Most jurists, except those of the Hanafi school, assert that the Islamic state cannot break any lawful treaty unless it is broken first by dar al-'ahd.

It should be noted here that while political issues related to truce agreements with non-Muslim states are determined by political authorities, with or without reference to legal opinions of Muslim jurists, personal contacts between Muslims and non-Muslims living inside and outside dar al-Islam for trade or other reasons are left to individuals to decide via aman. According to all the legal schools, any Muslim man or woman could extend the rights and privileges of aman to any non-Muslim who requested it, allowing that person to reside and travel unimpeded in Muslim lands.[54]

Mobility

With the rise of an international system based on sovereign nation-states, Muslims have been forced to adapt Islamic principles to modern conditions. Dar al-Islam is today largely a cultural-religious construct, an ideal of the spiritual, if not political, unity of Muslims around the world. The political reality is of the existence of some 50 independent Muslim states which frequently find themselves bitterly divided and sometimes at war with each other.

Still, significant moral issues arise in any attempt to reconcile a world of sovereign territorial states with the Islamic ideals of a universal commonwealth including diverse races, religions, and linguistic groups. We have already seen one important concern in our preceding discussion, that of international distributive justice claims. Another issue, and one related to distributive justice, is that of mobility of peoples.

In the early centuries of Islam, Muslim communities traveled easily from one geographical boundary to another in search of their livelihood. Political frontiers meant little in their search for food and water. Individual Muslims also traveled easily and widely, sometimes holding positions in governments of various states without the complications of immigration and naturalization laws and regulations. Even non-Muslims were allowed to travel freely within and between the Muslim states. The Muslim centers of learning in Cordova, Granada, Fez, Salerno, Cairo, Baghdad, Damascus, and Bukhara were frequented by scholars and students of various religious persuasions from all over the world.[55] It was not uncommon for a noted religious personality or jurist to wander easily from one center to another, an itinerant scholar whose passport was his scholastic reputation. Two of the best known figures from Islamic history are Ibn Khaldun, the historian and jurist who taught and held government posts in Tunis, Fez, Granada, and Cairo, and Ibn Batuta, whose name is synonymous in the Muslim world with the irrepressible traveler. Ibn Batuta's travelogues of his visits to one Muslim land after another are packed with information on the people, flora and fauna, and natural and mineral products, and are written with a flair that still makes them among the best works in this genre.[56]

Up to the period of the three great modern Muslim empires, the Ottoman, Safavid, and Mughal, Muslim states placed little restriction on the movement of their peoples within and outside their territorial boundaries. Even though Islamic laws permitted Muslims to impose restrictions on the movements of *harbis* without *aman*, in practice these laws were not strictly enforced after Islam became the dominant power in the eighth century.

Ironically, though, in modern times some of the Muslim countries even treat Muslims from outside their political boundaries as if they are *harbis*. Some Middle Eastern states not only have imposed severe restrictions on the entry and domestic travel of Muslims from other countries within their territories, but also prevent them from owning landed property, and determine when they may leave their host countries through the issuance of exit visas. From the Qur'anic teachings and from the life and practices of the Prophet and the early Muslim rulers, we find this behavior, at best, contrary to Islamic values and deplorable. As long as the nonresidents do not engage in activities that are harmful and repugnant to the residents, there is no moral or religious reason to impose restrictions on them. Unfortunately, modern nation-states that justify their existence on the basis of national characteristics (race, ethnicity, language, religion, etc.) do impose upon nonresidents, and in some cases on their own citizens, limits on movements, ownership of property, and encroach upon their personal space. The ideals of the religion and the practices of Muslim governments are often in conflict in the real world.

Conclusion

Boundaries are essential for the growth and fulfillment of an individual's pursuit of life, liberty, and happiness. Islam encourages Muslims to acquire wealth, while bidding them to be mindful of the needs of others. It sanctifies ownership of landed property (and, hence, territorial boundary), yet places the responsibility of utilization and development of natural and environmental resources on the society (i.e., on the state) for the common good.

Islamic teachings make it clear that differences in ethnicity, culture, language, religion, and moral practices cannot be the basis of allocation (or assignment) of specific living spaces for specific communities. The minorities living in peace within the boundary of an Islamic state are entitled to receive protection of life and property and are to be treated humanely.

Muslims are part of the Islamic *umma*, no matter what their origin or nationality. Ideally, there should be no restrictions on the movements of nonresident Muslims from one country to another. People of other faiths, when they are not at war with the Muslims, cannot be considered as *harbis* and, as such, there should be no restriction on their movements either. Unfortunately, because of the rise of nation-states, but more so because of the rise of corrupt governments and/or ruling classes or families, the realities are just the opposite of the ideals.

Notes

1. William S. Sahakian and Mabel L. Sahakian, *Realms of Philosophy* (Cambridge, Mass.: Schenkman Publishing Company, Inc., 1965), 75.

2. See Taha Jabir al-'Alwani, *Usul Al-Fiqh Al-Islami: Source Methodology in Islamic Jurisprudence* (Herndon, Va.: International Institute of Islamic Thought, 1990).

3. See Fazlur Rahman, *Islam*, 2nd ed. (Chicago: University of Chicago Press, 1979), chap. 4.

4. See also al-'Alwani, *Usul al-Fiqh al-Islami*; N.J. Coulson, *A History of Islamic Law* (Edinburgh: Edinburgh University Press, 1964); and Majid Fakhry, *A History of Islamic Philosophy*, 2nd ed. (New York: Columbia University Press, 1983), intro.

5. For further detail, see Abdulhamid A. Abu Sulayman, *The Islamic Theory of International Relations: New Directions for Islamic Methodology and Thought* (Herndon, Va.: International Institute of Islamic Thought, 1987), 5.

6. The Pythagorean theorem of geometry was apparently known by the Egyptians as early as 2000 B.C., even though the record of its clear-cut deductive proof dates back only to the time of Pythagoras, around 550 B.C. See James R. Newman, ed., *The Harper Encyclopedia of Science*, rev. ed. (New York: Harper & Row Publishers, 1967).

7. Muhammad H. Haykal, *The Life of Muhammad*, 8th ed., trans. Isma'il R. al-Faruqi (Indianapolis: North American Trust Publications, 1976), 486–87.

8. Abu al-A'la Maududi, *Islamic Law and Constitution*, 3rd ed. (Lahore: Islamic Publications, Ltd., 1967), 202.

9. Syed Nawab Haider Naqvi, *Ethics and Economics: An Islamic Synthesis* (Leicester, U.K.: The Islamic Foundation, 1981), chap. 2.

10. I have used the translation and commentary of Muhammad Asad, *The Message of the Qur'an* (Gibraltar: Dar al-Andalus, 1993).

11. It is the uniqueness and individuality of each person that makes it impossible for one to bear the burden of another and, as such, the idea of redemption is rejected by Islam. See Muhammad Iqbal, *The Reconstruction of Religious Thought in Islam* (Lahore: Sh. Muhammad Ashraf, 1968), chap. 4.

12. Qur'anic references on this subject are 1:78, 2:2–7, 7:1–3, 20:6, and 32:9.

13. See Qur'an 2:43, 83, 110, 177, 277; 4:77, 162; 5:13, 58; 7:156; 9:11, 18, 60, 71; 19:55; 22:78; and 30:39.

14. See Imam Abi Ubayd al-Qasim ibn Sallam, *Kitab al-Amwal* (Beirut: Dar al-Hadathah, 1988). Originally published in the eighth century, this book remains a fundamental reference for ownership rights in Islamic law.

15. Baber Johansen, *The Islamic Law on Land Tax and Rent* (London: Croom Helm, 1988), 11–12.

16. For the Qur'anic injunctions with respect to the distribution of conquered land and war booty, see (8:41, 67–69). See also M. A. Z. Nawawi, *Minhaj et Talibin: A Manual of Muhammedan Law According to the School of Shafii*, trans. E. C. Howard (London: W. Thacker & Co., 1914), bk. 31.

17. Though *waqf* is a kind of charitable trust, there are material differences between the two. Nasir (1986) points out eight characteristics that differentiate the two. See Jamal J. Nasir, *The Islamic Law of Personal Status* (London: Graham & Trotman, 1986), 252.

18. See B. Ahmed and A. D. Mahajan, *Questions and Answers on Mohammadan Law (Including Leading Cases)*, 14th ed. (Allahabad, India: Allahabad Law Agency, 1974).

19. Ibid., 91–92.

20. Ibid., 93.

21. Ibid. See also Charles Hamilton, *The Hedaya: A Commentary on the Mussulman Laws* (Delhi: Islamic Book Trust, 1982), 547–65 for details on laws of preemption.

22. See Nawawi, *Minhaj Et Talibin*, bk. 18.

23. See Hasan Askari, *Society and State in Islam: An Introduction* (New Delhi: Islam and the Modern Age Society, 1978). See also M. Raquibuz Zaman, "Economic Justice in Islam, Ideals and Reality: The Case of Malaysia, Pakistan, and Saudi Arabia," in *Islamic Identity and the Struggle for Justice*, ed. N. H. Barazangi, M. R. Zaman, and O. Afzal (Gainesville: University Press of Florida, 1996), chap. 4.

24. See the commentary on this Qur'anic verse by Asad, *Message of the Qur'an*, 149.

25. Ibid., 150.

26. A proposal for collection of *zakat* and distribution of some of the proceeds to poor countries like Bangladesh was prepared by this author in 1981–82 while he was on sabbatical leave to teach at the King Abdulaziz University in Jeddah, Saudi Arabia. See M. Raquibuz Zaman, *Some Administrative Aspects of the Collection and Distribution of Zakat and the Distributive Effects of the Introduction of Zakat in Modern Economies* (Jeddah, Saudi Arabia: Scientific Publishing Center, King Abdulaziz University, 1987).

27. For a detailed exposition of the subject, see M. Raquibuz Zaman, ed., *Some Aspects of the Economics of Zakah* (Indianapolis: American Trust Publications, 1981).

28. See Iqbal, *Reconstruction of Religious Thought in Islam*, 141.

29. See Abu Sulayman, *Islamic Theory of International Relations*, 29.

30. See Manzooruddin Ahmed, *Islamic Political System in the Modern Age: Theory and Practice* (Karachi: Saad Publications, 1983), 73.

31. Abu Sulayman quotes the discourse of Imam al-Haramayn (d. 1085) on this subject. See Abu Sulayman, *Islamic Theory of International Relations*, 30, and 53, n. 44.

32. For an eloquent discussion of the modern political thinking in Islam, see Rahman, *Islam*, 226–31. See also W. Montgomery Watt, *Islamic Political Thought* (Edinburgh: Edinburgh University Press, 1968).

33. See Ann K. S. Lambton, *State and Government in Medieval Islam* (New York: Oxford University Press, 1981), 203.

34. See James Piscatori, *Islam in a World of Nation-States* (Cambridge: Cambridge University Press, 1986), 45.

35. See Maududi, *Islamic Law and Constitution*, 248.

36. See W. Montgomery Watt, *The Majesty That Was Islam* (London: Sidgwick and Jackson, 1974), 46–49.

37. See Isma'il R. al-Faruqi, in his intro. to Abu Sulayman, *Islamic Theory of International Relations*, xxv–xxvi.

38. See Watt, *Majesty That Was Islam*, 47–48.

39. See Abu Sulayman, *Islamic Theory of International Relations*, 30–35.

40. Ibid., 7.

41. Treatment of non-Muslims in a Muslim society has been a subject of interest to Muslims as well as non-Muslims. Among the non-Muslim writers who are critical of Islamic laws, one may consult Bat Ye'or, *The Decline of Eastern Christianity under Islam: From Jihad to Dhimmitude: Seventh–Twentieth Century*, trans. by M. Kochan and D. Littman (Madison, N.J.: Fairleigh Dickinson University Press, 1996); and Bat Ye'or, *The Dhimmi: Jews and Christians under Islam*, trans. by D. Maisel and P. Fenton (Rutherford, N.J.: Fairleigh Dickinson University Press, 1985). For a Muslim point of view, see Syed Amir Ali, *The Spirit of Islam* (Karachi: Pakistan Publishing House, 1976). For other viewpoints, see Nicolas P. Aghnides, *Mohammedan Theories of Finance* (Lahore: Premier Book House, n.d.); and Gustave E. von Grunebaum, *Classical Islam: A History—600–1258*, trans. by K. Watson (New York: Barnes & Noble, 1970).

42. See Ali, *Spirit of Islam*, 212–16, for details on *dar al-aman*.

43. This category is coined by Shafi'i. See Abu Sulayman, *Islamic Theory of International Relations*, 17.

44. Ali, *Spirit of Islam*, 215.

45. Abu Sulayman, *Islamic Theory of International Relations*, 8.

46. Ibid.

47. Ibid., 10.

48. Ibid., 11.

49. The Buwayhid sultans controlled Iraq and Persia between 932 and 1062. The Abbasids succeeded the Umayyads in 749 and ruled the Muslim empire until 1258, when the Mongols overran Baghdad.

50. See Qamaruddin Khan, *Al-Mawardi's Theory of the State* (Delhi: Idarah-i Adabiyat-i Delhi, 1979).

51. See Majid Khadduri, *The Islamic Law of Nations*, trans. from Arabic of Muhammad al-Shaybani's *al-Siyar al-kabir* (Baltimore: Johns Hopkins University Press, 1966), 16–17.

52. See Abu Sulayman, *Islamic Theory of International Relations*, 18.

53. For a detailed explanation, see the commentaries by Asad, *Message of the Qur'an*, on the Qur'anic verses cited. He has cited *hadiths* as well as earlier commentators on the subject.

54. See Majid Khadduri, *War and Peace in the Law of Islam* (Baltimore: Johns Hopkins University Press, 1952), 162–69.

55. See Ali, *Spirit of Islam*, 397.

56. On the life of Ibn Khaldun, see Franz Rosenthal, *The Muqaddimah: An Introduction to History*, 2nd ed. (Princeton: Princeton University Press, 1967), vol. 1, xxix–lxvii. For an account of the journeys of Ibn Batuta, see Ross E. Dunn, *The Adventures of Ibn Batuta: A Muslim Traveler of the 14th Century* (Berkeley: University of California Press, 1989).

Ten

Religion and the Maintenance of Boundaries

AN ISLAMIC VIEW

SULAYMAN NYANG

RELIGION is one of the oldest sources of boundaries among human beings. It remains one of the most important means of demarcating and maintaining boundaries in our time. The necessity of taking account of religious values is particularly acute for men and women living in states and societies where notions of boundaries—geographical and metaphysical—are related to notions of divine will, expressed through revelation of a sacred law, as is the case in Islam. M. Raquibuz Zaman's review of the Islamic tradition in the preceding chapter highlights this way of thinking, for he cites several Qur'anic verses and Prophetic statements to justify the right of ownership and the sanctity of private property. This treatment is certainly warranted, for the *shari'a* prescriptions for ordering human relations remain perhaps the first and most essential consideration that most Muslims employ. I want to approach the topic in a slightly different manner, however, focusing on both the metaphysical and physical aspects of boundary formation and maintenance from an Islamic point of view.

Religion as a Source of Boundaries

Religions claim transcendence beyond time and place. But the historical fact is that in most human societies religions arose from and responded to the conditions of specific human groups. These ethnic or geographic origins of religious beliefs have been well documented by anthropologists, historians, and social scientists.[1] Boundary lines in the early human communities were erected and maintained through some ritualistic expression of shared faith. Since one human being cannot read the mind of another, the only way to determine belief is by some explicit profession and affirmation of membership in a belief system.

Some religious systems have erected elaborate means of admission to their community. Others make fewer demands on those who would enter their fold. Nevertheless, all religious systems create boundaries between their believers and outsiders by requiring some overt demonstration of conviction. In Islam, the means of crossing the boundary from non-Islam to Islam is relatively straightforward: through the *shahada* or the profession of faith that "There is no god but God, and Muhammad is the messenger of God." This first pillar of the Islamic faith is the moral equivalent of a public declaration delimiting the borders of one's mind. A non-Muslim who decides voluntarily to embrace Islam is making both a mental and a social/physical decision. By declaring his faith as a Muslim, he is telling members of his immediate family and the rest of society that the mental borders defining his family and the culture with which he identifies have been redrawn in accordance with the teachings of his newly adopted faith.

This geography of the mind has a number of social consequences. The new believer must now be trusted by all members of his new religion. His faithfulness to Islam cannot be challenged within the community because no other believer can directly probe his mind and know absolutely whether he is a true believer or not. From the point of view of external verification of his faith, the only means by which the border guard of the faith can attest to his fidelity and sincerity is through his compliance with the rituals of the new faith. This is why rituals are crucial for the maintenance of boundaries and in the perpetuation of social solidarity among the members of a particular religion. We will return to the role of ritual in maintaining boundaries shortly.

Religions not only establish boundaries between believers and unbelievers, they also frequently create or legitimate boundaries among believers. I am referring now not to spiritual boundaries, which shared conviction is supposed to tear down, but to physical boundaries such as the rights of property ownership. As Zaman's elaboration of the Islamic laws on property demonstrates, Islam has been closely aligned through the centuries with private property. Under the *shari'a*, property may be acquired in three ways: by *iktisab* (earning), *wiratha* (inheritance), and *hiba* (gift). Maulana Muhammad 'Ali, a leading Indo-Pakistani intellectual of the twentieth century, describes the right of an individual to acquire property as "one of the basic laws regulating human society."[2] The Qur'an makes clear that this right is enjoyed by both men and women: "Men shall have the benefit of what they earn and women shall have the benefit of what they earn" (4:32). Both sexes also have a right to inherit property: "Men shall have a portion of what the parents and the near relatives leave and women shall have a portion of what the parents and the near relatives leave" (4:7). While no formal legal limitations are placed upon the property or wealth that an individual may acquire or dispose of, moral injunctions certainly circumscribe the behavior of the faithful in this area.

The Qur'an warns Muslims not to seek wealth through immoral means, such as through deceit (e.g., 4:29), bribery (2:188), usury (2:275–76), and the misappropriation of wealth held in trust (4:58)—for example, the property of orphans (4:6). Moreover, a number of other proscriptions in Islam may be seen as related to honest dealing in property acquisition. For example, the strong condemnation of gambling is coupled with a rebuke against consumption of alcoholic beverages in Q. 2:219. The connection between gambling and obtaining or losing property is obvious, but the connection with intoxicants is perhaps not so straightforward. Certainly, consumption of alcohol may be condemned for other reasons as well. In Q. 4:43 Muslims are told not to approach their daily prayers in a state of intoxication. But finally when the Qur'an proscribes intoxicants altogether in a later revelation (5:90), alcohol is once again linked with gambling because "they excite enmity and hatred among you." Producing, selling, and imbibing liquor and other forms of intoxicants are all condemned, like gambling, because they promote, among other things, fraudulent and harmful exchanges of wealth, potentially threatening the stability of society.

The Qur'an gives full rights of disposal of property to its legitimate owners, whether male or female, but at the same time it requires that the owners be most careful in spending the resulting wealth.[3] There are many injunctions of a general nature to this effect. Thus, the Qur'an describes the righteous servants of Allah ('ibad al-Rahman) as "they who, when they spend, are neither extravagant, nor parsimonious, and keep between these the just mean" (25:67). And elsewhere: "And do not make your hand to be shackled to your neck (in miserliness), nor stretch it forth to the utmost limit of its stretching forth, lest you should (afterwards) become blameworthy and destitute" (17:29). These restrictions on the exercise of rights of property by individual owners is described as *hajr* in a number of *hadiths* from the prophet Muhammad. One widely cited report from Imam Bukhari's collection of *hadith* reads as follows: "There is no charity unless a man has sufficient to give, and whoever spends in charity and he is himself in want or his family is in want or he has a debt to pay, it is more in the fitness of things that the debt should be paid than that he should spend in charity or free a slave or make a gift, and such a gift or charity shall be annulled, for he has no right to waste the wealth of the people (*amwal al-nas*)."[4] The reference to the "wealth of the people" in this *hadith* is a clear example of the Islamic view that though an individual owns property, that ownership *in the moral sense* is not exclusive to him or her. Spending one's wealth in even the worthiest of causes, as in charity, may be objectionable if the prior claims of one's dependents are not met.

In short, we can conclude that the owner of movable or immovable property, whether male or female, has the right to sell, barter, or bequeath it in any fashion deemed moral in light of Islamic teachings. Overarching all such transactions is the fundamental Qur'anic injunction: "Woe to the defrauders, who, when they take the measure from men, take it fully; but when they measure out to others or weigh out for them, they are deficient" (83:1–3).

The preceding discussion of private property rights is fundamental to our discussion of territorial boundaries, not only because individual owners are the building blocks of any national economy, but because the legal rulings and the general moral precepts we have outlined above apply equally to the state in its own business transactions. What is permitted the individual is permitted the state; what is prohibited the individual is prohibited the state. On the basis of the Qur'anic statements discussed above, general agreement has existed among Muslim scholars that in light of Islam's protection of individual property rights, governments have no right to deprive citizens of such ownership. This is not to say, of course, that the moral purview of the state is not broader than that of the individual. Whereas the individual is responsible to family and perhaps immediate neighbors, the state must take account of the welfare of all those residing within its jurisdiction. This obligation was historically fulfilled through the collection and distribution of the alms tax (zakat), which has already been discussed in the previous chapter. During the past two centuries, under the influence of socialist ideologies from Europe, a few Muslim intellectuals have sought to portray the Qur'anic vision of mutual obligations in society as a form of proto-socialism, while rejecting some of the more extreme aspects of Marxism. As Maulana Muhammad 'Ali argues: "Islam is thus opposed to Bolshevism, which recognizes no individual rights of property; but it is at the same time socialistic in its tendencies, inasmuch as it tries to bring about a more or less equal distribution of wealth."[5] The question is, how far does Islamic ethics permit the state to move down the path of distributive justice?

The debate among Muslims on this issue is rich and ranges along the spectrum from total rejection to acceptance of various degrees of state intervention. Much of the controversy centers around the right of modern nation-states to nationalize private property in the name of social welfare and economic development. All modern Muslim states have to various degrees pursued such policies, and, in the face of religious opposition, have mobilized religious supporters to provide Islamic sanction for their policies. Thus, when Nasser undertook his Arab socialist schemes in Egypt, Mahmud Shaltut, the shaykh of al-Azhar, the leading religious functionary of the state, produced a treatise arguing that Islam and Arab socialism were compatible. Other, "independent" Muslim intellectuals, such as Mustafa Siba'i, a leader of the Syrian Muslim Brotherhood, and the Indo-Pakistani scholar Khalifa 'Abd al-Hakim, have also promoted the idea of "Islamic socialism." In their view, the goal of state intervention should be to alleviate poverty and class differences, not eradicate them as the Communists wanted to do, because such goals are contrary to the natural order described in the Qur'an.[6]

Such arguments have been strongly challenged by other Muslim thinkers, and in some cases of state intervention, the 'ulama, the guardians of the religious law, have led a conservative backlash. Particularly susceptible to challenge from the 'ulama have been land reforms, which represent an obviously dramatic claim on the part of the state to reinterpret shari'a laws for the sake of the national good. When the shah of Iran undertook land reforms as part of his White Revolution in the mid-1960s, the Iranian *'ulama*, including Ayatollah Khomeini, were almost unanimous in their opposition to the redistribution of private property.[7] Such reactions have been evident in other major instances of land reform, including in Pakistan and Egypt. In the case of Iran, the *'ulama*'s mobilization against the shah during the White Revolution (which incidentally did little to improve the condition of the nation's peasant farmers) proved a harbinger of the revolution that came fifteen years later.

Religion as a Maintainer of Boundaries

Linking religion to private property, as most Muslims have done over the centuries, produces significant social and political consequences. The right to enjoy private property is meaningless without the existence of law and order. Hence, Islamic political thought has historically emphasized the need for law and order, leading even some of the greatest Muslim thinkers to accept tyrannical or, in modern parlance, authoritarian rule. "For," as al-Ghazali (d. 1111) famously put it, "if we were to decide that all wilayat [political authority] are now null and void, all institutions of public welfare would also be absolutely null and void. How should the capital be dissipated in straining after the profit?"[8] The "capital" al-Ghazali refers to here is the *shari'a*, which establishes and regulates all institutions of public welfare.[9] These institutions allow men and women in society, both individually and collectively, to carry out the primary purpose of life, the worship of the Most High God. But they also promote social peace and harmony through the regulation of human institutions, including the right to own and dispose of one's property. Surely, the preservation of such physical boundaries would be among the chief "profits" al-Ghazali had in mind.

All religions, no matter how universalistic their claims, are in the final analysis boundary maintainers, not just in the physical domain as discussed with regard to property, but also in the metaphysical realm.[10] This is largely because of their doctrine and their definition of reality. In the particular case of Islam, though Muslims claim that all human beings are the creatures of Allah and descendants of Adam and Eve, they strongly emphasize the line demarcating believers from unbelievers. Hence the juristic terms discussed by Zaman, *dar al-Islam* and *dar al-harb*. The first realm is that which harbors the men and women who embrace the belief in one God (*tawhid*), and the other is inhabited by the unbelievers (*kafirun*). *Dar al-Islam* and *dar al-harb* are as much metaphysical as physical constructs. We see clearly in these concepts how boundary lines are drawn not on geographical or biological differences, but on matters of faith. These concepts require us to distinguish between mental and physical boundaries among humans.[11]

Mental boundaries are those boundaries that are visible only to the perceiving agent. One can never know with certainty who else shares one's mental boundaries. This raises some acute problems for ideologically based human groupings whose physical and metaphysical integrity rests on trusting others who claim to hold the same convictions.

Hypocrisy and dissimulation have been the two most formidable threats to the integrity and security of social formations in human history. All religions as social groups have historically tried to maintain and protect their boundaries from penetration and infiltration. We know, for example, that the ancient Israelites were very much aware of the dangers posed by infiltration. According to linguists familiar with the Israelites' language, the Hebrew word *shibboleth* was used to distinguish aggressors and hypocrites from the devout; although the word simply meant "stream," its special use, as a test of pronunciation, gave it a special function (as can be seen in its English meaning). The very creation of a word like this reveals the strategic and social consciousness of the Israelites that the preservation of their community required both physical and mental tests.

In the case of Islam, inner acceptance of the faith has entailed the public performance of various ritual obligations, such as the pilgrimage, alms-giving, fasting, and most conspicuously, prayer. Yet from its very origins as a social phenomenon, Islam has grappled with the problems of false expressions of faith. The Qur'an repeatedly warns the faithful to beware the deceptions of hypocrites, who may give physical indications of their sincerity, but have not fully crossed the mental boundary separating believers and unbelievers: "Woe to the worshippers, those who are neglectful of their prayers, those who (want but) to be seen (as Muslims), but refuse (even) the small kindnesses" (107:4–7).

In more extreme cases, that of the renegade apostate (*murtadd*) who renounces his religion, the penalty adduced by most medieval jurists was execution. The legal rationale for this penalty was that his apostasy signified that he was either a hypocrite or an unbeliever disguised as a believer. In either event, he was a spy who posed a danger to the physical integrity of the Muslim community rather than to its spiritual integrity. This danger was considerable in the early days of Islam—from which the punishment is derived—because the community was constantly threatened by enemies from within and without.[12]

Cases like this one illustrate how the ethical questions are virtually indistinguishable from the legal and political ones. Since membership in an ethnic, national, or religious community confers social, political, and psychological protection and benefits upon those who are eligible and certified, it becomes problematic if someone who was at one time deemed worthy of privileges turns out to be an outsider posing as an insider. This is why words become an important means by which Muslims hold one another accountable for their deeds in this life. Historically, under Muslim rule, those who converted to the faith by declaring the *shahada* immediately became eligible for all the rights and prerogatives of the community, including ownership of land, just as those who were born Muslim. Conversely, those who recanted became subject to sanctions.

The problem of dealing with hypocrites and renegades was not confined to legal disputations. The early history of Islam witnessed philosophical and theological controversies among Muslim intellectuals trying to demarcate the mental boundaries, especially as these boundaries influenced the social and physical realms of human belief and action.[13] The question was: What actions signify an absence of faith? How can the community discern the true believer from the hypocrite? The intellectual contests between the Mu'tazilites and other schools of thought during the ninth and tenth centuries is perhaps the best-known case of such philosophical wrangling. The Mu'tazilites believed that human beings are responsible for their actions within the human realm, producing a view of human agency and hence responsibility that is not contingent on external factors. The Ash'arites took the view that a combination of human will and divine sanction underlie all human activity, that no result in the physical or metaphysical universe is the product simply of human intent. This view leads logically to a predeterministic view of one's own place in the universe. The Murji'ites sought to chart a middle course on the question of human agency. Their leaders preferred to defer judgment to the end of time, when the Truth will be known only through divine revelation. This metaphysical "fence-sitting"—eventually adopted as a sort of compromise position among Muslim theologians—could well be construed as a sanction for the politics of indifference. Such a theological attitude of course yields a variety of outcomes. On the one hand, it promotes an ethic of toleration by removing judgment on matters of faith from human hands. But on the other hand, this position can easily become the basis for the acceptance of the status quo and the unenthusiastic conformity with changes brought about by revolutionary means. It may yield as fatalistic a view of human life as some of the predestinarian principles of the Ash'arites, making the maintenance of mental and physical boundaries not a human activity, but a divine will.

Regardless of how one feels about the different strategies developed by religious communities to maintain their boundaries, the fact remains that social and political order can only become a reality when men and women live in peace. This is where Islam provided the ancient world with a new paradigm of social definition and identification. Using what we might term "Adamic" and "Abrahamic" criteria to determine who belongs where and why, Islam holds all human beings to be essentially the same because they are all the children of Adam. This universal category confers upon all human beings the attributes of a creature deemed as God's representative on earth through genetic links to Adam and Eve.

However, a being devoid of faith in the Creator is considered *kafir*, a word which conveys both the sense of lack of belief and lack of gratitude. For this and other related reasons, he or she is excluded from the Abrahamic common-wealth. This commonwealth consists of the Islamic *umma* and those members of the human race who are called *ahl al-kitab* (peoples of the Book)—a cate-gory including Jews and Christians, who also began with the Abrahamic ethic, but in one crucial way or another departed from it in the course of their evolu-tion. As Zaman points out in the preceding chapter, the category was ex-tended to include Zoroastrians, Hindus, and Buddhists when Islam expanded east of the Arabian peninsula. In describing the Islamic view of boundaries, therefore, we can argue that Muslims at the height of their power—when they might have succumbed to the temptations of exclusivism—recognized the utility and reality of both mental and physical boundaries, and they tried to defend and protect the rights of members of the various groups under their rule by formulating a public policy which allowed mental space to determine phys-ical space. This is to say that the Muslims in their quest for a just order among human beings saw the relationship between the geography of religion and the theology of space.

The Islamic geography of religion made it impossible for the Islamic con-querors of the Middle East to uproot and relocate the vanquished as other conquerors had done in the ages before them. It also enabled them to articu-late a policy of accommodation which respects the property rights of the de-feated through the assessment of a special kind of tax (*kharaj*). The theology of space, it must be emphasized, allowed the Muslims to recognize and protect the rights of all property owners, Muslim and non-Muslim.[14]

Two points made by Zaman bear repeating in our discussion of the Muslim approach to property rights. The first issue relates to the belief that the uni-verse is a created *entity*, with humans as temporary custodians of this world. Unlike many Western exponents of the principle that a piece of land belongs to the person who mixes his labor with it, the Islamic view categorically states that private ownership is justifiable, but it is and must be seen always as hold-ing property in trust. In his exposition, Zaman has shed ample light on the different schools of jurisprudence and their rulings on ownership.

What needs to be emphasized here is that the ethics of ownership in this case is so religiously bound that the believer's acts can be read ethically and legally simultaneously. In other words, ownership cannot in itself be the goal of a righteous individual; it is always merely a means to the pursuit of higher goals, and Islam always enjoins the promotion of family and communal well-being as among the highest. The Qur'an and the *hadith* literature identified with the prophet Muhammad convey to Muslims that this life is temporary and human beings should not be too fixated upon it. However, Islam does not teach its followers that this life is an illusion, as some creeds maintain. Rather, it teaches that compared to the next life (*al-akhira*), this life is insignificant. This is why Muslims pray for success in this life and success in the next life.

No strand of Muslim thought has grappled so deeply with the moral importance of physical and mental boundaries as has that of the Sufis, who came to the understanding that ownership is socially acceptable but mentally unnecessary. To most Sufi masters the idea of owning a thing is acceptable, but one must not forget that ownership brings only temporary utility. Investing too much emotional and psychic energy in such items of passing value can be spiritually counterproductive. In the logic of the Sufi master, material things, which are seen by many human beings as extensions of their egos, erect unwarranted boundaries among people. To the Sufi master, the only boundary worth preserving is that which separates the believer from the unbeliever. Though unbelievers share with believers common ancestry from Adam and Eve, their lack of faith in the Creator disqualifies them as reliable associates in this world. Again we return to the ingratitude implied in the term *kafir*: The unbeliever does not give credit to the very one who gives his life and ultimately takes his life in death. By being an unbeliever the neighbor who shares physical space with the Muslim in a human society is a traveling partner on the highway of life, but one fated sooner or later to part ways with the believer. The Muslim's destination is heavenward, whereas that of her unbelieving neighbor is earthbound.

Notes

1. For a discussion of the variety of human religious thought and the impact of ethno-cultural history on human societies, see Ninian Smart, *Worldviews: Crosscultural Explorations of Human Beliefs* (New York: Charles Scribner's Sons, 1983).

2. Maulana Muhammad 'Ali, *The Religion of Islam* (Columbus, Ohio: Ahmadiyya Anjuman Isha'at Islam, 1990), 509.

3. Ibid., 510.

4. *Sahih al-Bukhari*, bk. 24 (*kitab al-zakat*), chap. 17. Cited in ibid., 511.

5. Ibid., 509.

6. For a convenient anthology of Muslim arguments on socialism, see John J. Donohue and John L. Esposito, *Islam in Transition: Muslim Perspectives* (New York: Oxford University Press, 1982), 98–139.

7. See Ervand Abrahamian, *Khomeinism: Essays on the Islamic Republic* (Berkeley: University of California Press, 1993), 10, 55.

8. Quoted in H. A. R. Gibb, "Constitutional Organization," in *Law in the Middle East*, ed. Majid Khadduri and Herbert Liebesny (Washington, D.C.: Middle East Institute, 1955), 19.

9. Ibid., 20.

10. Almost all students of religion will agree that, though the world religions claim to be universal, their distinctiveness demarcates them from others making similar

claims. For some recent discussions on this phenomenon and the challenge of pluralism, see Harold Coward, *Pluralism: Challenge to World Religions* (Maryknoll, N.Y.: Orbis
Books, 1985).

11. For a discussion by modern Muslims of the relevance of these terms, see Hasan
Moinuddin, *Charter of the Islamic Conference* (New York: Oxford University Press,
1987), 42–53; and Mohammed Talaat al-Ghunaimi, *The Muslim Conception of International Law and the Western Approach* (The Hague: Martinus Nijhoff, 1968), 184.

12. Al-Mawardi summarizes some of the opinions regarding the treatment of renegades who departed from the Islamic fold but later recanted. Abu al-Hasan al-Mawardi,
al-Ahkam al-Sultaniyya: The Laws of Islamic Governance, trans. Asadullah Yate (London: Ta-Ha Publishers, 1996), chap. 5.

13. For details on these medieval theological disputes, see Fazlur Rahman, *Islam*
(Chicago: University of Chicago Press, 1979), chap. 5.

14. For a balanced discussion on the treatment of religious minorities by both Muslims and Christians in the medieval period, see Mark R. Cohen, *Under Crescent and
Cross: The Jews in the Middle Ages* (Princeton: Princeton University Press, 1994).

Eleven

Land and People

ONE JEWISH PERSPECTIVE

DAVID NOVAK

THE QUESTION of territorial boundaries has been ubiquitous in political discourse throughout history. That is because human life is inconceivable outside
of a finite community and its structures. Those who do not need such a defined
community are either gods or beasts, as Aristotle so well put it.[1] Now one of
the structures of any such defined human community is the place that it occupies. One could very well say that even when a human community does not
regard its present place of occupation as permanent (as has been the case with
the Jewish people for much of her history in exile), it nevertheless aspires to
eventually occupy its own place in the world (as in the Jewish doctrine of the
return to Zion).

The political question of territorial boundaries that has always been with us
is the question of defining the proper limits between one place and another,
and then determining just how the inhabitants of one such defined place are
to interact with those who dwell within their own boundaries, as well as with
those who dwell outside these same boundaries. The question of these boundaries is ubiquitous because it is historically inescapable. None of us are either
from nowhere or on our way to nowhere. We are all both historical and geographical beings. Indeed, just as time and space cannot be separated in physics,
as Einstein taught us, so it would seem that history and geography cannot be
separated in political discourse. Even in the version of the Jewish messianic
vision that sees one world polity as the goal of all human history, such a world
polity is still oriented around Zion as the *axis mundi*.[2] We can no more intelligently conceive of ourselves outside of a particular place than we can conceive
of ourselves outside our own bodies. (Indeed, it is significant that the Jewish
doctrine of the return to Zion is closely connected to the Jewish doctrine of
the bodily resurrection of the dead.)[3]

As we can already see, for Jews, the question of territorial borders cannot be
addressed outside of the whole issue of Zionism, not only Zionism (taken in
the broadest sense of the term) as a doctrine of Jewish tradition, but Zionism
as a historical reality that has led to the presence of the state of Israel among
the nation-states in the world in which we now live. Territorial borders are

usually seen as a practical political question. However, they are also a theoretical one: the ontological question of *place*, which seems to underlie the political question of territory.

Now there are those who would deny the validity of ontological questions altogether, or the relevance of ontological questions to real political concerns. For them, law (even religious law) and politics require no more fundamental grounding. They are simply to be posited as such. But for any Jewish reflection on the political question of territory, such positivism becomes indefensible. For even though one need not engage in ontology before beginning coherent political discourse, the fact is that the Jewish tradition has certainly taken itself to be theologically grounded. Ultimately, even if not immediately, deeper theological issues cannot be intelligently avoided. And, theology (usually called "revealed theology," namely, a theology constituted out of a historical revelation), like metaphysics (inevitably culminating in what is usually called "natural theology," namely, a theology constituted out of that which is taken to be universal nature), is a way of engaging in ontology: the reflection on being. For Judaism, the connection between politics and theology is unavoidable, so much so that even that quintessential modern defector from Judaism, Baruch Spinoza, entitled his deconstruction of Judaism *Tractatus Theologico-Politicus*. (Spinoza knew Judaism very well from the inside, and then attempted to answer the theologico-political question differently from the outside, but with respect for the validity of the question nonetheless.[4])

Ownership

Territorial boundaries are essentially connected to the question of ownership. If I have a right to be in a certain place and you do not have such a right, or only the right to be there because I have invited you in as my guest, then it seems that my right is one of ownership. In modern times, with the rise of a commercial class of individual property owners, a theorist like Locke could develop a whole political philosophy based on the notion of individual possession of property and the rational principles to govern its development and transfer.[5] But this philosophy seems to assume that money and property are interchangeable terms. In fact, though, they are only interchangeable when property is primarily conceived of as movable goods, which are detached from any particular place. In this case, property and its ownership come down to being that which an individual can move around at will and trade for anything anywhere. The essence of money is its anonymous transferability; as we often say, it has no "earmarks."[6] Nevertheless, movable property originally is derived from a particular place on earth and must ultimately be set down somewhere on earth. Therefore, the question of ownership is still fundamentally one of territory, however less apparent it is now than was the case in pre-commercial society.[7] But it is still territory, much more than movable goods and money, for which peoples have been willing to risk the own lives and especially the lives of their most able-bodied sons and daughters in war.

One can see the legal and political question of ownership inevitably leading into the ontological question of creation. Thus the modern concern with the individual or collective ownership of property reflected in capitalist and socialist theories respectively is primarily concerned with the greatly expanded role of human creativity that came with the commercial-then-industrial revolution in history. But as the various ecologies that have been emerging of late well remind us, this exaltation of the human creation of "goods" (hence the equation of "good" and "value" in much modern ethical theory) has been at the increasingly heavy price of the abuse of the earth and its limits, which certainly precede all of our own creative efforts and which these efforts can ultimately never transcend. The question, though, is whether the crisis of our human relationship with the earth is one that can be solved by eliminating the institution of ownership altogether, or whether its solution requires a correction of our presently flawed notions of ownership. This latter option seems to assume that the issue of ownership cannot be avoided in any human relationship with the earth. The attempt of all socialisms, ancient and modern, to solve the problem of ownership by transferring it from individuals to collectives simply begs the real question altogether. Indeed, to simply avoid it means that it will come back inadequately resolved like any other "return of the repressed." Clearly, though, if we regard what has been called the "territorial imperative" as an essential aspect of human political nature, then correction and guidance of it as it has been manifest in history are our only rational options.

In the Jewish tradition, beginning with its sources in Scripture, the question of ownership and the question of creation are seen in tandem. Thus Eve, upon the first human birth in the world (she and her husband having been fully made by God and placed in the world as adults), that of her first-born son Cain (Qayin), calls him by this name because "I have acquired/made (qaniti) a manchild (ish) with (et) the Lord" (Genesis 4:1). What she is acknowledging is that she has become the co-creator of a child with God.[8] The question is just what the moral/political significance of any co-creation/acquisition is. This is very much connected with our issue of territory inasmuch as our original connection to anyplace is that of our being heirs of our ancestors, now preparing a heritage to pass on to our children. It is the necessary connection between the particular historical time and the particular location that lies at the core of human experience and action in the world. Thus when this firstborn child finally settles down as the builder of the first city, he dedicates (that is, perpetuates) it by calling the city by his son's name Enoch (Genesis 4:17), which itself (Hanokh) means "dedication." The perpetuity of the city and the perpetuity of the family/clan are the subject of the very same word.[9]

The question of ownership is the question of the right relationship between God as the absolute owner/creator of everything in the world and humans as limited participants in what is to be seen as creation, which is an ongoing process rather than a once and for all event. Thus providence (*hashgahah*) is not an addition to creation but a property of it. God does not lose interest in anything He has made. God never transfers true ownership of anything. For without God's continual care and concern, the world would revert to primordial chaos. "If My covenant (*briti*) is not there day and night, then I have not put in place the laws (*huqqot*) of heaven and earth" (Jeremiah 33:25).[10] This truth requires that God's ownership be continually emphasized by a number of practices, both communal and individual. When it comes to the relation to landed property, at most, various creatures are given leases on certain areas of the created order, and these leases require regular renewal. The basis of the renewal procedure is whether the continuing surveillance of the true owner has determined that the tenants are treating His property properly or not.

This point comes out quite clearly in the legislation of the Pentateuch that deals with the acquisition of the Promised Land by the people of Israel and their continuing domicile therein. Thus the Torah rules out any permanent transfer of the agricultural real estate that is considered the original patrimony of the tribes of Israel to whom it has been *given* by God conditionally. Land is only a relative commercial entity, which can only be leased to a tribal outsider for a maximum of forty-nine years from one Jubilee year to the next. (The rent was to be prorated based on the number of years left at the time of the "sale" before the next Jubilee year, when all such real estate would be returned to its original tribal owners.) Unlike most of the legislation of the Torah, a reason is supplied for this whole institution of removing agricultural land from the realm of commercial transfer: "For the land shall not be sold into perpetuity (*la-tsmitut*), since the earth is Mine, hence you are sojourners and tenants with Me (*gerim ve-toshavim immadi*)" (Leviticus 25:23). This theological reason is surely that "the earth is the Lord's and the fullness thereof, the world and all who dwell therein" (Psalms 24:1).[11] And, although it is taught "and the earth He has given (*natan*) to humans" (Psalms 115:16), this only means that God has allotted various parts of His earth to various peoples.[12] All of these peoples are to be aware of the fact that it is God who both moves peoples from one place to another and settles them therein, and all of them are to be aware that their domicile is conditional, that it is for the sake of their obedience to the law of God. "Are you not unto Me like the Ethiopians, children of Israel. . . . Have I not brought up Israel out of Egypt, and the Philistines from Caphtor, and Aram from Kir? Behold the eyes of the Lord God are on the sinful kingdom, and I shall destroy her from the face of the earth" (Amos 9:7–8). But, since the Torah is primarily concerned with the people of Israel, it is the various laws which have been given to her and for her, such as the restrictions of the Sabbatical and Jubilee years, that enable us to see just how divine ownership is practically emphasized in her national life.

To lose sight of this truth, and the practical results it entails, is a form of the primal sin, which for Scripture is idolatry. Thus the Torah warns the Israelites not to make the same mistake in the land of Israel because of which God transferred its tenancy from the earlier Canaanite residents to them. "You shall not practice all these idolatrous acts (ha-to'evot). . . . For all these idolatrous acts were practiced by the people of the land before you, and the land became defiled (va-titma). Let not the land vomit you out because of your defilement of it as it vomited out the nation before you" (Leviticus 18:26–28). The idolatry for which the Canaanites forfeited the land is closely bound up with sexual license and bloodshed (sins that later rabbinic tradition saw as unconditional prohibitions for both Jews and non-Jews).[13]

This does not mean, though, that the displacement of the Jewish people from the land of Israel by another people is that other people's moral/political entitlement from God. Indeed, in history, such displacements by other nations have been for purposes of their own political/military conquest pure and simple, and these nations have been castigated by the prophets, speaking in the name of God, as severely as they castigated Israel for her sins. "O Assyria the rod of My anger; my wrath is a staff in their hand. . . . But he does imagine it and in his heart he does not consider it, for to destroy is what is in his heart and to annihilate not a few nations" (Isaiah 10:5,7). Those nations have been used and discarded by God without their knowledge and consent of what their aggression against Israel means theologically. They have only temporarily displaced Israel. To borrow words from T. S. Eliot, they did "the right thing for the wrong reason."[14] Hence, Israel's precarious situation in the land can only be understood in the context of the covenant with God. The threat of displacement is because Israel must be aware that her right to unique domicile in the land is contingent on the purposes for which such domicile is to be conducted. Unlike the election of Israel itself, which the preponderance of Scripture and rabbinic tradition see as unconditional and hence irrevocable by either Israel or even God, the presence of the Jewish people in the land of Israel must be recognized as a contingent matter by them. That is why the people could survive with their identity intact even when exiled from the land, but could not survive without the Torah, which is the constitution of the irrevocable covenant between God and the people. And, whereas God has no covenantal justification for rejecting Israel, God does have covenantal justification for exiling Israel from the land when she has grossly violated the precepts of the Torah. Hence Israel's domicile in the land and her taking possession of it is for the sake of the covenant. As Martin Buber saw with great insight, the Zionism that emerges out of the Jewish tradition itself is no ordinary nationalism.[15]

Distribution

The right to live within the boundaries of the land of Israel is one that must be seen differently before and after the destruction of the First Temple in 586 B.C.E. Before the destruction of the First Temple, it is assumed that all twelve tribes of Israel are living intact upon the portions of the land that were assigned to them in the days of Moses, and of which possession was taken in the days of Joshua. Although the boundaries of the land expanded during the reigns of David and Solomon due to their successful military campaigns, the essential tribal pattern of domicile was taken by the rabbinic tradition to be intact before the destruction of the Northern Kingdom of Israel by the Assyrians and the destruction of the Kingdom of Judah (along with the much smaller tribe of Benjamin) by the Babylonians, of which the destruction of the Temple was the main defining event.[16] Thus the Torah speaks of the process of taking possession of the land as an essentially tribal undertaking. While still waiting on the plains of Moab, poised to enter the Promised Land, the people of Israel are told, "You shall inherit (ve-horashtem) the land and dwell therein, for to you have I given the land to inherit it. You shall apportion (ve-hitnahaltem) the land by lot for your clans (le-mishpehoteikhem): to the larger ones you shall apportion more of a share, and to the smaller ones less of a share" (Numbers 33:53–54).[17]

This tribal apportionment of the land had important distributional consequences for both Jews (at that time, more accurately, "Israelites") and non-Jews. For Jews, it meant that no one was allowed to permanently sell or purchase their tribal inheritance. So, when the daughters of Zelophehad successfully petitioned Moses for the right to inherit their deceased father's land, as they would have automatically had they been males, their request was approved by God. However, this caused a problem for the members of their tribe of Manasseh which their leaders expressed as follows: "If they become the wives of members of one of the other tribes of Israel, then their portion will be subtracted (ve-nigra'ah) from the portion of our ancestors and added to the portion of the tribe they have married into" (Numbers 36:3). The compromise finally effected is that "the daughters of Zelophehad may become the wives of whomever they please, but they must become the wives of a family of the tribe of their father" (Numbers 36:6).[18] From this we see that even "personal" matters such as marriage were ultimately matters of tribal identification within tribal territory. Full political personhood was only possible for those men—and women—who had claims to tribal land.

For non-Jews, this meant that their status in what might be seen as this "landlocked" society would at worst be that of foreign slaves, either purchased from other nations or captured in war, or at best that of resident-aliens (gerim). In both statuses, non-Jews had some rights clearly defined, although they occupied an inferior status in the polity. In the case of slaves, they were entitled to their bodily integrity: they were not to be mutilated or raped. They were, also, to be included in a number of cultic observances such as the celebration of the Sabbath and Passover, which were certainly the most important communal religious celebrations in ancient Israel. In the case of non-Jewish free men and women in ancient Israel, they had the right to the full protection of civil and criminal law. Thus after the Torah prescribes capital punishment for a man who was the son of an Egyptian father and an Israelite mother, which would have meant that he was at least like a gentile resident-alien in having no claim to an ancestral portion in the land of Israel, a number of laws are set down pertaining to interhuman relations. Foremost among these laws is the requirement to execute the murderer of "any human person (*kol nefesh adam*)" (Leviticus 24:17). The general principle behind these laws is that "one judgment (*mishpat*) shall there be for you: the sojourner (*ka-ger*) and the native-born shall be treated alike" (Leviticus 24:22).[19]

From this we do see that even those who were not permanent property owners in the land of Israel were not totally disenfranchised in the national covenant. Indeed, the experience of landlessness, which was that of the resident-alien, is seen to be a reminder of Israel's own state during her sojourn in Egypt, hence "You may not oppress the sojourner, for you know the life of the sojourner (*nefesh ha-ger*) having yourselves been sojourners in the land of Egypt" (Exodus 23:9). Since Israel's experience in Egypt was indeed one of oppression, one where all her rights were eliminated, she is now commanded to treat sojourners in her own land differently. This is clearly an example of the later rabbinically formulated norm that "what is hateful to you, do not do to any fellow human being."[20] Thus the land of Israel is not to be a place that is ever to be "ethnically cleansed."[21]

The tribal form of land distribution was only effective when the society as a whole was constituted as a tribal confederation. In this political system, one's primary identification was tribal and only secondarily national. However, already before the First Temple was even built, military vulnerability caused the people of Israel to adopt a centralized monarchy, primarily because only such a centralized form of government could maintain the standing army necessary to defend Israel from the threat of highly organized Philistine aggression. (The Canaanites, Israel's earlier enemies, on the other hand, seem to have been as decentralized as were the tribes of Israel.) This was to have very important ramifications for the whole issue of territoriality in ancient Israel. For the power of the king very much included his redistribution of property. As such, even before the first king is actually selected, Scripture tells of how the prophet Samuel, at the time the highest religio-political official in Israel, warned the people of the high price they would have to pay for the new institution of monarchy. Part of that overall price was territorial. "And your fields and your vineyards and your good olive trees he will take, giving them to his servants. Your produce and your vineyards he will tax [literally, 'tithe'], giving it to his officials and his servants" (I Samuel 8:14–15).[22]

The monarchy, with its greater centralization of political power and authority, also led to a greater urbanization of society. One of the main features of a more urban society as opposed to a more rural society is the greater role that money plays in it. And the very anonymity of money reflects the greater anonymity of urban society in general, but especially as pertains to the question of territorial domicile. Already in the Torah, one notes there is a fundamental difference between urban property (specifically, property held in a walled city) and property held in rural fields or villages. Property in rural fields or villages cannot be permanently purchased because it must return to the original tribal owners in the Jubilee year; hence it can only be leased. But concerning urban property, it is stated that if it is not redeemed within the year of its sale, then "it is permanently (la-tsmitut) the purchaser's" (Leviticus 25:30), which means that he or she can pass it on to heirs, or sell it to someone else. Only in cities does land become a truly commercial entity. And that reflects a different relationship of people to their territory than in a rural setting, which is in many ways closer to the earth.

By the time that the Jewish people returned from the Exile beginning around 516 B.C.E., the old tribal territorial divisions were no longer in effect. For it was only the Judeans (hence the name "Jews," now the "remnant of Israel") who came back to the land of Israel, and the territory they occupied was not the same as that of the old twelve tribes.[23] Thus, as it were, the whole society became urbanized, at least in the legal sense, even though the physical presence of agriculture was obviously still in place. The political impact of this changed geographic and economic reality is not to be underestimated.

First, it led to the gradual obliteration of the old distinctions between those who owned land and those who were landless. Thus the Levites, who were only assigned a number of villages that could not support sufficient agriculture for their needs and thus had to live off of the tithes that the rest of the people paid them, were eventually integrated into the rest of the population. That seems to be the case because in what has been called by historians the "Second Jewish Commonwealth," the Levites no longer had their old villages, and because most of the people had ceased to pay them the old tithes. To be sure, some of this may have been due to the assimilation of many of the Levites into Babylonian society, thus preventing very many of them from returning to the land of Israel under Ezra and Nehemiah.[24] But it seems more likely that their status had largely depended on the role they had played among all the tribes of Israel when they were all living on their old ancestral territories. But the new political realities could not restore that ancien régime, however much it remained a messianic hope. Aside from their secondary role in the service of the Temple, which only involved a minority of them anyway, the Levites had lost the unique territorial role they had formerly played in the covenantal society. And this might well explain why only the most exceptionally pious people felt it necessary to continue to support them with their tithes, especially when during the Second Temple period the people were paying taxes to the various empires (Persian, Macedonian, Ptolemaic, Seleucid, Roman) under whose rule (sometimes distant; sometimes quite immediate) they had to live.[25]

The most radical social change that came in the wake of the territorial changes during the Second Temple period was that possessing rural land or living in rural areas, which had alone given one full social status in the pre-exilic period, by the time of at least the Roman occupation actually became a sign of social inferiority, for the urbanization of society had greatly increased the opportunities for learning, and learning took on a new importance in the very governance of society. In many ways, the portability of sacred texts and their rabbinic expositors took on the importance that had formerly pertained to the landed gentry and the institutions that depended on their support.

This seems to have been the result of the Exile itself, where the identity of the now landless Jewish people was dependent on the centrality of the Book in their communal life. Thus, when the people were being reestablished in the land again, the central feature in their celebration of this great event was that Ezra the Scribe (and not, significantly, Nehemiah the territorial governor) had the people "read the law of God that was explicit in the book (*ba-sefer*), and they intelligently understood the reading (*ba-miqra*)" (Nehemiah 8:8).[26] From that time one, where the leadership of the people would lie became a struggle between those who had political power based on territory and those who had political power based on learning (viz., the scribes and sages). After the time of the destruction of the Second Temple in 70 c.e. (the final loss of their own place by the Jewish people), the political victory was that of the scribes and sages. Only they, through their mastery of the Book, had not lost the basis of their authority. In fact, based on that authority, these scribes and sages conceived what the return to national sovereignty in the land of Israel would be like, even including the rebuilding of the Temple.[27]

But those who lived in rural areas were rarely able to take advantage of the newer social institutions of the synagogue (*bet ha-keneset*), whose main function was the public reading and exposition of Scripture, and the academy (*bet ha-midrash*), whose main function was the development of post-scriptural forms of normative teaching (what came to be called the "Oral Tradition").[28] Thus the old scriptural term *am ha'arets* (literally, "people of the land"), whose originally meaning was probably the name of a council of local landed gentry, became by the time of the Pharisees a name designating an ignoramus, who would be called today a "country bumpkin."[29] Organized learning is very much a result of greater urbanity; only cities have the number and variety of people to enable learning to function on an institutional level. So, even though the overall sacred status of the land of Israel was continually emphasized in rabbinic jurisprudence and theology, the fact was that its distributional significance had radically changed.

Now, in an unprecedented manner, the entire Jewish people had an equal share in the land of Israel, and the old differences between the various types of landowners and non-landowners became less and less significant. Furthermore, even though there probably was some sort of Jewish diaspora already in the time of the First Temple, the reality of the Jewish diaspora was not fully established until the time of the Second Temple. This was due to the fact that many Jews did not return to the land of Israel when Cyrus the Great had permitted them to do so under the leadership of Ezra and Nehemiah. Although some of this was because of gradual assimilation, more of it seems to have been because large numbers of Jews believed that their religious and social identity did not depend on their physical presence in the land of Israel. And, although some of these Jews do seem to have cut off their ties altogether to the ancestral homeland (as evidenced, for example, by the construction of a temple to rival the one in Jerusalem by Egyptian Jews in Leontopolis sometime in the second century B.C.E.), the vast majority of diaspora Jews seem to have maintained their connection to the land of Israel.[30] This is especially evidenced by the pilgrimages many of them made regularly to the Temple in Jerusalem, and the offerings that were regularly sent there even by those who could not come in person.[31]

Of course, tensions did arise from time to time between Israeli and non-Israeli Jews. Frequently, the tensions were over issues of political sovereignty that occasionally erupted when diaspora communities balked at the idea of being treated as mere colonies of the motherland. Nevertheless, at least from what we know from rabbinic sources, even at the time of such political tensions, the religious uniqueness of the land of Israel was not challenged. What was challenged, especially after the demise of the Israel-centered Sanhedrin as the central legislative-juridical body in Jewry, was the notion that all authority was to be contained within the borders of the land. But the diaspora communities refused to surrender their own authority even when there was a politically viable community in the land of Israel.[32] And they were able to do this without cutting off their ties to the land and their hopes for its messianic redemption. We shall examine this idea of a land encompassing more than its actual inhabitants when we deal with the question of national autonomy.

Diversity

The breakdown of the old tribal system as well as the development of Judaism as a basically urban phenomenon also led to a different mode of relationship between Jews and non-Jews, both in the land of Israel and in the Diaspora.

In the land of Israel during the pre-exilic period, non-Jews were related to

Jews as either foreigners (*nokhrim*) or resident-aliens (*gerim*). Foreigners were those who occupied what was taken to be essentially gentile space. Their territorial integrity was to be respected, however. Even in the event of imminent war, the people of Israel were commanded to "offer peace terms" (Deuteronomy 20:10) before entering into any acts of conquest. But here the distinction was made between the lands of the Canaanite tribes, which God entitled Israel to conquer, and the lands whose "cities are far away from you" (Deuteronomy 20:15). Yet even that distinction was also broken down in the development of the rabbinic tradition.[33]

The resident-aliens, as we have already seen, were those people living among the people of Israel in a subordinate capacity, although one having definite rights and duties and enjoying the protection of the due process of law. The only way they were able to gain full status in that landed society was to somehow or other assimilate with the people of Israel. The process seems to have taken a number of generations in order to be complete. It was usually done through intermarriage, especially the marriage of gentile women with Israelite men.[34] At least in the explicit norms of Scripture, intermarriage was only prohibited with the sons and daughters of the Canaanite nations.[35]

The changed situation of the post-exilic Jewish community in the land of Israel, with its new relationship to territory, made the relationship of the Jews with the non-Jews living among them different. Not only were the old tribal distinctions between the Jews themselves largely a thing of the past, but the distinctions between the non-Jews themselves that the Torah had recognized in its legislation, especially as pertains to marriage, were also regarded to be a thing of the past. Thus, whereas in the past some non-Jews had been more privileged than others in their right to live in the land of Israel as resident-aliens, after the Exile these distinctions were considered impossible to detect. As the Mishnah put it, "And are the Ammonites and the Moabites still in their [original] locales? [After all] Senacherib the king of Assyria ascended and mixed up (*u-bilbel*) all the nations."[36] Indeed, the very process whereby the people was exiled—first the Northern Kingdom of Israel by the Assyrians and then the Kingdom of Judah by the Babylonians—was the same process that led to what seemed to be universal disruption of territorial and ethnic boundaries; just as the Jewish people had now become more of a homogeneous people, so were the nations of the world whom they faced as "others" now, at least for them, more homogeneous too. For this reason, the old distinctions pertaining to intermarriage could no longer apply. But, instead of becoming more lenient because of this, the distinctions became stricter. Ezra's strictures against intermarriage applied across the board to all gentiles. And these strictures were promoted at the time that the people of Israel were retaking the land of Israel (albeit, in effect, as Persian colonists). The connection between marriage, domicile, and territory is integral.[37] As Ezra is reported to have put it, "the officials approached me saying that the people of Israel and the priests and the Levites had not separated themselves from the peoples of the lands. . . . for they have taken their daughters for themselves and for their sons, and they have assimilated (*ve-hit'arvu*) the holy stock with the peoples of the lands" (Ezra 9:1–2).

The lack of full Jewish sovereignty in the land of Israel during the entire period of the Second Temple made the question of non-Jewish domicile within traditionally Jewish territory one that was essentially out of the hands of the Jews. Non-Jews were living in close proximity to Jewish settlements in the land, and that was a fact of life that the Jews had to face in a way other than by exercising the kind of control they formerly had over non-Jews under the pre-exilic monarchy.[38] Thus the Talmud assumed that the formal institution of the resident-alien (*ger toshav*) could have only been in force when all the tribes of Israel were intact in their respective ancestral territories.[39] This situation had a number of important ramifications as regards the diversity of population in the land of Israel.

First, it meant that the Jews had to recognize that in their own land (that is, their own land by virtue of their own theological-legal criteria) there was a permanent non-Jewish presence. Although by messianic criteria this may have been a situation to be ultimately overcome, in the present political reality it was a factor that had to be taken into serious consideration in communal policy decisions. For example, the Talmud notes:

> In Ammon and Moab the tithe for the poor is to be given even during the Sabbatical year, as an earlier authority indicated: Many towns were captured by those who left Egypt but were not captured by those who left Babylonia. For the sanctification of the land in the first instance was only established in the first instance for that time (*le-sha'atah*) but not for the future. They excluded these towns from the latter conquest in order that the poor might rely on them during the Sabbatical year.[40]

Whether any such exclusion was intentionally made at that earlier time is somewhat questionable. But what this passage does show is that Jewish policy decisions, having important economic and social consequences, were more likely made on the assumption that the non-Jewish presence within the larger historical borders of the land of Israel was a factor that could be accepted, and a factor that could be usefully employed in making policy decisions for the common good of the Jewish people herself.

Second, the disappearance of the old resident-alien status, for reasons we have seen above, also made any non-Jewish integration into the Jewish community and its territories harder, yet at the same time more immediate. For it is during the Second Temple period that we see the whole phenomenon of conversion to Judaism emerge as distinct from gradual assimilation into the Jewish people and her territories. By "conversion" I mean an event whereby one who is formerly a gentile becomes a Jew. That is quite different from the process of becoming either a permanent or temporary (a process of several generations) resident-alien that seems to have been in effect in earlier times.[41]

With the institution of conversion (*gerut*), a gentile had the opportunity to become a full member of the Jewish people by his or her own choice. Of course, the conversion itself was not done by converts themselves but, rather, by a tribunal, which functioned very much on behalf of the entire people if not, in effect, on behalf of God (since conversion seems to be based on the theological doctrine that the covenantal election of Israel by God can extend to individuals who are not themselves literal descendants of Abraham and Sarah).[42] Nevertheless, the consent of the convert himself or herself is a necessary, if not sufficient, condition for the conversion itself to be legally valid.[43] (This latter qualification may have been the result of the disastrous results the Jewish people experienced from the forced conversion of the people of Edom by the Hasmonean king, John Hyrcanus, in the second century B.C.E.[44]) Although a more immediate way to become part of the Jewish people and whatever territory they inhabit or control at the time, it is harder inasmuch as converts are required to demonstrate their willingness to adopt the full regimen of Jewish law.[45] To be sure, native-born Jews are also required to observe it, but their status as permanent members of the Jewish people is not dependent on any such prior commitment. At least in the Diaspora, becoming part of Jewish polity requires one's full religious integration into the life of the Jewish people.

The return of the Jewish people to national sovereignty in the land of Israel brought about by the state of Israel has raised some important new issues for the question of diversity in a Jewish polity. That is largely the case, it seems to me, because the new Jewish state (forty-nine years is a very short period of time in relation to the more than four-thousand-year history of the Jewish people) as a *secular Jewish state* is unprecedented in history. (The fact that the state of Israel does not have a written constitution makes the legal ramifications of its undefined character often quite problematic.) The main issue centers around the question of the status of non-Jews in a Jewish polity; indeed, how their very presence therein is to be designated politically and legally.

In ancient Israel, the status of the resident-alien, at least as the rabbinic sources retrospectively defined that status, partakes of both religious and secular aspects. This status has a religious component inasmuch as the rabbinic view is unanimous in presuming that the right to resident-alien status in ancient Israel required that the candidate for this status agree not to engage in any public idolatry (*avodah zarah*).[46] That, in effect, meant that resident-aliens were proscribed from practicing their native religion in the land of Israel. (The notion of a "private" religion is a peculiarly modern fiction that would have been unintelligible until very recent times.) This did not mean, though, that they had to adopt Jewish religious practices. (The scriptural sources do mention such "sojourners" being able to observe some Jewish cultic celebrations, but whether there was any actual legal pressure for them to do so is unclear.) The status has a secular component, too, inasmuch as the positive requirements of resident-aliens and the positive rights they enjoyed are all taken to be within the realm of interpersonal relations, such as the right to be protected from harm to one's person or one's property. In fact, this predominantly secular aspect of this institution very much impressed the great German Jewish philosopher, Hermann Cohen (d. 1918), so much so that he saw it as a precedent for modern notions of citizenship that are meant to be unconnected to religious or ethnic origins.[47]

Nevertheless, as we have seen, this type of citizenship (or, at least, the idea of this type of citizenship) presupposes a basically religious polity, which also includes within itself the fully intact presence of all twelve tribes of Israel dwelling on their respective ancestral portions. And, even if the latter criterion is effectively a messianic one, the former criterion—the presupposition of a basically religious polity—does not hold in the land of Israel at present or in the foreseeable future. Accordingly, a peculiar paradox pertains to the way distinctions involving citizenship are made in the state of Israel. The paradox can be seen as follows: On the one hand, if the state of Israel is a secular, democratic polity, then there should be no ethnic or religious distinctions made between one group of *Israelis* or another. However, were this to be so, the essentially *Jewish* character of the state, including its significance for the majority of Jews who still live in the Diaspora, would no doubt be lost. (And there are, indeed, radically secularist Israelis who would like to see Israel as a state for Israelis in the same way, let us say, that Canada is a state for Canadians—of whatever religious or ethnic background.) On the other hand, if the state of Israel is to be a state for Jews governed by traditional Jewish law, then the only full citizens should be those Jews willing to live under the rule of this law. As for secular Jews, or liberal religious Jews, let alone non-Jews, their obviously second-class status would have to be determined by the rabbinical interpreters of that law.[48]

The fact is, though, that despite the officially secular character of the state of Israel, secular Jews, liberal religious Jews, and non-Jews all live at some sort of political disadvantage there. Secular Jews are required to submit themselves to Orthodox religious authorities in all matters pertaining to marriage and divorce. Liberal religious Jews do not have the government support for their institutions, and their leaders have no official clerical status. (Thus they may not officiate at marriage or divorce procedures.) As for non-Jews, although their religious institutions are officially recognized, they are not the subjects of the most basic right to which Jewish Israelis are entitled: the "Law of Return" (*hoq ha-shevut*), which entitles any Jew from anywhere to immediate citizenship upon arrival in Israel. (The passage of this law was the first official act of Israel's parliament, the *Keneset*, after the establishment of the state in 1948.)

And as for Arabs living on the West Bank (as distinct from Arabs living within Israel's pre-1967 borders), their whole political status is still very much in limbo.

Israel's problem of diversity within her territory, like several other such matters of identity, lacks a satisfactory solution because Israel has had neither the time nor the energy so far to more clearly define the character of her own society. But such a definition is surely a desideratum: first, for Israeli Jews themselves; second, for Israeli non-Jews; and third, for diaspora Jews, the over-whelming number of whom see the state of Israel as a Jewish polity to which they are connected politically, even if not in the strictly legal sense of citizen-ship. Being such a desideratum, the quest for clearer definition calls for theo-retical reflection whenever possible.

This problem partakes of the inherent paradox of a secular state enforcing religious criteria of identity. It is best illustrated by a landmark decision of the Israel Supreme Court in the late 1960s. The case involved the petition of an Israeli naval officer, Binyamin Shalit, for his wife and children to be given Jewish citizenship in Israel. The problem was that Mrs. Shalit was a Scottish-born gentile. Their children, by virtue of the rabbinic principle of matrilineal descent (the mother's identity determines that of her children), are therefore gentiles.[49] The only solution would have been for Mrs. Shalit and her children to have converted to Judaism. However, such a "conversion" is by definition a religious act, involving full acceptance of the universal kingship of the God of Israel and the commandments of the Torah and Jewish tradition. That proved to be an insuperable impediment for Mrs. Shalit, since both she and Mr. Shalit are committed atheists who refused on principle to submit them-selves to religious standards and rites which they could not in good conscience accept. Their argument was that their *Jewishness* was a secular matter, evi-denced by their choice to live in the secular, Jewish state of Israel and raise their children in that society. They, in effect, requested a secular means for affirming the Jewishness of Mrs. Shalit and their children. But the problem was, of course, that no such means exists. The only way for one to become a Jew, even in this secular state, is through religious—and in Israel that means Orthodox—auspices. The Shalits' petition was thus denied.[50] The status of Mrs. Shalit and the Shalit children could only be that of gentiles (*goyyim*) living in the Jewish state as gentile citizens.

Now as is well known, the political reason for this secular concession to religious standards, indeed only one kind of Jewish religious standard, is that no secular party in Israel has ever been able to win its own majority in the Keneset and thus be able to form a government (a *memshalah* as distinct from the state itself: *medinat yisrael*) by itself. All Israeli governments since 1948 have been formed by coalitions, coalitions that have always included Ortho-dox religious parties. The price these religious parties have exacted for their participation in these coalition governments has been their increasing control of such areas of society as familial and personal status. But what many Is-raelis—and non-Israelis—have argued is that this emphasizes the paradox of confusing religion and secularity, the result being that the worst elements of both worldviews emerge. For what we have is, in effect, a secular contract as the basis of religious coercion.

More and more people are becoming increasingly aware of just how unsatis-factory this approach to the question of diversity, both among Jews themselves and with respect to Jews and non-Jews, really is. The approach has heretofore been unable to deal with dangerous tensions between Jews themselves and the even more dangerous tensions between Jews and non-Jews. This grave practi-cal problem seems to be very much with us for, at least, the near future. How-ever, theorists should, whenever possible, attempt to imagine some way out of it, because intelligent public policy requires a basis in coherent theory. Thus let me make a suggestion here.

Although every society has to employ coercion from time to time to protect public order from those whose disrespect for the rule of law would endanger it, no society can hold the moral allegiance of its members if coercion is the very basis of that public order. One need not be an advocate of any sort of social contract theory as the basis of society to appreciate this point. It also pertains to a society that is based on a covenant between God and a people, which is the way Judaism has consistently constituted any Jewish polity. A covenantal society is based on God's initiation of a political relationship between Himself and a people. Unlike a contract, it is not the coming together of equal parties, nor do the people have any right of initial refusal or subsequent termination of the covenant. (Indeed, the only basis for any such termination would be the permanent absence of God or Israel from the world.) Both possibilities are in fact precluded by the very divine promises that founded the covenant in the first place. Thus only God has the right—the autonomy—to initiate the cove-nant, and God has promised away any right He could have had to terminate it.[51] At that level, then, the covenant could be said to be forced upon the people by God. Yet, however valid the covenant might be on the ontological level as an act of divine coercion (the rights of the Creator over any of His creatures), on the practical level it would be inoperative. In what might very well be one of the most theologically striking discussions in the entire Tal-mud, it is emphasized that although at Mount Sinai God "suspended the mountain over them [Israel]," it was only during the Exile, when Israel finally accepted the covenant and its Torah out of inherently free love, did the whole covenantal system—including its law—become truly effective.[52]

The upshot of all this is that the Jewish religious system of law and polity cannot operate coherently unless it is based on a continually renewed cove-nant between God and the people. To base it on a contract between religious political parties and a secular state, as is the case now in Israel, where the interpreters of religious law derive coercive power from secular authority, can only lead to widespread contempt for what is being presented by them as "the Torah." The contempt of the secular (or, at least, non-Orthodox) majority is due to their being forced to live under a law they do not wish, in good conscience, to accept. Moreover, there are a number in the religious communities as well who suspect this political situation, being pained to see what they love become the object of hate by so many others. And they see that this unnatural marriage between secular authority and religious enforcement leads to numerous compromises with secularity that threaten the very integrity of Jewish religious law itself.[53] Thus, for example, if matters of personal status and their legal ramifications, which could well be considered the most important aspect of a religion that is a communal covenant, are the subject of the legislation of the Keneset, then these matters are being practically determined by a body whose majority consists of religiously nonobservant Jews—as well as its non-Jewish, Arab members. One need not be a religiously observant Jew to be troubled by all this.

The reemphasis of the covenantal basis of Judaism itself requires due (albeit critical) appreciation of the modern experience of democratic pluralism. For it is from this type of polity that Jews have derived such enormous political benefits wherever it has been in force. (It would be very hard to find a Jew who could make any sort of politically convincing argument for the political alternatives to democracy today, primarily because Jews have been so victimized in those societies where they have been operative.) That reemphasis has some rather direct implications for the problem of diversity in a society where political power and authority are constitutionally Jewish. (However vague that Jewish basis has been constituted heretofore, the state of Israel, by virtue of its Declaration of Independence, designates herself as a *medinah yehudit*, a "Jewish state.") These ramifications apply to both Jewish and non-Jewish diversity.

As for Jewish diversity, which in practice means the differences between Orthodox and non-Orthodox Jews as well as the even greater differences between religious and secular (better, "secularist") Jews, the question is how to find sources in the tradition itself for the employment of an absolute minimum of coercion by religious authorities. This is the only way, I think, that a rationally persuasive case could be made for a truly religious foundation for a Jewish polity, especially at this point in history. (And how could anything but a rational case be persuasive rather than intimidating?) The case could be made that such a religious foundation would alone be able to provide enough continuity with Jewish tradition to justify calling the polity a "Jewish state," and it would have enough in common with modern democratic notions of a minimum of coercion and a respect for individual rights to prove attractive to the vast majority of Jews who have, quite understandably, grown attached to these notions.

As regards Jewish diversity, there would have to be a reliance on authoritative sources within the classical literature that indicate that the use of coercion is often a matter of judicial or legislative discretion. For example, there is a principle that laws which are the result of rabbinic legislation should not be enforced if they prove to be practices which the majority of the community have already quite clearly neglected.[54] (Needless to say, any such reticence could not be cogently advocated when the sin to be committed, or which has just been committed, involves physical harm to persons or property.) Of course, all these procedural principles need to be very carefully nuanced when we reach the level of legal application.[55] All I am saying now is that the tradition has within it the potential for their development for the moral/political needs of the present.

The problem of diversity in a Jewish polity that includes non-Jews is harder to approach, let alone resolve, because the classical rabbinic sources, upon which we always have to draw, were all written during the very long period of time between the close of Scripture and the reestablishment of the state of Israel when Jews had no real political power over any group of non-Jews. At most, they sometimes did have power over individual non-Jews whom they held as slaves; however, considering the scarcity of this institution in the world today due to virtually universal moral revulsion, we should not look to it for any precedents or parallels. Fortunately, there is no legal obligation (*hovah*) for Jews to impose themselves or allow themselves to be imposed over any non-Jew in this way.[56] Furthermore, that the Jewish experience of slavery in Egypt and redemption therefrom surely provided much of the historical inspiration for the outlawing of slavery in the English-speaking (and Scripture-reading) world in the nineteenth century is a fact that should not be lost on Jews today when contemplating what their newly regained political power over others means.

Fortunately, though, real political solutions do come out of theoretical imaginings. One such theoretical imagining is the rabbinic concept of the "Noahide Laws," which were taken by the ancient rabbis to be those laws that God requires both Jews and non-Jews to accept and obey (although Jews are required to accept and obey much more because of the covenant at Sinai). They are theoretical because they did not arise out of any real juridical authority of Jews over non-Jews actually in operation in history.[57] The core of these laws concern what we today would consider proper political matters, such as prohibitions of murder, robbery, and incest. There are many ramifications of this concept, which has played an important role in Jewish thought since rabbinic times. One such ramification is that it provided the rabbis with the means to imagine (since there seem to have been no explicit records extant) just what was required of the resident-alien (*ger toshav*) in the days when all Israel was living intact in the land of Israel.[58]

However, the question eventually arose as to who was to administer and enforce these laws for the gentiles living under Jewish rule. (Since the concept of the "Noahide" was taken to pertain to all of humankind universally, it is wider than the concept of the resident-alien, which only pertains to the land of Israel under optimal political conditions. Therefore, it is clear that in the absence of Jewish political authority, there is no question that it is the gentiles themselves who are to administer and enforce these laws for themselves among themselves.) Since the question was hypothetical in his day, there being no real precedents to cite, Maimonides (d. 1204) offers the following imaginative answer:

> The Jewish court [the Sanhedrin] is obligated (*hayyavim*) to appoint judges for those who are resident-aliens (*ha-gerim ha-toshavim*) to adjudicate for them according to these [Noahide] laws. This is to be done so that civilization (*ha'olam*) not be destroyed. If the court decides it is appropriate to appoint judges from among them (*me-hen*), it may do so; but if it decides it is appropriate to appoint Jewish judges for them (*la-hen*), it may do so.[59]

Now the question is just how much political and legal autonomy Maimonides is willing to allow to the non-Jewish residents of a Jewish polity. It seems that, at best, they are to be allowed some sort of subordinate status of partial internal rule over themselves. However, one of the most perspicacious students of Maimonides's jurisprudence and himself a distinguished jurist in the same Egyptian community Maimonides had served three centuries earlier, the late fifteenth-century authority, Rabbi David ibn Abi Zimra, in his notes *ad locum*, opines: "if they themselves did not [already] appoint a court for themselves, or there was no one among them fit (*ra'ui*) for the task, then (*az*) the Jewish court is obligated to appoint judges for them."[60] Whether he is actually interpreting Maimonides's own statement here, or is in fact emending it, is arguable either way.

Nevertheless, one can derive from his note that a Jewish polity may grant total juridical authority to a group of non-Jews living under its control, which suggests political sovereignty as well. The only proviso would be that the Jewish authorities be assured that the Noahide laws would be respected by this newly empowered juridical entity. In the case of Christians and Muslims, this would be so *ipso facto* inasmuch as we could rely on the widely influential opinion of the fourteenth-century Provençal jurist, Rabbi Menahem ha-Meiri, who judged both Christians and Muslims to be "nations bound by the ways of [religiously acceptable] law (*ummot ha-gedurot be-darkhei ha-datot*)."[61] The question is, though, how closely one can connect juridical authority to what we would call political sovereignty today. (We shall return to this question in the last section of this chapter.)

Mobility

The question of the right of passage of nonresidents through the territorial boundaries of a polity, for Jews, goes back to the time when Moses and the Israelites requested passage through the land of the Edomites and the land of the Amorites on their way to the Promised Land. "I wish to pass through your land. . . . We shall go by way of the royal road (be-derekh ha-melekh) until we will have crossed your border" (Numbers 21:22). (The "royal road" seems to have been some sort of international highway that was to be open to all peaceful travelers.) Since they requested this right, with the qualification that they would be careful not to take what was not theirs or cause any damage during their passage to the land they were to be passing through, it would stand to reason that they could not in all fairness deny such a right to others passing through their own land. In fact, one rabbinic midrash (exegesis) connects Moses's request for passage through the land of the Amorites with the commandment "to offer peace terms to her [a foreign city]" (Deuteronomy 20:10). In fact, this rabbinic exegete imagined God to have congratulated Moses for reminding him of His own commandment here.[62] Following this analogy, it would seem that just as peace terms are to be both offered and accepted, so is the right of safe passage through one's land for nonresidents something that can be requested and is to be fulfilled. So it would seem that no one could argue against the right of passage—that is, under normal peacetime conditions. Like the negative experience of slavery in Egypt, so the negative experience of being refused the right of passage through the land of the Edomites and the land of the Amorites should cause Jews to infer the positive from the negative, thus seeing what was denied them to be a universal human right.

Autonomy

As we have already seen, one cannot argue for modern notions of autonomy within the Jewish tradition, for "autonomy" has come to mean a law made by myself for myself, but that is a property that belongs to God alone, not to any creature, not even the human creature created in His image. This is so, whether one means "autonomy" in the Kantian sense (the power to legislate duty for oneself and anyone else in one's same general situation) or in the liberal sense (the right to do whatever I want, so long as no one else is harmed thereby). Because of this, the closest we can come to affirming a notion of "autonomy" is to affirm "sovereignty," that is, when a community has the power to govern itself based on the law it has accepted for itself.[63]

Jews have always aspired to a maximum of such sovereignty in the world. They have often had to settle, though, for the minimum of simply being able to govern their "religious" life, which is how they conduct their relationship with God within their own community. (Anything below that minimum makes Jewish life impossible as a public phenomenon, as witnessed by the Marranos, the "secret Jews," who continued to practice Judaism in absolute privacy after it had been banned in Spain and Portugal at the end of the fifteenth century. Their inability to publicly practice Judaism led to the demise of virtually all of them as Jews after a few generations.) But this sovereignty is relative even when maximal. Even the sovereignty of a king in Israel, whether a past historical king or the future Messiah, is subordinate to that of God, the only true king. [64]

That being the case, the maximal liberty that Jews have in any polity of their own is juridical liberty: the right to judge what is the true meaning of law, all of which is taken to be God's law, whether directly revealed in Scripture and tradition or surmised by human reason—none of which could be called autonomy in the strict modern sense of the term.[65] A number of implications can be drawn from this.

First, since the polity is defined by its adherence to the law of God and the perpetuation of it, no matter how important territory is in the covenant between God and Israel, the polity cannot be limited to those who live within the land of Israel. At most, it is the optimal place for the life of the covenant to be led and centered, but it is not the only place.[66] It is only at the time when the Messiah will gather all of the exiled into the land of Israel that polity and territory will coincide. (That will be similar to the recoincidence of bodies and souls that is promised to take place at the resurrection of the dead, an event that is closely linked, if not identical, with the messianic redemption.) And yet, even then, polity will transcend territory inasmuch as Zion is meant to be the capital of a united humankind living under the explicit kingship of God throughout the earth. Therefore, the notion of the "disappearance of the Diaspora (*shelilat ha-golah*)," which some Jews have entertained, is not only bad historical prognostication (in many ways the reestablishment of the state of Israel has strengthened Jewish life in the Diaspora), it is also bad theology. It goes back to the claim made by the Jews of the first Exile in Babylonia that because they were in exile from the land of Israel, "we will become like the nations, like the families of the [other] lands" (Ezekiel 20:32).

Second, there is an implication for the granting of sovereignty to non-Jewish communities living at present under Jewish rule. For if the greatest sovereignty that even the Jews themselves have is essentially juridical, it would seem that if they can recognize the juridical independence of a non-Jewish community presently living under Jewish rule, then they have recognized as much liberty in and for that community as they can recognize in and for their own. This would be based on the notion of a legally constituted state (*Rechtsstaat*), which is not only a state that recognizes the rule of law, but one that is itself the creature of a prior law.[67] At this stage, this point about the priority of the juridical realm over the political realm needs much more specific thought to even be coherent in theory. However, that law itself is rooted in *the* covenant between God and Israel. And other covenants can be made between humans based on that prior covenant. Perhaps, then, the same covenantal thinking, which is the only cogent way I can see, both theologically and politically, for the return of Jewish law in and for a modern nation-state, can lead to a coherent *modus vivendi* with the other communities who now share life with the Jews within the borders of the greater land of Israel.

Notes

1. *Politics*, 1.1/1253a29.
2. See Isa. 2:1–4, 56:6–7; Mic. 4:1–4.
3. See Ezek. 37:1–14; *Babylonian Talmud* (hereafter "B."): Sanhedrin 92b.
4. See David Novak, *The Election of Israel* (Cambridge: Cambridge University Press, 1995), 26ff.
5. See *Second Treatise of Government*, chap. 5.
6. See Aristotle, *Nicomachean Ethics*, 5.5/1133a30.
7. That is why the Talmud rules that certain forms of commercial transfer must still take place "on the ground." See B. Kiddushin 27a.
8. See Rashi, *Commentary on the Torah* thereon; also, B. Kiddushin 30b and B. Niddah 31a.
9. See *Midrash Aggadah* thereon re Ps. 49:12, ed. S. Buber (Vienna: A. Panta, 1894), p. 13.
10. See B. Pesahim 68b.
11. See *Palestinian Talmud*: Berakhot 6:1/9d.
12. See Deut. 32:8–9; B. Berakhot 35a-b and B. Shabbat 119a re Ps. 24:1. The earth and any of its goods are only to be enjoyed *after* acknowledgment that they have all been given by God and, ultimately, remain God's sole property.
13. B. Sanhedrin 57a.
14. *Murder in the Cathedral*, pt. 1, *The Complete Poems and Plays 1909–1950* (New York: Harcourt, Brace, and World, 1971), 196.
15. *Israel und Palaestina* (Zurich: Artemis-Verlag, 1950), 8.
16. B. Arakhin 32b re Lev. 25:10.
17. For the exact status of the commandment to dwell in the land of Israel, see David Novak, *The Theology of Nahmanides Systematically Presented* (Atlanta, Ga.: Scholars Press, 1992), 95.
18. See B. Baba Batra 120a–121a.
19. See David Novak, *The Image of the Non-Jew in Judaism* (New York and Toronto: Edwin Mellen Press, 1983), 53ff.
20. B. Shabbat 31a.
21. Thus even the apparently unconditional scriptural commandment to wipe out the Canaanite inhabitants of the land of Israel (Deut. 20:16) was interpreted by the rabbis to be enforceable only upon the prior refusal of the Canaanites to abide by universal moral law; if they chose to abide by it, they were to be politically recognized by Israel and left unmolested. See David Novak, *Jewish Social Ethics* (New York: Oxford University Press, 1992), 189ff. re *Palestinian Talmud*: Sheviit 6:1/36c.
22. See B. Sanhedrin 20b.
23. See *Mishnah*: Sheviit 6:1, Yadayim 4:4 re Amos 9:14.

24. See B. Yevamot 86b re Ez. 8:15; B. Ketubot 26a; also, Josephus, *Antiquities*, 20.8.8.

25. See B. Sotah 48a; *Mishnah*: Demai 2:2–3.

26. See B. Megillah 3a.

27. See B. Sanhedrin 52b; *Mishnah*: Zevahim 12:4.

28. See B. Berakhot 8a re Ps. 87:2.

29. For the original meaning of *am ha'arets*, see Gen. 23:7; for the later meaning, see B. Berakhot 47b.

30. Hence the ancient Jewish custom to have the worshipers in all synagogues, both in the land of Israel and the Diaspora, face the site of the Temple in Jerusalem. See *Tosefta*: Megillah 3:22 re Num. 3:38; B. Berakhot 6a and Tos., s.v. "ahorei bet ha-keneset."

31. See *Mishnah*: Sheqalim 3:4.

32. See B. Gittin 88b.

33. See n. 21 above.

34. See Novak, *The Election of Israel*, 177ff.

35. See B. Avodah Zarah 36b re Deut. 7:3–4; B. Kiddushin 68b.

36. *Mishnah*: Yadayim 4:4.

37. See B. Shabbat 118b and B. Gittin 52a.

38. See *Tosefta*: Avodah Zarah 4:3.

39. B. Arakhin 29a.

40. B. Hagigah 3b.

41. See n. 34 above.

42. See *Palestinian Talmud*: Bikkurim 1:4/64a re Gen. 17:5.

43. See B. Ketubot 11a; also, B. Yevamot 47a.

44. See Josephus, *Antiquities*, 13.9.1.

45. *Tosefta*: Demai 2:4; B. Berakhot 30b.

46. B. Avodah Zarah 64b.

47. See *Religion of Reason out of the Sources of Judaism*, trans. S. Kaplan (New York: Frederick Ungar, 1972), 124ff.

48. See B. Sanhedrin 27a re Exod. 23:1.

49. B. Kiddushin 68b re Deut. 7:4.

50. See M. Silberg, *In Inner Harmony*, ed. Z. Terlo and M. Hovav (Jerusalem: Magnes Press, 1981), 404ff (in Hebrew).

51. See B. Berakhot 32a re Exod. 32:13; B. Sanhedrin 44a re Josh. 7:11.

52. B. Shabbat 88a re Exod. 19:17.

53. See I. Englard, "The Problem of Jewish Law in a Jewish State," in *Jewish Law in Ancient and Modern Israel*, ed. H. H. Cohn (New York: KTAV, 1971), 143ff.

54. B. Avodah Zarah 36a-b; also, B. Baba Batra 60b.

55. See Maimonides, *Mishneh Torah*: Rebellion, 2.2–7.

56. See David Novak, *Law and Theology in Judaism* 2 (New York: KTAV, 1976), 87ff.

57. See Novak, *The Image of the Non-Jew in Judaism*, 3ff.

58. See B. Avodah Zarah 64b.

59. *Mishneh Torah*: Kingship, 10.11.

60. Ibid., note of Radbaz thereon. Cf. Nahmanides, *Commentary on the Torah*: Gen. 34:13.

61. *Bet ha-Behirah*: Baba Kama 38a, ed. K. Schlesinger (Jerusalem: Mosad ha-Rav Kook, 1967), p. 122. See David Novak, *Natural Law in Judaism* (Cambridge: Cambridge University Press, 1998), 77ff.

62. *Bemidbar Rabbah* 19:20.

63. See Aristotle, *Politics*, 3.11/1287a25–30.

64. See Maimonides, *Mishneh Torah*: Kingship, 12.1.

65. See Novak, *Natural Law in Judaism*, 82ff.

66. See B. Ketubot 110b–111a.

67. See Oliver O'Donovan, *The Desire of the Nations* (Cambridge: Cambridge University Press, 1996), 234.

Twelve

Contested Boundaries

JUDAIC VISIONS OF A SHARED WORLD

NOAM J. ZOHAR

THE TASK of producing, from within the Jewish tradition, significant responses to a specific set of questions regarding territorial boundaries called for extensive reexamination—and sometimes, imaginative extension—of traditional sources. Because of the character of Judaism as a religious tradition focused on one particular people, the analysis often appears to deal exclusively with Jewish or Israeli experience. But my intent, paralleling that of David Novak in the preceding chapter, is to draw insights from this experience that may be applied to a more general context. My remarks below—even where they take issue with Novak's position—are deeply indebted to his original analyses and insights.

Broadly speaking, I endorse the view expressed by Novak, which accords priority to the definition of communal boundaries over the definition of territorial boundaries. In terms of the Jewish tradition, however, I wish to emphasize the contrasting vision of a world shared by all humanity together, contesting the rigidity of political boundaries, territorial and communal alike.

Territorial Boundaries and World Community

Novak begins by positing that "human life is inconceivable outside of a *finite* community"; then in the next sentence, he speaks of a "*defined* community" (emphases added). But "defined" need not be "finite," at least not in Novak's sense of a community which is one of many into which the human race is divided. Why not a world community? This question is raised in the next paragraph, which cites a "version of the Jewish messianic vision that sees one world polity as the goal of all human history." But I find Novak's answer to this insufficient, for he only stresses that even the future world polity is seen as "oriented around Zion as the *axis mundi*."

What is the nature of this "orientation"? It might be spiritual, akin to the Catholic Church's orientation around Rome; this does not require maintaining territorial boundaries between communities worldwide. But suppose it is meant in a more strongly political sense, as in the famous prophetic vision of world peace (Isaiah 2:1–4) which Novak cites. In that vision, Zion's spiritual centrality facilitates resolution of disputes by the messianic king: ". . . Thus he will judge among the nations and arbitrate for the many peoples; and they shall beat their swords into plowshares," and so on. On a minimalist reading, Jerusalem is depicted here simply as the site of the world court. But it is hard to imagine effective adjudication of international disputes without some form of world polity. Indeed, the language of the biblical vision—and certainly its elaboration in post-biblical Judaism—points clearly to Jerusalem as the capital of a world state.[1]

It is true that in traditional messianic visions, the world's peoples are normally seen as retaining their distinct identities. But within the framework of a worldwide polity, this does not imply that the nations will continue to be divided by firm political boundaries. The suggestion seems rather to be one of a federation under which peoples maintain their ethnic and cultural diversity.

Moreover, according to the biblical account, even the division of humanity into separate communities is not part of the original scene. In the Bible, human history begins without inter-communal boundaries, and some versions of the messianic vision include elimination of even linguistic boundaries between the world's nations.

Throughout the first ten chapters of Genesis, humanity is one family. The rabbis stressed the anti-racist significance of this common origin: "That is why Adam was created only one—so that none should say to his fellow, 'My forefather was greater than your forefather'" (*Mishnah* San. 4:5). Only at the Tower of Babel does God decide to frustrate human unity and inflict on humans a division of languages (Gen. 11:1–9). The nature of the human trespass which supposedly called for this punishment is far from clear. In any case, latter-day prophetic visions clearly express the hope of a reunited humanity (cf., e.g., Zeph. 3:9).

In actual history, however, humanity is divided into disparate communities. Novak's analysis rightly stresses the primacy of communities over territorial states. It is not that the world is first divided by territorial boundaries and then the human aggregate within each area forms a community; rather, humanity is divided into communities, who then in fact maintain territorial boundaries between their distinct living spaces. It is worth adding that this too is illustrated nicely in the Tower of Babel story: it was mutual incomprehension that reduced humanity to many different tongues, causing them to scatter "over the face of the whole earth" (Gen. 11:7–9).

The primacy of communities leaves room for wondering whether they must necessarily be coextensive with particular territories. Here the Jewish people seems to furnish a classic counterexample: a community that has maintained its identity over millennia without territorial integrity or continuity. Against this, Novak points to the Jewish aspiration to return to Zion. But toward the end of his chapter (under "Autonomy"), he seems to relegate this return to a point beyond history, connecting it to the resurrection of the dead, and asserts that denying the significance of Jewish existence in the Diaspora is "bad theology," as it suggests that access to God is restricted to one land. Similarly, at the end of the section on "Ownership", he writes that "the people could survive with her identity intact even when exiled from the land."

Thus the Jewish people do seem to illustrate that a community *can* exist in dispersion. And Novak apparently holds that there is no inherent deficiency in such existence, as long as Jews preserve a utopian dream of return to their land. Against this, it is worth citing the Zionist counterclaim that such existence was always more or less precarious, and in the era of the modern nation-state was destined to produce catastrophe, as it did most infamously in the Holocaust.

On another level, we might ask whether the community's existence in dispersion and without sovereignty was in fact viewed as satisfactory in terms of the Jewish religious tradition itself. If we look to rabbinic records from the years following the fall of the Second Commonwealth (70 C.E.), it is possible to reconstruct a debate on whether there was any sense at all in continued observance of the Torah's commandments in exile.[2]

The upshot of rabbinic discussions on this point was that outside the land of Israel, an entire class of commandments do not, in fact, apply. These include, first and foremost, the laws relating to agriculture and to the earth's yield—the very same laws that embody most of the Torah's instruction pertaining to social justice. The concern for social justice continued to find partial expression in the communal institutions of *tzedakah* [welfare]; but as a minority in foreign lands, Jews could not aspire to mold the shape of economic life around them.

It is perhaps possible that in modern democracies, Jewish communities will be able to flourish and even to extend their commitments to impact society at large, while respecting the traditions and commitments of other communities. If this proves viable, then the long Jewish experience of diaspora life will have yielded a striking example of full communal existence without a territory. Against this, some religious Zionists have argued that the vitality of Judaism in the modern world can be sustained only through life in a Jewish land.[3]

Ownership, Exclusionary Rights, and Violence

Even if people must exist in distinct communities, and even if each community has to exist in some specific place, it does not follow that any local community has a "right to be in a certain place" in the exclusionary sense intended by Novak. The "territorial imperative" on the collective level (Novak's usage—to my mind a dubious extension of the term) is grounded in the fact that control over land is indispensable for producing and maintaining property, to be passed on from one generation to the next. Novak compellingly connects this with ancient agricultural society and its urban centers, pointing to humanity's first child (Cain), who calls the first city by the name of his own child, linking "The perpetuity of the city and the perpetuity of the family/clan."

There is, however, a "missing link" in this narrative, namely, pre-agricultural society. There were—and, indeed, still are—human groups who do not settle down in one place, from the prehistoric hunters and gatherers to various nomadic tribes. The Bible posits the selfsame Cain as the first "tiller of the soil," in juxtaposition to his brother Abel—whom he murdered—the first "keeper of sheep" (Gen. 4:2).

In their classical midrashic commentary, the rabbis describe the altercation which led to the first murder (fratricide): "The one [i.e., Cain] said, 'The land upon which you are standing is mine!' while the other [i.e., Abel] said, 'The garment you are wearing is mine!'"[4] From the perspective of Novak's analysis we might add that the landowner may be able to survive without the wool garment, while no place at all is left for the nomad if title to the entire land is claimed by others. This reveals the inherent connection between agricultural communities, exclusive ownership, and lethal violence. Thus, besides recognizing the territorial forms of social organization covered in Novak's discussion, the Judaic tradition also echoes the moral rebuke implicit in the conception of a nomadic mode of communal existence.

This moral rebuke may be extended to form a critique of certain contemporary theories of political obligation. Specifically, it seems to apply to Locke's grounding of commitment to local laws in "tacit consent," given through one's continued residence within a polity—and particularly one's possession of land therein.[5] After all, Locke was a primary exponent—in modern political philosophy—of the biblical teaching (emphasized by Novak) regarding divine ownership of the world and all its resources. God had given over these resources to humanity collectively, and individuals are permitted to assert ownership only if sufficient similar resources remain for others to take. This seems to imply a significant qualification of Locke's "tacit consent" argument. Locke posits, in effect, that the initial members of the commonwealth make acceptance of its laws a condition for possessing land therein. Now, they can rightly require such a condition only if they may legitimately bar a prospective dweller from taking possession of land in their midst. Their own initial right of (exclusive) possession, however, holds only insofar as the supply of free land is not exhausted. Hence the "tacit consent" grounding of political obligation is valid only if there is land elsewhere, free for the taking—or at least if persons are permitted to reside in a land without incurring the full duties of citizens.[6]

The emphasis on divine ownership of the land—indeed, of the entire world—is certainly a central motif in both biblical and rabbinic Judaism. Minimally, this implies—as Novak notes—that human "domicile is conditional"; God may expel a people from His land because of their "abominations." But (*pace* Novak) in the Hebrew Bible these "abominations" seem *not* to include idolatry: the Canaanites are expelled because of various forms of incest, or particularly heinous modes of idolatrous worship, such as child sacrifices.[7]

While the Israelites too might be expelled for similar iniquities, their tenancy is dependent on living up to various additional demands. Regarding the nature of these crucial demands, the several books of the Bible do not speak in one voice. While some focus on idolatry,[8] others emphasize social injustice as the prime cause of the downfall of Israel and Judea.[9] This latter emphasis is perhaps closer to the strictures of Leviticus 25, where divine ownership of both land and persons is invoked as a principle of freedom.

The laws of Leviticus 25 forbid the full alienation through sale of either an individual's personal freedom or his inherited portion of the ancestral land. As a piece of "utopian legislation," this probably expressed a revolutionary voice against the supremacy of a landed gentry—corresponding to the prophetic critique: "Ah, those who add house to house and join field to field, till there is room for none but you to dwell in the land!" (Isaiah 5:8).[10] Nevertheless, this notion of unalterable, male-inherited ownership can also become a conservative or even reactionary force.

Similarly, on the collective level, the notion of a holy land allotted by God is liable to produce opposition to pragmatic compromises over internationally disputed boundaries. Such opposition is by no means a necessary implication of the idea of a holy land itself;[11] still, it is voiced by more than a few speakers in contemporary Israeli politics.

Distribution: Boundaries and Commons

Novak, focusing on the internal boundaries between the holdings of tribes, clans, and individuals in ancient Israel, shows how the ownership of land first gave access to status and to (an ancient form of) "citizenship," and then was eventually superseded by the valuation of Torah. This is, then, a story of gradual erosion in the importance of territorial boundaries. Insofar as status came to depend on Torah learning and observance, its attainment became independent of holding land or even of living within the boundaries of the Holy Land.

This does not address, however, the question of what territorial boundaries *do* serve to distribute. Specifically, do they—or should they—function in distributing (1) living space and (2) access to natural resources? The first of these questions will be discussed below, in connection with the issue of diversity. Here I shall touch on the second question, that of natural resources.

It is hard to find anything in traditional Jewish sources about (re)distribution of natural resources across international boundaries. The common assumption in these sources seems to be that inhabitants of each land rightly control whatever it yields: for example, there is mention of international trade, or of Hiram, King of Tyre offering to supply cedars from Lebanon (1 Kings 5:15–25). I, too, will seek, therefore, to extrapolate from discussions concerning the boundaries established *within* the land of Israel, between the territories of the several tribes, or even between individuals.

The Talmud (B. Bava Kama 80b–81a) cites a list of ten stipulations attributed to Joshua, the leader who divided the land among the tribes. The idea seems to be that the initial title to discrete tribal territories was qualified by these stipulations. They include, for example, fishing rights in the Sea of Galilee (whose shores touch more that one tribal territory); collective rights to a water source that emerges in private land; rights of pasture in untilled open spaces (although they are privately owned); certain rights to free passage; and use of another's land for particular emergencies.

Thus, even though the tribal boundaries distribute living space and main title to the land as agricultural means of production, they are not taken to distribute rights to *all* uses of the territory or of the resources therein. Particular areas (like the Sea of Galilee) or scarce resources (like water) are retained for common access.

Now the Talmud (B. Bava Kama 81b) also appears to hold that these stipulations apply not only in the land of Israel, but also in other locations. This implies that they are seen not as idiosyncratic rules fashioned by a particular ruler, but rather as universal limitations upon land ownership by both individuals and tribes. There thus seems little reason not to extend a similar approach to international boundaries.

The particular details of these "ten stipulations," contained in a text composed roughly two thousand years ago, cannot conceivably serve, of course, as a recipe for industrial (or post-industrial) societies. But they can yield meaningful insights into a Jewish traditional stance favoring "universal commons" as qualifying—both spatially and functionally—the effects of territorial boundaries.

It is worth adding that another rabbinic tradition affirms that Jerusalem "was not included in the distribution to the tribes" (B. Yoma 12a), that is to say, it remained the holding of all in common. This may imply a conception that, insofar as a holy place is deemed crucial for access to spiritual fulfillment, it must not be owned by any particular group.[12]

Diversity: From Community to Nation

With the demise of the First Commonwealth and the exile to Babylon, the territorial boundaries of the Israelite people were dissolved. This eventually produced two opposite responses. Novak mentions one response, that of Ezra the scribe, who fiercely struggled against the assimilation of "the holy stock with the people of the lands." But this view, which may well be characterized as racist, was not universally shared. The post-exilic Isaiah prophesied: "Let not the foreigner say, who has attached himself to the Lord, 'The Lord will keep me apart from his people.' . . . For My House shall be called a house of prayer for all peoples" (Isa. 56:3,7).[13]

Eventually, the Jews established what we might call a *social boundary*, in lieu of a spatial boundary, to retain their identity as a distinct people. As Novak indicates, this was the setting in which the institution of *giyyur* (Novak: *gerut*) was born: a formal procedure deemed both necessary and sufficient for a non-Jew to become a Jew. To the extent that non-sovereign Jewish communities were political units, the *giyyur* procedure—conferring membership in the community—can be seen as akin to naturalization. But given the political and geographic conditions of Jewish existence, attaining such membership did not often carry significant material advantages.[14] Thus the "social boundary" that defined the Jewish community, permitting scarce internal diversity, excluded outsiders from little other than membership in the community itself.

All of the above cannot be applied in any straightforward way to a sovereign state. Novak rightly notes the extreme novelty of contemporary Israeli concerns over diversity and pluralism; but I believe he is wrong in attributing the novelty solely to the emergence of a *secular* Jewish state.[15]

The significant transformation in Jews' self-understanding with regard to the nature of their collectivity preceded the founding of the Jewish state and even the rise of the Zionist movement. The political emancipation of Jews in the various European countries, which proceeded throughout the nineteenth century—combined with the cultural effects of "enlightenment" and secularization—greatly undermined the definition of the Jewish collectivity in exclusively religious terms[16] (indeed, it was mostly secular Jews who opted for Zionism, essentially a modern national movement).

Hence, the Jewish internal problems of accommodating diversity derive from the contrast between the narrowness of the traditional social-cultural boundaries on the one hand, and the actual diversity amongst modern Jews on the other hand. In the late nineteenth century, (Jewish) Orthodoxy defined itself by splitting away from the wider Jewish society, founding separate communities. All this has yielded a duality in contemporary conceptions of the Jewish collective: Is it a religious community or a nation?

At a crucial point in Novak's discussion, these two conceptions are insufficiently distinguished. He states that

> if the state of Israel is a secular, democratic polity, then there should be no ethnic or religious distinctions made between one group of *Israelis* or another. However, were this to be, the essentially *Jewish* character of the state . . . would no doubt be lost. . . . On the other hand, if the state of Israel is to be a state for Jews governed by traditional Jewish law, then the only full citizens should be those Jews willing to live

under the rule of this law. As for secular Jews, or liberal religious Jews, let alone non-Jews, their obviously second-class status would have to be determined by the rabbinical interpreters of that law. [17]

This assumes that "Jewish" must imply adherence to the Jewish religion and to its rabbinic laws. Those who would "like to see Israel as a state for Israelis in the same way, let us say, that Canada is a state for Canadians" are accordingly described as "radically secularist."

What this leaves out is the possibility of Israel as a Jewish state in the same way, let us say, that France is a French state: a national home to the Jewish people. Surely for most Israelis, and for many Jews worldwide, Jewish identity is a matter of *national identity* rather than religious faith or praxis. I will turn shortly to the implications of such nationalism for non-Jewish minorities in Israel; at this point, I wish to emphasize that secular Israelis do not see themselves as less Jewish—and certainly not as enjoying a diminished citizenship in the "Jewish state"—on account of their rejection of religious traditions.[18] This has implications for both the question of joining the Jewish people and the status of non-Jewish citizens in Israel. Let us briefly address each in turn.

The struggle (which has recently received some notoriety) over the procedure for joining the Jewish collective is also not best understood in terms of the difficulties that Israel, as a Jewish-hence-religious state, has with democratic egalitarian ideals. Rather, this struggle reflects the same opposition noted above between two rival conceptions of the Jewish collective.

Those Orthodox Jews who adhere to a narrow definition of Judaism as a religious community have struggled to define the procedure of *giyyur* as the formal expression of a religious conversion. Novak's discussion appears to echo this understanding of *giyyur* in terms of a "prior commitment" to adopt "the full regimen of Jewish law." But others have argued that this understanding of *giyyur* is a modern innovation; classically, it was primarily a mode of joining the Jewish people. True, as long as the Jewish people as a whole adhered to religious faith and praxis, choosing to join them involved a willingness to share their religion. But the primary character of the procedure lies in being symbolically "reborn" into the people, joining an ethnic collective rather than a religious community.[19]

I believe that it is such an understanding of *giyyur* that has facilitated its retention as the only mode of joining the Jewish people recognized by Israeli law. Yet coalition politics leave the control of the procedure in the hands of rabbinic courts, whose members commonly subscribe to the Orthodox, narrow conception of the Jewish collective, and therefore prevent the "conversion" of the great number of persons who would want to do so without making a deep commitment to the Jewish religion.

This gap between popular sentiment and institutional behavior has resulted in a change in the Law of Return, which now grants the right of immigration to Israel, and of immediate conferral of Israeli citizenship, to (so-called) "non-Jewish" relatives of (legally recognized) "Jews." In effect, this gives legal expression to widespread support for an ethnic-national conception of Jewish identity.

That non-Orthodox Israelis have failed, to date, to remold *giyyur* in light of their own intuitive self-understanding is a fact that may have more general significance for theories of nationalism, beyond this specifically Jewish quandary. Insofar as a national state may adopt selective immigration laws, it gives preference to the repatriation of members of the nation living abroad. Such immigration rights would require formal criteria, and the question might easily arise: Who is a (legitimate) member of the nation? Can anyone join (and thereby gain a right to "repatriation")—and if so, how?

In the foregoing discussion I have assumed that if a nation-state, with regard to repatriation, distinguishes between would-be immigrants on the basis of their national affiliation, this does not constitute illicit discrimination. This does not apply, of course, to the treatment of the state's own residents. If "Jewish state" is understood, as I suggested above, as a political home to the Jewish nation, then the status of non-Jewish citizens should be addressed in terms of the normal discourse on the rights of ethnic and national minorities in a democratic nation-state.[20]

The particularly Jewish character of this nation is of concern here mainly to the extent that Jewish national culture, including the strong influence of biblical and post-biblical traditions, produces special obstacles (or, conversely, enhancements) to the toleration of some forms of diversity. Among such obstacles, surely the most serious is the strong Jewish tradition of uncompromising battle against "idolatry."

Novak properly cites here the teaching of Meiri, who excludes adherents of other monotheistic religions from the strictures against idolaters. Meiri taught that, unlike the barbarian pagans of old, these are civilized people and must be treated with full respect. It is worth emphasizing that, with regard to such people, Meiri stipulates that they are "[to be treated] exactly like Jews ... without any distinction."[21] This is not, however, because they adhere to "religiously acceptable" law (Novak's translation, imprecise in my view), but rather because they are subject to the civilizing force of religion. It is not that social norms require religious scrutiny; quite the contrary, the quality of particular religions may be known by their (civilizing) fruits. The problem with the ancient idolaters was not, according to Meiri, in their religion *per se*, but in its barbaric moral import.

This difference in translation has great importance for contemporary issues. Meiri certainly did not imagine that people could be civilized without *any* religion, and he would perhaps be greatly perplexed by the phenomenon of, say, civilized (and polytheistic) Hindu society. But since the importance he accords to religion in this context is *only* as (what he took to be) an indispensable force for inculcating civilized norms, his position paves the way for adherents of the Jewish religion to abandon traditions which allow (or even invite) discrimination against heretics or "idolaters."[22]

Mobility

Here I have little to add, except one consideration pertaining to resource allocation. Redistributive taxation is an integral part of the Jewish tradition: this is called *tzedakah*, sometimes imprecisely translated as "charity." Now the scope of *tzedakah* collection and distribution alike includes first of all the residents of a particular polity. Thus the funds collected in the communal *tzedakah* chest are meant primarily for meeting the needs of local indigent persons. The needs of persons in transit are to be met to a far lesser degree.[23]

Hence the halakhic tradition may well endorse making it known that the right to move within a group's territorial boundaries does not entail claim-rights (above a certain minimum) to services offered to indigent residents.

Autonomy: The Jewish Traditions of Rabbinic and Political Authority

Novak's emphasis on subordination to God is valid insofar as its intent is a moral-spiritual constraint on politics. But those voices within the Judaic tradition that give greater weight to human autonomy are underrepresented in his exposition in two important senses.

First, it is true that the Torah's underlying premise is a commitment to live by God's law. But this does not confine rabbinic interpretation and implementation of that law to a mode of "discovery" as opposed to "creation" of norms. On the contrary, rabbinic *midrash* is markedly bold in its (re)interpretations of God's "written Torah."[24]

A second point has greater direct bearing upon Novak's proposal of how to deal with aspirations for autonomy by non-Jewish communities within the boundaries of a Jewish polity. Novak claims that if non-Jewish communities are able to have their own autonomous courts of law, they will suffer no political deprivation. This is because, from a traditional point of view, the Jews themselves wield no more than "essentially juridical" sovereignty.

This seems to me a vast understatement of the role of politics and of the autonomy of political authority in Jewish law. True, when the people turned to Samuel seeking a king, God perceived this as a rejection of divine kingship (1 Sam. 8, 12). But much has transpired since then in the Jewish political tradition. Eventually, Nissim Gerondi (fourteenth century, Spain) formulated a doctrine of parallel authority, virtually secularizing politics. Torah law reflects ideal justice, but the requirements of social order call for something

else, which the king provides, guided not by Torah but by prudential considerations. And this was not mere speculation about a kingdom long lost, but a
reflection of the autonomous powers of the *berurim* (selectmen) who acted as
legislators and judges in medieval Jewish communities.[25]

There are many who view the ultimate grounds for such non-rabbinic authority as residing in the consent of the governed, and therefore extend the
same recognition to democratically elected legislatures and governments.[26]
Non-Jewish citizens of a Jewish state are subject to the authority of such bodies
insofar as they too consent and participate in electing them (as well as being
elected to them). And if they insist instead on a significant degree of self-
government, their claim has *prima facie* merit—subject, of course, to whatever
valid constraints there are on a right to full or partial secession; but that is for
another essay.

Notes

1. Novak himself, toward the end of his chapter (in the section on "Autonomy"),
writes that "Zion is meant to be the capital of a united humankind living under the
explicit kingship of God."

2. See *Sifre: A Tannaitic Commentary on the Book of Deuteronomy*, trans. R. Hammer
(New Haven: Yale University Press, 1986), secs. 43–44.

3. For example, David Hartman has at one point argued that "The circumstances of
Diaspora existence prevent the development of Judaism as a total way of life," suggest-
ing that even the viability of diaspora communities may depend on the Israeli reality.
See David Hartman, "Israel and the Rebirth of Judaism," in his *Joy and Responsibility*
(Jerusalem: Ben-Zvi–Posner, 1978), 276–86 (quote from p. 285).

4. *Genesis Rabbah* 22:7 (the text here is in my own translation).

5. John Locke, *Two Treatises on Government*, 2nd ed., ed. Peter Laslett (London:
Cambridge University Press, 1967), Second Treatise, secs. 116–19.

6. See the discussion by Harry Beran, *The Consent Theory of Political Obligation*
(London: Croom Helm, 1987).

7. This is clear from the specific sins enumerated in Lev. 18 and from numerous
other biblical passages.

8. Notably the books of Deuteronomy (e.g., 11:17) and Kings (e.g., 2 Kings 17:7–
23).

9. Notably the so-called "classical prophets," e.g., Micah 3:1–12. On all this, see
Yehezkel Kaufmann, *The Religion of Israel, from Its Beginnings to the Babylonian Exile*
(Chicago: University of Chicago Press, 1960).

10. Or also as protection against usurpation by a monarch; cf. the story of Navot in
1 Kings 22.

11. See Yeshayahu Leibowitz, *Judaism, Human Values, and the Jewish State*, ed. and
trans. Eliezer Goldman et al. (Cambridge: Harvard University Press, 1992), 223–28.

12. See the discussion in S. Lieberman, *Tosefta Ki-Fshuta: A Comprehensive Commentary on the Tosefta*, 2nd ed. (Jerusalem: JTS, 1992), Order Zera'im, pt. II, pp. 722–23
(in Hebrew).

13. See M. Weinfeld, "The Universalistic Trend and the Isolationist Trend in the Period of the Return to Zion," *Tarbitz* 33 (1964): 228–42 (in Hebrew).

14. On the contrary; the traditional response to persons seeking to join the Jewish fold was the warning: "Do you not know that Israel at the present time are persecuted and oppressed?" (B. Yevamot 47a).

15. Indeed, the very conception of a state as both "Jewish" and "secular" appears, in Novak's account, to be a definite oxymoron. Against this, we should recognize a distinction between the realm of Torah and the realm of politics, a point to which I shall return below.

16. See, e.g., Jacob Katz, *Tradition and Crisis: Jewish Society at the End of the Middle Ages*, trans. and with an afterward and bibliography by Bernard Dov Cooperman (New York: New York University Press, 1993).

17. See Novak in chapter 11 above, under "Diversity."

18. As noted by Novak, instances in which state mechanisms are harnessed to enforce religiously inspired norms are experienced by such persons as unjust intrusions, extracted by an Orthodox minority through a lamentable process of coalition politics—*not* as proper expressions of the state's "Jewish" character.

19. See A. Sagi and Z. Zohar, "The Halakhic Ritual of Giyyur and Its Symbolic Meaning," *Journal of Ritual Studies* 9:1 (1995): 1–13; and more fully in their *Conversion to Judaism and the Meaning of Jewish Identity* (Jerusalem: Bialik Institute and Shalom Hartman Institute, 1994) (in Hebrew).

20. On the notion of a democratic—and liberal—nation-state, see Yael Tamir, *Liberal Nationalism* (Princeton: Princeton University Press, 1993); and David Miller, *On Nationality* (Oxford: Clarendon Press, 1995).

21. Meiri's novellae to tractate *Bava Kama* 113b; for a discussion, see Jacob Katz, *Exclusiveness and Tolerance: Studies in Jewish-Gentile Relations in Medieval and Modern Times* (London: Oxford University Press, 1961), 114–28.

22. Should anything at all be retained from the old war against idolatry? Is there any creed today which should be opposed with the zeal of the biblical prophets? For an illuminating discussion, see Avishai Margalit and Moshe Halbertal, *Idolatry*, trans. Naomi Goldblum (Cambridge: Harvard University Press, 1992).

23. See *The Code of Maimonides* (*Mishneh Torah*), trans. Isaac Klein (New Haven: Yale University Press, 1979), bk. 7 (Agriculture), pt. X, "Laws of Gifts to the Poor," chap. 7.

24. See David Hartman, *A Living Covenant: The Innovative Spirit in Traditional Judaism* (New York: Free Press, 1985), 21–108; and Noam Zohar, "Midrash: Amendment through the Molding of Meaning," in *Responding to Imperfection: New Approaches to the Problem of Constitutional Amendment*, ed. Sanford Levinson (Princeton: Princeton University Press, 1995), 307–18.

25. For a discussion and analysis of Gerondi's views, see Menachem Lorberbaum, "Politics and the Limits of Law in Jewish Medieval Thought: Maimonides and Nissim Gerondi" (Ph.D. diss., Hebrew University, 1992).

26. For detailed sources (in translation) and commentaries, see Michael Walzer et al., eds., *The Jewish Political Tradition, Vol. I: Authority* (New Haven: Yale University Press, 2000), esp. chaps. 8–10.

Thirteen

Territorial Boundaries

A LIBERAL EGALITARIAN PERSPECTIVE

WILL KYMLICKA

TERRITORIAL boundaries are a source of embarrassment for liberals of all stripes, and particularly for liberal egalitarians. It is not clear what principles liberal egalitarians should invoke when drawing or redrawing political boundaries. Indeed, it is not clear that liberal egalitarianism can justify the existence of territorial boundaries at all, at least if these boundaries prevent individuals from moving freely, and living, working, and voting in whatever part of the globe they see fit.

There are two separate problems here for the liberal egalitarian. The first has to do with the role of boundaries in the allocation of rights. What is the justification for distinguishing the rights of citizens inside the borders from those of aliens outside the borders? The problem here is that liberalism is premised on the inherent moral worth of *persons*, each of whom is seen as a "self-originating source of valid claims," to use Rawls's well-known phrase. This assumption of the moral worth of persons is invoked by liberal theorists to defend various claims of individuals against the state. The state must not violate people's physical integrity, or restrict their freedom of religion, or association, or their right to earn a living. For liberal egalitarians, respect for the moral worth of individuals requires the state not only to protect these negative rights, but also to provide various forms of positive assistance (e.g., publicly funded health care, education, social assistance). Respect for the moral worth of individuals even entails acknowledging the right to resist and overthrow political authority which denies people these basic rights and freedoms.

In virtually all liberal theories, however, a subtle but profound shift takes place in terminology. What begins as a theory about the moral equality of *persons* typically ends up as a theory of the moral equality of *citizens*. The basic rights which liberalism accords to individuals turn out to be reserved for some individuals—namely, those who are citizens of the state. Only citizens have the right to move freely into a country, or to earn a living, or to share in collective self-government.

To be sure, liberal egalitarians have an inclusive conception of citizenship, which allows for, and indeed encourages, all people who are long-term residents on a territory to become citizens of that country. So, in principle, there is no permanent class of "resident aliens" who are denied equal citizenship.[1] But even if the class of "citizens" is more or less coextensive with that of "permanent residents," that still leaves all the people who live outside the territory, and who are denied the rights which are accorded to citizens. As people with an inherent moral worth, why aren't they entitled to enter, work, and vote in a liberal democracy?

As Samuel Black notes, this shift from the language of "persons" to "citizens," while ubiquitous in liberal theory, is rarely noticed, let alone defended, by liberals.[2] Yet it has profound consequences for people's well-being. In a world marked by massive global inequalities, the idea that one's freedoms and opportunities are limited to the state in which one is born means that some people are born into a legal status which guarantees them personal security, ample opportunities, and a decent standard of living, while others (through no fault of their own) are born into a legal status which condemns them to poverty and insecurity. As Joseph Carens notes, this is the modern equivalent of feudalism. People who are born on one side of the Rio Grande are born into the modern equivalent of the nobility, while those who are born a few miles across the river are born into the modern equivalent of serfdom.[3]

It is difficult to see how such a practice can be justified within a liberal egalitarian framework premised on the moral equality of persons. The logic of their principles, then, seems to commit liberal egalitarians to a defense of "open borders": while states may continue to have territorial boundaries, these boundaries should not form obstacles to mobility, and one's rights to live and work within a state should not depend on which side of the boundary one is born.

Needless to say, a policy of open borders would be a radical departure from the actual practice of liberal democracies. Indeed, it is so radical that, apart from a few academic philosophers, no one takes it seriously. To even mention it is to brand oneself as hopelessly naive. Since liberal egalitarians wish to be taken seriously, and typically think of themselves as articulating the basic norms and values of our existing political culture rather than elaborating some utopian scheme of values unrelated to people's existing convictions, they are reluctant to push this issue of open borders. The result is a conspiracy of silence on the role of boundaries within liberal egalitarianism.

The second problem for liberal egalitarians concerns the *drawing* of boundaries. Whether borders are open or closed, we are still faced with the question of where the boundaries should be drawn. In the real world, the locations of boundaries have almost always been determined by factors which we now recognize as illegitimate—conquest, colonization, the ceding of territories from one imperial power to another without the consent of the local population, and so on. We know, in short, that existing boundaries are largely the product of historical injustice.

This would suggest that liberal egalitarians should accord little or no moral weight to existing boundaries, and instead allow people to redraw them on the basis of legitimate moral factors. But what are the legitimate grounds or principles for determining the locations of boundaries? For liberals, the most obvious candidate here—as with any other issue—is freedom of choice, constrained by respect for the rights of others. If the majority on any particular territory does not wish to remain part of a larger state—perhaps because they were unjustly included in that state in the first place—why shouldn't they be allowed to secede, or to join some other state? So long as people's civil and political rights will continue to be respected under the new arrangements, what basis is there within liberalism for resisting such claims to redraw boundaries?

Presumably a group will only seek secession if it feels discriminated against within the larger state (e.g., the Kurds in Turkey). But even if the group desiring its own state is treated fairly and is economically prosperous within the larger state (e.g., Quebecers in Canada)—what some commentators call a "vanity secession"—why should liberals resist it? To force a group to stay within a larger state against their will seems to violate liberal principles of freedom and consent. As John Stuart Mill put it, recognizing a prima facie right to secede "is merely saying that the question of government ought to be decided by the governed. One hardly knows what any division of the human race should be free to do if not to determine which of the various collective bodies of human beings they wish to associate with."[4]

A very broad right of secession—what commentators call a "plebiscitary right of secession," since all it requires is that a group gain a majority in a free vote in favor of secession within a given territory—would seem, therefore, to be the natural conclusion of liberalism's commitment to freedom of association, and to the principle that legitimate authority requires the consent of the governed. As Allen Buchanan puts it, liberalism, unlike some other ideologies, does not see the state as an "unalterable fact of nature," but rather as "a human creation to serve human needs," and if a group thinks that another political arrangement will better serve their needs without violating anyone else's rights, then liberalism would seem to support their claim to redraw the political boundaries. Any political philosophy which "places a preeminent value on liberty and self-determination, highly values diversity, and holds that legitimate political authority in some sense rests on the consent of the governed" is driven towards affirming a broad plebiscitary right to secede.[5]

But here again, this position is radically at odds with the actual practice of liberal democracies and of international law. Indeed, as with open borders, it is a position which no one takes seriously outside of academic philosophy. It is seen not only as naive, but as dangerously irresponsible, and an invitation to instability and ethnic conflict. For most people, secession is only permissible as a last resort, if it is the only way to remedy great oppression and injustice like genocide or slavery. Under all other conditions, existing boundaries should be treated as sacrosanct. People who adopt this view need not deny that existing boundaries were drawn in an unjust manner. On the contrary, it is precisely because so many of the world's borders were formed unjustly, without the consent of the local population, that it would be a recipe for disaster to give a right to secede to any group which wishes it. No part of the world would be safe from the ensuing instability.

Liberal egalitarians are understandably reluctant to push this issue of a right of secession. The result, as with open borders, is silence on the question of the drawing of boundaries. Indeed, many liberal egalitarians tacitly accept the prevailing view that political boundaries are sacrosanct, and that groups which find themselves within a larger state as a result of history must accept that this is their fate in perpetuity, no matter how little they like it.

In short, territorial boundaries are the source of two acute embarrassments for liberal egalitarians. Liberal egalitarian principles seem, at first glance, to justify a policy of open borders, and of granting groups a plebiscitary right of secession. Yet these two positions are so radical that most liberals avoid discussing them. To avoid them, liberal theorists often assume that the answers to the question of boundaries and membership can be taken as givens for the purposes of developing a political theory. For example, John Rawls starts with the assumption that we already know where the boundaries of the state are located, and that we can assume that these boundaries exist "in perpetuity." We also already know who is permitted to live within those boundaries, and we assume that no one enters or leaves this society, and that every person lives out his life in the same country he was born into.[6] In this way, Rawls defines the problem of boundaries out of existence. He does not attempt to apply the principles of liberal egalitarianism to the questions of boundaries and membership. Rather, he assumes that these questions have been resolved in advance of the theory, and so can simply be taken as given for the purposes of developing and applying liberal egalitarian principles. In effect, Rawls says, "I have nothing to say on these questions. Go sort them out on your own, and come back to me when they've been settled. Then we can talk about how to apply liberal egalitarianism."[7]

The result is somewhat paradoxical. Liberal egalitarians have avoided pushing their radical views on boundaries and membership for fear that this would make them irrelevant to the debate; yet in the process, they have made themselves irrelevant in a different way, by treating these issues as ones which fall outside of their theory.

This is an unsatisfactory approach to some of the world's most urgent problems. In the real world, we can't assume that existing boundaries are accepted, let alone that they will be accepted in perpetuity. Nor can we assume that people outside these boundaries have no desire or claim to enter the country. Any political theory which has nothing to say about these questions is seriously flawed. Moreover, the result, intentional or unintentional, is to tacitly support the very conservative view that existing boundaries and restrictive membership rules are sacrosanct. Unwilling to advance the sorts of radical proposals for open borders and rights of secession which their own principles seem to entail, liberal theorists have tacitly accepted the opposite view: that people who are not members of the political community, because their place of birth happened to fall outside its boundaries, have no right to demand inclusion; and that those groups which are inside the boundaries of the state, because they happened to have been involuntarily included at some point in the past, have no right to exit.

This raises the question of whether liberal egalitarianism has anything useful to contribute to the debate about boundaries. I believe it does. I will proceed in a slightly unusual way. Most of the time, liberal political theorists start with their foundational principles of freedom and equality, and then try to work out the implications of these principles for particular political issues. But as I've already noted, when this method is applied to questions of boundaries and membership, it seems to lead almost immediately to conclusions which are unrealistic, and which liberal egalitarians have themselves been reluctant to promote. These may indeed be the only conclusions which are compatible with liberal egalitarian principles, in which case liberals should presumably have the courage of their convictions and actively promote what they see as the just approach.[8]

But I want to try a different approach. I will start with "actually existing" liberal democracies, to see which practices have developed over time within them regarding boundaries and membership, and then see if we can identify some normative rationale for them.

If we examine the actual practice of liberal democracies, we see that questions about the function and location of boundaries are often resolved by reference to principles of *nationhood*. That is, the location of boundaries is intended to demarcate discrete national political communities, and the function of these boundaries is, in part, to protect national cultures. As a general rule, both the location and function of boundaries are determined by principles of nationality—that is, by the goal of creating, recognizing, empowering, and protecting "nations."

This connection between boundaries and conceptions of nationhood lies very deep in the actual practice of liberal democracies, but until very recently it has not been seriously studied by liberal egalitarian theorists.[9] The question is whether we can close this gap between practice and theory: Can we find a theoretical justification, consistent with liberal egalitarianism, for the practice of privileging national identities, national cultures, and national communities in decisions about the location and function of territorial boundaries?

The fact that the boundaries of actually existing liberal democracies are rationalized on the basis of ideals of nationhood does not show that they are morally justified. The privileging of national identities within liberal democracies may simply reflect ethnocentrism or power politics, disconnected from any deeper set of liberal values or principles.[10] We should not exclude this possibility. But nor should we exclude the possibility that the privileging of nationality within liberal democracies is not a denial of liberal values, but rather an evolution and application of liberal principles. Perhaps nationality has turned out to be important for liberal democracies in a way which liberal theorists did not predict, and have not yet fully recognized.

That is the hypothesis I will explore in the rest of this paper. I will begin by discussing the actual practice of liberal democracies with regard to boundaries, and how these practices relate to conceptions of nationhood, and then ask whether liberal egalitarians can endorse these nationality-based practices.

Definition

The sorts of "boundaries" I am interested in are those which involve the territorial demarcation of contemporary democratic nation-states. In the first instance, these boundaries have a legal significance: they tell us which laws we are subject to, and which people and institutions exercise authority over a territory. In the past, this may have been the only significance of political boundaries. But in modern democracies, the boundaries of nation-states do more than this. They also define a body of citizens—a political community—which is seen as the bearer of sovereignty, and whose will and interests form the standards of political legitimacy. A democracy is the rule of and for "the people," and "the people" is usually defined as all those individuals permanently residing within the state's territorial boundaries.

It is important to remember how new this idea is. In earlier periods of European history, elites tried to dissociate themselves from "the plebs" or "the rabble," and justified their powers and privileges precisely in terms of their alleged distance from the masses. Political boundaries specified the scope of a lord's fiefdom, but did not demarcate a single people or community. The idea that serfs and lords belonged to the same society would have been incomprehensible to people in the feudal era, when elites were not only physically segregated from peasants, but also spoke a different language. The lords were seen not only as a different class, but as a different and superior race of people, with their own language and civilization, unrelated to the folk culture of the peasants in their midst, and this was the basis of their right to rule.

The rise of nationalism, however, valorized "the people." Nations are defined in terms of the people—that is, the mass of population on a territory, regardless of class or occupation—who become "the bearer of sovereignty, the central object of loyalty, and the basis of collective solidarity."[11] National identity remains strong in the modern era in part because its emphasis on the importance of "the people" provides a source of dignity to all individuals, whatever their class.

The use of the vernacular in modern political life is a manifestation of this shift towards a national identity. The use of the language of the people is confirmation that the political community really does belong to the people, and not to the elite. And while national communities still exhibit major economic inequalities, the different economic classes are no longer seen as separate races or cultures. It is seen as right and proper that lower-class children are exposed to the high culture of literature and the arts (which itself has become expressed in the vernacular), while upper-class children are exposed to the history and folk culture of the people. All individuals within the territory are supposed to share in a common national culture, speak the same national language, and participate in common educational and political institutions.

In short, nationalism created the myth of a single national community which encompasses all classes on the territory. And within the Western democracies, this myth has gradually moved closer to reality, as the achievement of both a wider franchise and mass literacy has enabled almost all citizens to participate, however unequally, in common national cultural and political institutions operating in the vernacular.

Boundaries, then, do not just circumscribe legal jurisdictions, but also define "peoples" or "nations" who form a common political community, and who share a common national language, culture, and identity. Of course, the boundaries of states rarely coincide exactly with people's national identities. Most states contain people who do not feel a part of the dominant national community, either because they are perceived as "aliens" by the majority, and so have been prevented from integrating into it (e.g., illegal immigrants; Turks in Germany), or because they have and cherish their own distinct national identity, and so do not wish to integrate (e.g., the Québécois in Canada). I will discuss these cases later in the chapter.

As a general rule, however, liberal democracies have aspired to forge a common national identity amongst the people permanently residing on their territory. Moreover, they have been surprisingly effective in this "nation-building" project. Who would have known that the French language, which was limited to a small region around Paris at the time of the Revolution, would become a defining feature of the national identity of the people of France? Who would have known that immigrants from all over the world, arriving on American shores with no knowledge of English or of American institutions, would so quickly adopt an American national identity, and accept the principle that their life chances will be bound up with participation in common national institutions operating in the English language?

This surprising degree of coincidence of territory and national identity has been achieved in two ways. In some cases, it has been achieved by redrawing boundaries to better match people's preexisting national identities. This is the case with the secession of Norway from Sweden in 1906, or of Slovakia from the Czech Republic. But more often, the aim has been to revise people's national identities to better fit existing boundaries. This is the aim of the classic "nation-building" programs undertaken by all Western democracies, in which common institutions operating in a common language are established through the entire territory of the state.[12]

In some countries, the result of these nation-building programs has been to extend a common national culture throughout the entire territory of the state. These are the paradigmatic "nation-states"—for example, England, France, Germany, Italy. But in other countries, territorially concentrated minorities have resisted integration into the dominant societal culture. In such "multination states"—for example, Canada, Switzerland, Belgium, and Spain—one or more national minorities, with their own distinct languages and separate institutions, exist alongside the dominant societal culture.

In multination states, people share citizenship but not a national identity. For most people in Flanders, their citizenship is Belgian, but their national identity is Flemish. For most Quebecers, their citizenship is Canadian, but their national identity is Québécois. It is within such multination states that questions of secession typically arise. Multination states are in effect federations of peoples, and the question may arise whether one of the federating peoples will seek to exit and form its own nation-state. There is no necessity for such multination states to dissolve, but if they do remain together, it is often by creating and strengthening an *internal* boundary between the constituent national units. In crossing from one region of the country to another, one is not only subject to different laws, but also to different institutions operating in different languages, and perhaps even different legal systems, so that passing from one region to another is, in important respects, like entering another country.

In short, multination states are the exception which proves the rule that the boundaries of liberal democracies demarcate not only distinct legal jurisdictions, but also distinct national political communities. For multination states are, in effect, federations of national political communities, each with its own national institutions operating in its own territory.[13]

Ownership

To say that the boundaries of modern nation-states demarcate national political communities is not to say that these states, or their territories, are the "property" of the dominant national group. To be sure, many nationalists make such claims, and some of the new constitutions in Central and Eastern Europe endorse them. It is not entirely clear what nationalists mean when they say that the state and its territory are the property of the titular national group. This is obviously not property ownership in the usual legal sense, since no one owns a state, and nonnationals are often allowed to own land or resources.

Generally speaking, the claim that the state and its territory belong to the titular nation is a claim not about the allocation of private property rights, but about control over public space. The heart of the claim is the belief that this part of the world is the homeland of the majority national group. The implication of this claim, sometimes made explicit, is that the presence of minorities on the nation's territory is somehow "unnatural" and regrettable. In earlier times, such minorities may have been expelled or stripped of their citizenship. In the post–World War II era, where the discourse of human rights is the international lingua franca, even virulent nationalists typically accept that "ethnic cleansing" is not permissible. But while the personal and privacy rights of minorities must be respected, nationalists often insist that the institutions of the state, and public space more generally, belong solely to the titular national group.

This can be enforced in various ways. For example, the use of minority languages can be prohibited in public forums. More subtly, the political process can be restricted to people who are loyal to the constitution—a constitution which declares that the state must uphold the "national" character of the state. Any individuals, or political parties, which question the privileging of the dominant national group can then be prohibited from holding public office on the grounds that they reject the constitution. Or various gerrymandering techniques can be used to ensure that everyone in senior positions of power comes from the majority national group.[14] There is no single or specific legal implication of the view that the state belongs to the titular national group. Rather, it is a more diffuse sense that public space should bear the mark of the dominant national group, while minorities are denied public visibility even as their individual rights are respected.

This is not an acceptable view from a liberal egalitarian perspective. As I noted earlier, the boundaries of states never coincide exactly with people's national identities. There are always some individuals within a state who do not belong to the dominant national group. And it is a fundamental principle of liberalism that the state treat all individuals subject to its authority with equal concern and respect. Since liberalism denies that anyone has a natural right to govern over others, respecting the moral equality of individuals is a precondition for legitimately acquiring authority over them. Political power, and public institutions generally, belong to all individuals subject to them, not just to those individuals who belong to the majority national group.

In opposition to the view that the state belongs to the titular nation, many liberal theorists have endorsed the view that the state should be "neutral" amongst all ethno-cultural groups, neither promoting nor suppressing any

particular national identities, languages, or cultures. On this view, the liberal
state should adopt the same strategy towards ethno-cultural groups that it
takes towards religious groups. Just as there is a separation of state and church,
with the state neither assisting nor impeding the ability of religious groups to
reproduce, so too there should be a separation of state and ethno-cultural
groups.[15]

But as we've seen, this is not the actual practice of liberal democracies.
Liberal democracies have engaged in extensive campaigns of nation-building
in an effort to diffuse a common set of institutions operating in a common
language throughout the entire territory of the state, and thereby to promote
a common national identity. Liberal democracies, as much as illiberal ones,
attempt to give a distinctly "national" character to public space.

What then distinguishes liberal nation-building from the sort of illiberal
nationalism which views the state as the property of the dominant national
group? This is an interesting—and inadequately studied—question. I will
highlight nine differences:

One difference is in the degree of coercion used to promote a common
national identity. It wouldn't be true to say that liberal states only use voluntary means to promote nation-building. Historically, at least, liberal states
have been quite willing to use coercion in the service of nation-building.
There was nothing voluntary about the imposition of the French language on
the Bretons after the Revolution, or the imposition of the English language on
the Mexicans living in the territory annexed from Mexico by the United
States after the war in 1848. And even today, as I will discuss later on, there
are coercive aspects to the way immigrants are pressured to integrate. But it is
generally true that liberal states impose fewer penalties or disadvantages on
those who remain outside the dominant national group. For example, while a
liberal state may not provide public funds to minority-language schools, they
are unlikely to prohibit such schools if they are privately funded.

This is related to a second difference—namely, that liberal states have a
more restricted conception of the relevant "public space" within which the
dominant national identity should be expressed, and a more expansive conception of the "private" sphere where differences are tolerated. For example,
parliamentary debates in a liberal state may be conducted exclusively in one
language, but liberal states are unlikely to insist, as some states in Eastern
Europe do, that election posters and brochures be printed only in the dominant language, or that weddings be conducted in the dominant language. Liberal states may insist that the official language be used when filling in govern-
ment-mandated health and safety reports in the workplace, but they are
unlikely to insist that union meetings be conducted in the majority language.

Third, liberal states are unlikely to prohibit forms of speech or political
mobilization which challenge the privileging of a national identity. People
who wish to give public space a different national character—perhaps by

adopting a different official language, or even by seceding to form a separate state—are not forbidden from holding public office. Advocating such changes is not seen as disloyalty, or even if it is seen as disloyal, this is not viewed as sufficient grounds for restricting democratic rights.

Fourth, liberal states typically have a more open definition of the national community. Membership in the nation is not restricted to those of a particular race, ethnicity, or religion. Generally speaking, anyone can join the nation who wants to do so. When liberal states have prohibited the public expression of a minority's national identity, they at least have ensured that the minority could become full and equal members of the dominant nation. However coercive the French were towards the Basques, there was never any question that Basques could become French. By contrast, in some countries, nonnationals are prevented from integrating into the dominant national group even as they are prohibited from expressing their own national identity. Bulgarian nationalism is currently undergoing major transformations, but until recently it used to be that to be a "true" Bulgarian, one must have a Bulgarian surname, be descended from ethnic Bulgarians, belong to the Orthodox Church, speak Bulgarian without an accent, and dress like a Bulgarian. Needless to say, it was very difficult for Turks living in Bulgaria to ever be accepted as members of the "Bulgarian" nation, even if they wished to integrate.

Fifth, partly as a result of this inclusiveness, liberal states exhibit a much thinner conception of national identity. In order to make it possible for people from different ethno-cultural backgrounds to become full and equal members of the nation, and to allow for the maximum room for individual dissent, the terms of admission are relatively thin—say, learning the language, participating in common public institutions, and perhaps expressing a commitment to the long-term survival of the nation. Joining the nation does not require one to abandon one's surname, or religion, or customs, or recreational practices.

Insofar as liberal nation-building involves diffusing a common national culture throughout the territory of the state, it is a thin form of culture—what we could call a "societal culture," centered on a shared language which is used in a wide range of societal institutions (schools, media, law, economy, government, etc.). I call it a societal culture to emphasize that it involves a common language and social institutions, rather than common religious beliefs, family customs, or personal lifestyles. Societal cultures within a modern liberal democracy are inevitably pluralistic, containing Christians as well as Muslims, Jews, and atheists; heterosexuals as well as gays; professional women as well as traditional housewives; conservatives as well as socialists. In non-liberal states, by contrast, acquiring a national identity typically requires a much thicker form of cultural integration, involving not only a common language and public institutions, but also elements of religion, ritual, and lifestyle.

Sixth, partly as a result of this cultural thinning, nationalism in a liberal nation is less likely to be viewed as the supreme value. Illiberal nationalisms often see the nation as sacred, and as the ultimate value to which all else is subordinate and instrumental (e.g., defining women's role as the "bearers of the nation"). Liberal nationalism, by contrast, seeks to thin the content of the national identity and culture so that other areas of social life have room to flourish on their own terms (e.g., religion, family life, personal lifestyles, hobbies, and careers). These are not seen as subordinate and instrumental to the goal of national greatness or the achieving of a national destiny. Rather, they are accepted as having independent and intrinsic value. If anything, it is the nation which is seen as having instrumental value. The nation is primarily valuable not in and of itself, but rather because it provides the context within which we pursue the things which truly matter to us as individuals—our family, faith, vocation, pastimes, and projects. As Jonathan Glover puts it, a useful maxim for liberal nationalists is: "Always treat nations merely as means, and never as ends in themselves."[16]

Of course, even in a liberal society, some individuals will view their nation as sacred, particularly if they subscribe to a religion which says that they are a chosen people who have made a covenant with God, and whose national destiny is ordained by God. A liberal society allows such views to exist and to be expressed as part of freedom of religion. But these are not the views of the state or of the constitution, and are not the basis for liberal nation-building programs. In separating church and state, and in thinning the content of national identity, liberalism also desacralizes the nation, and makes room for other values to flourish on their own terms.

Seventh, and also a result of this cultural thinning and ethnic inclusiveness, liberal national cultures become more "cosmopolitan." I don't mean that citizens in a liberal nation adopt the *ideology* of cosmopolitanism. As an ideology, cosmopolitanism rejects all forms of nationalism, and opposes efforts by the state to protect national identities and cultures. It is clear that citizens of Western democracies are not "cosmopolitan" in this sense: instead, they overwhelmingly accept that it is a legitimate function of the state to protect and express a particular national identity. But while liberal citizens remain committed to the practice of nation-building, the actual substance of their day-to-day life is increasingly influenced by the beliefs, practices, and products of other parts of the world. This cultural interchange is the inevitable result of liberal freedoms, ethnic inclusiveness, and the thinning of the official national culture.

Put another way, in a liberal nation, the societal culture is an open and pluralistic one, which borrows whatever it finds worthwhile in other cultures, integrates it into its own practices, and passes it on to subsequent generations. Moreover, this sort of cultural interchange is seen as a good thing. Liberal nationalists reject a notion of culture that sees the process of interacting with and learning from other cultures as a threat to "purity" or "integrity," rather than as an opportunity for enrichment. In short, liberal nationalisms wish to

become cosmopolitan in practice, in the sense of embracing cultural interchange, without accepting the cosmopolitan ideology which denies that people have any deep bond to their own language and cultural community.[17]

Illiberal nationalisms, by contrast, often aim to protect the "purity" or "au-
thenticity" of their culture from "corruption" by external influences. The
claim of illiberal nationalists to be protecting their "authentic" national culture is often a sham, since all forms of nationalism involve reshaping and
modernizing traditional cultures. But even if just a pretence, the rhetoric of
protecting cultural purity can have xenophobic consequences, both in formal
policies (e.g., prohibiting "foreign" religions from proselytizing; prohibiting
foreign ownership of land) and public discourse (e.g., criticizing local NGOs
for cooperating with international agencies).

Eighth, liberal nations are less likely to insist that national identity must be
exclusive. One can be a true "Canadian" and also think of oneself as a member
of the Irish or Vietnamese nation. Moreover, one can publicly express both of
these national identities. Canadians of Irish descent can celebrate Irish national symbols and holidays as well as Canadian ones—there is no formal or
informal prohibition on flying an Irish flag on one's property, or marching in
a St. Patrick's Day parade. By contrast, illiberal nationalisms tend to be more
exclusive in their conception of national identity, and to insist that to be a
true member of the nation one must renounce all other national identities.
Here again, this difference is reflected both in formal rules (e.g., whether dual
citizenship is legally permitted) and in informal interactions (e.g., whether
singing the anthem or flying the flag of another nation is seen as disloyal or
provocative). This tolerance for dual nationality is obviously most relevant for
immigrants and for the children of mixed marriages.

Finally, liberal states have, at least recently, been willing to accord public
recognition to, and share public space with, those national minorities which
consistently and democratically insist upon their national distinctiveness.
Unlike France after the Revolution, or the United States in 1848, liberal
states today recognize that territorially concentrated groups which were involuntarily incorporated into the state cannot and should not be forced to adopt
the majority's national identity. If groups like the Québécois, Catalans, Flemish, or Scots see themselves as distinct nations within the larger state, then
their national distinctiveness should be recognized in public life and public
symbols, through such things as official language status, self-government
rights, and recognition of their distinct legal traditions. In accepting the legitimacy of these minority nationalisms, states accept that they are the sort of
"multination" state which I discussed earlier.

These nine differences are interconnected, and often mutually reinforcing.
But it is possible for nationalist movements to be more liberal in some respects, and less liberal in others. It is also important to distinguish the formal
level of laws and constitutions from the informal level of public discourse and

attitudes. For example, it is possible to have a liberal constitution which affirms equal rights for women, and yet an illiberal public discourse which says that women who exercise their rights are betraying their duties to the nation. Similarly, liberal naturalization rules can coexist with an illiberal discourse which denies that immigrants or children of mixed marriages are "true" members of the nation. Removing illiberal exclusionary or discriminatory laws is obviously the first step, but nationalism can only become truly liberal if a wider public culture of tolerance develops. Liberal nationalism is not just about legal formalities, but also about the respect for dissent and diversity shown in everyday discourse and interaction amongst citizens.

There are undoubtedly many other ways in which liberal nation-building differs from illiberal nationalisms.[18] But enough has been said already, I hope, to show that the issue is not *whether* states engage in nation-building, but rather what *kind* of nation-building. While liberal states see themselves as having the right to promote a particular national identity, and to try to diffuse it through the territory of the state, this nation-building project is a qualified and self-limiting one. Minorities are not seen as "unnatural" blots on the nation's territory, but as full citizens whose interests must be given due concern, and not just weighed on the basis of how they affect the dominant national group. This means that any nation-building programs must involve only limited coercion; must leave ample room for the expression of differences in the private sphere; must allow nonmembers to become full and equal members of the nation if they choose; and must agree to share public space in cases where national minorities insist on maintaining their distinctiveness. In all of these ways, liberal democracies reject the view that the state belongs exclusively to the dominant national group.

Mobility

The admission and naturalization of aliens provides a good example of this distinctively self-limiting form of nation-building found within liberal democracies. The inevitable result of using boundaries to demarcate national communities is to create a category of "aliens" or "foreigners" living beyond these boundaries. And this raises one of the fundamental questions of this volume— what should states do when aliens wish to cross these boundaries and enter our national territory?

In many illiberal nation-states, aliens are denied admission, since they are seen as a source of cultural or racial impurity, and as a threat to national security. Other states allow aliens to enter as "guests," but deny them the option of becoming citizens, no matter how long they live in the country. For nations which adopt a culturally thick and racially exclusionary definition of nationhood, aliens can never really become "one of us," and so they must either be kept outside the borders or at least denied the vote.

In most liberal democracies, by contrast, legally admitted aliens are able to gain citizenship and become full and equal members of the nation. Many liberal democracies allow, sometimes even welcome, people from other countries to enter, settle within their boundaries, and join the nation. Such immigrants are seen as potential contributors to the nation, not as a threat to it.

But this openness is neither unrestricted nor unconditional. Since boundaries define not just legal jurisdictions but also national communities, admission to liberal democracies is regulated in such a way as to protect the national community. This means, firstly, that immigrants are expected, encouraged, even pressured, to integrate into the national society. This expectation of integration is enforced in a variety of ways. In the United States, for example, immigrants must learn English to gain citizenship (unless they are elderly), as well as some basic information about the nation's history and institutions. Similarly, it is a legal requirement under state laws that the children of immigrants learn English, and learn a common core curriculum. Typically, immigrants must know English to gain access to government-funded job training programs. In most countries, immigrants must know the official language in order to receive professional accreditation, or to have their foreign training recognized. The most highly skilled pharmacist won't be granted a professional license to practice pharmacy in Canada if she can only speak Portuguese. And knowledge of English is a precondition for working in the bureaucracy, or to gain government contract work. These policies designed to prompt the linguistic and institutional integration of immigrants are found in virtually every Western democracy.[19]

So liberal democracies not only allow immigrants to integrate, they also pressure them to integrate. Immigrants not only have a right to become full and equal members of the nation, they also have a duty to join the national community. Of course, immigrants are free to choose not to naturalize, and thereby avoid some of the pressures to integrate into the national community. But as we've seen, this is a costly decision, which limits the immigrant's right to earn a living, to vote, or to be free from the threat of deportation.

Secondly, liberal democracies impose limits on the *numbers* of people admitted, based on the capacity of the nation to absorb such immigrants. If immigrants integrate, then they help to strengthen a national community; but if too many arrive in too short a time, then the resources which assist immigrants in integrating (e.g., language training, citizenship classes, job-training programs) may be stretched too thin. Moreover, the pressures on immigrants to integrate may be ineffective if a massive number of immigrants from the same country arrive and settle together and form a sizable and economically viable enclave. Both the incentives and the pressures for integration work better when immigrants realize that they are too small and dispersed to form their own separate society.

So liberal democracies use control of their boundaries as a way to protect and strengthen their national society. Aliens are admitted only in limited numbers, and under terms which encourage and pressure them to integrate into the national community. If the number of immigrants currently admitted exceeds the absorptive capacity of the society, then the quotas are reduced. If the existing incentives and pressures for integration are not sufficient, then additional ones are added (e.g., strengthening the language or loyalty requirement for citizenship, or extending the residency requirement). The number of admissions, and the terms of admission, are constantly modified to reflect assessments of the interests of the national community.

As I said, this is a good example of how the liberal state privileges a national identity, but in a distinctively open and self-limited way. This is not the utopian "open borders" policy, since the rights of aliens to enter and settle are tightly regulated to protect the national community. But nor is this a xenophobic policy of closing the borders to all aliens, or of denying citizenship to aliens who live within the country. Since the nation is defined in a thin, inclusive, and democratic way, aliens who are admitted under these regulated conditions are able and encouraged to join the nation, and are seen as potential contributors to the nation, not as threats to its cultural purity or national security.

Diversity

So far, I have simply been describing the practices of actually existing liberal democracies with respect to borders. I've argued that liberal states use boundaries to define and protect national identities and cultures, but they do so in a distinctively self-limiting way which distinguishes them from illiberal forms of nationalism. But is this privileging of nationality defensible from a liberal egalitarian point of view? The fact that these self-limiting forms of nation-building are distinctive to liberal democracies does not prove that they are genuinely consistent with liberal principles. It could instead reflect a regrettable compromise between liberal egalitarian values and illiberal nationalist values.

At first glance, it may appear that liberal democracies are compromising their liberal principles when they engage in nation-building. As we've seen, liberals reject the idea that the state is the property of the dominant national group, since this idea would be a denial of the equal status which liberalism accords to all citizens. But nor are liberal democracies neutral towards the various national identities present within their territory. They are nation-states, and as such engage in nation-building programs. How can this privileging of national identities, however limited, reflect anything other than an unstable compromise of liberal and illiberal values? Even if a liberal state does not *exclusively* belong to the members of the dominant national group, doesn't this privileging of national identity imply that they are in some sense preferred shareholders in the state?

In this section, I will argue that limited forms of nation-building are indeed permissible from a liberal egalitarian point of view, and that differences in nationality provide a valid basis for determining the location and function of boundaries. I will set aside, for the moment, the fact of gross economic inequality between nation-states, which means that restricting mobility into rich countries is not only a matter of protecting a national culture but also of protecting an unequal share of resources. I will argue in the final section that claims by national communities to an unequal share of the world's resources are problematic from a liberal egalitarian point of view. But for the moment, I will set aside issues of economic inequality, and ask whether there is anything wrong with the privileging of national identities as such, even in the absence of economic inequality between states. To simplify the issue, imagine that the world contains ten nation-states, all of which have a comparable standard of living. Is there anything wrong with each country using its boundaries to define and protect its national identity in the various ways I've been describing?

There are several reasons, I think, why privileging nationality in this way can assist in the achievement of basic liberal egalitarian values. Some of the most interesting work in contemporary political theory has been exploring these connections between liberal values and national identities, and my discussion here draws on this emerging literature.[20]

Consider, first, equality of opportunity. A modern economy requires a mobile, educated, and literate workforce. Standardized public education in a common language has often been seen as essential if all citizens are to have equal opportunity to work in this modern economy. Indeed, equal opportunity is defined precisely in terms of equal access to mainstream institutions operating in a dominant language. Liberal nation-building—including the requirement that immigrants learn the dominant language to gain citizenship, and that their children learn it in school—makes this possible.

Second, participation in a common national culture has often been seen as essential for generating solidarity within modern democratic states. The sort of solidarity required by a welfare state presupposes that citizens have a strong sense of common identity and common membership, so that they will make sacrifices for each other, and this common identity is assumed to require (or at least be facilitated by) a common language and history. David Miller and Margaret Canovan have recently defended the importance of nation-building in motivating citizens to fulfill their obligations of justice to the disadvantaged.[21]

Third, participation in a national culture may enhance individual freedom. For example, Avishai Margalit and Joseph Raz argue that membership in a national culture provides people with meaningful choices about how to lead their lives, in the sense that "familiarity with a culture determines the boundaries of the imaginable." Hence if a culture is decaying or discriminated against, "the options and opportunities open to its members will shrink, become less attractive, and their pursuit less likely to be successful."[22] For this reason, the foundational liberal commitment to individual freedom can be extended to generate a commitment to the ongoing viability and flourishing of national cultures.

Finally, nation-building may be important for democratization. Shared political deliberation is only feasible if participants understand and trust one another, and this surely is promoted when citizens share a common language and national identity. Indeed, John Stuart Mill went so far as to claim that

> Free institutions are next to impossible in a country made up of different nationalities. Among a people without fellow-feeling, especially if they read and speak different languages, the united public opinion, necessary to the workings of representative government, cannot exist. The influences which form opinions and decide political acts are different in the different sections of the country. An altogether different set of leaders have the confidence of one part of the country and of another. The same books, newspapers, pamphlets, speeches do not reach them.[23]

Some people think that Mill's reasoning has been rendered obsolete by the arrival of radio, television, and the Internet. I will explain in the next section why I think Mill's analysis remains relevant, and why a strong connection still exists between democratic deliberation and territorially bounded national communities.

However, I hope enough has been said already to show that liberal egalitarians can find grounds for supporting limited forms of nation-building. When liberal states attempt to diffuse common educational and political institutions operating in a common language throughout the territory of their state, and pressure immigrants to learn this language and integrate into these institutions, they are promoting important values of equal opportunity, solidarity, individual freedom, and democratic deliberation. These nation-building programs need not reflect the illiberal idea that the state is the property of the dominant national group, but rather may reflect sincere attempts to promote basic liberal egalitarian values.

Despite initial appearances, then, liberal nation-building is not a regrettable compromise between liberal egalitarianism and illiberal nationalism, but may be the most effective vehicle for the achievement of liberal egalitarian aims.[24] One way to test the consistency of nation-building with liberal egalitarianism is to ask how parties in Rawls's original position would deal with issues of boundaries. In my view, Rawls's idea that we should test principles by asking whether they would be adopted behind a "veil of ignorance" is a useful way to determine whether our practices are consistent with norms of impartiality. As I noted earlier, Rawls himself does not apply this theoretical device to the question of boundaries. Instead, he tells the parties in the original position that the issue of boundaries is already settled. But what if we put this question to the parties in the original position? What would people, who do not know their race, class, ethnicity, or language, choose as a principle for the drawing and functioning of boundaries?

In light of the arguments given above, I think they would accept that boundaries should be drawn, wherever possible, to create distinct national communities. They would also accept that states can adopt limited forms of nation-building to further consolidate and protect the sense of national identity within each state; and that, so long as there is no gross economic inequality between nations, states should be able to regulate the admission and naturalization of aliens.

Why wouldn't parties in the original position favor a system of open borders, where people could freely cross borders and settle, work, and vote in whatever country they desire? After all, such a system would dramatically increase the domain within which people would be treated as free and equal citizens. Yet open borders would also make it more likely that their own national community would be overrun by settlers from other cultures, and that they would be unable to ensure their survival as a distinct national culture. So parties in the original position face a choice between, on the one hand, increased mobility and an expanded domain within which people are free and equal individuals, and, on the other hand, decreased mobility but with a greater assurance that people can continue to be free and equal members of their own national culture. Most people in liberal democracies favor the latter, and I think that parties in the original position would make the same choice. They would rather be free and equal within their own nation, even if this means they have less freedom to work and vote elsewhere, than be free and equal citizens of the world, if this means they are less likely to be able to live and work and participate politically in their own language and culture.

The constructing of national political communities needn't take the form of secession to create nation-states. It could instead take the form of drawing federal boundaries within multination states so as to enable national groups to exercise territorial self-government within a larger state. Indeed, this option might well be preferred by parties in the original position, since it combines the benefits of increased mobility with protection of national identities.[25] But the principle would still be to create political units, wherever possible, which share a common national identity, since such units are likely to provide the best context for the achievement of people's interests in freedom, justice, and democracy.

Autonomy

I briefly raised the issue of autonomy in the previous section, when I noted Mill's claim that meaningful democracy is only possible within political units which share a common national identity. I want to return to that claim, since it remains relevant to issues of democratization today. We can rephrase Mill's point this way: Democratic deliberation requires mutual understanding and trust, and there is good reason to think that such understanding and trust in turn requires some underlying commonalities. Some sense of commonality or shared identity may be required to sustain a deliberative and participatory democracy.

But what sort of shared identity? If we examine different existing democracies to see what sorts of commonalities have proven necessary for deliberative democracy, I think we would find that deliberative democracy does *not* require a common religion (or common lifestyles more generally); a common political ideology (e.g., right vs. left); or a common racial or ethnic descent. We can find genuinely participatory democratic forums and procedures which cut across these religious/ideological/racial cleavages.

When we turn to language, however, things are more complicated. Many democracies are effectively monolingual, and having a common language has clearly helped in their democratization. Of course, there are several multilingual democracies—Belgium, Spain, Switzerland, Canada. Each of these countries contains at least one sizable national minority whose distinctive language has some official status. But if we look at how democratic debates operate within these countries, we find that language is increasingly important in defining the boundaries of political communities, and the identities of political actors.

There is a similar dynamic which is taking place in all of these countries, by which (a) the separate language groups are becoming more territorialized— that is, each language has become ever-more dominant within a particular region, while gradually dying out outside that region (this phenomenon— known as the "territorial imperative"—is very widespread);[26] and (b) these territorialized language groups are demanding increased political recognition and self-government powers through federalization of the political system. (These processes of territorialization and federalization are of course closely linked—the latter is both the cause and the effect of the former.) Political boundaries have been drawn, and political powers redistributed, so that territorialized language groups are able to exercise greater self-government within the larger federal system.

In short, language has become an increasingly important determinant of the boundaries of political community within each of these multilingual countries. These countries are becoming, in effect, federations of self-governing language groups. These self-governing language groups often describe themselves as "nations," and mobilize along nationalist lines, creating the sort of "multination" state I discussed earlier.

There are good reasons to think that these "national" linguistic/territorial political communities—whether they are unilingual nation-states or linguistically distinct subunits within multination states—are the primary forum for democratic participation in the modern world. They are primary in the sense that democracy within national/linguistic units is more genuinely participatory than at higher levels which cut across language lines. Political debates at the federal level in multination states, for example, or at the EU, are almost invariably elite-dominated.

Why? Put simply, democratic politics is politics in the vernacular. The average citizen only feels comfortable debating political issues in his or her own tongue. As a general rule in Western democracies, it is only elites who have fluency with more than one language, and who have the continual opportunity to maintain and develop these language skills, and who feel comfortable debating political issues in another tongue within multilingual settings.[27] Moreover, political communication has a large ritualistic component, and these ritualized forms of communication are typically language-specific. Even if one understands a foreign language in the technical sense, without knowledge of these ritualistic elements one may be unable to understand political debates. For these and other reasons, we can expect—as a general rule—that the more political debate is conducted in the vernacular, the more participatory it will be.

There are "public spaces" and forms of civil society which cut across language lines. However, these tend to be issue-specific and/or elite-dominated. If we look for evidence of a genuinely popular process of "collective will formation"—or for the existence of a mass "public opinion"—we are likely to find these only within units which share a common language (and common mass media using that language). I quoted Mill's claim, made in 1861, that genuine democracy is "next to impossible" in multilingual states, because if people "read and speak different languages, the united public opinion necessary to the workings of representative institutions cannot exist." The evidence from Europe suggests that linguistic differences remain an obstacle to the development of a genuine "public opinion." As Dieter Grimm notes, it is the presence of a shared mass media, operating in a common language, "which creates the public needed for any general opinion forming and democratic participation at all," and

> the absence of a European communication system, chiefly due to language diversity, has the consequence that for the foreseeable future there will be neither a European

public nor a European political discourse. Public discourse instead remains for the time being bound by national frontiers, while the European sphere will remain dominated by professional and interest discourses conducted remotely from the public.[28]

So the evidence suggests that language is profoundly important in the construction of democratic political communities. It has in fact become increasingly important in defining political communities, and these language-demarcated political communities remain the primary forum for participatory democratic debates. Insofar as this is true, then territorially bounded national communities will, and indeed should, continue to serve as the primary locus for the exercise of collective autonomy and self-government.[29]

Distribution

I have offered a qualified defense of the view that limited forms of nation-building are permissible from a liberal egalitarian point of view. If I am right, the existing use of boundaries to define and protect distinct national languages, cultures, and identities is not inherently in conflict with liberal egalitarian values.

However, there is one respect in which the current practice of liberal democracies cannot, I think, be defended—namely, reserving a country's resources for the exclusive use and benefit of its citizens. I began this chapter by noting that liberal egalitarians view *people* as moral equals. It follows that each person's well-being matters equally, from the point of view of liberal theory. Liberal egalitarians cannot accept, therefore, any system of boundaries which condemns some people to abject poverty while allowing others a life of privilege. Yet this is precisely what occurs today, given the grossly unequal international distribution of resources between states, combined with limitations on mobility.

As several theorists have persuasively argued, parties in Rawls's original position would not accept an international regime which perpetuates such gross inequalities.[30] These are the very paradigm of the sort of undeserved and morally arbitrary inequalities which liberal egalitarianism is committed to remedying. The parties in the original position, not knowing where they will be born, will want to ensure that any system for drawing and policing boundaries will not create gross disparities in people's chances for a decent life.

But how would they seek to prevent or remedy these sorts of international inequalities? One option would be to insist that borders be eliminated, or at any rate left fully open, so that the less well-off can move to wealthier countries. But if my earlier arguments are correct, parties in the original position would not choose this option, since it would undermine or inhibit the benefits from creating cohesive national communities. Moreover, open borders would often be of no use to the very poorest, who cannot afford a ticket to fly from Mozambique to Germany.

Instead, I think that parties to the original position would choose some form of redistributive tax—perhaps a global resource tax—which requires wealthier countries to share their wealth with poorer countries.[31] The goal would be to ensure that all people are able to live a decent life in their country of birth, without having to leave their culture and move to another country to gain access to a fair share of resources.

If rich countries are unwilling to share their wealth in this way, then I think they forfeit the right to restrict admission into their borders. It is not permissible, in the liberal egalitarian view, to restrict admission if this involves hoarding an unfair share of resources. However, if states do meet their obligations of international justice, then it is permissible for them to regulate admissions so as preserve a distinctive national community. This regulation of mobility is consistent with liberal egalitarianism, I believe, since it would not involve claiming an unfair share of resources, but would only reserve for the nationals of a country what aliens already have in their own country—namely, the chance to be free and equal citizens within their own national community. This is the sort of freedom and equality which most people value, and in the absence of gross economic inequalities, there is no invidious inequality in saying that each nation should be able to take limited steps to protect its national distinctiveness.

The claim that wealthy countries can only restrict admissions if they share their wealth with poorer countries will strike many people as wildly unrealistic. And many liberal egalitarians have attempted to avoid this conclusion. Some argue that justice only applies where people are in relations of interdependence, and that the level of interdependence between countries is insufficient to raise issues of justice. Others argue that the very meaning of justice is inevitably culture-bound, since it depends on "shared understandings" of goods, and that it is therefore unintelligible to ask what justice requires across boundaries.[32] In my view, these claims are both factually incorrect and morally irrelevant. There are in fact extensive relations of interdependence and shared understandings of justice across boundaries, and even if there weren't, this still would not justify a scheme of boundaries which condemns some people to abject poverty while others live in affluence. The principle of the moral equality of persons which lies at the heart of liberal egalitarianism requires that we care equally about the well-being of all individuals, wherever they are born, and however little we interact with them. People in different cultures may disagree about the meaning of certain social goods, and this may affect how different cultures allocate their share of the world's resources, but no one wishes to live in abject poverty, and liberal egalitarians cannot justify an international distribution which condemns people to poverty based solely on the accident of their place of birth.[33]

Notes

1. This is not only the principle, but also the practice, in most Western democracies. The major exception concerns illegal immigrants, who may in fact be permanent residents, yet legally excluded from gaining citizenship. Of course, not all countries adhere to this principle of inclusive citizenship—Germany and Austria, in particular, have resisted granting citizenship to their so-called "guest-workers," and indeed to their children and grandchildren, even if they were born and raised on German or Austrian soil.

2. Samuel Black, "Individualism at an Impasse," *Canadian Journal of Philosophy* 21:3 (1991): 347–77.

3. Joseph Carens, "Aliens and Citizens: The Case for Open Borders," *Review of Politics* 49:3 (1987): 251–73.

4. John Stuart Mill, "Considerations on Representative Government," in *Utilitarianism, On Liberty, Considerations on Representative Government*, ed. H. B. Acton (London: J. M. Dent, 1972), 392.

5. Allen Buchanan, *Secession: The Morality of Political Divorce* (Boulder: Westview Press, 1991), xi, 4. Buchanan himself resists this conclusion, and argues instead that liberals should accept secession only where it is necessary to remedy some serious injustice. Daniel Philpott, however, argues that Buchanan's arguments against a wider right of secession do not work. See Philpott, "In Defense of Self-Determination," *Ethics* 105:2 (1995): 352–85.

6. John Rawls, *Political Liberalism* (New York: Columbia University Press, 1993), 277.

7. Cf. Ronald Dworkin's claim that in his theory "we treat community as prior to justice and fairness in the sense that questions of justice and fairness are regarded as questions of what would be just or fair within a particular political group"—a "political group" whose boundaries and membership are taken as givens. Ronald Dworkin, *Law's Empire* (Cambridge: Harvard University Press, 1986), 208. Donald Galloway discusses the tendency of liberals to take boundaries and membership as given in his "Liberalism, Globalism and Immigration," *Queen's Law Journal* 18 (1993): 269.

8. For liberal egalitarians who have bit the bullet on these issues, see Bruce Ackerman, Joseph Carens, and Veit Bader on open borders; Daniel Philpott, David Copp, and Kai Nielsen on plebiscitary right of secession.

9. The first major systematic exploration of the theoretical links between liberalism and nationalism is Yael Tamir, *Liberal Nationalism* (Princeton: Princeton University Press, 1993).

10. See M. Raquibuz Zaman, chap. 9 of this volume, where he notes that actually existing Muslim countries typically privilege national identities, but argues that this is indefensible, and indeed "anathema" from the standpoint of Islamic ethics.

11. Liah Greenfeld, *Nationalism: Five Roads to Modernity* (Cambridge: Harvard University Press, 1992), 14.

12. For the ubiquity of this process around the world, see Ernest Gellner, *Nations and Nationalism* (Oxford: Blackwell, 1983); Benedict Anderson, *Imagined Communities: Reflections on the Origin and Spread of Nationalism* (London: New Left Books, 1983).

13. I discuss "multination federalism" in my *Politics in the Vernacular: Nationalism, Multiculturalism and Citizenship* (Oxford: Oxford University Press, 2001), chap. 5.

14. Commentators often call countries which use these techniques "ethnic democracies," since they combine democratic procedures with the institutional privileging of the dominant ethnic group. The term was developed in accounts of Israeli democracy, but has been applied to several of the newly democratizing countries of Eastern Europe. See Sammy Smooha, "Minority Status in an Ethnic Democracy: The Status of the Arab Minority in Israel," *Ethnic and Racial Studies* 13:3 (1990): 389–413; Graham Smith, "The Ethnic Democracy Thesis and the Citizenship Question in Estonia and Latvia," *Nationalities Papers* 24:2 (1996): 199–216.

15. The extent to which there is a complete separation of church and state differs in the Western democracies. Some countries still have an official state religion, although few of these actively encourage citizens to join this official church. In any event, most liberal theorists have tended to endorse a more strict separation of church and state, and have wanted to implement a similar separation of state and ethnocultural group.

16. Jonathan Glover, "Nations, Identity, and Conflict," in *The Morality of Nationalism*, ed. Robert McKim and Jeff McMahan (New York: Oxford University Press, 1997), 29.

17. For more on this distinction between cosmopolitanism as an ideology and as a reality of modern cultures, see my "From Enlightenment Cosmopolitanism to Liberal Nationalism," in *Politics in the Vernacular*, chap. 10.

18. Some commentators have attempted to summarize these differences under the labels of "civic" versus "ethnic" nationalism. Civic nationalism, in this standard view, defines national membership purely in terms of adherence to democratic principles; whereas ethnic nationalism defines national membership in terms of a common language, culture, and ethnic descent. But this is misleading. Even in the most liberal of democracies, nation-building goes beyond the diffusion of political principles. It also involves the diffusion of a common language and national culture. What distinguishes liberal nation-building from illiberal nationalism is not the absence of any concern with language, culture, and national identity, but rather the content, scope, and inclusiveness of this national culture, and the modes of incorporation into it. For further discussion, see my "Misunderstanding Nationalism," *Dissent* (Winter 1995): 130–37.

19. Just as there are "thicker" and "thinner" conceptions of a national culture, so there are thicker and thinner conceptions of linguistic integration. On a thinner view, immigrants are expected to learn how to use the common language in public life; on a thicker view, it is also important to speak the language in a particular way (e.g., without an accent) or to revere the language as a sacred inheritance, or to give up using one's mother tongue even in private life. Here again, liberals will prefer a thinner conception of the role of a common national language.

20. See, in particular, David Miller, *On Nationality* (Oxford: Oxford University Press, 1995); Avishai Margalit and Joseph Raz, "National Self-Determination," *Journal of Philosophy* 87:9 (1990): 439–61; Charles Taylor, "The Politics of Recognition," in *Multiculturalism and the "Politics of Recognition,"* ed. Amy Gutmann (Princeton: Princeton University Press, 1993); Tamir, *Liberal Nationalism*; James Nickel, "The Value of Cultural Belonging," *Dialogue*, 33:4 (1995): 635–42; Jeff Spinner, *The Boundaries of Citizenship: Race, Ethnicity and Nationality in the Liberal State* (Baltimore: Johns Hopkins University Press, 1994); Margaret Canovan, *Nationhood and Political Theory* (Cheltenham: Edward Elgar, 1996); and my *Multicultural Citizenship* (Oxford: Oxford University Press, 1995).

21. Miller, *On Nationality*; Canovan, *Nationhood and Political Theory*.

22. Margalit and Raz, "National Self-Determination"; similar arguments are made in Taylor, "Politics of Recognition"; Tamir, *Liberal Nationalism*; Nickel, "The Value of Cultural Belonging," and my *Multicultural Citizenship*.

23. Mill, "Considerations on Representative Government," 392.

24. I am not saying that states have adopted nation-building *because* it promotes liberal values. Nation-building policies have been supported for different reasons at different times by different groups of people. Some of these reasons are liberal, others not. My main claim in this paper is with the theoretical consistency of liberal values and nation-building, not the causal relationship between liberalism and nationalism. However, I would claim that the consistency of nation-building and liberal values helps to explain the ubiquity of the former. Even if liberal values haven't always been the main motivation for adopting nation-building policies, these policies would be less common if they threatened liberal values.

25. Even if liberal egalitarians can give prima facie support to the idea of nationality-based political units, this does not mean that they must support a right of nations to their own independent states, or a general plebiscitarian right to secede.

26. On the territorial imperative in Belgium, see Robert Senelle, "Constitutional Reform in Belgium: From Unitarism towards Federalism," in *Federalism and Nationalism*, ed. Murray Forsyth (Leicester: Leicester University Press, 1989), 51–95; on Switzerland, see Gerda Mansour, *Multilingualism and Nation Building* (Clevedon: Multilingual Matters, 1993), 109–11. For a theoretical account of the "territorial imperative" in multilingual societies, see Jean Laponce, *Languages and their Territories* (Toronto: University of Toronto Press, 1987).

27. This is not the case in many Third World countries, where most people would be familiar with both a local indigenous/tribal language and the European language which was imposed by the colonial rulers, and which was maintained as a national language after independence. But in the Western democracies, the vernacular has become the national language, and few people outside the elites are comfortable discussing politics in the national language of other countries.

28. Dieter Grimm, "Does Europe Need a Constitution?" *European Law Journal* 1:3 (1995): 296. This same dynamic can be seen even within the various multilingual states in Europe, where it has become increasingly obvious that "public opinion" is divided on language lines.

29. This is not to deny that we need international political institutions, transcending linguistic/national boundaries, to deal with economic globalization, environmental problems, and issues of international security. And we need to figure out ways to make

these organizations more accountable, within the constraints of a nation-based world order. On this, see my "Citizenship in an Era of Globalization," in *Politics in the Vernacular*, chap. 17.

30. Charles Beitz, *Political Theory and International Relations* (Princeton: Princeton University Press, 1979); Thomas Pogge, *Realizing Rawls* (Ithaca: Cornell University Press, 1989).

31. For the details of such a scheme, see Thomas Pogge, "Migration and Poverty," in *Citizenship and Exclusion*, ed. Veit Bader (London: St. Martin's Press, 1997). As Pogge notes, this would only be appropriate if there was some assurance that the resources being redistributed went to help the citizens of poorer countries, rather than simply enriching corrupt elites or increasing military expenditures. Similarly, it's important, from a liberal point of view, to ensure that such a redistributive scheme does not undermine the ability of liberal democracies to protect themselves in a world composed mainly of non-liberal states. But neither of these factors justify the almost complete disregard for international injustice amongst the Western democracies.

32. Yet others argue that restrictions on immigration benefit the least well-off within a rich society, and so are justified on Rawlsian grounds. Restrictions on immigration are said to help the poor either by (a) helping to maintain support for the welfare state, since citizens are unlikely to make the same sorts of sacrifices for poor newcomers that they make for the native-born poor; or (b) helping to maintain high wages, since immigrants might agree to work for less than native-born citizens. These are debatable empirical assumptions, but in any event I agree with Loren Lomasky, who argues in chap. 3 of this volume that it is indefensible to help the local poor by keeping out even poorer people from elsewhere.

33. The fact that people around the world have different understandings of social goods means that we should not rely on any single simplistic measure of equality, such as disposable income. The role of individual income differs across cultures—some place more emphasis on disposable personal income, others on publicly provided goods; some encourage high incomes with less leisure; others encourage reduced working hours and reduced income; and so on. As a result, different cultures will display different patterns of income, consumption, leisure, savings, risk-taking and so on, without necessarily involving any invidious inequality. But there are other measures of inequality which are less culture-specific, such as those adopted by the United Nations Human Development Index—life expectancy, infant mortality, literacy, health and safety, and so on. If two societies differ dramatically in their rates of literacy or life expectancy, this almost certainly reflects the sort of unjust inequality in resources which liberal egalitarians should be concerned with. By contrast, if two societies have similar levels of literacy and life expectancy, but differ in their levels of average income, this may simply reflect benign differences in the way cultures think about the relative value of different goods, such as income and leisure, or private goods and public services.

Fourteen

Group Boundaries, Individual Barriers

RUSSELL HARDIN

IN ONE major strand of contemporary liberal thought, the core of liberalism is autonomy. In a parallel strand of political thought, it is supposed that what might be good for individuals is good for groups, because individuals typically or at least commonly are members of groups, and if their interests and values are to be secured, they may have to be secured for and through the groups. Many liberal egalitarians therefore assert the value of national boundaries to protect national values and the value of similar protections for subnational groups, such as aboriginal peoples in North America or ethnic minorities in many mixed societies. I wish to focus here on the latter issue, the protection of subnational minorities whose members assert values substantially different from those of their larger society. In particular, they—or their leaders—often demand autonomy in the form of some degree of autarky from the larger society. De facto they want social boundaries between themselves and others in their society. (They also often want national autonomy with physical boundaries, as in recent moves for regional autonomy in several European nations, but I will not address this stronger variant of the problem of demands for subnational autonomy.)

There are two quite distinct arguments one might make for the autonomy of groups. First, one might suppose with many of the most conservative communitarians that groups are the source of the lives and values of their members and that, for the benefit of these members, the groups must be sustained. Second, one might suppose that individual autonomy is itself dependent on the support of the groups that are the sources of the self. In the first argument, individual autonomy is not at issue; indeed, one often suspects that the proponents of the harshest versions of communitarianism do not much care for individuals as such, and they surely do not care much for individual autonomy, which might seem to threaten loyalty to the group.[1] The harshest versions of communitarianism are openly antiliberal. But those who defend group rights and group autonomy *as the basis for individual autonomy* are typically liberal. I wish to question the coherence of this liberal defense of group rights and group autonomy.

After discussing the tensions between traditional liberalisms that focused on individuals and the contemporary focus on groups, I will take up three major classes of objection to claims for group autonomy of the kind that contemporary liberal moral philosophers want to defend for various ethnic, linguistic, and cultural groups. First, the very idea of group autonomy as defended on liberal—typically Kantian liberal—grounds is causally incoherent if it requires, as it often does, the suppression of opportunities for the next generation for the benefit of the current adult generation. Autonomy for some comes at the necessary cost of loss of autonomy for others. Second, the concern for distributive justice that motivates some ostensibly liberal policy recommendations cannot be coherently met. The central issue in maldistribution is not wealth but capacity that resides in human and organizational capital. But these can be redistributed only by violating the group autonomy of those with high levels of such capital or, alternatively, of those with low levels of such capital. And third, the claim of Will Kymlicka, that societies should go even further than merely to protect minority cultural groups but also, in many cases, to subsidize them, makes little moral sense because there is no ground for such an obligation.[2]

There are other defenses of the protection of minority cultures. Charles Taylor supposes that such cultures are intrinsically valuable and are therefore worthy of protection.[3] Typically, communitarians suppose that the values of such cultures are inherently right for their members, and some communitarians seem to think it right for communities to impose their values on their young. This vision recalls a remark of Yael Tamir that the "idea of nationalism tends to be associated with its most fanatic versions, which assume that the identity of individuals is totally constituted by their national membership and that personal will is only free when fully submerged in the general one."[4] These are not liberal defenses, and I will not address them here.

Throughout the discussions, there is the question of how group boundaries turn into individual barriers for the group members, as they often do. Political boundaries commonly pose no barrier to those within the boundaries. When there is a political boundary without a right of exit, as was true of many east European nations in the era of Communism, it is clear that the boundary is a barrier to individual choice within the very group that the boundary delineates. But social boundaries can also be powerfully effective in blocking individual opportunities. Shunning and ostracism can make anyone an outcast from a group. Groups might welcome the return of members, so that membership can be more or less objectively defined by ethnicity, family line, religion, or other attribute. But marriage and even friendship outside the group, taking jobs outside, failing in the group's religious or social practices, using the language or even the accent of a larger community, and many other supposed faults can lead to reactions ranging from criticism to complete ostracism. Hence, membership in a group can be a forceful barrier to any of these choices. Moreover, the only form of leaving may be leaving completely.

I will not focus on the ways group boundaries can and commonly do become individual barriers but will merely suppose that such barriers are common. Such barriers are commonly illiberal in the sense of suppressing individual autonomy—often extremely illiberal, as illiberal as any autocratic regime's hostility to free choice. Indeed, they can be more pervasively invoked than mere boundaries because they are often spontaneously enforced by almost everyone against any miscreant. If I complain against my regime's strictures, I might find widespread sympathy. But if my group's strictures are effective, that might mean that I cannot find much sympathy for my contrary views because those strictures may be widely honored and sometimes brutally enforced norms of exclusion.[5]

Liberalisms

In the following, I simply write of liberalism without qualification. Note, however, that there are two very different universalistic positions on liberalism. In keeping with a sad trend of our times, Kymlicka assumes only one of these: roughly a Kantian deontological position that values liberalism per se as *the political theory of personal autonomy.* This is a peculiar turn in modern political philosophy in that virtually all actual liberal societies have principles that are generally pragmatic, Millian, and utilitarian rather than Kantian. In a pragmatic or utilitarian account, liberal institutions are valued for what they enable us to accomplish. In our time, deontological liberalism is the special vision of academics, not of the general populations or political classes of North America, Europe, and other liberal democratic societies, most of whom are primarily concerned with having institutions that work for the benefit of citizens.

Many of the issues discussed above would not arise in a Millian understanding of groups and their effects on, or their values to, their members. A Millian would immediately blanch at the thought of a society that can impose massive strictures on its young to block their opportunities on some kind of claim that somehow being strapped into their society gives them eventual autonomy or that their long-lifetime losses are outweighed by the short-lifetime gains of their elders for generation after generation to come.

It may well be that having nations with at least somewhat stiff boundaries enables us, under present technological, demographic, and other conditions, to accomplish many things better than we could without such boundaries. Many of the positions of Kymlicka and advocates of liberal nationalism fit under this claim.[6] On this pragmatic view, the creation and maintenance of national states is not per se good or right. Rather, the state is merely a device that arguably works for good.

Kymlicka and the liberal nationalists generally take the main conditions of contemporary international and national politics for granted and therefore argue within the constraints of these conditions. For example, virtually no one today would argue, in the manner of Woodrow Wilson, that every cultural or linguistic community should be an independent nation-state. There are two devastating problems with Wilson's arrogantly ignorant vision. First, a world of thousands of independent states seems unlikely to be as good a place to live as the world of vastly fewer such states in which we actually live. And second, few Wilsonian "nations" live in geographically contiguous areas without interlacing with other nations. But anyone who takes the conditions of contemporary international and national politics for granted in arguing for policies of liberal nationalism and group autonomy is inherently making contingent, not abstractly rationalist claims. It is not trivially obvious how Kantian arguments from the individual autonomy of rational agents in "the kingdom of ends" (that is, rational agents) can be brought down to such contingent ground. Without argument for how to do this, the assertion of the value of an autonomy that is massively constrained by communal values and history seems unserious because it is at best merely an uncritical, intuitionist assertion. Or worse, it is merely a politically correct acquiescence to the claims of anyone, no matter how silly or incoherent those claims are.

The supposed autonomy that matters to communitarians and to those, such as Kymlicka, who assert the rights of groups is particularistic in an odd way at the collective level. It is about sociological facts that matter to people *once their habits, tastes, and values have been formed by those sociological facts.* Especially important among these in many discussions is language, which is both enabling and heavily constraining.[7] Charles Taylor has argued that language is an "irreducibly social good" and is therefore intrinsically and not merely instrumentally good.[8] Anthropologists and linguists have long been encouraging the maintenance of dying languages, among about three thousand of which are many that are spoken by almost no one and that are being learned by no children.[9] It is claimed that about half the currently spoken languages of the world are spoken by no children. And the last known speakers of various languages have died in recent decades. There are older people who have no language in common with their own grandchildren and who are, in effect, losing their own communities as they age.

The linguist Kenneth Hale thinks that language loss is a disaster because most of the dying languages he studies are essential to the cultural identities of the now tiny groups that speak them. The last known speaker of Eyak in Alaska says of the disappearance of fellow speakers, "It hurts. I feel as though I lost someone in my family."[10] The idea that such languages are intrinsically valuable, however, despite the fact that they are essentially useless to anyone and could be taught to children only at great opportunity cost to those children, recalls the silliness of G. E. Moore's value theory that says a beautiful world in the vast reaches of the universe where no sentient being will ever see or experience it is intrinsically good.[11]

Although missionaries and governments have often suppressed native languages, the loss of minute languages is an intergenerational process that commonly today comes from choices of members of the relevant language groups. For example, Red Thunder Cloud died, at 76, as the last remaining speaker of Catawba, an oral language with no written form, although there are estimated to be from several hundred to a thousand surviving Catawba.[12] Thunder Cloud evidently chose to learn the language from his grandfather and other elders even when its use was passing and other children were not learning the language. The last other speaker of Catawba died forty years ago. To say that those of Thunder Cloud's generation who did not learn Catawba sacrificed their autonomy in making the choice to speak a more generally useful language is perverse.

Intergenerational Issues

A boundary for a group is a potential barrier for the individual. For a typical individual past age fifty, the barrier might be of no concern because it might block off no opportunity that those of middle age would find appealing. For an individual at age twenty, it might seem catastrophic because it might block off virtually every opportunity the individual would find appealing. The function of the barrier then is to protect the older members of the group from the freedom of choice of the younger members of the group.

Virtually all of the argument for group rights of exclusion and separatism in actual communities today is grounded in the values and commitments of communal leaders and elders or, one might say, those who fear the loss of their own communities as they age. Such rights are in fact not merely protections for many group members. Rather, they are barriers to alternative opportunities. They are virtual impositions on the next generation, many of whom might well prefer to have the other opportunities that are closed to, for example, anyone who speaks only a minor language with any fluency. The actual working purpose of enforcing so-called group rights is commonly therefore not to protect groups from outsiders but to protect them *against their own insiders* by suppressing choices by insiders.

Kymlicka says, for example, that "the viability of Indian communities depends on coercively restricting the mobility, residence, and political rights of both Indians and non-Indians."[13] And this is the point of granting such communities group rights. The oddity of such group "rights" is that they are characteristically coercive more than they are enabling, whereas classical individual rights are typically enabling by protecting us from coercion. Indeed, some classical individual rights enable groups more than they enable individuals. For example, the right of free political speech enables not so much the speaker as the audience of the speaker. It enables by making it possible for that audience to know what audience members might wish or need to know that would benefit them. For example, the somewhat scurrilously used freedom of the press that President John Adams's Sedition Act of 1798 was intended to suppress and that newly democratic governments in east Europe still today want to suppress is a causally necessary part of a genuinely open democratic process.[14]

There are, of course, group rights that are enabling both for groups and for their members. For example, rights of equal opportunity for members of groups that have suffered or might otherwise suffer from discrimination enable individuals to have opportunities that might, without legal protections, be denied on grounds of group membership alone. Hence, such rights can be coherently grounded in their beneficial effects for all individuals covered by them. These rights are, in essence, universalistic in their appeal because they merely extend rights that are already de facto available to others, to individuals who suffer discrimination based on their group membership. Their force is generally to counter the effects of social norms, such as racist or sexist norms, that are de facto barriers to individual exercise of rights. In many instances, when legalized, such rights do little more than assert forcefully that the usual rights that should protect everyone also must be taken to protect individual members of some identifiable group, by giving heightened scrutiny in relevant cases or by promulgating guidelines to make sure that the rights are protected. Hence, these so-called group rights are genuinely universalistic and not at all about group preference.

The so-called rights that many cultural groups want—or that are wanted by the leaders of such groups—are not enabling in this way, and they are not at all universalistic. Their actual effect is commonly to disable, as the deplorable decision of *Wisconsin v. Yoder et al.* disables young Old Order Amish in Wisconsin by allowing their parents to cut short their schooling so that they have no more than an eighth-grade education.[15] This means they have little more than the qualifications for staying at home on Amish farms or for taking at best menial jobs outside the Amish community. So-called language rights to be educated in, say, an Inuit language are similarly grossly disabling if the way those rights are enforced is by suppressing education in an economically—because nationally and internationally—more useful language such as French or English.

Liberal proponents of ethnic nationalism and group separatism must address the intergenerational issues at the center of such policies if they are to be taken seriously morally. Intergenerational issues do not necessarily trump concern for group autonomy. But *the moral argument for group autonomy is inherently violated by the intergenerational effects of group autonomy.* The moral argument is that group autonomy is necessary to enable individual autonomy. But group autonomy that is maintained by curtailing the opportunities of the young blocks or reduces their autonomy. The ostensible moral defense of group rights and group autonomy is therefore logically and substantively incoherent.[16] To argue the case for group rights as though they were to affect only the current adult generation and no one else trivializes the very difficult issues at stake. Yet, most of what is written in defense of such group rights trivializes the issues in just this way.

The very idea of group autonomy is subject to a grand fallacy of composition. If genuinely everyone in a group shares all relevant values with everyone else, then the group's desire for separate status is meaningful. If not, and there are some who do not share the desire, it is specious to speak of the group as though it were an entity with a will and a coherent desire. Given that minority groups are composed of more than one generation and given that the desires of different generations are likely to be systematically different and potentially contradictory, we cannot take the idea of group autonomy as pristine or simple enough merely to defend it in the abstract. In practice, it is likely to be utterly indefensible except by some simplistic majoritarian and likely paternalistic assessment.

The historical point of rights has been *to protect individuals against majorities*. Commonly, this means protecting individuals against the excesses of majoritarian government and its agencies and agents. It is a corruption of the tradition of rights even to speak of group rights in the face of the reality of group desires. In that reality, group rights all too likely must be primarily directed against members of the group. That is to say, group rights are commonly a device *to protect majorities (or even only leaders) against individuals*. They therefore cannot be defended as merely beneficial for members of the group. The idea of group rights is all too often a canard.

Distributive Justice for Autonomous Groups

Kymlicka thinks that egalitarian liberals shy away from facing the real difficulty, which is not nations per se but radically unequal distribution of resources. I think it is a gross mistake to focus on resources in defense of minority group autonomy. What is most acutely maldistributed in the world is *human capital* and *organizational capital*. Human capital is the result of education and training, much of it on the job. Organizational capital is the array of networks and connections of variously talented people that, along with physical and financial capital, stands behind any organization's capacity to produce whatever it does. Organizational capital can be dissipated quickly when the individuals scatter. For example, if a rocket program at NASA is closed down, the organizational capacity may be very hard to rebuild, nearly as hard as it was to build it originally. In a sense, much of technological knowledge is collective knowledge that is available only while the collectivity is together.

To see the importance of human and organizational capital and the relatively limited importance of standard resources, consider the example of

Japan. Japan's wealth is not from natural resources—Bangladesh has about as much natural wealth as Japan, and Malaysia probably has radically more than Japan. What Japan has is human and organizational capital and the products of these. The human and organizational capital cannot simply be shared out with other societies, because they are intrinsically built out of or into contemporary Japanese individuals and Japanese society. If several Japanese factories were transported to Bangladesh without their employees, those factories would not soon be very productive there. But the people left behind in Japan would soon be producing again in new factories that could be paid for out of their expected productivity.

We can go further to say that most of the physical capital of any modern industrial state is primarily the product of human and organizational capital. If we attempt radical redistribution of such capital, the result will not be that the value of, say, Manhattan gets redistributed across the world but, rather, that the market value of Manhattan falls drastically. Suppose I sell my house (whose value is primarily the value of its land) and redistribute the proceeds to the Third World. It is incoherent to suppose the value of the land per se could be redistributed from the United States to elsewhere—it is fixed in Manhattan and the property can be sold at all only if someone can buy it. But radical redistribution of wealth would mean that no one would be able to buy a townhouse in the Village or on the Upper East Side for the several million dollars at which it is now valued. Hence, such houses would lose value. Of course, those houses currently represent a large fraction of the wealth of their owners. That wealth cannot be withdrawn from all of them in the form of transferable money and therefore it cannot be transferred to the people of Kenya or Bangladesh. The money at issue does not exist, because the value of, say, the U.S. dollar is grounded in the wealth that includes the value of such houses. We could reduce that wealth by redistributing personal and corporate wealth so that demand and supply relations would not drive up land costs, but then the original value of, say, land in Manhattan would no longer be available for redistribution. Hence, redistribution that would equalize the spread of value would destroy value, so that what was redistributed would be woefully less than what exists. The idea of radical redistribution is therefore profoundly misguided if it is supposed that we could simply share out the wealth of the world in a way that would give each person a share equal to the current average wealth.

Gerrard Winstanley and other proponents of equality in seventeenth-century England at least seemed to recognize that the way to level their society was to *level down* the prosperity of many, even most people.[17] Contemporary proponents of massive international redistribution for the sake of equality seem to miss that point. John Rawls's theory of justice recognizes the possibility that redistribution might destroy what is to be redistributed by impeding the incentive to produce it. His difference principle is therefore a compromise answer to the contrary claims of economic possibility and moral philosophy.[18] He supposes that moral philosophy requires equality but economic possibility says this can be achieved only by leveling down to universal poverty. The concern of Rawls is the incentives for productivity that inequality offers.

Friedrich Hayek argues the related thesis that progress inherently entails and even depends on inequality.[19] The concern of Hayek is with the productivity that *inequality directly enables*. In the face of these issues, the most we could accomplish without massive destruction of productive economies is relatively modest, not radical, redistribution of wealth. Rawlsians, such as apparently Kymlicka, would settle for such modest redistribution if they agreed with the causal account here.

Unfortunately, although such transfers of wealth would change immediate consumption patterns, *they might not affect human capital*. They would therefore be a short-term palliative that might even have negative longer-term consequences on group autonomy by harming incentives to be productively engaged in the group's own economy. Arguably, the most straightforward way to overcome this distributional problem would be to open borders, at least gingerly, to allow a sort of apprenticeship transference or learning of human capital. This is essentially what followed from the foreign guest-worker programs of West Germany, Switzerland, and other European nations during the decades after about 1960. Southern Italians, Spaniards, Portuguese, Croats, Turks, and others first became industrial workers in Germany, Sweden, and so forth, and then took their skills back to their homelands, where industries developed more effectively and quickly than they might otherwise have done. Wealthy nations might go further and subsidize the creation of firms in developing nations to put the new human capital more effectively to use, but developing nations are often hostile to foreign investment as destructive of local autonomy.

Note, however, that *if the way to address inequality of human capital is to open borders, considerations of distributive justice conflict with boundaries*. Human capital is largely the product of communities, but its redistribution from highly capitalized to poorly capitalized nations conflicts with concern for communities as such. It is virtually inconceivable that considerations of distributive justice are consistent with any demand for autarkic, closed communities. It is closure that leaves communities far behind while more open communities develop economically.[20] The slogan "Socialism in one society" was a chimera because a closed society is likely to be a relatively impoverished society. "Culture in one society" is also a chimera if wealth is a concern, as it must be if distributive justice is a concern.

Finally, the point of distributive justice seems misplaced for such minority cultures as the Inuit and other indigenous minorities, the Amish, the Lubavitchers, and many other groups defined, in essence, by their extremely narrowly circumscribed cultures. If the Inuit or the Amish become wealthy, their way of life is deeply threatened. Why hunt and fish in the extreme conditions of Hudson Bay if not out of need? Why work a traditional farm with traditional tools, why work at small craft production of religious articles for the larger Jewish community, when the economic returns from those activities are swamped by the returns from redistribution from the larger society? The Amish and many Indian tribes in the United States know well that wealth destroys their cultures through its insidious effects on desires and incentives. The traditional culture that many political leaders of such communities wish to maintain is through and through a culture of extreme limits, not of plenty. Economic equality with the rest of Canada or the United States at their current levels of wealth is utterly contrary to that traditional culture.

In sum, both for causal reasons of the nature of wealth that is fundamentally grounded in human capital and for essential reasons of the economically limited nature of many minority group cultures, substantial, equalizing redistribution would destroy such groups. Hence, claims of distributive justice are likely to be irrelevant to the defense of such groups.

Fairness to Minority Cultural Groups

Kymlicka makes the moral claim that justice requires not merely protecting minority ethnic groups but also subsidizing them to enable them to sustain their cultures. He says such subsidy is only fair, because majority groups can readily sustain their cultures without any special effort, while minority groups are constantly at risk of being bulldozed by the majority culture.[21] It is remarkable that this argument is similar to that used for generations by various economic groups that begin to lose out in the pattern of economic development that renders old occupations and industries relatively less remunerative than newer occupations and industries. The outstanding instance, of course, is the steady, massive decline of agriculture in modern societies. Agriculture was the life of more than eighty percent of populations historically, as it still is in some nations today. It is the life of about two percent of the U.S. population today.

The history of American politics includes many episodes in which the central political issue was protection of farmers against the declining fortunes they faced. Indeed, this was perhaps the chief issue in contention for most of the period between the Civil War and the end of the Great Depression. Had early efforts at such protection really succeeded, the American economy today would be comparable to that of an impoverished Third World nation, with more than half the workforce producing basic foodstuffs, which constitute a very small part of what Americans consume today.

It would be perverse to suppose that the massive decline of agriculture relative to other activities was a harm to Americans generally, although it was devastating to particular farm families along the way, just as the threatened decline of tobacco farming may be hard on many American farmers in the near future. Not so long ago, the idle aristocracy of Europe was faced with harsh decline, and craft workers everywhere have been displaced by industrial production. Similarly, in the economic transition of many nations from inefficient centrally controlled to market economies, many bureaucrats whose chief talent was to oversee the command economy are instantly obsolete. Must societies support these people by maintaining the economy that was dominated by aristocrats or craft workers or by keeping the bureaucrats on the job of commanding their economies? The parallel to Kymlicka's argument for minority cultures is that justice requires that the larger American society of non-tobacco farmers subsidize these farmers to protect them against losses *and to keep their children on the farm growing tobacco,* that the aristocrats and craft workers not be displaced by economic developments, and that the larger Russian society keep its command bureaucrats on the job. These claims, however, sound outrageous. It is not clear how one could argue that the parallel claim for minority cultures is not similarly outrageous. Cultural Luddism may be no more defensible than economic Luddism. Yet the defenders of minority protection simply assume this arguably outrageous Luddite principle for cultural minorities.

It is not a necessary part of the protection of all cultural groups that their economic way of life be protected. A minority group might be fully integrated into the economy of its larger society even while its social organization in other respects is autarkic. But protection of an economic way of life is commonly a part of the protection of the culture of aboriginal peoples such as the Inuit. The mere fact that some people leave hunting and fishing behind to enter the industrial age of remarkably expanding wealth does not seem to yield a moral requirement that they therefore fund the efforts of others to stay in the life of hunting and fishing. One might suppose that societies, although perhaps not individuals, have some duty to help their members prosper economically by enabling them to enter the modern economy. But this, of course, is contrary to the program of protection of the group's culture by helping it keep itself autarkic, economically backward, and unproductive.

Kymlicka argues that granting merely equal individual rights to members of cultural minorities is insufficient to gain them equal opportunity, because the worth of those rights is much higher for those who identify with the ethos of the governing institutions.[22] One might similarly note that individual rights to ownership of property in a market economy are worth more—far more—to some than to others. They are, of course, generally worth more to those who identify with the ethos of the property regime and the governing institutions that protect it, as well as to those who own substantial shares of property.

To maintain their land for traditional uses, Kymlicka notes, the Inuit would have to outbid non-aborigines just to ensure that their cultural structure survives. This could mean they would have few resources to pursue particular goals.[23] The way that their land would get away from them would be that individuals would sell parts of it. Hence, as Kymlicka argues more generally, if individual Inuit could sell their land, unfettered individual actions would have the perverse and unintended external effect of destroying the landed basis of the Inuit culture.

The Rabbi Schneerson long ago argued an analog of this point very articulately in Crown Heights, the Lubavitch community of Brooklyn. As reported by David Remnick, in 1969 the Rebbe said,

> "In recent times, a plague has spread among our brethren—the wholesale migration from Jewish neighborhoods. . . . One result of this phenomenon is the sale of houses in these neighborhoods to non-Jewish people. Even synagogues and places of Torah study are sold." Citing Talmudic sources, the Rebbe said that it was prohibited for Jews to sell their houses to Gentiles when the sale would have negative consequences for the community. "Such stringent prohibitions of Torah law would apply if the sale of the house to a non-Jew caused damages to only one person," he declared. "How much more so does it apply when, as in our case, the damage is suffered by all neighborhood residents."[24]

Under such conditions of the market, protection of a group's way of life might indeed require some restrictions on individual actions that would undercut that way of life. One might suppose that all of the Lubavitch homeowners in Crown Heights would agree that it would be best overall if they would all somehow commit to selling only to others in the community or to new joiners of the community and not to other outsiders. If such a restriction could be made binding, all in the community might benefit in their own view.[25] If there were agreement but no way to make it binding, some might sell because of the fear that others will, so that their commitment to staying, while strong if the community stays, is weakened by the threat of others' departures. In such a case, group barriers might be individually favored as a resolution of a collective action problem, whose resolution is beneficial to all members of the group.

Much of the out-migration from Crown Heights, however, may have been intergenerational. (The Lubavitch community has one of the highest rates of reproduction of any group in the industrial world, a rate comparable to that of the ultra-Orthodox Jews of Israel, whose population more than triples in each generation.) Asking the next generation to sign on to an agreement to restrict mobility might push more of them to leave. Indeed, given the employment prospects in the community, many parents might choose to leave in order to provide their numerous children with better economic prospects. If Lubavitch community leaders could erect barriers to the departure of such people, those barriers would not be mutually beneficial.

Cultural Preservation

Perhaps the harshest criticism one should make of many of the defenses of minority cultures is that they seem to entail not the support of living communities, but the museum-like preservation of mummified cultures. Part of the objection to subsidizing minority cultures in order essentially to protect them from influences for change is that the subsidies seem to entail such preservation of cultures, as in the restoration of ritual whaling among the Makah Indians in Washington State.[26] Oddly, few if any liberals who advocate static preservation of minority cultures would demand such preservation of *mainstream* cultures. Of historical necessity, cultures change with the generations and the times, and much of what is good in any modern society is the ways that that society differs from its predecessor societies. Somehow, defenders of minority cultures implicitly forget this fundamental fact in their seeming urge to preserve those cultures. Much of the defense of such cultures is part of the political philosophy of the museum. Museums preserve; societies develop and change in manifold ways.

Ironically, a Makah says of opposition to his tribe's planned whale hunt: "They want us in the museum. . . . They want us to have a dead culture. But it's been our way of life. . . . [We] feel we not only have a legal right but a moral right to whale."[27] Another calls whale hunting "our sacred tradition." But no living Makah had ever before participated in a whale hunt. It had never been the way of life of any now living Makah. Generations before whaling ended in U.S. waters, the Makah had stopped whaling of their own accord and had lost the taste for whale blubber. If there was originally a reason for the whaling tradition, it was not as a sacred ritual but as a way to provide food. One of the quasi-religious legends of the Makah is of the god Thunderbird, who delivers a whale in a time when the Makah are without food. It is therefore not the opponents of their renewal of whaling who have an eye on the museum, it is some of the Makah who wish to inhabit one—although when they caught their first whale, they killed it with an assault rifle.[28] But in their case, relegation to a museum is particularly perverse because it requires not merely preservation but retrogression to an earlier state. They wish to inhabit an archeological museum. Efforts to recreate Inuit societies in Canada have a similarly perverse character. They are retrograde, insofar as they wish to bring back a way of life that is no one's way of life.

What might the state owe to a group to protect its culture? Protection or subsidy of its religion, language, status, or economic choices? As Tamir asks, does respect for a group's religious rituals imply that others must subsidize them (for example, to help group members afford kosher meat)?[29] To some extent, the answers to these questions depend on whether the state supports any cultural group at all (as many states do, for example, a religion), in which case it must treat all equally. And one might argue that language is so important for citizenship that it must be taken into account by the state, as it is in multilingual India, Canada, and Belgium, at least insofar as to enable political participation.[30] But this makes little sense for locally very tiny minority languages, such as those of aboriginal tribes in North America or of scattered immigrant groups. Establishing language rights for such groups is tantamount to coercing the next generation to be worse off for the benefit of their elders.

Liberal Nationalism

Variants of the concern for indigenous minority groups are concerns for minority immigrant groups and for historically intermingled minority groups. For such groups, the most important problems are arguably finding a way to include them politically without working against their cultures. Tamir argues that the liberal tradition—with its concern for personal autonomy, reflection, and choice—and the national tradition—with its concern for belonging, loyalty, and solidarity—can be accommodated. She also supposes that the traditional nationalist emphasis on the importance of particular circumstances for the construction of personal identity does not contradict the universalist view of human nature.[31] A liberal nationalism would permit the coexistence of different cultural groups while leaving all individual members of such groups free to participate in or to leave the culture. In such a liberal system, no individual could be bound to a culture.[32] She argues that cultural subgroups in a nation do not have an automatic right but only that it is liberal to allow individuals their own cultural choices.

Both Kymlicka and Tamir are forced to argue in the shadow of the American and other nations' experience with racial minorities and radically illiberal racism. Their arguments in defense of group practices cannot be generalized because they could not, as liberals, support *majority* suppression of a cultural or ethnic minority even though that might be a central feature of the majority culture. Their task is to suggest something between full-blown individual rights with no attention to group claims, on the one hand, and coercive group rights that would be used to suppress others, on the other. Kymlicka's solution to this quandary is to allow "groups" (the term in this context is a fallacy of composition) to suppress their own members and to have the state support them in doing so. Tamir's solution is to allow states to support groups in various ways so long as they do so equally.

In their defenses of liberal nationalism, both Tamir and David Miller argue that co-nationals have obligations to each other.[33] Tamir speaks of "associative obligations," which are not grounded on consent but on a feeling of belonging and connectedness. Traditional arguments for obligation do not seem to underlie this claim. Indeed, Tamir does not establish that there is an obligation derivable from some principle, but only says it is an intuition that many of us have that we do owe something to those with whom we associate in various ways, as we do with family members and co-nationals.[34] Miller argues that distributive justice cannot be achieved without a defined group among whom it is to be achieved, a group that is in essence governed by the same law. This is a more generally compelling argument, at least for utilitarians, for whom the pragmatic facts of nationality argue for making distributive justice partially a local concern, because there is some hope of achieving it in particular communities but less hope of achieving it globally. My obligation in this case is little more than the usual utilitarian duty to contribute to the general welfare. Nations are contingently morally good for what they can achieve— although they are also contingently morally bad for what they can achieve.

Miller's argument generally is about nations as actual states with boundaries, whereas Tamir's is about national groups within states. In Miller's argument, there is reason to defend national boundaries even though these are commonly individual barriers against outsiders. The only ways we have to achieve important benefits to people in general involve reliance on big and often powerful institutions. National boundaries merely define some of the biggest and most powerful institutions; and, if those institutions do good, we can defend them and the implications of having them in place, including their barrier to individuals. I doubt that this defense could justify the unduly exclusive policies of big, prosperous states against immigration from far poorer states. But in principle it does ground a genuinely liberal defense of boundaries.

Conclusion

The chief ostensibly liberal argument for protecting minority cultures is that the autonomy of their individual members is dependent on the survival and autonomy of the cultural group. This argument fails intergenerationally, because it is internally contradictory. Group autonomy likely enhances the individual autonomy of some while it cripples that of others. Unless this grievous conceptual flaw in the argument can be adequately addressed, the whole defense of minority culture rights and autonomy as grounded in individual autonomy fails. The flaw might be addressed by arguing for tradeoffs between the gains of older and the losses of younger members of the group. But such a move is evidently repulsive to autonomy theorists. An alternative might be to adopt a brutally paternalistic stance toward the young and not to count their interests until they have been either socialized or broken by the group. Such a move might lose most of the support any minority culture might expect to get from citizens in the larger society.

The argument for distributive justice to minority cultures might be sustained even despite this flaw in the argument from autonomy. But that argument would often be fundamentally contrary to the claims for group autonomy in any case, because the achievement of distributive justice would destroy many minority cultures. Kymlicka's claim for fairness to minority cultures in the face of the corrosive influence of a majority culture must commonly run afoul of the difficulties in the moral claim for group autonomy that inhibits individual autonomy. It is the corrosive influence of the majority culture that leads the young of many minority cultures to see that their opportunities might be far richer and more varied than what is offered by the minority culture. If fairness to a minority culture entails letting it stand outside the law of the larger society by restricting its children's education to disable them, adopting property laws that drastically penalize exit from the culture, violating fairness internally, for example, with respect to gender, and adopting other measures whose point is to suppress exit, it is hard to see how that fairness can be justified by appeal to the individual autonomy that is supposedly enhanced—not blocked—by group autonomy.

The argument for group autonomy as an entailment of the claim for individual autonomy is often incoherent. This is not merely a factual matter, although it appears to be factually overwhelming. Rather, it is a logical matter in many instances. Group boundaries commonly pose individual barriers. The boundaries around groups have two purposes: to keep others out and to keep community members in. One can imagine a culture that poses no obstacles to exit of its members while making entry very hard—local social elites in such cities as Boston and New Orleans have historically done this, as have whites more generally in much of the United States and many other racially mixed societies. But the minority cultures of our time that are seemingly in need of protection by the larger societies in which they are geographically embedded are not like such groups. Their main problem is not keeping outsiders out; outsiders do not want in. Their problem is keeping insiders in, especially the next generation of potential insiders. They seem to be like those nationalists who conceive obligations to the group as not elective but dictated by the fate of birth. It is finally inconceivable that devices to forcibly keep people in a culture can enhance individual autonomy.

Despite the incoherence of the argument from autonomy, there might be grounds, both trivial and profound, for protecting minority cultures. Trivially, one might, for example, suppose that a reason for many anthropologists to want to keep alive many currently dying languages is that those languages are their field of study, not that they are otherwise good or beneficial for their native speakers or their non–native-speaking children. One might similarly suppose that many people like the fact of extant minority cultures as a kind of comparison set for their own culture or as a field for exotic vacations.

More profoundly, one might feel great compassion for those whose culture threatens to die out from under them.[35] If there were a way to keep their culture vibrant without drafting the next generation into service for their elders and without massive other costs, we might readily agree that it should be done. But if the costs of sustaining a particular minority culture are enormous and especially if they entail use of the young against their own interests, then that culture might better be left alone to go the way of craft workers, tobacco farmers, aristocrats, and command bureaucrats, as sad as that might be for the lingering elders of the culture. Indeed, many people regularly make the choice to abandon their culture for the benefit of themselves and their children, as when millions have migrated to the Americas. Presumably, theirs were often autonomous choices. Barriers imposed by their cultures of origin against their emigration would have been contrary to individual autonomy.

We may see minority cultures that seem threatened with collapse as an analog of one of Albert Hirschman's declining organizations, whose members have three options available to them: the members can exit from the organization, they can exercise voice within the organization in order to try to effect changes that would stop the decline, or they can simply express loyalty to the organization.[36] Exit is likely to destroy a culture; voice is likely to alter it dramatically. The role of group rights is essentially *to impose loyalty* on members of minority cultures in order to block or at least impede their exit. Imposed loyalty might keep such a culture alive a bit longer than it might otherwise last. But it cannot guarantee longer-term survival because it cannot block the blandishments of the larger world, blandishments that entice people into exiting from the limited opportunities offered by minority cultures.

In many cases, the very fact that a culture needs such artificial supports suggests that it cannot survive such blandishments, which is to say, that its individual members value alternatives more than they value the culture. Kymlicka and others speak of the value of cultural membership.[37] But a minority or any other culture is a disvalue if its members choose to leave it because they have other values. Hence, giving power to the leadership of a minority group to impose loyalty on its members cannot be defended as a liberal policy.

Cultures need protection from their own internal forces for collapse and dispersal only when they are not economically or culturally viable in the sense that they cannot spontaneously maintain themselves through their own members' actions. Kymlicka supposes we must have some principle for giving cultural claims priority over individual claims, perhaps always, perhaps only in certain ranges of cases.[38] Coercing the relevant actions—turning so-called group rights into individual obligations and burdens—cannot, no matter how argued, be a liberal resolution of their problem. This is not an analog of the standard legal enforcement of behavior to stop harmful external effects, as Kymlicka suggests. Pollution commonly harms even the polluter. My departure from a stifling and constraining culture does not harm me. If individual concerns conflict enough with maintaining the culture, that is finally simply too bad for the culture. The most pointed and harsh conflict between individual and group concerns is typically likely to be the massive intergenerational burden placed on the young to conform to rather than to leave their culture. It seems likely that this is by far the most important issue in the maintenance of aboriginal cultures. We can protect tribal leaders in their urge to keep their future generations in a museum, or we can protect individuals against such coercion, as we do in the larger society.

Notes

I wish to thank Yael Tamir for extensive discussion of the issues raised in this essay.

1. This is also commonly the view of ethnic nationalists, who hold that the nation is prior to the individual. Individuals are their cultural inheritance and nothing more, and they owe their lives to the nation. It is a misfortune that many of the leaders of the aboriginal groups whose autonomy Will Kymlicka defends are essentially ethnic nationalists.

2. For this argument, see Will Kymlicka, *Liberalism, Community, and Culture* (Oxford: Oxford University Press, 1991); Kymlicka, *Multicultural Citizenship* (Oxford: Oxford University Press, 1995).

3. Charles Taylor, "Irreducibly Social Goods," in *Rationality, Individualism and Public Policy*, ed. Geoffrey Brennan and Cliff Walsh (Canberra: Centre for Research on Federal Financial Relations, 1990), 45–63. Julius Moravcsik makes a similar claim for the intrinsic value of certain communities in "Communal Ties," *Supplement to Proceedings and Addresses of the American Philosophical Association* 62 (September 1988): 211–25.

4. Yael Tamir, *Liberal Nationalism* (Princeton: Princeton University Press, 1993), 79.

5. I analyze norms of exclusion in Russell Hardin, *One for All: The Logic of Group Conflict* (Princeton: Princeton University Press, 1995), chap. 4.

6. As discussed further below under "Liberal Nationalism."

7. For further discussion, see Hardin, *One for All*, 65–70.

8. Taylor, "Irreducibly Social Goods."

9. *Science* 251 (11 January 1991): 159 and 267 (3 March 1995): 1272. Also see Burkhard Bilger, "Keeping Our Words," *The Sciences* (September/October 1994): 18–20. Only about five percent of extant languages—about 300—are safe against extinction in the sense that they have at least a million speakers and some degree of state support. Some linguists question the significance of their colleagues' claims in part because they question the way languages are counted.

10. *Science* 267 (3 March 1995): 1272. Such stories are frequently reported and are commonly accompanied by claims of linguists that they are a "cultural disaster." See an

account of the last speaker of Chamicuro in Peru, "Cultural Loss Seen as Languages Fade," *New York Times*, 16 May 1999, sec. 1.

11. G. E. Moore, *Principia Ethica* (Cambridge: Cambridge University Press, [1903] 1959), 83–84.

12. *New York Times*, 14 January 1996, sec. 1, p. 3.

13. Kymlicka, *Liberalism, Community, and Culture*, 146.

14. The complexity of the politics and purpose of the Sedition Act is well, if tendentiously, laid out in William Winslow Crosskey, *Politics and the Constitution in the History of the United States*, vol. 2 (Chicago: University of Chicago Press, 1953), 767ff.

15. *Wisconsin v. Yoder et al.*, 406 U. S. 205–249, at p. 211.

16. It is perhaps not strictly illogical. But because a society is necessarily a series of overlapping generations, it is illogical in application to a society.

17. For religious reasons, Winstanley held a frugal, not bountiful, existence to be a morally superior state in any case. See Gerrard Winstanley, *The Law of Freedom in a Platform or, True Magistracy Restored*, ed. Robert W. Kenny (New York: Schocken Books, [1652] 1973).

18. John Rawls, *A Theory of Justice* (Cambridge: Harvard University Press, 1971).

19. Friedrich Hayek, *The Constitution of Liberty* (Chicago: University of Chicago Press, 1960), 44.

20. See further, Russell Hardin, "Communities and Development: Autarkic Social Groups and the Economy," in *A Not-So-Dismal Science: A Broader, Brighter Approach to Economies and Societies*, ed. Mancur Olson, Jr., and Satu Kähkönen (Oxford: Oxford University Press, 2000): 206–27.

21. Kymlicka, chap. 13 above. Yael Tamir similarly notes that, even if social resources are fairly distributed, minority groups may be more limited in their ability to practice their national claims, and that liberal nationalism entails readiness to compensate minority groups to reduce the hardships of their status. Tamir, *Liberal Nationalism*, 56, 163.

22. Kymlicka, *Liberalism, Community, and Culture*, 146.

23. Ibid., 189.

24. David Remnick, "Waiting for the Apocalypse in Crown Heights," *New Yorker* (21 December 1992), pp. 52–57, at p. 54. See further, Hardin, *One for All*, 195–198.

25. In an earlier era, many communities in the United States were protected by legally binding covenants that prohibited the sale of houses to blacks, Jews, Asians, Latinos, and members of many European ethnic groups, such as Italians and east Europeans. Although such covenants are no longer legally enforceable, some of those communities still today are overwhelmingly white. A defender of minority cultures might defend such covenants for their use while, presumably, condemning them when used by dominant cultural groups to keep minorities out.

26. Robert Sullivan, "Permission Granted to Kill a Whale: Now What?" *New York Times Magazine*, 9 August 1998, pp. 30–33.

27. Ibid., 32.

28. *New York Times*, 23 May 1999, sec. 4, p. 2.

29. Tamir, *Liberal Nationalism*, 41. See also, David Miller, *On Nationality* (Oxford: Oxford University Press, 1995).

30. Hardin, "Communities and Development," 220–23.

31. Tamir, *Liberal Nationalism*, 6–7.

32. Ibid., 32.

33. Ibid., 137; David Miller, "The Ethical Significance of Nationality," *Ethics* 98 (July 1988): 647–62.

34. Tamir, *Liberal Nationalism*, 99–102.

35. See further, Hardin, *One for All*, esp. 69–70, for discussion of the painful cases of Ota Benga, Ishi (the so-called last wild Indian in the United States), and Kurt Tucholsky, after they were cut off from their cultures.

36. Albert O. Hirschman, *Exit, Voice and Loyalty: Responses to Decline in Firms, Organizations, and States* (Cambridge: Harvard University Press, 1970).

37. Kymlicka, *Liberalism, Community, and Culture*, 200.

38. Ibid., 198.

Fifteen

Boundaries, Ownership, and Autonomy

A NATURAL LAW PERSPECTIVE

JOSEPH BOYLE

THE CORE IDEA of natural law, as a thesis about morality, law, and other forms of social authority, is that some action-guiding thoughts and statements, that is, some precepts or practical principles, are natural in the sense that they are not dependent for their validity on human decision, authority, or convention. Standard natural law accounts of precepts and principles held to be natural in this way maintain that they are accessible to human reason,[1] and so can be judged on critical reflection to be valid independently of social enactment or acceptance. I will take this thesis about the accessibility of moral truth to human reason to be part of the core idea of natural law.

Stoic and Christian natural law theories agree that the ontological basis for this accessibility is divine reason. But the theism of natural law theory, however essential to a complete story about it, is not part of the core idea, nor is it necessary for addressing the obvious epistemological questions the core idea raises. Similarly, natural law theories characteristically hold for a close connection between human nature and moral precepts; some natural law theories are strongly naturalistic in holding for a tight logical derivation of moral conclusions from human functions that can be identified as essential to humans independently of moral judgment. The exact relationship between human nature and moral precepts is disputed among natural law theorists, and the alleged naturalism of natural law morality is controversial. Moreover, like the theism of natural law theory, the full range of issues about the relationship between morality and human nature need not be settled in order to draw, from principles widely understood to be natural law convictions, the ethical and political considerations relevant to many normative issues, including those raised by the de facto existence of territorial boundaries and the de jure claims made about their significance.

The idea that human reason provides enough access to moral principle that established social arrangements can be evaluated morally can be liberating, but some actual deliverances of human reason thus engaged are needed if light is to be shed on questions of political morality such as those raised by practices concerning borders. I will begin by indicating some of the normative content of a natural law approach and the analytical categories by which natural law norms could be specified in the political context in which questions about borders arise.[2]

The relationship between the core idea of natural law and the actual content of the deliverances of human reason is not as simple as is suggested by the natural law claim that some moral principles are universally accessible. The natural law which all humans know or can know is capable of a variety of formulations, some of which can include mistaken assumptions. Moreover, the implications of what is naturally accessible to human reason are understood only through a process of conceptual clarification and reasoning. There is room for error here as well; the natural law conviction is not that there cannot be mistakes in moral reasoning, but that humans have the wherewithal to detect and correct them. It is not surprising, therefore, that those in agreement on the core idea of natural law should disagree on the formulations of basic moral principles and, even more, disagree about the exact formulations of the precepts derived from those principles.[3] I propose to set aside the conceptual and historical exploration of alternative natural law precepts and principles, for the issues before us can be illuminated by taking one form of natural law theory and developing it in the relevant way. I focus here on the form of natural law that finds its classical exposition in the ethical writings of St. Thomas Aquinas and has been developed in a set of interrelated interpretations and applications by a group of (mostly Roman Catholic) theologians, philosophers, and social theorists, who together comprise a loose tradition of inquiry that can be called Catholic or Thomistic natural law theory.[4] This contribution will, therefore, be an essay in Thomistic natural law thinking. Since, as far as I know, there has not been extensive reflection by exponents of Thomistic natural law on moral questions raised by borders, this essay will attempt to construct a natural law approach to these problems from the norms and categories developed in the tradition. I will indicate when the development of Thomistic natural law is well established in the tradition and when the development is largely my own attempt to construct broadly Thomistic responses to the questions that define the inquiry of this book.

Aquinas put forth an extensive, complex, and interrelated set of precepts governing private and public life.[5] He held that these precepts were implications of general moral considerations which he characterized as the principles of natural law. Aquinas formulated what he took to be the most basic of these principles in several ways: most notably as the prescription to act in accord with right reason, or to act in accord with its basic moral deliverance, namely, to love God above all things and one's neighbor as oneself. However difficult it might be to explain how this precept can be the basic and self-evident moral principle of natural law, Aquinas plainly thought it to be so, and indeed could hardly have considered any other principle to be preferable.[6] Still, the twofold love commandment has obvious similarities to other prescriptions thought to be fundamental in moral life, most notably, to several of Kant's formulations of the categorical imperative: actions respecting rational nature as an end in itself surely express something of the love of neighbor which Aquinas thought implied the Decalogue. Kant's kingdom of ends seems a secularized version of the human community shaped by compliance with the love commandments.[7]

The precepts of the second tablet of the Decalogue are the immediate implication of the principle that one is to love one's neighbor as oneself. These precepts—prohibiting killing, stealing, lying, and adultery and requiring respect for parents—provide the normative shape for social life. In most cases they provide moral limits beyond which a person or group must not go if decent social existence is to be maintained. But this hardly amounts to a complete political morality.

The normative core of Thomistic natural law contains the basis for a further step in that direction. A component of the second love commandment itself—the Golden Rule—provides a principle that does more than delineate outer moral limits for social life. The Golden Rule provides a rational basis for scrutinizing the bias that our feelings can generate in favor of ourselves and those with whom we identify. So it provides a moral ground for evaluating actions compatible with the precepts of the Decalogue. By revealing partiality that is not in conformity with reason, the Golden Rule serves as a consideration in the justification of duties and rights, and in the reasoning that determines the ranking of duties and sometimes the overriding of rights. This principle, then, is an essential working principle in social and political morality.

Still, the love commandments, including the Golden Rule, together with the precepts of the Decalogue, do not by themselves constitute a complete social or political philosophy. For they cannot, by themselves, answer many of the moral questions which arise for groups acting corporately and for individuals acting as authorities within communities or as members under authority. Included in these questions are many of the key questions of political philosophy, including those discussed here. Thus, for example, use of the Golden Rule can reveal that certain of a country's policies about aliens crossing its borders are unfair. But the Golden Rule cannot by itself provide the rationale for having borders in the first place, or decisively criticize the rationales for some kinds of differential treatment of people inside and outside borders.

To deal with these questions, and more generally with questions of social and political morality, we seem to need, in addition to strictly moral principles and precepts, some way of understanding the conditions for common action and cooperation. Only by clarifying the character of common action by groups of people does it become clear what it is that moral norms and principles direct and evaluate in social contexts. Thus, if the human actions by which borders are created, respected, and given social significance by political society are understood as purposeful acts of communities, then moral puzzles about the fairness of acts that treat borders as significant can begin to be resolved.

Thomistic natural law makes use of two interrelated ideas to understand human cooperation: the notion of the common good and a conception of practical authority. The notion of the good, as what is desirable for humans because of its capacity to perfect or fulfill the human person, both individually and in community with others, is the analytical foundation of practical reasoning, including moral reasoning. The goods that motivate human beings are intelligible: they provide reasons for action.[8]

As intelligible, goods can be understood to be desirable by anyone and perfective of anyone. This allows the same goods to be pursued by groups of people: life by a survival community, health by a health-care team, including professionals, patients, and family supporters, victory and excellence in performance by a team of athletes, good relations with God or the gods by a religious congregation, and so on. When the same good is pursued by a group of people, that good is common to them.[9]

Goods common in this way are a necessary condition for the existence of a community, understood as something specifically distinct from a group, namely, as a group that engages in common action. Not all groups of human beings sharing some form of common identity are communities in this sense; for example, people whose only connection to one another is their ethnic origin are not. But any such group can find in its identifying features grounds for common action, that is, common goods, the pursuit of which will make them communities in this stronger sense.

Since many uncoordinated actions of distinct and separated individuals and communities could aim at the same human good as, for example, isolated survival communities all aim to stay alive, a common good is not sufficient for community or common action. Indeed, many if not all individual and communal actions have purposes that are common in the sense that they have good-making or desirability-making features that are the same as those of the actions of other people. Thus, common action requires, in addition to goods common in this way, a goal that is common, that is, a state of affairs at which the various individual actions aim. A goal is common to a group of people when each person chooses actions which he or she understands as a means towards the realization of the goal. In short, action of many towards a common good becomes a common action only if each member of the group understands his or her action as a contribution to the realization of the same goal, only if each sees his or her actions as part of a larger project or enterprise. But even aiming at the same goal, such as the defeat of a common enemy by communities completely out of touch with each other, is not sufficient for common action.[10]

At least one further condition is needed if community and common action are to exist, that is, some form of coordination of individual action towards the common goal. This coordination of action towards a common goal occurs if each participant's contribution to the achievement of the goal is understood by him or her as dependent for its success in the project on the success of actions of other parties—coordination towards a common goal includes the idea of taking account of the contribution of others to the project and adjusting one's actions accordingly.

I think these two necessary conditions are together sufficient for actions directed towards a common good to be considered common action. If a person acts for a goal he or she thinks is common and makes relevant choices by taking into consideration actions of others for that goal, then that person's actions are joined to the actions of the others. He or she does what is possible to realize a goal understood to be others' goal as well and to take into account their actions for its realization. To the extent that mutuality exists between these acting parties, the actions for common goals are more fully common and the acts of the group.

These conditions can be met when there is a very considerable unanimity within a group of people, not only about the common goods and common goals to which they are committed, but also about each person's contribution to realization of the common goal by his or her choice of the appropriate action to pursue it. Absent that kind of unanimity, practical authority is needed for the coordination of individual action necessary for common action.

Practical authority is recognized by one's willingness to allow choices to be settled not by one's own preferences or practical judgments, but by the decision of another person—the one accepted as having practical authority. This surrender of discretion to a person or group intent on the common goal has the same effect as unanimity: it allows the actions of the obedient to be integrated into the project of realizing the goal.

It is reasonable to accept practical authority if one believes there are goods that either cannot be achieved without it or cannot be as easily or surely achieved without submitting to that restraint in choosing. Thus, whenever there is reason supporting common action and no prospect of securing the coordination necessary for common action by unanimity, then there is reason for accepting authority. When the reason supporting common action is moral obligation, then, absent unanimity, accepting authority is morally obligatory.[11]

The notions of the common good and of authority introduced here are formal notions that apply, *mutatis mutandis*, to all communities and common actions. Moreover, the internal logic of these formal notions raises, but does not provide detailed resources for answering, questions about how to identify a community and its authorities. Aquinas's method of political analysis allowed him to set aside questions of this kind,[12] and such later natural law efforts to answer them do not seem to provide much progress beyond the abstract question the formal analysis suggests: will accepting this leadership best serve the common good in the de facto circumstances?[13]

To sum up these introductory remarks: The core of natural law is the rejection of legal and moral positivism or conventionalism grounded on the claims of human reason to attain moral truth. That position alone, though relevant to political and social philosophy, throws little light on the issues under discussion in this volume. Since there is no developed natural law analysis of territorial boundaries, I will try to construct one from key elements of a natural law normative theory and social analysis. The characteristic principles and precepts of Thomistic natural law provide the needed normative framework. The conceptions of the common good and of authority provide the needed account of common action.

Definition

The bodies of animals, including human beings, have limited and fairly precise dimensions. There is a clear limit to the extension of our bodily selves, and that is a kind of boundary. Other natural things have boundaries of this kind, although often they are vague. The boundaries of geographically significant things like bodies of water or mountains are sometimes discovered to have human significance as limits on the activities of a group of people. Impassable rivers, oceans, or forests are examples.

Of course, the humanly significant boundaries which exist in most of the world today are far less naturally based than the boundaries in these examples; most such boundaries are thoroughgoingly if not completely conventional. Property lines and political boundaries divide much of the world insofar as it is social space shared by human beings. Although such thing as rivers, oceans, and deserts are often used to define boundaries, the division of property and of polities is frequently by boundaries that are necessarily more precise than such natural features, without human specification, can provide. Moreover, many humanly significant boundaries are drawn with no basis in natural boundaries, on the basis of deals, negotiations, and other human actions such as wars.

Some boundaries are humanly significant as property lines. Others are significant because they indicate which political authorities have jurisdiction within them. This is an obvious function of political boundaries, even when they are not boundaries between polities claiming sovereignty, but between provinces, states, or administrative regions of a country.

It seems promising, therefore, to define political boundaries as the geographical limits to the jurisdiction of a political authority. By "jurisdiction" I do not mean "political authority," for members of a polity can be obliged to obey their political leaders on some matters even when they are not in their jurisdiction. Rather, I mean the capacity of political authorities to back their directives with sanctions without the consent of others outside the polity's authority structure.

Many political authorities claim some jurisdiction beyond their borders, for example, by demanding extradition of extraterritorial criminals, or by trying to convince extraterritorial citizens to pay their taxes. Still, claims such as these, when plausible, are qualified in such a way that they are not unequivocal claims to jurisdiction. For when these claims are made against those who are not members of the polity claiming the extraterritorial jurisdiction, they generally suppose the consent or agreement of the foreign political authority having jurisdiction in the region where the claim must be made good. Thus, a request for the extradition of a criminal either is a simple request, and not an authoritative intervention, or it is an appeal to a treaty or other covenant, and this appeal's force comes from the promise involved in the treaty, not the appellant country's authority beyond its borders.

The authority that a polity claims over its citizens when they are beyond its borders is also importantly qualified. Although that authority may sometimes bind such citizens morally, their obedient or disobedient response cannot be rewarded or punished while beyond the borders and the reach of the polity claiming allegiance. Moreover, citizens of a polity traveling or residing in other countries are for most purposes reasonably under the legal authority of the jurisdiction where they find themselves. Visitors should obey local traffic laws, pay appropriate taxes, and so on. Resident aliens should be cooperative members of the community and not usurp rights of citizenship.

In short, the fact that polities have interests that are not limited by their borders seems to imply that political authorities have reason, sometimes morally binding reason, to act for such interests. But the soundness of this implication does not further imply that political authorities must have extraterritorial political jurisdiction to act for these interests. They can act by pleading, threatening, going to war and so on; such initiatives imply the possibility of acting beyond a polity's borders, but ordinarily include negotiating with representatives of other polities, which are not under their authority. Even when they do have authority beyond their borders, it is qualified and in many matters superceded by the local political authority.

I have developed these reflections to indicate a significant, geographically based limitation on the authority of the leaders of a political society which I believe to be essential to a natural law view on the moral issues raised by boundaries. Because of the dependence of authority upon the common good of the community it serves, this limitation makes sense on natural law terms only if there is a strong tie between the common good of a political society and the more or less limited territory in which the community lives. I believe that, although the natural law tradition assumes rather than explores it, this relationship between a region and the common good of the polity established there is an important element in the natural law conception of political life.

To show this connection, I must first say something about how natural law elaborates the generic idea of common good as the common good of political society. Although there is considerable debate among natural law theorists about how the common good of political society is to be defined, several key aspects are clear and uncontroversial. First, the common good is not simply a sum of individual interests defined independently of people's interests in cooperating politically with others. It is the object of certain, politically defined human interests such as justice and social harmony.

Second, human cooperation generally is an instrumental good for the achievement of other goods, such as life and security. Political society is no exception. But various forms of social communion, such as friendship and marriage, are intrinsically desirable, as are many of the cooperative practices that social life makes possible—for example, games and sports. Again political society is no exception. Some aspects of the good that unites people into political society also seem intrinsically good—for example, the fair play that a decent legal system allows upright citizens to pursue harmonious relationships with others in ways not otherwise available. So, the common good of political society appears to be in some respects at least an intrinsic good of human beings, that is, something that can be sought as a benefit or end in itself and not simply as an empowerment or means.

Third, the consequence of the preceding two considerations is that natural law's rejection of an individualistic conception of the common good as a sum of individual goods does not imply that the common good is only a deontological notion. It is a good, something in which people can take an interest and find fulfillment.

Fourth, the common good of political society is sufficiently inclusive of the range of basic human concerns that it can justify both a legal system that regulates some aspects of virtually all people do, and the coercive power of legal authorities. This inclusiveness is part of the sense of the natural law idea that political society is a complete or perfect community.[14] The extent of the inclusiveness of the claims of political society is a matter of debate among exponents of natural law. In particular, there is controversy over whether all aspects of the human good are comprised within the political common good, or whether some aspects of human fulfillment are beyond the competence of political society.

It seems to me that the second alternative is the correct natural law view. For there are human goods, such as the development of virtue, the forming of friendships and familial relationships, and the authentic practice of religion, which political society cannot directly promote because the actions that realize them simply cannot be acts of political authority and obedience. At best political society can contribute to these goods by creating the social conditions that foster the private actions of individuals and nonpolitical communities that realize these goods. In the spirit of this line of reasoning, and in accord with Aquinas's limitation of the common good of political society to the public concern for justice and peace,[15] recent formulations of the common good suggest that it is the ensemble of conditions, including such things as a legal system and established rights, that allow citizens to live their lives fully and well.[16]

This limitation of the common good of political society does not address geographical limits. But the entire picture of social life which natural law develops assumes that a set of concerns of people living together in the same place creates a motive and a justifying reason to cooperate in political society.

The fact that human beings and their most elementary communities are in some particular place, interacting with others who share adjacent and nearby places, seems to be an implication of the fact that humans are animals and animals are bodies. This fact becomes morally significant because people living together have reasons to negotiate their interactions and to cooperate in various ways just because they are in proximity in one region of the world.

People living together have security interests in preventing harms to life and its conditions by criminals and unfriendly outsiders. These interests are plainly basic and are virtually impossible to satisfy without cooperation among neighbors. People living in contiguity also have interests in establishing conventions for getting along: rules for property rights, opportunities for trade, mechanisms to resolve conflicts, rules for marriage, protections for the practice of religion, a framework for voluntary associations, and the creation and maintenance of public services such as roads. All these human interests are common to people who physically interact or could because they share a region of the earth.

The defense of life and property are basic ingredients in any criminal law, and the laws of contracts, marriage, and so on comprise a significant part of what any legal system must regulate and any polity must ensure. In short, the natural law identification of the political common good as primarily a matter of peace and justice supposes that the precise kinds of harmony and justice at stake are those which arise from the common concerns of people living together.

Although these interests include the community's dealings with outsiders, and with members of the group when they are outside the community's region, the interests that reach beyond borders are also connected to the community's common life—for example, defending the community's region by wars that extend beyond its borders, insisting on citizens' rights to travel and do business beyond national borders, and insisting that traveling citizens fulfill their civic responsibilities. Therefore, there is an essentially geographical element in political society and the cooperation of its members. Thus, the limits of the region in which people cooperate as a political community—ordinarily borders— mark a limit to the community itself, and so to the authority and jurisdiction of its leaders.

The thesis about the essential geographical element in political society is not a claim about communities as such. People can form communities that are significantly independent of where they live and immediately do their business. Scholarly associations, for example, are not significantly territorial, nor are many religions. Although every scientist must work in some definite place or places, the community of scientists depends only on scientists' ability to communicate. Although the possibility of joining in an assembly with co-religionists is usually required for religious community, there is no need for them to live in the same region, or to have anything in common except religious conviction.

Nor does my thesis concerning the geographical nature of political society have any implications about the merits of huge empires or even a world polity. Cooperation on a global level requires coordination of individual and social activity across polities and boundaries. Throughout history, such coordination has been required whenever people of different countries have had reason to cooperate. Given the current level of such cooperation, more comprehensive polities, even a single global polity—or perhaps a more robust and less piecemeal legal arrangement than current international law— may be desirable and justified. But even if there were only one sovereign polity in the world, the need for local jurisdiction would remain. If there were only one legal system, it would not, on account of this unity, be able to dispense with addressing interests that give people living together reason to cooperate politically.

A political society capable of addressing such interests, however extensive its unifying reach among the people and places on the earth, must establish boundaries. Some specified people and laws must be in authority in every part of the world in which people interact. These laws and authorities must take into account local realities and deal with issues that arise locally—policing, arbitrating disputes, establishing housing regulations, and so on. Authority capable of effective presence in one place and capable of dealing with local concerns cannot be equally present everywhere.

In short, some political boundaries are necessary for doing the things the political common good requires. This normative inevitability would retain its force in a world in which modern nation-states did not exist, and so is justified even if the nation-state system is not. Whether or not all politics is local, local politics is unavoidable and justified. And locales are limited; they have borders or at least frontiers.

Ownership

Thomistic natural law holds that the non-personal realities in the world are properly used to satisfy human need. This does not imply that nonpersonal realities belong to everyone. The relationship of possession is established by custom or convention and allows various forms, such as private and common, and, no doubt, various grades or modalities of possession, such as exclusive use and some level of shared use. So, possession is not a natural relationship. Moreover, the conventions and customs which define possession do not override what is "natural" in the morally relevant sense, namely, the reasonable use of things to satisfy human need. What current exponents of natural law call the "universal destination" of earthly goods—that is, the morally proper use of earthly goods fairly to meet the needs of all who can benefit from them—can morally trump conventions assigning property to some rather than others. Moral principle trumps these conventions when their working causes harm that can be justly remedied either by setting them aside in particular cases or by revising the conventions. Aquinas's famous discussion of a person in urgent need taking something from another not in such need is the classic example of the first possibility. Modern natural law defenses of the wide dispersal of property among poor and working class people is an example of the second.[17]

Within the framework set by the traditional assumption that earthly goods are to be used to meet human need, Aquinas gave three reasons he judged sufficient to justify a regime in which there is private property, that is, control over some thing by an individual or smaller group within a group of people. First, people tend to be more careful about things that are their own responsibility than they are about things that are the common responsibility of many people. Second, it would be more orderly if one person had the responsibility for the thing than if everyone were equally in charge of it. Third, it is more conducive to peace if each has his or her own goods to use and care for; when people hold things in common and without division, conflicts are frequent.[18]

The first of these considerations appears to be an argument from efficiency. Private property allows the best use of many of the things of the earth. But the second two are essentially political. The orderliness achieved by having some and not all be owners of an item involves an element of cooperation among people who have access to the same useful things and so have reason to desire an authoritative ruling as to who is to be in charge of them. In the most elementary cases, the useful things to which many have access are those in reach physically by all, such things as plots of land, watering places, tools, and dwelling places. More complicated forms of property, for example, intellectual property or partial ownership by investments in enterprises, would not be possible without regulations governing ownership in the elementary cases. So, it seems to me that the orderliness which Aquinas judged to be a benefit of a regime including private property is an element of the peace and justice he thought characteristic of the common good of political society. Similarly, the conflicts avoided by private ownership of certain useful things are conflicts between people having access to those things. In the first instance that access is physical reach, and so the peace achievable by private property is not only familial and informal but also essentially civic and political.

Thus, the same features of human life—that people live together in a place and interact with one another—figure in the rationale for private property and in the motivation for creating political society. Therefore, the relevant implication of natural law thinking is that political society carries out some of its essential tasks by creating the legal framework to create and give precision to the division of land, resources, and other items people who share a region use, so that the items will be well used and order and peace maintained.

This does not imply ownership by the polity of the territory in which it has jurisdiction. The institutionalization of political leadership in a government ordinarily implies a need for various things that must be under government control—for example, government buildings are correctly thought of as the government's private property. Similarly, political society can maintain some parts of its territory as common, and set regulations for fair common use. These cases of public and common ownership, and even the right of authorities to override the property rights of owners, do not imply that political society is a kind of super-owner of all the useful things that fall within its borders. Just as the universal destination of earthly goods does not imply that everyone owns everything, the existence of humanly useful things in a certain region does not mean that the political community in place there owns those things. The political community is obliged to do what it can to see that these goods are well used to meet human need. That generally requires a property regime that includes private, public, and common ownership of various things. This division creates ownership or formalizes and improves customary ownership conventions. It does not presuppose that the country owns its territory.[19]

As with other aspects of the life of a political community, the jurisdiction and authority of its law and leaders with respect to property is in important ways limited by its borders. The property of citizens and others outside a polity's borders are often beyond its reach to control, and when such property is not beyond the polity's reach, that is because some other property, within its borders or available because of the cooperation of other polities, can be taxed or seized.

Although property regulations, including tax law, vary considerably from jurisdiction to jurisdiction (even within sovereign polities), there are aspects of possession that are so important for human life and so entrenched in custom that they are part of a *jus gentium*.[20] Thus, rules that would deprive merchants of the opportunity to do business outside their borders, or would deny their or other travelers' rightful possession of goods they bring for trade, or of their clothes and tools, are unjust. For such rules would establish conventions that could not pass Golden Rule tests and so could not assure morally good use of earthy goods.

Distribution

Political society has a responsibility to distribute various burdens and benefits among its members, for example, taxes and offices. However, the intrinsic benefits of political life are ordinarily not distributable. The benefits of being a law-abiding member of a polity having just laws and harmony among members are available to those who are members of such a society and not available to others. In whatever ways political society is limited, so are such benefits, but there is no distribution decision in addition to group decisions to have a just society and individual decisions to be good citizens of such a polity. In this regard territorial limits are not different than others: the decision to have a polity is not a decision per se to deny its benefits to those beyond its borders or frontiers. Other goods, closely related to the common life of a group of people organized politically, may also be difficult if not impossible to distribute—for example, the beauty of cities or countryside.

Still, the realization of the common goals of a polity ordinarily facilitates the development of many goods that are both distributable and valuable to people within and outside the polity's borders. The welfare benefits which technologically advanced and wealthy countries are able to provide for their citizens are generally limited to citizens and residents within the country's borders. Some of the resources used in such countries for health care or welfare for the poor could be redirected to the much needier sick and poor of the Third World. Similarly, the prosperity in skills and goods resulting from trade and private enterprise provides useful things that both citizens and foreigners can use and sometimes desperately need. Yet the property regimes in wealthy countries ordinarily require no distribution to the needy except what is required by law, usually modestly redistributionist tax law for the local needy, and, for outsiders, what the free market requires.

The recent natural law tradition, as represented in the body of Catholic "social teaching," affirms the existence of significant and "natural" welfare rights. I believe that these rights are natural in the sense that (1) the fundamental moral obligation—in this case the requirement of neighbor love itself—is natural, and (2) every step in institutionalizing personal moral obligation as a set of duties to which welfare rights correspond is itself required by moral principle, not convention or decision. In other words, a welfare right is natural if and only if the de facto conditions of social life, and not conventions or decisions, require a political community to establish that right on the ground that the fundamental requirements of neighbor love will not be met—or not be met as effectively—by individual or informal group initiative as by politically coordinated action, and on the condition that no other moral obligation prevents the needed initiatives. In many countries today these conditions are met. In such countries goals like health care for all and food and shelter for the poor, goals everyone capable has a moral obligation to help realize, are better realized by action coordinated by the government than by private and voluntary initiative. The actions by which political society coordinates such action, most notably taxation, need not be so extensive or oppressive as to interfere with other goals of political life.[21]

Rights justified in this way are essentially political because the entitlement presupposes the common action of the polity—at least taxation. Without that common action, the entitlements involved in welfare rights could not exist because there would be no agent or agents having the duties corresponding to the rights. The individual obligation of neighbor love cannot by itself establish the duties to provide health or shelter, since that is ordinarily beyond any individual's capacity. It seems to me, therefore, that welfare rights are necessarily tied to membership within a polity and ordinarily to citizenship or residence within its borders. Outsiders do not have similar political entitlements, even if individual citizens and the community as a whole continue to have moral responsibilities towards them.

Of course, the benefits delivered by entitlement systems— health or housing or food— are not essentially political in this way, and these benefits can sometimes be given by one community to the needy of another. There can be barriers to doing this that are connected to borders. Some outside a polity's borders may be technologically or geographically beyond its reach. A foreign regime may refuse the help outsiders seek to give, or it may make it impossible for the help to get to those who need it. But the underlying obligation to help the needy one can help remains binding on every person. To whatever extent borders do not completely remove the possibility of helping those beyond them, to that extent responsibility to help remains. For, to reemphasize the fundamental moral point: The morally variable capacities of political societies to organize to meet basic need do not cause variation in the basic moral principle, only in the ways people are to respond to it.

It is hard to see how this should not also be an obligation of groups, not only families, churches, and charitable organizations, but also political communities. For political communities have interests and can act in various ways beyond their borders. And political societies can often, without compromising other responsibilities, coordinate the morally required actions of citizens into more effective common actions. I don't see why the limitations which borders impose on the effectiveness of such action should excuse political society from acting. One country cannot guarantee welfare rights for citizens of other countries, but when it can fairly help them, it should.

Diversity

Twentieth-century exponents of natural law have distinguished between the nation and the political society which organizes it politically and provides its legal structure.[22] The nation is the proper object of patriotism, and often is taken to essentially include the ethnic, religious, and cultural character of the people who reside together in a region.

The set of interests that constitute a group of people as a nation needing political organization necessarily includes interests based on the fact that they

share a region of the world. Other interests that are connected to living together in the same region over time can become part of national identity: for
example, the common language and culture that must develop over time
among people who interact, and the religion such people often share. But
these do not seem to me essential to national identity, and do not by themselves form a basis for politically dividing people having territorially based
interests in cooperating politically.

People from different ethnic backgrounds, with (initially) different languages, cultures, and religions can have the set of interests that makes them a
people needing a political organization. They can be organized politically
while maintaining significant differences in other respects, as the experience
of the multicultural nations of North America, and, to some real extent, of the
multinational empires of the ancient world indicates.

Recent exponents of natural law have made clear that political society
should not seek to enforce religious practice, but instead should limit activity
bearing on religion to establishing public conditions fostering authentic religious practice and maintaining public order.[23] That implies that religion as
such should not be the basis for defining limits to a polity—including its
borders.

Similar developments of natural law thinking with respect to the civic significance of ethnic, linguistic, and other cultural factors have not, to my
knowledge, been made. But the current natural law reasoning on religion
seems to have parallel applications: religion deals with a basic human interest
that has obvious social dimensions. Political society should respect and foster
religion as it can. But that requires refraining from promoting one religion
over others or identifying the polity by religious affiliation. Similarly, ethnic
and linguistic affiliations and cultural interests are often connected to basic
and social human interests. Political society should respect and promote those
interests in appropriate ways. But identification of the polity by those affiliations and interests when the interests of those sharing a region require defining
the polity more broadly appears unjustified, for it denies to some the opportunity to cooperate politically with their neighbors on grounds that are arbitrary.

This is not meant to deny that there are often good reasons to maintain the
boundaries of countries originally established on ethnic or religious grounds.
Rather, it is to make the normative claims that denying the benefits of political membership to those within the borders on these grounds is wrong, and
that refusing on these grounds to consider expanding political cooperation to
neighbors is also wrong. So, it is not religion or ethnicity as such, but the risks
of tinkering with established borders and of causing other avoidable harms,
that render them indirectly relevant to the definition of borders and membership in a political society.

Still, there are tensions and conflicts between people in the same region
that are based on ethnic and religious differences. Such hostilities, when they

arise from legitimate grievances on both sides, do not necessarily prevent reasonable political cooperation and even unity. But such hostilities are often unreasonable, at least on one side; and they are often so intense that they prevent cooperation that would otherwise be mandatory for the reasonable party. In cases of that kind, the existence of hostilities among separate but adjoining communities might well justify significant political division of the communities. This solution does not work for the more common problem caused by hostile communities intermingled and sharing the same space. In this case, political separation is not possible, and the interests that lead people to form political society become moral obligations for the reasonable people in the situation.

Mobility

As suggested above in the opening section of this chapter, the natural law tradition accepts as part of the *jus gentium*[24] certain rights of people to move across borders. The only reasonable limits on such movement, whether by immigrants, merchants, or other travelers, are those imposed by the common good of the polity in question.

Plainly, the common good of any polity will require the exclusion of people entering with hostile intent. That is why border crossings by hostile armies are presumptively causes of war. Perhaps some forms of colonization and foreign efforts to exploit a region's natural resources are also hostile, and rightly resisted by political authorities and citizens.

Things are not so clear, however, when one enters a country for one's own peaceable purposes—such as visiting, doing business, or immigrating. How are such actions related to the common good of a country? Presumptively and ordinarily such actions of nonmembers of a political society are compatible with and contribute to the common good of a polity. Visits by outsiders are among the things most citizens have reason to desire, and so they are among the activities political society should facilitate and coordinate. The same is obviously true of foreign commerce conducted within one's borders.

Immigration may seem to present different moral issues, since it is at least conceivable that immigrants might swamp one's economy or become a threat to political order. These possibilities, do not, in my opinion, remove the presumption in favor of easy passage across borders; for often immigrants are in desperate need which all but the most straitened political communities have duties to address.

The mere possibility that accepting immigrants who seek entry might harm some legitimate interests of a political society or its citizens is not sufficient grounds to exclude them, for two reasons. First, any argument that the common good of a polity excludes some kinds of immigration must make reference to the particular circumstances, such as the state of the economy of the polity excluding the immigrants. While one cannot exclude in principle the possibility that some such arguments are sound, examples of sound, common-good-based arguments to limit immigration are not easy to find. Second, the requirements of the common good of any group do not override other moral considerations, such as those based on Golden Rule reasoning. The common good is a basis for common action and a ground for authority, not a moral principle capable of dispensing with the principles and precepts of the natural law.

These considerations, plainly, do not prevent a government from rightly controlling its borders, requiring visas and imposing reasonable taxes and quarantines. On its face, the scrutiny of those who wish to enter a country and the determination of the reasons for entry is a reasonable exercise of political authority, an activity capable of abuse but nevertheless of service to the common good.

Autonomy

Autonomy is not a prominent category in natural law analysis, and its absence may not be ascribed simply to the premodern character of natural law's classic texts. Rather, natural law is preoccupied not with creating social space for people to do as they wish, but with exploring the practical rationality of individual and group decisions. Consequently, its focus in social and political philosophy is on whether and how social decisions serve the common good. In questions about decisions affecting the relationships between polities, natural law has not focused on sovereign rights but on moral principle and the common good of the entire group of communities and people affected by the decisions.

If natural law's conception of social life and international relations does not focus on autonomy and sovereignty, it nevertheless does acknowledge that some individuals are in authority in some matters, and that the exercise of authority is not simply drawing inferences from the principles of practical reason. Authorities have discretion, limited by moral principle and by the rulings of other relevant authorities. On this conception, owners have considerable discretion over their property, as do political authorities in making social choices. The latter may sometimes lawfully limit the discretion of owners, even within the general terms of that discretion.

The part of autonomy that I have called "discretion" is, therefore, an irreducible element in decent society, and its exercise is required in any human life that rises above mechanistic routine. The natural law version of the question about the relationship between autonomy and boundaries is, therefore, a question about whether boundaries are importantly connected to the exercise of discretion over their lives by the people and political authorities in a certain part of the world. The answer for which I have been implicitly arguing is affirmative, and that answer is independent of whether the local political authority is understood to be sovereign.

However coordinated the interactions of people may become by developing ever more encompassing political communities to guarantee common action, there will be local interactions which require local coordination. Some boundaries, however otherwise arbitrary, are needed if there is to be local community, since authority competent to deal with the particulars of local interactions cannot be responsible for the whole world. The (practically impossible) removal of such local authority would not relegate to more global authorities the needed discretion over local particulars, it would eliminate that discretion. The elimination of local political discretion would in turn significantly limit the discretion over the lives of people who would lack the resources for common action, including such things as mechanisms for dispute resolution.

In other words, the interests that cause upright people to endorse political arrangements or to create them when lacking are vital to their living their lives in a decent way. These social, political, and legal interests can extend very far—to any human interaction within physical or technological reach. But however far these interests extend, and with them the political community they justify, they reach out from the person's body, workplace, and home. They extend the possibilities of common action available to those who are literally neighbors to many and perhaps all other people. But the extension cannot supercede the reality it extends. For if these foundational elements of social life are not politically organized, the pursuit of a life rich and fulfilling by the person's own judgments and commitments is put at risk, and so the human interests justifying political organization are undercut. And there is no relevant political organization unless some authority has jurisdiction; in practice that means jurisdiction limited by borders.

There is, of course, a richer concept of autonomy than the combination of the discretion over one's life which is implied by the natural law concept of property and authority, and the freedom to do as one pleases which is valued by many today and apparently disdained by natural law. This richer idea is the autonomy of those who have significant options for major life choices and for the shape of many lesser choices within their chosen way of life. This kind of autonomy allows a person to be in a significant way the creator of his or her own life.[25] Plainly, this kind of autonomy exists in some societies and cultures and not in others. It may require some features of modern urban life as a necessary condition. It presupposes certain social conditions, at the very least an array of different ways to live a human life, and social permissiveness sufficient to allow the array to present several live options to many people.

Although this kind of autonomy is socially dependent, it is not so obviously politically dependent. It may be one of the nondistributable empowerments or benefits of modern urban life. In particular, it does not appear to be necessarily included in the interests of people interacting in the same region and so to be importantly related to borders, but rather to be dependent on general features of modernity, such as urbanization and economic mobility In any case, natural law theorizing, and perhaps much other political and moral philosophy, has had relatively little to say about the human goodness or social importance of autonomy as a person's self-creation of his or her life. Still, the natural law argument for the necessity of territorially limited political authority is as necessary to preserve the conditions under which this value is realized as it is for social life generally.

Notes

1. See Alan Donagan, *The Theory of Morality* (Chicago and London: University of Chicago Press, 1977), 1–9.

2. For an account of the natural law approach to international ethics generally, see Joseph Boyle, "Natural Law and International Ethics," in *Traditions of International Ethics*, ed. Terry Nardin and David Mapel (Cambridge and New York: Cambridge University Press, 1992), 112–35.

3. The extent of moral diversity, both among those who style themselves natural lawyers and among other moral theorists who hold for basic and accessible moral principles (for example, utilitarians), is a fact that needs explaining by those who believe that moral principles are universally accessible. For an attempt at such an explanation from a natural law perspective, see Joseph Boyle, "Natural Law and the Ethics of Traditions," in *Natural Law Theory: Contemporary Essays*, ed. Robert George (Oxford: Oxford University Press, 1992), 18–28. Aquinas recognized the possibility of mistakes about the conclusions of the principles of the natural law: the classic text is *Summa Theologiae* I-II (First Part of the Second Part), q. (question) 94, a. (article) 4. Since Aquinas's *Summa Theologiae* is available in many editions and translations, I will refer to this book in accord with the commonly used conventions, which allow identification of the text in most editions and translations.

4. The interpretation of Aquinas and its implications for developing natural law theory which I think best is that represented by John Finnis, *Aquinas: Moral, Political, and Legal Theory* (Oxford: Oxford University Press, 1998).

5. Aquinas devoted a large volume, the second part of the ethical treatise in his *Summa Theologiae*, to detailing the complex normative picture of individual and social life which he inherited from canonists, theologians, and Greek philosophy. These norms are plainly meant to be related to, and in some way derived from, the general ethical considerations in the first part of his ethical treatise, which contains his famous treatment of civil and natural law. But the connection is neither tight nor explicit. Since ethics comprises the second part of the *Summa Theologiae*, the first part of the second part, dealing with ethical theory, is distinguished in references from the second part of the second part, which deals with precepts.

6. See *Summa Theologiae* I-II, q. 100, a. 3, body of the article and ad 1 (reply to the first objection), for a classic Thomistic statement of the primacy of the love commands and of the role in moral reasoning of this and other "primary and common" precepts.

7. See Donagan, *Theory of Morality*, 57–66, for a discussion of the relationships between various formulations of the first moral principle.

8. See *Summa Theologiae* I-II, q. 94, a. 2; for commentary, see Finnis, *Aquinas,* 79–102.

9. See Finnis, *Aquinas*, 111–17.

10. The preceding paragraphs are my own analytical reconstruction of the natural law account of the common good and common action. My distinction between common goods and common goals is tacit in the tradition. For the reasons given, it is essential to the story. For the basis of the distinction, see Germain Grisez, Joseph Boyle, and John Finnis, "Practical, Moral Truth and Ultimate Ends," *The American Journal of Jurisprudence* 32 (1987): 103–5.

11. Here I follow the classic exposition of the natural law conception of authority: Yves Simon, *Philosophy of Democratic Government* (Chicago: University of Chicago Press, 1966), 1–71; see also John Finnis, *Natural Law and Natural Rights* (Oxford: Oxford University Press, 1980), 231–59; for the roots in Aquinas's text, see Finnis, *Aquinas*, 35–37.

12. See Finnis, *Aquinas*, 219–22.

13. See Finnis, *Natural Law and Natural Rights*, 248–49. For a critique of the position stated here and a good general discussion of this question, see Mark C. Murphy, "Consent, Custom, and the Common Good in Aquinas' Account of Political Authority," *The Review of Politics* 59 (1997): 323–50, esp. 348–50.

14. See Finnis, *Aquinas*, 219–22.

15. See *Summa Theologiae* I-II, q. 96, a. 3; for commentary and related texts see Finnis, *Aquinas*, 222–28.

16. See Jacques Maritain, *The Person and the Common Good* (Notre Dame: University of Notre Dame Press, 1966), 47–56; Vatican Council II, *Gaudium et Spes*, par. 26; Germain Grisez, *The Way of the Lord Jesus: Volume 2: Living a Christian Life* (Quincy, Ill.: Franciscan Press, 1993), 846–51.

17. The classic source for the natural law evaluation of property is Aquinas's discussion of stealing; see *Summa Theologiae* II-II, q. 66; for commentary see Finnis, *Aquinas*, 188–96; more generally see Joseph Boyle, "Natural Law, Ownership and the World's Natural Resources," *The Journal of Value Inquiry* 23 (1989): 191–207; and Grisez, *Way of the Lord Jesus: Living a Christian Life*, 789–99. Grisez provides references to the recent Catholic teaching about the universal destination of goods and reflection on this idea. In *Summa Theologiae* II-II, q. 66, a. 7, Aquinas allows that one in desperate need may take from another not similarly situated something that, by the conventions of ownership, belongs to the latter. This, he says, is not stealing. Aquinas represents the common natural law view.

18. See *Summa Theologiae* II-II, q. 66, a. 2; my summary is adapted from Boyle, "Natural Law, Ownership and the World's Natural Resources," 195.

19. I am not aware that Aquinas or other natural law theorists have either affirmed or denied that political society has anything like ownership of its territory. For the reasons given, however, I think it would not illuminate these institutions as human undertakings to assimilate the rights and duties of political rulers with those of owners.

For a distinct but compatible argument for this conclusion, see Michael Walzer, *Just and Unjust Wars* (New York: Basic Books, 1977), 55–58.

20. For the dominant natural law idea of *jus gentium*, see Bernice Hamilton, *Political Thought in Sixteenth-Century Spain* (Oxford: Oxford University Press, 1963), 98–109; sixteenth-century exponents of natural law, in discussing the colonization of the New World, held that some property rights were part of the *jus gentium* (p. 132). For an English translation of relevant excerpts from Francisco de Vitoria, *De Indis*, Relectio I, see J. Eppstein, *The Catholic Tradition of the Law of Nations* (Washington, D.C.: Catholic Association for International Peace, 1935), 443–49.

21. For references to Catholic social teaching and a development of the reasoning in this paragraph, see Joseph Boyle, "Catholic Social Justice and Health Care Entitlement Packages," *Christian Bioethics* 2 (1996): 282–92.

22. For the idea of "nation" in natural law and its relationship to the virtue of patriotism, see Grisez, *Way of the Lord Jesus: Living a Christian Life*, 836–46.

23. The classical statement of the new natural law position on religion and politics is Vatican Council II, "Declaration on Religious Freedom (*Dignitatis Humanae*)," pars. 2–9, in W. Abbott, ed., *The Documents of Vatican II in a New and Definitive Translation* (New York: Herder and Herder, Association Press, 1966), 678–88. For a fuller account of why religion is socially important but not to be directly promoted by political society, see Joseph Boyle, "The Place of Religion in the Practical Reasoning of Individuals and Groups," *The American Journal of Jurisprudence* 43 (1998): 1–24.

24. See note 17 above.

25. For this concept of autonomy, see Joseph Raz, *The Morality of Freedom* (Oxford: Oxford University Press, 1987), 369–90.

Sixteen

In Defense of Reasonable Lines

NATURAL LAW FROM A NATURAL RIGHTS PERSPECTIVE

JEREMY RABKIN

JOSEPH BOYLE'S account of natural law in the preceding chapter starts with the duty "to love God above all things and one's neighbor as oneself." From this starting point, his account emphasizes the obligation to share with others. Boyle's version of morality thus tends to minimize the importance of boundaries.

Boundaries are more important—much more important—in the tradition of thought associated with natural rights. In an era of disorienting globalization, this fact may be a quite reassuring feature of natural rights thinking. Before turning to specific contrasts on this theme, however, it might be useful to say a bit about the general difference between natural law and natural rights.

Natural Rights v. Natural Law

Boyle's essay claims to be applying a tradition of Catholic social thought that goes back to Thomas Aquinas in the thirteenth century. Thomas himself clearly drew on philosophic traditions stretching back to the Stoics in ancient Rome and to Aristotle in ancient Athens.

Talk about "natural rights" is, by contrast, relatively modern. It was not until the early seventeenth century that Hugo Grotius, an immensely learned Dutch jurist, initiated the modern practice of speaking about rights in the subjective sense—viewing legal claims from the perspective of the claimant, as in "my rights" rather than what is right.[1] In the mid-seventeenth century, Thomas Hobbes became the first thinker to erect an entire scheme of politics on the doctrine of natural rights. And Hobbes presented natural rights doctrine as the opposite of natural law, since rights convey a choice, while law imposes the obligation to obey.[2]

A more familiar and congenial version of natural rights doctrine was published by John Locke in the immediate aftermath of the Glorious Revolution in England. The Lockean version of natural rights greatly influenced the

American and French revolutions and still influences constitutional doctrine and practice in most Western countries down to the present day. Unlike Hobbes, Locke and his followers were not eager to emphasize the novelty of their doctrine, and this has helped to win a wider following for the Lockean version of natural rights.

Whatever background connections these later theorists might have acknowledged with older political traditions, however, they were, at the least, very selective in their appropriations. Over a period of more than two millennia, natural law doctrines have been invoked to inspire or interpret a wide range of political regimes—including, for example, both the pagan republics of antiquity and the feudal empires of medieval Christendom. By contrast, natural rights doctrine since Locke has been associated almost exclusively with nation-states governed under liberal constitutions. Natural rights doctrine seeks to limit the range of issues in political dispute by limiting the reach of government itself. Natural rights doctrine thus works to justify limited, constitutional government and has not had much attraction for the champions of other kinds of authority.

It is true that Locke speaks of a "law of nature" that complements or reinforces the doctrine of natural rights.[3] And if a natural right implies a duty in others to respect that right, then it might seem largely a matter of style whether one speaks of natural rights or (in reference to the corresponding duties) of natural law. But a natural law that is the converse of natural rights is a much reduced natural law.

All versions of natural rights doctrine agree that individual human beings are the original or primary bearers of rights, because in the natural state—in the "state of nature"—there are individual human beings and no settled communities or governments. So if natural law looks only to establish the claims of natural rights, it will leave out a whole range of duties which we might owe to the community or to the government or to past and future generations. Natural rights theorists, in presenting government as an artificial device to secure natural rights, teach that government has much more limited ends; accordingly, the individual's obligations to government or to the community or to humanity at large are much more limited and much more questionable than earlier thinkers had supposed.

If government is for the sake of rights and rights are for the sake of the individual, the whole doctrine might seem to reduce to the claim that political life rests, for the most part, on individual self-interest. Boyle sees the Golden Rule as the foundation of natural law because it corrects against the "partiality" to one's self which he associates with irrationality. It is only a slight exaggeration to say that natural rights theorists have taken the opposite view: Natural rights allow and even encourage such "partiality" because they are grounded in the right of each person to preserve himself, which is also, in the natural rights perspective, a duty. We are each of us responsible, in the first instance, for taking care of ourselves.

Is it really necessary or sensible to present the claims of self-interest as a moral doctrine? Should natural rights doctrine even be described as a moral doctrine? By the nineteenth century, many thinkers, accepting the Lockean foundations of liberal constitutional government, no longer saw any reason to talk about natural rights and analyzed all political questions in utilitarian terms. But utilitarian arguments—stressing the greatest good for the greatest number, over all—invite a sacrifice of the rights of the minority. Other thinkers, following the lead offered by Kant, looked to moral ideals abstracted from human nature, ideals which could be achieved only by remaking human nature in the interest of equality—or community or dignity or some other vast abstraction. Monstrous tyrannies were built on such formulas in the course of the twentieth century. The resort to mass murder showed that they had strayed much further from the teachings of biblical religion than the theorists of natural rights—all of whom took very seriously at least the commandment against murder.

In a number of ways, Boyle's version of natural law actually seems to have more in common with utopian schemes of the twentieth century than with the constitutional systems founded on natural rights doctrine. Natural rights doctrine rests on a distrust of power. Boyle, who wants to found legal obligations on a universal love, is plainly impatient with limits on power. It is not surprising, then, that Boyle's view of boundaries reveals such fundamental differences with the constitutional systems founded on natural rights doctrine. Boundaries are, after all, a kind of limit.

Sovereignty

Boyle's disdain for boundaries appears most vividly in his approach to what he calls "jurisdiction." Though he wants to preserve a role for local government, Boyle minimizes the importance of national boundaries. He does so because he wants to emphasize responsibilities which transcend the bounds of any one nation. In Boyle's account, we start with the duty to love our neighbor and then find that our "neighbor" may include anyone on the planet.

Territorial boundaries, as Boyle acknowledges, generally define the limits of a government's lawful authority. Boyle is halfway through his exposition, however, before he mentions the word "sovereign," and then it is to disparage the relevance of that status. He acknowledges that "a single global polity" might be "desirable and justified." His general "thesis," he says, has no "implications" regarding "huge empires" or "one sovereign polity in the world." Boyle thinks the relevance of boundaries has to do only (or at least, primarily) with "the need for local jurisdiction," and this "need" would "remain" even in "a single global polity."[4]

Here at the outset is a very large and revealing difference with the natural rights account of government. All natural rights theorists agree that government is in some sense an artificial construction: the rights of individuals come from nature or God, but the powers of government are instituted by the consent of the governed. The naturalness of freedom and the questionableness of government is expressed by the claim that in the state of nature, there is no government. Locke and later theorists acknowledge that there is law—of a sort—in the state of nature. But it is law without a reliable authority to expound or enforce it. Consequently, this law is always in danger of collapsing into hostility and aggression—into a state of war, as Locke says. People cannot rely on a law which cannot be reliably enforced against others.

Locke points to the relations between independent states as a continuing model of what the state of nature is like. Hobbes had made the same point.[5] Whole treatises on international law were subsequently elaborated from this premise of natural rights theory—most notably by the German jurist Samuel Pufendorf, in the late seventeenth century, and by the Swiss diplomat Emerich de Vattel, in the mid-eighteenth century. Both Pufendorf and Vattel follow the logic of the natural rights analysis by emphasizing that each sovereign state must give priority to its own preservation, since every government is established to protect the rights of its own people and self-preservation is not served by excessive trust in others, especially when there is no higher authority to enforce a common law.[6]

Though they have acknowledged—and even emphasized—the insecurities arising from a world of separate, sovereign states, no natural rights theorist has ever suggested that global sovereignty should be established to resolve this insecurity. Their rejection of this solution seems to have rested on the following considerations: If government derives its authority from the consent of the governed, then it must be possible for the governed to withdraw consent. At the individual level, this means the right to leave; one who stays within the territory of a particular government implies that he does tacitly consent to its authority. If all the world is governed by the same global sovereign, however, there can be no escape, hence no easy way to withdraw consent.

Similarly, Locke (as later, Vattel) endorses a right of revolution by which a whole people change their government. This is the argument, of course, of the American Declaration of Independence. But to make a revolution, it must be possible for a whole people (or most of its members) to act in common, which means that a certain degree of national solidarity is necessary for the defense of popular rights against oppressive government.[7] A global sovereignty might make such revolutions impossible—in which case it would invite global tyranny. If global sovereignty did not exclude such revolutions, however, then spirited or self-reliant peoples might indeed break off from the rest and we would be back to a situation of separate, rival states. What would be the relations among them? The American Declaration of Independence, extrapolating from Locke's account and perhaps paraphrasing Vattel, says that when a people separates itself from another, it is "entitled" by the "law of Nature and Nature's God" to a "separate and equal station among the powers of the earth."[8]

Local governments within the same territory do not, of course, have such a "separate and equal station." Instead, the town is subordinate to the county, the county to the state or province, the state or province to the national government. There may be elaborate divisions of responsibility, as in federal systems, but when there is a dispute over the allocation of responsibilities, the matter is resolved, in the end, by the higher authority. And nobody expects localities, within a sovereign state, to respond to such disputes by launching a revolution. That is what makes the higher authority sovereign and the local unit subordinate. In disputes between independent nations, on the other hand, neither side can simply force its will on the other—unless it comes to outright war between them.

Boyle's account, abstracting from all such questions of force and authority, suggests that it does not much matter where sovereignty lies. Locke, by contrast, holds that delegating legislative power to a foreign government would constitute a betrayal and bring on a revolution.[9] Boyle's view is trusting toward higher authority in a way that is quite contrary to the inclinations of the natural rights tradition.

The contrast might have something to do with Boyle's claim to be articulating a Catholic version of natural law. Catholic tradition might be influenced by the traditions of empire in continental Europe, while natural rights doctrine draws on the political traditions of Britain—an island apart. But Boyle's view may finally have less to do with traditional Catholic doctrine than with contemporary political fashion. Certainly, older natural law theorists were quite prepared to assert that a world-state would not be in accord with natural law.

A notable example is Francisco Suarez, the seventeenth-century Spanish Jesuit who was, in his day, regarded as the foremost expounder of Thomistic natural law. Suarez was quite explicit in rejecting a universal empire as impractical.[10] He was also quite explicit about an issue which Boyle seems eager to obscure. What is the difference between a sovereign state and a "local jurisdiction"? Following traditional authority, Suarez identified sovereignty with the authority to make war (which is still the view assumed by the United States Constitution).[11] And the authority to make war on outsiders implies the authority to wield the necessary force to uphold laws at home or settle disputes about what is the proper law at home.

Yet Suarez softened the import of his own doctrine by insisting that the Pope has the ultimate authority to license or prohibit wars and the ultimate authority to limit tyranny by declaring some rulers to have forfeited their claim to the obedience of their subjects.[12] Natural rights theorists were extremely hostile to the notion that the Pope could rightly direct the political loyalty or civic conscience of people in other countries. Locke, for example, insisted that religious toleration should not be extended to Catholics if they would not disclaim any political allegiance to papal directives.[13]

Boyle's version of natural law does not seem to follow Suarez in placing the Pope as the ultimate authority over sovereign states. Perhaps Boyle wants to avoid affronting the sensibilities of non-Catholics by declining to specify the precise nature of his contemplated global authority. Yet the current Pope is widely admired even among non-Catholics and certainly has more moral authority than the secretary-general of the United Nations. If even so admirable a figure as John Paul II would not be trusted to exercise ultimate power, who would be trusted? It is characteristic of Boyle's approach that he does not find it necessary to consider this question.

Property

What is true for sovereignty in Boyle's account is also true for property. Boyle has a remarkably trusting view. With property as with national authority, legal boundaries separate mine from thine. And in both cases Boyle focuses on neighbor love and reason, making little allowance for the natural partiality of the ordinary human being—toward what is his own. Boyle does acknowledge a place for property, as for "local jurisdiction." But he does not provide any special safeguard for property any more than he does for sovereignty or nationality. His general view of property rights is somewhat dismissive.

Yes, Boyle concedes, even Thomas Aquinas recognized that private owners are more careful with their own property than with common responsibilities. But Boyle promptly characterizes this as a matter of "efficiency"—which he then treats as if it were a matter of small importance. Instead, he emphasizes two other aspects of Thomistic teaching on property which Boyle dubs "political" (that private property is more conducive to "orderliness," and that it is less likely to provoke disputes). Clearly, the "political" considerations predominate in Boyle's approach to property.

So "possession," Boyle insists, is "not a natural relationship." What this means is rather obscure, but it seems for Boyle to justify the conclusion that "conventions" of property need "revising" when such changes will secure "the wide dispersal of property among poor and working class people." Only a few pages further along, Boyle admonishes us that "nature" and "neighbor love"—which he treats here as if interchangeable—require "institutionalizing personal moral obligation as a set of duties to which welfare rights correspond."[14]

These claims illustrate several points of difference with the natural rights perspective. To begin with, Locke says, over and over again, that there is private property—that is, "possession"—in the state of nature, and he insists that protection of private property is, in fact, one of the main purposes for which men establish government.[15] Locke does not deny (and in fact, he expressly acknowledges) that positive law may redefine property rights, so the sense in which property is "natural" even for Locke is somewhat complicated.[16] But clearly property rights have a moral priority for Locke that they do not have for Boyle.

The reason for Locke's priority is entirely clear to anyone who reads his *Second Treatise* with a bit of attention. Property, he says, is founded in labor, and it is human labor that makes nine parts out of ten—or rather, as he corrects himself, 99 parts out of 100, or finally, as he belabors the claim, actually 999 parts out of 1,000—in establishing the value of things.[17] What we get from nature alone is nearly worthless; nearly all things of value are generated by human labor. Originally, Locke says, an individual could only appropriate land or other resources when this appropriation still left enough for others to appropriate in the same way. But with the invention of money, individuals could sell their surplus produce and therefore not feel any scruples about enclosing larger tracts of land for their own productive effort, because the fruits of this enclosure would not go to waste.[18] Everything that serves as a spur to productivity and production is a contribution to human well-being. The security of private property is necessary if people are to have incentives to acquire—by producing things of value for others.

Boyle seems entirely indifferent to these elementary economic facts. Some "political" reason suggests that property should be more widely dispersed, so the government is entitled to set aside existing property rights in pursuit of this objective. Will this sort of upheaval make the economy more productive overall? Will a government which does this once in the name of "equality" or "justice" be able to refrain from doing it again and again, simply to gratify the eagerness of some to take the property of others? Is it safe to accord this sort of power to government? Will people be as willing to save and invest in a country where government does this sort of thing on a large scale? None of this seems to matter to Boyle, because he assumes that "property" is just something out there—like firewood in a forest—which can be redistributed without much concern for how it is produced in the first place.

Besides opening the door to what might prove to be massive redistributions of property, Boyle demands ambitious public welfare programs: "goals like health care for all and food and shelter for the poor, goals everyone capable has a moral obligation to help realize, are better realized by action coordinated by the government than by private and voluntary initiative." Boyle grounds this prescription in a rather metaphysical doctrine regarding "the morally proper use of earthly goods"—from which he leaps to the conclusion that "reason" can tell us what resources are needed and in what amounts for all members of society. Or at least, he thinks this is so in some areas. He speaks of "food and shelter *for the poor*"—implicitly acknowledging that the sort of food or shelter provided for the poor might not be quite the same as what people of more means will buy for themselves. When it comes to "health care," however, he treats it as a single thing to be distributed—uniformly, it seems—"to all."[19]

In real life, "health care" covers a vast range of services, some of which are extremely expensive, some of which are directed to enhancing appearance rather than preserving life, some of which are disputed as to their efficacy or value. Meanwhile, people differ in their health priorities and concerns, as much as in their preferences regarding shelter. Some hold themselves to strict diets and rigorous exercise routines; others binge on fatty foods, drink and smoke to excess, take dangerous narcotics, or engage in reckless forms of recreation. Some people seek out medical specialists for minor ailments; others prefer to endure suffering or severe disability rather than enter a hospital. Why assume that what counts as "health care" must come in a preformed package, established by the state?

True, some people enter the market with very limited purchasing power. It is also true that a rich country can afford to help people with the most limited means. But the larger truth remains that everything—including health care—is subject to many conflicting demands and inevitable trade-offs. Countries with government-financed health care usually end up controlling costs by rationing or limiting services, reducing the overall quality of care. For this reason, tens of thousands of Canadians come to the United States each year for surgery or other specialized medical treatments. Canada's system of government-provided health insurance imposes long delays and many restrictions on the quality of care, so many Canadians prefer to pay on their own for the improved treatment available in the United States.

It would be foolish to suggest that all disputes about government policy in this area can be settled by a few philosophic principles. But even if we place a very high priority on protecting physical health—as natural rights doctrine asserts that we should—it hardly follows that a government-run health system is the way to achieve it. Boyle's approach seems so indifferent to real world problems that one may question whether it really does aim to maximize health or simply to demonstrate neighbor love—which might have a rather different logic.

In Boyle's world, it seems, we don't need to worry about over-consumption of medical resources or about how medical costs should be balanced against other costs and needs. We don't need to worry about how individuals differ in their preferences and needs, because a loving government knows what is reasonable for all of us. Nor need we worry about where life-saving drugs or new devices for the handicapped come from. A loving government will just see that we, as a society, develop as many of them as reason tells us we "need." Questions about incentives for drug companies or inventors can be readily answered by government bureaucrats, contemplating the Golden Rule. Natural rights theorists might have recognized a religious impulse in Boyle's approach, but would probably have been much less ready to associate this impulse with the dictates of reason.

Consent

Natural rights doctrine seeks to restrain governmental power. It is focused on political or constitutional norms rather than moral aspirations. Earlier natural law teachings certainly had a much wider scope. It is characteristic of Boyle's version, however, not only that it goes much beyond questions of government, but that it tends to blur basic distinctions between public authority and private life. For this reason, the doctrine of government by consent of the governed, which is crucial for most natural rights theorists, is scarcely mentioned at all in Boyle's essay. Boyle's indifference to consent is very much related to his underlying indifference to boundaries.

One can see the point from the outset in the way Boyle's account obscures the difference between moral precept and legal obligation. An admonition to give to charity is, one might think, quite a different thing from the threat to send you to jail if you do not pay your taxes. The constitutional principle derived from natural rights doctrine holds that taxes cannot be imposed without the consent of the taxpayers. That is Locke's precise teaching.[20] Locke does not say that moral precepts should never be articulated except when the preceptor has received the prior consent of his intended audience. Actual coercive measures require consent (meaning some sort of formal act by a representative body) as a precaution against abusive government. Boyle finds no place to mention this doctrine, because he does not focus, as natural rights doctrine does, on the need for precautions against abusive government. Boyle never acknowledges that coercive force is something dangerous and therefore a power to be hedged with firm legal boundaries.

In the natural rights perspective, even government by consent does involve coercion. In the terms of the Declaration of Independence, the "just *powers*" of government are derived from "the consent of the people"—which is quite different from saying that every act of government must meet the approval of every citizen or every affected citizen. Still, once one speaks of "the consent of the people," it is necessary to define the relevant people. A democratic government is accountable to a particular demos—a particular body of citizens.

What makes Boyle's doctrine particularly odd, from a natural rights perspective, is that it does not even focus its redistributionist enthusiasm on the poorer citizens *within* a polity. A government that depends on consent will be pulled to some degree toward the concerns of the needier portions of the electorate. One can, to some degree, think of this as a matter of self-interest for others: a more harmonious and contented community may be a more stable community and one more respectful of rights, including property rights. But Boyle's approach, grounded in an open-ended moral obligation to "neighbor love," seems to have no necessary connection to one's own political community. He is at least highly ambivalent—if not simply inconsistent or confused—on the limits of this broader obligation to the world at large.

So he points to the way in which "welfare rights" are "essentially political" because their delivery "presupposes the common action of the polity—at least taxation." He then advances the following non-sequitur: "It seems to me, therefore, that welfare rights are necessarily tied to membership within a polity and ordinarily to citizenship or residence within its borders."[21] On Boyle's own premise, all we can say is that organized communities may be required to deliver welfare rights, but this says nothing about how the recipients must be defined. There is no inherent reason why France could not organize itself to provide extensive welfare rights for Senegal or Lebanon, as indeed the United States now does for people in Puerto Rico and Guam.

In fact, Boyle's view seems to be that wealthy nations do, after all, have a strong obligation to provide assistance to the needy outside their own borders. The "benefits delivered by entitlement systems—health or housing or food . . . can sometimes be given by one community to the needy of another." He acknowledges that needy persons outside the borders of a particular country "may be technologically or geographically beyond its reach," and foreign governments may sometimes prevent outsiders from delivering assistance. "But the underlying obligation to help the needy one can help remains binding on every person. To whatever extent borders do not completely remove the possibility of helping those beyond them, to that extent responsibility to help remains."[22]

This seems to indicate that every nation, or at least every wealthy nation, is obliged to finance as much foreign aid as it is physically able to deliver. What this obligation would actually mean in practice is very hard to determine. Should a rich nation devote half of its GNP to foreign aid? Certainly, Americans or Europeans could survive on a per capita income reduced by half—they did so in the past. Must they, then, keep giving so long as other countries say they need more? Since Boyle's doctrine accords little respect to private property, it gives no attention to consent as an institutional protection for private property. The preferences of foreigners about the distribution of American wealth seem to be at least as relevant—morally or naturally, as Boyle would have it—as the preferences of Americans. The fact that Americans themselves have produced the wealth which they now own does not seem to have any moral standing with Boyle, so it is not clear why Americans should have the decisive say about the distribution of this wealth.

If this seems to be an exaggeration, one should consider what Boyle says about immigration. There should be a "presumption in favor of easy passage across borders" for immigrants, he says, because "often immigrants are in desperate need which all but the most straitened political communities have duties to address." Even if immigration seems to threaten the common good of the receiving country, moreover, "the requirements of the common good of any group do not override other moral considerations, such as those based on Golden Rule reasoning."[23] So, if three hundred million Chinese wish to relocate to the United States, it seems to be the obligation of the United States to take them in.

This astonishing conclusion follows from Boyle's premise that "neighbor love" knows no bounds. Pufendorf and Vattel, relying on natural rights reasoning, held that every sovereign state has the right to deny entrance to would-be immigrants if its own self-interest so dictates.[24] With minor exceptions, this is, in fact, still the accepted doctrine of international law. Boyle says there is no reason to put limits on immigration. He insists that "sound" arguments about economic detriment from immigration are "hard to find" (though his own arguments for generous welfare rights would suggest many such arguments). After dismissing the economic risks, Boyle also rejects any concerns that excessive immigration might generate dangerous social tensions. He sees no reason to worry about too much heterogeneity: "ethnic and linguistic affiliations and cultural interests are often connected to basic and social human interests. . . . But identification of the polity by those affiliations and interests when the interests of those sharing a region require defining the polity more broadly appears unjustified, for it denies to some the opportunity to cooperate politically with their neighbors on grounds that are arbitrary."[25]

What this seems to be saying is that the United States, for example, would be morally wrong to require immigrants to learn English and adapt to Anglo-American social norms. Yet ethnically divided societies—and in practice, ethnos is largely a matter of language and outward culture—find it very hard to operate as stable democracies. The continued challenge of Quebec separatism to Canada is not something a sensible country would want to import into its borders. It is entirely reasonable to think about restricting immigration to manageable levels to maintain democratic stability. Even "such a champion" of tolerance as Thomas Jefferson—a great champion of natural rights doctrine, too—argued that restrictions on immigration were a prudent precaution for the maintenance of a stable democracy.[26] This consideration figures not at all in Boyle's thinking, however, because he does not think about democratic stability.

Yet, that is the fundamental meaning of national borders: they define a territory within which the people will be governed in common. Those who do not agree may leave. Those who have very different views may rightly be kept out. Otherwise, there would be no real meaning to the claim that people may "secure" their rights by instituting government on the basis of consent. That thought does not seem to trouble Boyle very much. He wants to extend neighbor love through the whole world. He does not focus on protecting the rights of people in any particular country.

Conclusion

Brought down to concrete policies, Boyle's vision of justice would seem to imply something like the following for the United States: First, Americans should place themselves under international authority. Next, they should let this international authority tax Americans for the support of needy people in other countries. Then, they should let this authority regulate passage over American borders, so that needy foreigners can immigrate to America in whatever numbers the international authority determines to be proper. Finally, Americans should let this international authority protect foreign immigrants by imposing new laws for their welfare or by invalidating American laws that are offensive or burdensome to immigrants. For Europeans, the prescription might be described even more succinctly: Expand the European Union to incorporate all of Africa and Asia.

This is not quite what Boyle advocates, but he offers an account of "boundaries" that provides no basis for opposing such projects. The federal government of the United States already exercises all these powers over the states (while the EU now exercises most of them over its member states). On Boyle's account, the authority remaining to the states in the American federal system is all that natural law can justify in the way of bounded "local" jurisdiction. At the same time, he insists, natural law condemns the use of borders to let Americans or Europeans hold on to their own earnings or protect the cultural character of their own countries.

Rooting moral obligation in the duty of loving our neighbor, Boyle implies that resistance to his doctrines is motivated by selfishness. To the extent that rejection of Boyle's program reflects a moral outlook influenced by natural rights thinking, the charge can hardly be denied. The natural rights doctrine rests on the premise that, generally speaking, the ordinary person is better able to look after his own interests than is anyone else. The doctrine appeals, more or less openly, to the self-interest of the ordinary person. It insists on boundaries—delimiting the rights of individuals, delimiting the powers of governments, delimiting the borders of nations—as a way of limiting responsibilities.

Boyle's relative disdain for boundaries reflects his insistence on imputing much greater responsibilities to people. Again, one might say there is an element of self-interest (or selfishness) in wanting to disclaim such broader responsibilities. But there is quite a lot to say in defense of the natural rights perspective here.

First, Boyle's notion of "responsibility" is, in its own terms, not entirely reasonable or responsible. During the debate over the American Constitution in 1788, *The Federalist* wisely noted that "Responsibility, in order to be reasonable, must be limited to objects within the power of the responsible party."[27] Boyle claims that all of us are "responsible" for alleviating suffering or deprivation, even if we did not cause it; we are "responsible" because we have not prevented it. Pursuing this logic, Boyle concludes that we must give government the power to correct these problems. Then, as Boyle extends this responsibility to encompass suffering or deprivation everywhere in the world, he logically suggests that some global authority should have power to direct resources throughout the world. But to whom will these authorities be held responsible for the way they perform their responsibilities? To a global electorate? And what if—as current experience suggests—the majority of people in the world do not much care about terrible delinquency or brutality in far-off places?

Boyle's notion of responsibility undermines reasonable efforts to limit, channel, focus power—and hence "responsibility" itself. "Responsibility" implies not only an agent (who accepts the responsibility) but an effective principal, who can hold the agent responsible for what the agent does. The natural rights philosophy, putting boundaries around personal rights and sovereign nations, works to put reasonable bounds on claims of "responsibility." Boyle's notion is disturbingly open-ended.

When the wrong people take up such appeals, the consequences can be horrendous. The twentieth century is filled with horrible examples of regimes that rose to power by attacking selfishness and urging solidarity—by class or race or nationality—and ended in murderous tyranny. Boyle's account seems rather innocent to the fact that selfishness is not, after all, the worst or most dangerous human impulse. If it is selfish or self-interested to demand the protection of boundaries, it can also be prudent.

And, after all, the world at large has reason to be grateful for this political prudence and the boundaries that have sustained it. When Europe went mad, the liberal nations—and most especially the United States—retained the strength and endurance to fight back, saving the rest of the world from the ferocious tyrannies of both the national socialists and the international socialists. That is not a small achievement to the credit side of the constitutional systems founded on natural rights doctrine.

Meanwhile, the American economy, driven for the most part by self-interest as it is, has generated tens of millions of new jobs in recent decades. It has thus provided incomes for tens of millions of new immigrants, while also helping to fuel a vast increase in international trade that has, in turn, helped to power economic growth in poor countries around the world. The more generous welfare states of western Europe, under socialist and so-called Christian governments, have experienced considerable economic difficulty in the past two decades. Generous welfare rights have gone hand in hand with chronically high unemployment. In Christian or socialist Europe, moreover, immigrants are viewed with more suspicion and resentment than they are in the United States because in Europe, immigrants are more likely to be competitors for scarce jobs or for overstretched welfare funds.

Do such facts matter? Not the least problem with Boyle's approach is that, looking to "love" as its ultimate foundation, it seems to put more stress on intentions than effects. The natural rights doctrine demands that government rest on the consent of the governed. Natural rights theorists do not suppose that a government's good intentions can substitute for actual performance. Boyle's insistence on religious duties implies that performance should not be judged by anything so crass as the self-interested assessments of an actual electorate. So he makes no provision for electoral consent.

Finally, one might say that Boyle himself pays a certain kind of compliment to the natural rights doctrine by appropriating its historic achievements for his own program. Boyle's notions about welfare entitlements are, of course, constructions based on modern conditions—among other things, modern conditions of great wealth and technical progress, which did not arise when the world was under the direction of those who followed medieval natural law. Though Boyle says that his program builds on the second tablet of the Decalogue,[28] he does not reckon with the Tenth Commandment, which prohibits "coveting . . . anything that is thy neighbor's."[29] Material security for the ordinary person may be a worthy goal, but it is not one that preoccupied earlier religious authorities as much as it does Boyle.

One might wonder, in a similar way, if Boyle's avowed support for religious toleration is not also a reaction to modern circumstances which would not have arisen without the intervention of natural rights philosophies, in place of Boyle's medieval framework. Suarez, for example, endorses the earlier Catholic teaching that, as government must act for the common good and true faith is part of that good, the Jews should be carefully confined and separated, so that ordinary citizens will not be lured from the true faith.[30]

Boyle takes for granted the benefits achieved by liberal constitutional government, erected on the doctrines of natural rights. Boyle wants the benefits without accepting the preconditions—personal rights and national independence.

Notes

1. In his great work, *De Jure Belli ac Pacis* (The Law of War and Peace, 1625), Grotius uses the same Latin term (*jus*) to mean rights in this modern sense and at other times in its traditional sense, meaning "law"—an ambiguity preserved in the French *droit*, the Spanish *derecho*, the German *recht*, etc. See Richard Tuck, *Natural Rights*

Theories: Their Origins and Development (Cambridge: Cambridge University Press, 1979), 66–69, on some of the wider implications of this innovation in usage and the philosophic premises behind it.

2. Hobbes, *Leviathan*, chap. 14, par. 3.

3. Locke, *Second Treatise* (hereafter, *ST*), par. 6.

4. See Joseph Boyle in chapter 15 above, under "Definition."

5. Locke, *ST*, par. 14; *Hobbes, Leviathan*, chap. 13, par. 12.

6. Samuel Pufendorf, *De Jure Naturae et Gentium* (On the Law of Nature and Nations, 1688), trans. C. H. and W. A. Oldfather (Oxford: Clarendon Press, 1934), bk. VIII, chap. 6, par. 14 (sovereign's first duty is to the protection of his own people, so there is no duty to adhere to treaties when adherence is not in the interest of the other party, hence not likely to be observed by the other party). It is notable that Locke himself recommended this work of Pufendorf as a better guide for students than the work of Grotius. See *Some Thoughts Concerning Education*, sec. 186, in James L. Axtell, ed., *The Educational Writings of John Locke* (Cambridge: Cambridge University Press, 1968), 294. Emerich de Vattel, *Le Droit des Gens* (The Law of Nations, 1758) trans. Charles Fenwick (Washington, D.C.: Carnegie Institution, 1916), bk. II, chap. 18, sec. 335 ("in virtue of the natural liberty of nations," each sovereign state must decide for itself whether to seek pacific means for resolving disputes or assert its rights—even when they are legally doubtful—by resort to force).

7. Vattel's endorsement of the right of revolution is in *Le Droit des Gens*, bk. I, chap. 3, sec. 31–35. In this, as in other things, Vattel follows Locke. I have tried to show how much Locke gestures toward some notion of national solidarity in his *Essay Concerning Human Understanding*, and how much he relies upon it in his explicitly political writings in "Grotius, Vattel, and Locke: An Older View of Liberalism and Nationality," *The Review of Politics*, 59:2 (Spring 1997): 293.

8. "Since men are by nature equal, and their individual rights and obligations the same, as coming equally from nature, nations, which are composed of men and may be regarded as so many free persons living together in a state of nature, are by nature equal and hold from nature the same obligations and the same rights. . . . A dwarf is as much a man as a giant is; a small republic is no less a sovereign state than the most powerful kingdom. . . . Since nations are free, independent and equal, and since each has the right to decide in its own conscience what it must do to fulfill its duties, the effect of this is to produce, before the world at least, a perfect equality of rights among nations in the conduct of their affairs and in the pursuit of their policies." Vattel, *Le Droit des Gens*, Introduction, sec. 18, 21.

9. Locke, *ST*, par. 217: "The delivery of the people into the subjection of a foreign power, either by the prince or by the legislative, is certainly a change of the legislative [power] and so a dissolution of the government. For the end why people entered into society, being to be preserved one entire, free, independent society, to be governed by its own laws; this is lost, whenever they are given up into the power of another."

10. Francisco Suarez, S.J., *De Legibus, ac Deo Legislatore* (A Treatise in Ten Books on Laws and God the Lawgiver,' 1612), in Suarez, *Selections from Three Works*, ed. James Brown Scott, trans. Gwladys L. Williams, Ammi Brown, John Waldron, and Henry Davis (Oxford: Clarendon Press, 1944), bk. III, chap. 2, pars. 5, 6 (p. 376).

11. Suarez, *De Triplici Virtute Theologica: De Charitate* (On Charity, from The Three Theological Virtues, 1621), Disputation XIII, sec. 2 ("Who has the legitimate power of

declaring war"), in *Selections*, ed. Scott, p. 805. Suarez explains, in the same context, that "when there exist a tribunal and an authority superior to both parties, it is contrary to the law of nature to strive for one's own right by force, and acting (as it were) on one's own authority [rather than submitting disputes to this appellate tribunal]" (par. 2, p. 807). U.S. Constitution, Art. I, Sec. 10 prohibits the states to "engage in war, unless actually invaded," and also prohibits the states to "keep troops or ships of war in time of peace" unless by express "consent of Congress."

12. Suarez, *Defensio Fidei Catholicae, et Apostolicae Adversus Anglicanae Sectae Errores* (Defense of the Catholic and Apostolic Faith in Refutation of the Errors of the Anglican Sect, 1613), in *Selections*, ed. Scott, bk. III, chap. 23, pp. 685–704.

13. Locke, *A Letter Concerning Toleration*: "That Church can have no right to be tolerated by the magistrate which is constituted upon such a bottom that all those who enter into it do thereby *ipso facto* deliver themselves up to the protection and service of another prince. For by this means the magistrate would give way to the settling of a foreign jurisdiction in his own country and suffer his own people to be listed, as it were, for soldiers against their own Government." *Treatise of Civil Government* and *Letter Concerning Toleration*, ed. Charles Sherman (New York: Irvington Publishers, 1979), 212.

14. See Boyle, chap. 15 above, under "Ownership."

15. Locke, *ST*, par. 94 ("government has no other end but the preservation of property"); par. 124 ("the great and chief end of men's uniting into commonwealths and putting themselves under government is the preservation of their property"); and similar statements at pars. 3, 88, 95, 120, 139. In this, as in so much else, Vattel follows Locke: "The end or aim of civil society is to procure for its citizens the necessities, the comforts and the pleasures of life and in general their happiness; *to secure to each the peaceful enjoyment of his property* and a sure means of obtaining justice; and finally to defend the whole body against all external violence." *Le Droit des Gens*, bk. I, chap. 2, sec.15. From Vattel's subsequent praise of commerce (e.g., I, 2, 24 and I, 7, generally), one can infer that he sees no contradiction and scarcely any distinction between procuring "necessities" and "comforts" and securing "peaceful enjoyment of property."

16. For Locke's acknowledgments that property depends on the standards set by positive law, after the establishment of civil society, see *ST*, pars. 38, 45, 50. Michael Zuckert, *Natural Rights and the New Republicanism* (Princeton: Princeton University Press, 1994), chap. 9, offers a particularly penetrating analysis of the paradoxes in Locke's account and the way Locke himself may have understood them.

17. *ST*, pars. 40, 43.

18. *ST*, pars. 36, 46–50, and especially 37: ". . . he that encloses land and has a greater plenty of the conveniences of life from ten acres than he could have from an hundred left to nature may truly be said to give ninety acres to Mankind. For his labour now supplies him with provisions out of ten acres which were but the product of an hundred lying in common." Vattel makes a somewhat parallel point in noting that peoples who live a nomadic existence, as hunters or even as shepherds, do not have full claim to exclude others from their territory: "Those who still pursue this idle mode of life occupy more land than they would have need of under a system of honest labor and they may not complain if other more industrious nations, too confined at home, should come and occupy part of their lands." He thus condemns the Spanish conquest of

Indian civilizations in Mexico and Peru but endorses English settlement in North America, because one simply rewarded plunder while the other gave a spur to productive industry. *Le Droit des Gens*, bk. I, chap. 7, sec. 81.

19. See Boyle, chap. 15 above, under "Distribution."

20. Locke, *ST*, par. 138.

21. Boyle, chap. 15, under "Distribution."

22. Ibid.

23. Boyle, chap. 15, under "Mobility."

24. Rejecting the argument of the Spanish jurist Francisco Vitoria, who defended Spanish incursions into the New World as "natural communication," Pufendorf comments: "The answer to this is, that this 'natural communication' cannot prevent a property-holder from having the final decision on the question, whether he wishes to share with others the use of his property. Furthermore, it is crude indeed to try to give others so indefinite a right to journey and live among us, with no thought of the numbers in which they come, their purpose in coming, as well as of the question whether . . . they propose to stay a short time or to settle among us permanently, as if upon some right of theirs. . . . [W]hoever wishes to lay upon others such a requirement for hospitality, ought surely be rejected as too severe an arbiter." *De Jure Naturae*, bk. III, chap. 3 (Oldfather trans., pp. 364–65). Vattel, while recognizing a right of the persecuted to claim refuge in a third country as a "right of necessity," nonetheless emphasizes that a host country must be the ultimate judge of its obligations: "Every State should, of course, give to so unfortunate a people [those "driven from their own country"] such help as it can furnish without neglecting itself; but to grant them a settlement within its national domain is a very serious step to take, the consequences of which the ruler of the State should weigh carefully. . . . If the sovereign anticipates danger or serious inconvenience from admitting these fugitive peoples, he is justified in turning them away, or, if he receives them, in taking such precautions as prudence may dictate. One of the safest will be not to permit these foreigners to dwell together in the same section of the country and preserve their national identity. Men who have not been able to protect their homes can claim no right to settle in the territory of another and remain there as a distinct body politic." *Le Droit des Gens*, bk. II, chap. 10, sec. 136 (Fenwick trans., p. 154).

25. Boyle, chap. 15, under "Diversity."

26. Jefferson, principal author of the Declaration of Independence, endorsed restrictions on immigration only a decade later: "It is for the happiness of those united in society to harmonize as much as possible in matters which they must of necessity transact together. . . . Every species of government has its specific principles. Ours perhaps are more peculiar than any other. . . . To these nothing can be more opposed than the maxims of absolute monarchies. Yet, from such, we are to expect the greatest number of emigrants. . . . These principles, with their language, they will transmit to their children. In proportion to their numbers they will share with us the legislation. They will infuse into it their spirit, warp and bias its direction and render it a heterogeneous, incoherent, distracted mass. . . . Is it not safer to wait . . . for the attainment of any degree of population desired or expected [rather than augment population by immigration]? May not our governments be more homogeneous, more peaceable, more durable?" *Notes on the State of Virginia*, Query VIII, in Thomas Jefferson, *Writings*, ed. Merrill D. Peterson (New York: Library of America, 1984), 211–12.

27. *The Federalist*, No. 63 (probably by James Madison), in Clinton Rossiter, ed., *The Federalist Papers* (New York: Mentor, NAL, 1961), 383.

28. Boyle, chap. 15, introduction.

29. Boyle's presentation simply edits out the Tenth Commandment from the original ten: "The precepts of the second tablet of the Decalogue are the immediate implication of the commandment that one is to love one's neighbor as oneself. These precepts—prohibiting killing, stealing, lying, and adultery and requiring respect for parents—provide the normative shape for social life." Boyle's summary should be compared with God's original: Exodus 20:14.

30. Suarez, *De Triplici Virtute Theologica: De Fide* (On Faith, from Three Theological Virtues, 1621), Disputation XVIII, sec. 6, in *Selections*, pp. 787–95. It is notable, however, that Suarez (following earlier authority) takes a more limited view of responsibility than Boyle, since such coercive measures—and others against nonbelievers—are held to be the responsibility of Christian kings within their own jurisdictions only, not something they should try to impose or promote outside their own jurisdictions. Ibid., sec. 4, pp. 768–71.

Seventeen

The Ethics of Boundaries

A QUESTION OF PARTIAL COMMITMENTS

DANIEL PHILPOTT

THE SOVEREIGN STATE, a polity in which a single authority reigns supreme over a people within a bounded territory, is the only form of political organization ever to cover the entire land surface of the globe. The vast majority of people on earth live inside a set of borders and under the authority of the constitution, the dictator, or the junta which holds sovereignty there. As borders have so formidably fenced the world's populations, the state's most ardent philosophical enthusiasts, along with many citizens of many actual states, have arrived at a corresponding ethical notion—that their obligations of justice are exclusive to, or at least may heavily favor, their fellow members. External defense, internal security, roads, education, health care, the vitality of an ethnicity, language, or religion: that citizens justly provide these goods for themselves disproportionately to, or even exclusively of, outsiders is a claim for the validity of what philosophers have called "partial commitments."[1] Two sorts of philosophies have most favored partial commitments. The first is political realism, the tradition of thought in international relations that conceives of the state as an organic body with its own interests, and asks the state's citizens to direct their highest political loyalty to it. The second sort is those forms of nationalism, mostly illiberal, which conceive of one national culture as superior to others and thus worthy of loyalty.

Partial commitments to the state, though, have never rested easy with universalistic systems of ethics, that is, ones which hold that humans come to know their rights and duties through divine revelation, reason, or both, and which aver that at least some of these rights and duties are applicable to all humans. Each of the papers in this volume expresses a universal ethic. Some of them—the natural law perspective and the religious perspectives—long predate the nation-state and deal with it as a new reality. As Richard Miller describes, "[Early modern Christian] authors did not generate normative principles for addressing questions of dominion and boundaries *de novo*; they drew on a tradition of categories, distinctions, and concrete practices that give substance to the Christian imagination regarding social and political issues" (page 16). The other traditions—the liberal traditions, international law—arose after the state did, but nevertheless challenge it or limit it. All of the traditions surveyed in this volume question the primacy of borders and the partial commitments which borders generate, some of them quite radically. Borders, they argue, exclude arbitrarily and hinder commitments to outsiders. This we might expect from traditions that assert a common humanity. But interestingly, neither do any of them wholly denounce the state's partial commitments; they all allow them, to some extent, at least provisionally. All of them grant the state legitimacy, but none an absolute, unqualified authority.

Can partial commitments be justified? If so, how? These are the central ethical questions which any tradition must face when it considers borders, and, indeed, the questions which each author confronts, even if the authors do not use the term "partial commitments." Partial commitments are, after all, exactly the sort of commitments that borders tend to create. Among the traditions, there are important differences in how they answer these questions. I propose that these answers fall into two broad categories. One kind of tradition is generally reluctant to endorse partial commitments, and approves them only insofar as these commitments are instrumental to other, politically relevant, ends. The other kind of tradition embraces partial commitments more readily, viewing them as constitutive of the good life of the members of a political community. The root of the difference, the key to what distinguishes the two approaches, I propose in turn, lies in their contrasting conceptions of the good of the person and the relationship of this good to political community. Differing conceptions yield differing approaches to the partial commitments of the territorial state.

What are these contrasting conceptions of the good? The two approaches are divisible according to John Rawls's distinction between "thin" and "full" theories of the good.[2] What conception of the person's good is relevant to politics? Thin theories of the good answer minimally. Most of these are in the liberal tradition; here they are represented by Loren Lomasky, Will Kymlicka, Robert McCorquodale, and their respondents. They conceive the person as free and equal in his dignity, but having no fixed set of goods that fulfill him. In John Rawls's theory, the person is free and equal in his capacity to form, revise, and rationally pursue a conception of the good. But no particular conception of the good is normative for politics. Most contemporary liberals are indeed committed to preserving the individual's autonomy to pursue his own good. Liberals are not altogether dismissive of goods, for they want various goods—wealth, income, power, opportunities—to be justly distributed and provided. For Rawls, these are "primary goods." But primary goods are not themselves constitutive of the good life; rather, they are goods which are necessary instruments to a wide variety of further pursuits.

What does all of this imply for partial commitments toward the state? What is most important about the thin theories is not those features of the person's good they deem essential for political justice, but those features which they do not. Namely, they prescind from asserting participation in the common life of the community and the provision of its common goods as essential to an individual's good life. As I will argue, in any universal ethic, the essential good of participating in the common life is the deep foundation of partial commitments. Liberalism's concept of the free and equal person, uninscribed with a conception of the good, indeed seems to eliminate any strong basis for distinguishing people within borders and people without as objects of commitment. Unsurprisingly, then, liberals like Charles Beitz have proposed a globalization of Rawls's principles of distributive justice, while others have proposed open immigration policies, arguing precisely against limiting cooperative schemes of distribution to single states.[3]

Some liberals, though, do argue for partial commitments within the state, not according to a deep principled distinction among persons, but rather with arguments like these: To be stable and robust, a state's liberal rights and distributive justice require the legitimacy which nationalist sentiments evoke; finite communities, limited in their size, are necessary for achieving economies of scale and optimality in the provision of social welfare. These are instrumental arguments. Institutions built upon partial commitments are a necessary means for promoting the demands of justice that arise out of liberalism's deeper commitments to freedom and equality. They are the strongest sort of argument for partial commitments that liberalism can provide. They are also open-ended. Partial commitments to the citizens of one's state do not rule out commitments to outsiders; how the two kinds of commitments are to be balanced is highly indeterminate.

Full theories of the good, by contrast, propose that an individual's good, her fixed good, her human fulfillment, lies in community—in some versions, political community, in others, religious community, in still others, both. Participation, friendship, worship, and sharing in the governance of common life are essential to the good life. Because of the finiteness of relationships for which anyone has the capacity, one can only realize this good through a set of commitments—partial commitments—to a limited group of people, the fellow members of one's community. The natural law tradition, here represented by Joseph Boyle, renders this principle as the common good. The religious traditions, Christian, Confucian, Islamic, and Jewish, generally affirm the natural good of community, conceived generally as human association, but also call for special commitments to particular communities—in the Abrahamic faiths, to the believers in revealed truth, in the Confucian tradition, to members of the Chinese community. In all full theories of the good, then, there are deeply principled reasons, not just instrumental reasons, for partial commitments. We must keep in mind, though, that partial commitments are not absolute, for each of the full theories also affirms obligations to outsiders. Nor are partial commitments in these theories necessarily commitments to the fellow citizens of the state.

I propose, then, to categorize the traditions according to the role they envision for community in furthering their members' good. They divide into thin and full according to their treatment of this good. From each theory of the good flows its basic approach to partial commitments toward the boundaried, territorial state. From this basic approach, in turn, flows its treatment of each of the cognate questions regarding boundaries which the essays address: ownership, distribution, diversity, mobility, and autonomy.

An Embarrassment of Partiality: Liberalism and State Borders

None of the liberals—egalitarian, classical, or international law—is comfortable with borders. Both Will Kymlicka and Loren Lomasky use the word "embarrassment" to describe liberalism's predicament. Hillel Steiner and Russell Hardin, as well as Robert McCorquodale and Raul Pangalangan, whose international law perspectives are broadly compatible with the liberals' perspective, all second this embarrassment, voicing skepticism toward partial commitments—toward group rights, toward absolute sovereignty, toward nationally or culturally exclusive distribution schemes. Each scholar's embarrassment clearly arises from the tension between liberalism's universal commitments and the exclusion that borders create. Lomasky expresses well liberalism's universalism: "The whole of humanity on the one hand and self-determining individuals on the other hand: these are the foci of moral forces with which liberalism is most at home" (56). Each of the liberals here questions what many philosophers in the liberal tradition have assumed (the legitimacy of borders) and focused upon (single societies as the locus of liberal justice).[4] The problem with borders is arbitrariness, which Kymlicka (250) and Lomasky (57) each locate on the Rio Grande: How can people who by unchosen circumstances of birth live ten miles apart across the U.S.-Mexico border justly experience a fantastic disparity in their life prospects? Not only borders, but also peoples enclosed within states who desire to secede, are difficult to reconcile with liberalism, at least for Kymlicka.

This concern with arbitrariness also leads each of the liberals to reject the political promotion of cultural or national ties, at least as a cause separate from liberal ends. Steiner, for instance, holds that even a culturally homogeneous state whose citizens unanimously desire the flourishing of their culture as a public good may not exclude outsiders from claiming against these citizens their legitimate universal entitlement to land and wealth (79–82).

Finally, all of the liberals root their political perspective in a liberal notion of the person. Kymlicka borrows Rawls's free and equal person; Lomasky proffers an autonomous chooser; Hardin trucks in the person as an equal locus of utility. The liberals here, then, generally share the commitments that I have described above: universalism, a skepticism toward borders, and a notion of the person who, for purposes of political justice, is free and equal in dignity, but has no fixed conception of the good.

The liberals clearly differ over some matters, too—most prominently, distributive justice. Lomasky, writing for the classic liberal tradition, is skeptical of distributive obligations; Kymlicka, a liberal egalitarian, favors a global redistribution of wealth. But this difference does not lead them to starkly different conclusions about partial commitments. For Kymlicka, boundaries are a hindrance to redistribution, a creator and perpetuator of inequality. Lomasky directs his criticism at the domestic welfare state, arguing that its requirement that outsiders be excluded ends up worsening their plight to the benefit of insiders. Though he reaches a different conclusion about distribution than Kymlicka, he, too, is concerned about the economically exclusive effects of borders.

Despite the centrality which all of the liberals give to their embarrassment over borders, some of them nevertheless allow some partial commitments toward the state—albeit limited ones. While generally arguing against "hard" borders, Lomasky does allow for "soft" borders—that is, the confinement of government to a finite group of people and limited barriers to outsiders. The reasons? Government is needed to provide public order, including basic civil rights, especially the right to acquire property. Though the intrinsic validity of these rights depends upon no convention or positive law, their enjoyment indeed requires a convention, a law, which is practically established only within a particular domain of people. Lomasky follows the philosophical reasoning of the contractarian tradition (61–65). But this only implies that a political community will be finite; nothing about this finiteness limits the number of people included in the community, or even obligations to outsiders. The only outsiders which a community may justifiably exclude, Lomasky argues, are those who would, upon entrance, violate the rights established by the convention. Here, Lomasky seems to have in mind criminals, a very limited set (69–70). Government is also needed to provide certain public goods like defense, goods that require collective action, which, in turn, requires a demarcated domain for the provision (65–66). A government might even promote the cultural and national identities of its citizens, but only if they freely and generally choose communal ends (66–68). But neither does the necessity of government for these tasks imply any limits to the size of the population under it or any particular "hardness" of its borders. In Lomasky's thought, there remains only a weak basis for the directing of commitments inward—and this is exactly the conclusion he draws.

Kymlicka argues more strongly for the promotion of a citizenry's national identities, through "nation-building" projects that strengthen and spread its language, and through immigration that is limited and shaped to build the national community. These projects sustain partial commitments, for they favor the national people over minority insiders and nonnational outsiders. Why does Kymlicka value these commitments? Because public education in a common language is essential to equal opportunity; a common national culture generates the solidarity for redistribution in the welfare state; national culture enhances individual freedom by giving people meaningful choices; and a national identity creates the fellow-feeling needed for democratization—John Stuart Mill's argument (265–67).

Both Kymlicka and Lomasky, though, carefully qualify their support for partial commitments. Following the logic of his position, Lomasky is uncomfortable in endorsing even soft boundaries. He calls them a necessary second-best solution in a world where order is necessary, but where assertions of state power ought to be minimized. He places the "onus of justification . . . squarely on the shoulders of those who promote the hardening of boundaries" (70). Even the goal of civility, he argues, "cannot be stretched to legitimate a generally exclusionary immigration policy" (70). He shies especially from his endorsement of policies to promote cultural solidarity, worrying about fomenting communal conflict between insiders and excluded outsiders, or creating secessionist tendencies among minority insiders whose rights are suppressed (66–68). Kymlicka takes pains to distinguish his liberal nationalism from illiberal nationalism, which most egregiously promotes national ends to the exclusion of the rights of minority insiders. Similarly skeptical of political measures to fortify cultures, Hardin is quite critical of even Kymlicka's liberal egalitarian proposals to promote the culture of groups, although most of his criticism is directed against arguments that Kymlicka has made elsewhere in favor of preserving the endangered cultures of minorities. He too, though, offers a qualified endorsement to nations as promoters of liberal justice (290).

What is most important about all of these liberal arguments for partial commitments is that they are instrumental. Consider Kymlicka's defense of nation-building: "[L]iberal nation-building is not a regrettable compromise between liberal egalitarianism and illiberal nationalism, but may be *the most effective vehicle* for the achievement of liberal egalitarian aims" (266, emphasis added). For Kymlicka, it is the achievement of liberal egalitarian aims that justifies nation-building. Hardin's instrumentalism is baldly explicit: "Nations are contingently morally good for what they can achieve—although they are also contingently morally bad for what they can achieve" (290). As a utilitarian, by "what they can achieve," he likely has in mind the maximization of social utility. Likewise, Lomasky stresses the prudential, second-best quality of his justifications for boundaries. Finally, Jeremy Rabkin articulates a similar logic in his response to Joseph Boyle. Criticizing Boyle's Thomist "natural law" perspective, he proffers a Lockean enlightenment "natural rights" framework, stressing the individual's rights against interference from government and other individuals. His strongest criticisms, though, are not deeply philosophical, but are aimed at what he perceives Boyle doing with his natural law perspective—attempting in utopian fashion to justify radical distributive commitments toward outsiders, loose immigration provisions, and even world government. He instead argues for a government limited in both the quality of its powers and the geographic extent of its obligations, and one whose citizens' obligations are based upon their consent. But his argument for limitedness is rooted not in any denial of the universal—which is implied in "natural rights"—but rather in prudential reasoning which concludes that limited government is the sort that is most likely to guarantee natural rights. Here again, the reasoning is instrumental.

Liberals are committed first to liberal justice—the enjoyment of autonomy, the practice of rights and liberties, a just distribution, the maximization of social utility. In each of these notions of justice, all people are equal subjects. Liberalism has no principled basis for privileging one person's entitlement over another's or for confining these entitlements to particular communities. This is its universalism. Some liberals argue, though, that achieving this equal justice nevertheless relies upon communities, ones with borders, with some limits on movement across these borders, with some privileging of its inhabitants in provision and distribution, and with sentimental ties of solidarity between members. Such partial commitments do not give to some what is being taken from others, but create measures of justice where there otherwise would be none, or less. For liberals, it is this positive sum of justice, rather than any intrinsic good that is realized in community, that justifies partial commitments.

Distribution, Ownership, and Partial Commitments

Liberals' general reluctance to endorse partial commitments to the territorial state, their willingness to endorse them only qualifiedly, as an instrument to liberal justice, shapes their approach to the several cognate issues associated with boundaries. It is with respect to issues of distribution and ownership that liberals' professed embarrassment toward the state is deepest. They share this embarrassment despite their widely different general views on distribution.

More than any of the other essays, Robert McCorquodale's chapter on international law perspectives expresses vituperative scorn toward the sovereign state and its confinement of obligations. His view is atypical of the international law field, most of whose scholars accept the sovereign state system as legitimate, and proceed to posit legal obligations between states, some of which permit limited infringements upon sovereignty. To McCorquodale, the international legal system, its boundaries and its laws, treat the state as a grand owner (140–42). It is unclear at first whether he means literal ownership or something analogous to ownership. After all, as Kymlicka writes, "[t]his is obviously not property ownership in the usual legal sense, since no one owns a state, and nonnationals are often allowed to own land or resources" (257). In his discussion of ownership, McCorquodale links it closely with sovereignty, the state's supreme authority within borders, its rule over people and territory—a concept analogous to ownership, but not identical with it. Sovereignty is above all an entitlement to political rule, not to land ownership. But the analogy with ownership and property is strong; others have drawn it, and have pointed out the mutual and connected origins of both concepts in early modern Europe.[5]

The effects of sovereignty, to McCorquodale, are "privileging and silencing"—the privileging of the state and the silencing of other parties, including indigenous peoples, national and ethnic minorities within states, refugees, women, and the poor. Historically, the roots of inequity lie in the colonial system, whose distribution of power was perpetuated when colonies became independent but maintained their colonial boundaries according to the legal principle of *uti possidetis* (142–46). These former colonies maintained their position in the global economic system, too. One result is that they are dwarfed by powerful states in their control over wealth and natural resources. McCorquodale mentions the 1982 United Nations Convention of the Law of the Sea as an international legal agreement that was designed to ensure an equitable sharing of "the common heritage of mankind," but was reshaped by powerful states seeking to preserve their nationals' economic ability to exploit maritime resources (146–48). The state and the free market, for him, are a strong alliance.

McCorquodale does not identify himself as a liberal. His language suggests something more radical: the influences of Foucault, radical feminism, theories which exceed liberalism in emphasizing the pervasive structures of power. But like the liberals, McCorquodale is deeply critical of the state's hindrance of justice for a more universally conceived set of parties—individuals and groups disenfranchised by the power structure created by the international legal system. The partial commitments of the state, at least the powerful state, are but a reflection of the advantaged position of those inside.

Pangalangan largely shares McCorquodale's critical perspective. "I will likewise challenge international law's fixation on the state as the preeminent actor, stifling collectivities within states (e.g., minorities seeking self-determination), and likewise deterring people from reaching out and finding common cause (e.g., human rights) with others beyond national borders" (164). For Pangalangan, though, the territorial state is not merely exclusive of non-state actors; it is also outmoded. Sovereignty is shifting away from its territorial aspect and toward its decisional aspect. That is, new wielders of power—including "owners" of resources and organizations which enforce human rights—are challenging the state, but are not necessarily territorially located themselves (170–74). Such organizations challenge the state as the exclusive locus of partial commitments. Like McCorquodale, Pangalangan is quite uncomfortable with such partiality; at least in the case of human rights organizations, he welcomes their challenge to sovereignty.

Like McCorquodale, too, Kymlicka is radically dissatisfied with the global distribution of wealth and radically critical of the sovereign state's role in perpetuating it. "Liberal egalitarians cannot accept," he argues, "any system of boundaries which condemns some people to abject poverty while allowing others a life of privilege" (270). His emphasis, though, is not on the character of the international legal system, but on the distributive obligations which his egalitarian liberal perspective requires. Like other egalitarian liberals such as Charles Beitz and Thomas Pogge, Kymlicka calls for a radical redistributive tax—he suggests a "global resource tax"—which transfers wealth from rich states to poor states (271). Here, he draws from his commitment to the moral equality of humans, borrowing Rawls's device of the original position to derive redistributive obligations, yet challenging Rawls's confinement of it to borders. Kymlicka recognizes that his proposal will likely be criticized as unrealistic, but exhorts liberals to take on radical convictions (253).

Yet even in asserting an overriding, universalistic egalitarian justice, Kymlicka wants to maintain his commitment to preserving national cultures. In his discussion of ownership, he raises, then rejects, the claim that the titular nation properly controls the public place of a state and its territory, and even more strongly rejects a nation's claim to own the state as property (257–62). But rather than replace this illiberal and unacceptable nationalism with a requirement that states adopt neutrality toward all national and ethnic groups within their territory, Kymlicka asserts a liberal nationalism which, once again, amounts to an endorsement of the state's promotion of a national language and culture, but with strict protections for minority rights. Liberal nationalism has an implication for redistribution: Kymlicka prefers an equality achieved not through open migration across borders, but through a redistributive tax. The reason? Mainly because unrestricted immigration would "undermine or inhibit the benefits from creating cohesive national communities"— the goal of liberal nationalism (271). But Kymlicka adds a proviso, which reveals the liberal egalitarian foundation of his judgments: If states do not pay their just share of a redistributive tax, then they forfeit their claim to restrict immigration (271). Either way, rich states must relinquish their hoarding. Such balancing and qualification reflects Kymlicka's overall approach. His highest priority is liberal egalitarian justice. States may foster partial national loyalty, but again, because such loyalty is instrumental to egalitarian justice. When nationalism is illiberal, then the partial commitments it fosters are indefensible.

Lomasky, a classic liberal, dissents from Kymlicka's and McCorquodale's commitment to global redistribution. He is skeptical of all such obligations, domestic or international; this is what makes him a classic liberal. Indeed, he seeks to criticize liberal distributivists by taking them on their own terms, exposing their own reinforcement of partial commitments. His target is the domestic welfare state which, he argues, distributes to its own members wealth that could conceivably be distributed more equitably to outsiders. Such a state hardens its borders and in fact harms outsiders (72–73). Here, Kymlicka and other liberal egalitarians might reply that their international conception of redistribution avoids this partiality problem. But in the existing institutional world, where domestic redistribution dwarfs foreign aid, Lomasky's criticism challenges the scope of obligations envisioned by liberal egalitarians who favor the welfare state.

But if he is a classical liberal, Lomasky is still a liberal. He, too, is troubled by the unjust partiality which borders create in the economic sense. Like other liberals, Lomasky also makes no distinction between what people are entitled to within and without borders. His emphasis differs somewhat in that he decries not inequalities in wealth so much as inequalities in life chances. It is the "prospects," not the stock of wealth, of the babies who live across the Rio Grande which differ so wildly (57). Lomasky's embarrassment is that of a free marketeer, not a distributivist. It is the opportunities for buying and selling labor, goods, and capital for which he demands equality. What follows from this demand is his "modest proposal," that people and goods flow across the borders of world states as readily as they do across states in the United States. Only in raising resources for public goods, in creating conventions for safeguarding civil rights, and in very modestly restricting the flow of people (those who might violate insiders' civil rights) may states organize and act inwardly, partially. Lomasky's liberalism, then, despite its dissent from the egalitarians toward distribution, shares other liberals' embarrassment toward borders.

Both Steiner and Hardin offer variations on distributive justice, but also echo liberal embarrassment. Steiner raises a criticism, along liberal universalist lines, of even Lomasky's "soft" defense of states' internal conventions for property rights—that is, laws which apply only to the state's members. He is concerned that internal conventions unjustly exclude outsiders, who do not belong to the convention, from appropriating property on the same terms as insiders. If the justification for appropriating property, he argues, emanates from universal reason, then no convention could justly demand insiders and outsiders to appropriate property on different terms. But if the justification is conventional, or if it amounts to a conventional implementation of a right that reason suggests but whose conventional form reason does not determine precisely, then what basis is there for only extending the convention to some and not others? Conventions themselves, Steiner argues, do not determine their own domains (82–85).

It is unclear how restrictive Lomasky intends his convention to be. Can outsiders enter within borders and own property on the same terms as insiders, according to the convention, in violation of nobody's rights? Or is there some sense in which insiders have property rights and privileges that outsiders do not? The more inclusive interpretation is suggested by Lomasky's analogy of international relations to relations between American states. A Pennsylvanian can generally buy property in Ohio on roughly the same terms as Ohioans, even if these terms are conventionally different in the two states according to their laws. Disparate conventional determinations of a general right to property suggested by reason carry no necessary exclusivity. Such a reading of Lomasky means that a convention may apply to the people in a domain without restricting who may enter the domain and thus become one of those people. If this reading is correct, then contrary to Steiner, conventionality does not necessarily imply exclusivity.

Whatever the outcome of this debate, though, Steiner clearly endorses the other liberals' criticism of boundaries. He endorses a "Global Fund regime," premised on the claim that every individual has an equal claim to property, which compensates individuals who have been deprived of such property with an "*unconditional basic initial endowment*" of income (emphasis his). He insists that this is not a positive right to a redistribution of wealth, but a negative right, along classical liberal lines, against the encroachment of others upon what is rightfully one's own (82–85). Unlike Kymlicka, Steiner's entitlement derives from the freedom to own property; but in contrast to Lomasky and more like Kymlicka, it amounts to a strong, distributivist scheme, though of an original sort—not one that would redistribute the products of human labor, whether through foreign aid or a redistributive tax, but would grant an equal share of the earth's resources to those who do not enjoy one. But like all the other liberals, Steiner holds the robust borders of sovereign states responsible for the denial of economic justice.

Among the liberals, it is Hardin who is least embarrassed by boundaries. The justification of boundaries apparently depends upon their effects on overall social utility. He endorses, for instance, this reasoning of David Miller regarding liberal nationalism: "National boundaries merely define some of the biggest and most powerful institutions and, if those institutions do good, we can defend them and the implications of having them in place, including their barrier to individuals" (290). Hardin is open in principle, then, to partial commitments, but only if they maximize welfare, to which they are instrumental. Yet, he focuses his critical energies on exposing the disutility, and even self-undermining character, of particular liberal proposals for partial commitments, especially Kymlicka's.[6] For instance, he takes issue with liberals such as Kymlicka who propose that liberal states respect the autonomy of minority groups whose culture is threatened, even if this involves permitting some of their illiberal restrictions on mobility, residence, and political rights. To Hardin, such policies, in the name of autonomy, undermine liberalism's own commitment to individual autonomy, most importantly by allowing communities to restrict future generations' ability to choose a viable life outside the community (285–88). Hardin also excoriates liberals who propose to redistribute wealth on a global scale—Steiner, Kymlicka, and possibly McCorquodale would fit here. His objection here is primarily practical. Wealth is not likely to be redistributed without eviscerating its very value; the redistribution of human and organizational capital, whose skewed dispersal is the true basis of inequality, would again violate the autonomy of groups (282–85). Hardin also questions Kymlicka's argument for subsidizing endangered minority cultural groups. There simply is no obligation to protect existing cultures, whether tobacco farmers or Inuits (285–88).

What is important for comparative purposes is the character of Hardin's objections. All of them are aimed at distributivist schemes, but also at partial commitments. Each of the arguments he challenges calls for channeling wealth toward particular groups. In general, Hardin is willing to countenance both redistribution and partiality, as his endorsement of liberal nationalism as an aid to domestic distribution shows—but only as instrumental promoters of utility, whose advancement must strictly be demonstrated. Such instrumentalism and such a placement of the burden of argument position Hardin quite near the other liberals in his moral consideration of boundaries.

Despite a wide variety of views on ownership and distribution, each of the above authors is critical of borders' confinement of moral commitments, except for Hardin, who is only moderately critical, but certainly not deeply committed to borders. Why are liberals so deeply embarrassed by the state when economic issues are involved, while some of them are willing to favor some partial commitments when it comes to preserving culture and nation? Unlike culture, economic wealth is a uniformly and universally valuable good in liberal theory. It is for all people a means to other goods, whatever their identity or beliefs. Wealth is the most universally denominated currency, and plays best into liberalism's universalism. Like basic civil rights, its enjoyment, or at least the capacity for acquiring it, ought to be available to insiders and outsiders alike.

Diversity, Mobility, Autonomy: Stronger
Partial Commitments

It is in their discussion of the cognate issues of diversity, mobility, and autonomy that some liberals defend partial commitments to the degree that they do. These issues are most directly invoked by some liberals' project of building national culture.

Kymlicka's project of liberal nation-building is the strongest example. Within the borders of a state, he wants to promote fellow-feeling by fostering a strong national identity and, most importantly, a common language. He insists, though, that this project is a liberal one. States should not prohibit minority languages even if they encourage a majority one; they ought to allow "private spheres" where citizens may use minority languages; they ought not to prohibit speech or political activity that challenges the national identity; they ought not to restrict membership in a national community to members of a single ethnicity, race, or religion; and so on (264–67). So the state is professedly not neutral in its promotion of a single nationality, but it does not prohibit the expressions of minority cultures, or still less expel or deny the civil liberties of minorities, all the notorious measures of illiberal national-ism—that is Kymlicka's general formula.

In his discussion of diversity, Kymlicka makes clear his reasons for nation-building. Each amounts to a liberal goal to which a common linguistic culture is a means. A standardized language fosters equality of opportunity; a common national culture builds solidarity; participation in a national culture enhances individual freedom by creating meaningful life choices for individuals; a common culture creates the trust needed for participatory democracy (265–67). To achieve these gains from a common culture, Kymlicka is willing to trade off a limited amount of mobility and autonomy. He wants to allow the admission of aliens, immigration, and the possibility of outsiders becoming citizens. But immigration is conditional. Liberal democracies may pressure immigrants to integrate into society, requiring that they learn its dominant language and become educated into its history and institutions. They may also restrict numbers of immigrants, not simply to allow easier absorption, but to discourage enclaves that are separate from, and potentially fragment, the national society (262–64). Generally, Kymlicka wants to require common education into a single language within territorial borders. But other kinds of autonomy—religious, ideological, racial—ought not to be restricted in order to further these other sorts of homogeneity. The reason? Participatory democracy requires a common language, but can function fine amidst other sorts of cleavages. For Kymlicka, any curbs on diversity, mobility, and autonomy in the name of nation-building can be justified only by nation-building's greater gains for other aspects of liberal democracy—deliberation, equality of opportunity, and the like. Nor does nation-building crowd out or eliminate obligations to outsiders, particularly distributive ones.

Lomasky's classical liberalism strongly favors curbs on autonomy, mobility, and diversity in the pursuit of nation-building. Throughout his essay, individual autonomy emerges as his central political value; he is loathe to yield to any abridgment of it in the name of nation or culture. Toward restrictions on immigration and mobility, he is generally skeptical. He makes a case for "a fundamental moral equivalence between international and intranational travel," qualified only by the proviso that those who threaten predatory violence or pose a (strictly defined) ideological or political threat to the liberal regime be excluded (58, 73–75). He is willing to allow policies which build cultural and national bonds when they are generally endorsed by the individuals within a polity, but he ends this discussion with an expression of strong concern for individuals who are minorities or who belong to the dominant culture, but choose not to identify with it strongly (66–68). Lomasky makes no stronger statement on behalf of nations, ethnicities, and cultures in his essay, and makes no mention of their instrumental value for promoting liberal democratic ends.

What all of the liberal perspectives have in common, then, is an affirmation of the universal freedom and equality of the individual that challenges borders and their confinement of commitments. Some liberals, like Kymlicka, will allow limited special commitments to the national group within the state, but only in order to promote the political institutions which in turn promote universal freedom and equality. Liberals will claim nothing stronger on behalf of partial commitments to the state and the national community. Unlike realists and illiberal nationalists, they will not claim that the state is an organic body which has its own interests separate from and superior to individuals' interests, or that a particular nation has a special value and status that other nations do not. They would also differ from other moral theories which privilege the individual as a bearer of a universally shared equal dignity, but which also view the individual's participation in the common life of the political community as essential to her fulfillment. Beyond the individual's dignity as a free and equal being, beyond her entitlement to certain primary goods with which individuals pursue further goods, liberals want politics to avoid promoting any particular conception of the good life. That is what makes their accounts thin theories of the good, and different from full theories of the good, to whose claims we now turn.

Religion, Natural Law, and Partial Commitments

Natural law and the religious perspectives—Christian, Confucian, Islamic, and Jewish—are far less embarrassed toward partial commitments in politics than the liberal and international law perspectives. In these perspectives, partial commitments to polities are far from being outright violations of the justice of some free and equal persons and far more than instruments of the good of individuals conceived as free and equal persons. These commitments, rather, are constitutive, integral, and fundamental—both to the just character of polities and to the good of their members. It is the members' good that roots these commitments. Objective, fulfilling of persons, and indispensably involving participation in community, this good grounds a full theory that contrasts with the liberals' thin theory.

But what do such "full" theories say about the book's central problem, the ethical significance of borders? We have already ruled out any categorization that simplistically renders all liberal theories as proponents of unlimited global commitments, without regard to borders, and casts natural law and religious theories as advocates of unqualified partial commitments to the state. Some liberal theories, as we have seen, argue for some partial commitments. The natural law and religious traditions depart from this crude dichotomy even further, affirming the value of partial commitments to the state, to be sure, but proposing the state as only one of several communities, and not even the most important community, to which people are to direct their partial commitments. Full theories of the good also summon their audiences to universalistic commitments toward an unlimited set of all outsiders, obligations which are, in turn, rooted in shared human dignity. Unlike liberalism, then, full theories of the good may endorse non-instrumental partial commitments toward the state; but they balance these commitments with partial commitments toward other communities and commitments to all of humanity.

This complex conclusion is the yield of the two broad sources of knowledge which, to differing degrees, inform traditions entailing full theories of the good. One is "religious sources"—divine revelation, and tradition, as it evolves and is bequeathed through authorities. These sources evoke commitments to the tradition's members and to strangers, as well as to the state. The other source of knowledge is "natural law," or the rational capacity of all humans to know truth. Not all of the full theories of the good draw upon this source; some do so only implicitly. But in those which do evoke it, morality demands not only commitments to the political community, but also to outsiders as well as to smaller communities.

Partial commitments to the people within the state's borders, but also to the members of one's tradition and to smaller communities, all constitutive of a person's good; obligations to outsiders; the roots of these commitments in both religious sources and in reason—full theories of the good justify and emphasize these factors diversely. Joseph Boyle's perspective is explicitly and entirely based upon natural law, accessible by human reason, though ontologically rooted in divine reason. He explains most forcefully and systematically how a person's good is fulfilled through his partial commitments to a political community. The key to natural law thought on the matter is the notion of the common good. The object of politically defined human interests such as justice and social harmony, the common good is realized through the common, cooperative action of individuals. Much of this cooperative action will be instrumental to the achievement of other goods, such as life and security. But Boyle makes clear that "some aspects of the good that unites people into political society also seem intrinsically good. . . . So, the common good of political society appears to be in some respects at least an intrinsic good of human beings, that is, something that can be sought as a benefit or end in itself and not simply as an empowerment or means" (303). As an intrinsic good, political society, like all basic human goods in a natural law framework, is fulfilling of, perfecting of, the person (303–4).

How, then, does the common good imply bordered political communities? Noting that "there is no developed natural law analysis of territorial boundaries," Boyle seeks to construct one (301). He observes that a natural law conception of social life—people interacting, cooperating, realizing basic goods through this interaction—assumes that the people involved are living together in the same place (304). They are animals; animals are embodied; their embodiment necessitates that they cooperate, at least for political purposes, in a particular physical locale. As many, if not most, political concerns are local, the authority which promotes the common good and its jurisdiction must, then, also be local. Boundaries, which define the community in which the common good is realized, are then a "normative inevitability" (305).

Now boundaries and finite authority do not necessarily imply the modern nation-state. But history has bequeathed us the state as the primary unit of authority; it is now the form of political community in which we express our partial commitments. It is not, though, the only form of political community. Echoing the concept of "subsidiarity," drawn from Catholic social teaching, Boyle argues that some common goods will be realized in more localized bordered communities; some, perhaps, in supranational ones (304–5). Boyle also argues that states have distributive obligations to outsiders and very little justification for limiting immigration—cosmopolitan commitments that also qualify partial commitments to the state. All of this amounts to a notion of partial commitments which is quintessential for full theories of the good, indeed offering a template by which we can compare the emphases of other full theories: Individuals may and ought to make partial commitments to the political community because it is in its common good that they realize their own good. But the state, even if the primary modern political community, is not the only community that demands our commitments; and its demands of loyalty do not eviscerate its citizens' commitments to outsiders.

The Abrahamic faith traditions share all of these features of full theories of the good. Distinctively, though, they look to the special revelation of God—His self-revelation, recorded in scripture—as a chief source of their knowledge about the partial commitments that fulfill us. But specially revealed knowledge hardly precludes natural knowledge (which Christian theologians often refer to as general revelation); in these traditions, the two are often treated as coexisting and complementary.

Consider Richard Miller's Christian perspective, for instance. A Christian understanding of boundaries, he argues, begins and ends with the most crucial boundary, that between creation and its Creator. The most fundamental sin, pride, consists in a trespass of this boundary. But this central, axial boundary says little about how we are to order our earthly boundaries, only that a Christian who avoids the pride of trying to become God will also avoid traversing the boundaries of respect for his neighbors (16). For guidance into earthly boundaries, Miller turns to a perspective much like Boyle's. God has ordered social life according to principles discernible by human reason, he claims. Natural law shows us that humans have an "innate tendency to develop a common life, that membership in community is a natural human good": for

Miller, too, the individual is fulfilled, perfected, in common life (17). Miller goes on to argue that this common life takes a territorial form; throughout his paper, he treats the state as this form. Not only do territories foster common life, but "as a natural fact, human beings seem to need a sense of place" (17). Borders encourage basic human goods—a perspective indistinguishable from a natural law one.

But then Miller turns back to revelation, to Christ, where he finds *agape*, unconditional, indiscriminate love, blind to nation, ethnicity, or social position. Cannot such a notion only be in tension with territorial borders, which ask us to "privilege local solidarities" (17)? Miller indeed stresses the tension, fearing that borders will weaken the radical message of Christianity, watering down the demand to love our neighbor. His solution is to render borders, and the common good which they promote, as "real but relative" goods, ones which are temporal, and lesser than the good of the Kingdom of God, where *agape* is realized. So Christians are to affirm the common good of political life as a real good, constitutive of the person's good, but to understand it as relative to, and limited by, the call to universal love.

Nigel Biggar argues for a Christian perspective that treats national commitments as less provisional, and more essential, than they are in Miller's analysis. Biggar disputes that either Christ's "hard sayings," calling us to leave behind marriage and family, or the nature of God's love for humans, contains implications for how we are to distribute our commitments among the millions of people who are potentially our neighbors. Rather, the very creatureliness of human beings, their natural dependence on historical communities, suggests that Christian love may well be directed toward one's most immediate neighbors. Biggar even argues that Christianity affirms national diversity as a created good, an affirmation manifested both at Pentecost and in the very character of the Trinity, a perfect community of love among differentiated divine persons. Finally, like both Boyle and Miller, he argues for a notion of the common good in which the good of the human individual is "bound up with the good of others" (43). The Christian's national loyalties must be qualified; nations are historically mutable and ought never to be identified with God. Nations, rather, are forums in which people may live out their love for God and neighbor. Even more strongly than Miller, Biggar asserts that national communities help to constitute the good of the individual.

What is curious about Miller's and Biggar's perspectives is that in their treatment of loyalty to the community, they discuss only in passing the central community in the Christian life: the church. Does the Christian have special commitments to members of the church that he does not have to others? How does his understanding of and involvement in the church shape his obligations toward those outside the church, and particularly toward the community of a nation-state? The answers to these questions are diverse in the history of Christian theology, and will have diverse implications for the question of borders. But as the church has been central to classical Christian theology, so a rich ecclesiology ought to be incorporated into considerations of ethical questions such as the status of borders.

Obligations toward the members of one's religious community are by contrast hardly lacking in the Jewish perspectives. Both David Novak and Noam Zohar explore the meaning of borders for people whose primary obligations, indeed, whose very destiny, is realized in a very particular community. As Novak writes, "for Jews, the question of territorial boundaries cannot be addressed outside of the whole issue of Zionism . . . as a historical reality that has led to the presence of the state of Israel among the nation-states in the world in which we now live" (213). What Zionism is, what the good, the destiny, and the calling of Jews are, begins with theology—that is, with God's historical revelation. Central to this theology is the notion of God's covenant with the Jewish people, a promise in which their history and their obligations are rooted. Place, here, plays a vital role—for Jews, history will culminate in a world that revolves around Zion as the *axis mundi*. In his discussion of the dilemmas surrounding territoriality, Novak's focus is on the contemporary state of Israel and the nature of Jews' partial commitments toward it. The most difficult questions revolve around the meaning of God's covenant for the obligations of Jews to non-Jews, especially those living in Israel. It is here that his and Zohar's treatments diverge somewhat. Novak emphasizes obligations to preserve Jewish law and tradition within Israel; Zohar stresses commitments to a shared humanity.

Novak does, however, hint at a more universalistic understanding of partial commitments to territorially bounded communities. He notes that place is central in all human life. "[H]uman life is inconceivable outside of a finite community and its structures"; "[w]e are all both historical and geographical beings" (213). Later, he discusses the "'territorial imperative' as an essential aspect of human political nature" (215). Is this the natural good of community, essential to human fulfillment? Novak does not make the claim, but his several statements point toward it. But the central considerations in both authors' essays are the status of the state of Israel, its boundaries, and its approach to attendant dilemmas, all of which revolve around the partial commitments of Jews to the community in which their destiny is fulfilled—a destiny revealed by God.

Islamic traditions, like Jewish traditions, center the community of believers in their analysis. Nyang proposes the key boundary in Islamic thought, from which all other Muslim thinking on boundaries derives: the boundary between believers and nonbelievers. All religions create such boundaries insofar as they demarcate communities of believers who are committed to their teachings. Boundaries, in Islam, indeed reflect a crucial assumption of the teachings—that the Muslim's self, his identity, his commitments, his destiny, are intimately tied to the Islamic community. His partial commitments to that community are, as they are in all thick theories of the good represented here, fulfilling of his person. From these partial commitments to community follows Nyang's claim for the inseparability of ethical questions from legal and political ones (208). The political order instantiates, promotes, and reflects the purposes of that community which fulfills the person. Only this understanding of the social order can make sense out of Nyang's claim that a person's compliance with ritual is a sign that he is faithful to the ethical commitments of Islam, and hence, a trustworthy member of the political community (207–9).

The Islamic political community, of course, is not first and foremost the territorial nation-state. It is obviously temporally prior to it, long predating it. But it is also ontologically prior to it: A reflection upon the nature and character of the Islamic political community is the starting point for inquiring into the status of the modern territorial state. Zaman notes that "[a]s in previous centuries, some contemporary Muslim scholars have attempted to reconcile Islamic ideals with prevailing political realities" (192). As the *umma*, the community of all Muslims, is the group to which Muslims owe their first allegiance, national boundaries are " anathema to Islam" (191). But many modern Muslim scholars have come to argue for an accommodation to current political realities, asserting the acceptability of an Islamic territorial state, governed by *shari'a*, or Islamic law. Such an arrangement need not unalterably reverse the unity of the *umma* (192). Nor does it alter the basic character of Muslims' partial commitments. Muslims have certain commitments to the welfare of their Islamic state which they do not have to outsiders, particularly to those of non-Islamic states. Why? Because it is within their state that Islamic law is realized, where their good is realized, and where the general good of Islam is realized. Like the Jewish tradition, the Islamic tradition views the religious community as the key locus of partial commitments. How these traditions regard the state is a subsidiary, derivative question.

The Confucian tradition, as presented by Joseph Chan and Michael Nylan, arrives through neither divine revelation nor pure natural reason, but through a body of doctrines which Confucius himself first synthesized. Like the Abrahamic religions, Confucianism long predates the nation-state. But its notion of community as a crucial component of the moral life yields conclusions quite relevant to boundaries, territory, and partial commitments.

At the heart of the Confucian ethical tradition, Chan tells us, is the concept of *ren*, the highest virtue, one expressed primarily through love of one's fellow human beings. It is, in turn, the family where *ren* is most naturally manifested (91–92). Clearly, in Confucianism, the good life is realized, the person fulfilled, through relationships. But *ren* is not to be limited to familial relationships. Society, even the entire world, constitutes an analogous "family," potentially a component of a person's web of constitutive relationships. Chan claims that "the Confucian family is . . . a highly elastic entity, and its spirit and care can be extended to places far away from home" (92).

Correspondingly, all humankind is a political association, the order of *tian xia* (the world under heaven). This order, claims Chan, "admits of no territorial boundaries" (94). Localized governments may exist, but never with sovereignty, and always as a part of the universal political order. Nylan holds similarly that boundaries are permeable, expandable, and blurry, dependent upon flow and change, much like the human body in Confucian thought (94–99).

Whether this framework can be reconciled with the territorial states system is unclear. Chan discusses the work of twentieth-century philosopher Mou Zongsan, who attempts precisely such a reconciliation (106–9). The key revision in contemporary Confucian thought that permits an embrace of the state is the assertion of equal respect for a diversity of cultures and the abjuration of the superiority of Chinese culture. As the nation-state is the best contemporary form of government to promote culture, it may be recognized as legitimate. Mou never developed any detailed thought on the ethics of boundaries, to what degree partial commitments within them are justified, or how they are balanced by universal commitments (107–8). But minimally, Mou's Confucianism allows the legitimacy of the state.

Confucianism amounts to a unique version of a full theory of the good. The person is undoubtedly fulfilled in relationship with particular others; one's family is crucially important, but not all-inclusive, among these others. This is its fullness. But beyond family, the identity and location of these others is unlimited. There is a universalism in Confucianism. In contrast to Aristotle, Chan argues, the Chinese conception of the political order involves no territorial boundaries (97–99). In the same spirit, Nylan distinguishes Confucianism from Realpolitik, the notion that the state is the possession of a single ruler within a territory, to dispose of as the ruler pleases (117). Likewise, though, Confucianism is very different from liberalism: "[A]ny society that celebrates mere freedom from intervention as its highest goal will inevitably pay a heavy price in terms of the physical, mental, and moral health of its members" (124). No person's good can be conceived in isolation from that of others.

Full Theories of the Good and Questions
Regarding Boundaries

What most distinguishes full theories of the good from thin theories of the good is their averment that the good of the individual is fulfilled in political community. The person's partial commitments to that community, then, are rooted in first principles, in the person's very nature. They are not justified instrumentally, as means to the more truncated good of the liberals' free and equal individual, as the thin theories of the good would have it. The full theories of the good propel this logic through the several cognate areas of justice related to boundaries. Goods may be distributed disproportionately within political communities; minorities may be given special outsider status; immigration may be restricted—all on the basis of noninstrumental principles.

It is the Islamic and the Jewish perspectives that most strongly defend partial commitments in the cognate areas. In both traditions, God has created a community of followers and given them law. It is within this community, on the basis of this law, that the members of these traditions answer specific questions regarding institutions and policies. In both traditions, obligations of ownership and distributive justice clearly emanate from scriptural passages concerning property, poverty, and taxation. In the Jewish perspective, interpretation of boundary issues often revolves around the relationship of the Jewish people to a specific piece of land. It only inhabits this land, Novak emphasizes, according to its covenant with God, to which the Jews are responsible. In the current state of Israel, it follows, the most difficult problems will be ones of diversity: How should Jewish law be interpreted with respect to non-Jews, diaspora Jews, and communities of Jews who differ with one another over orthodoxy? The question is only intelligible in a political community whose purpose is the good of a specific, divinely called people.

Likewise, the Islamic perspectives again and again answer questions about the justice of boundaries so as to reflect the division of the world between Muslims and non-Muslims. Only the Muslims within an Islamic state pay the *zakat*, a kind of tax. Zaman recounts only weak distributive justice obligations to non-Muslim outsiders (188–90). One of the central features of Muslim political community is the creation of *ahl al-dhimma*, non-Muslim communities which inhabit Muslim territories, but are not bound by Muslim laws: in return for taxes and tributes, such communities receive protection from enemies, internal and external, according to the terms of treaties (192–94). With respect to relations with outsiders, Islam divides the world into *dar al-harb*, *dar al-aman*, *dar al-sulh*, and *dar al-Islam* depending on whether the realm is at war, at peace, or under the sovereignty of Muslims. In the history of Muslim law, there is precedent for placing restrictions on the movement of enemies, *harbis*, within Muslim territory, although Zaman holds that in premodern times, they were little practiced, and in modern times are practiced unjustly, contrary to Islamic law (192–96). In all these ways, Islam settles questions of justice on the basis of who belongs to the community and who does not.

We should not make the mistake of thinking that in making determinations of justice with regard to boundaries, Jewish and Muslim traditions deny the dignity of outsiders and minorities. What is distinctive, though, is that in framing questions of justice, they begin with the religious community as the relevant unit of people and with revelation as the starting point of analysis. They ask first what scripture says to the Muslim and the Jew about ownership, distribution, diversity, mobility, and autonomy, and only then what this implies with respect to those who are not members. The character and content of revelation dictate this methodology; the same character and content yield such a strong notion of partial commitments.

Miller and Biggar conceive the demands of the Christian Gospel upon the Christian community quite differently than the Jewish and Islamic perspectives treat the demands of divine law upon their respective communities, at least with respect to boundaries and partial commitments. Indeed, in Miller's perspective, special revelation plays a nearly mirror opposite role to the divine law in the other Abrahamic faiths. Here, natural law and scripture are more distinct, yielding two sources of norms, with natural law more the robust. It is natural law that evokes the strongest notion of partial commitments, although not without the counterweight of universal obligations, while scripture offers the radical universalistic *agape* love that places limits on natural commitments to community, which Miller calls a temporal good. Natural law, then, establishes (qualified) rights of ownership; *agape* love commands the disposition to sell one's goods to the poor (19–25). Natural law allows people to make partial commitments to communities which are organized around culture, language, and ethnicity; radical *agape* love cautions against worldly loyalties, idolatry and rationalized provincialism, and calls for devotion to the outsider (25–27). The natural goods of community and participation imply restrictions on immigration; *agape* love calls for indiscriminate love of the neighbor in need (27–28).

It is only with respect to the autonomy issue, which Miller frames as one of respect for minorities, that the commands of special revelation can create partiality, rather than universalistic demands. Conquest, crusades, imperialism, holy war, the subjugation of the Amerindians—all were justified with the argument that true Christian belief ought to be defended and forcibly spread as a sign of God's sovereignty (29–33). At the same time, in the context of Anabaptist communities, scripture also translated into partial Christian commitments, but here in pacifist form. Living out the logic of the Christian community meant renouncing war (30).

Generally, though, Miller poses community as a natural good, and indiscriminate, universalistic *agape* love as the demand of the Christian gospels— this is the rubric by which he approaches the several cognate questions. Biggar's Christian perspective places a higher value on community as a natural good and describes less of a tension between this good and the demands of the gospel. He too, though, sees universal Christian love as a limitation on the restrictions, the exclusions, and the idolatries which can often attend loyalty to the nation.

Boyle's perspective, of course, contains none of the partial commitments that stem from divine revelation, as in the Islamic and the Jewish perspectives, nor the radical *agape* that stems from revelation in Miller's Christian perspective. His perspective is a natural law one—cast, to be sure, in the Catholic Thomist tradition, and intended to complement Scripture, but rooted entirely in reason nevertheless. But in its application to the areas of justice associated with boundaries, we find both partial commitments and universal obligations. The property laws which provide for the reasonable use of goods to satisfy human need are properly bounded by borders; but some obligations to respect commercial and property rights are properly a part of *jus gentium* (305–7). Welfare rights, required in principle by natural law, are enjoyed due to the common law and action of the polity; citizens of states, though, still have obligations to the welfare of outsiders (307–9). Ties derived from shared ethnicity, language, culture, and religion are a defensible basis for forming communities; denying the equality of minorities within these communities is indefensible (309–11). Some limits on immigration are reasonable in furtherance of the common good, but sound defenses for such limits are rare and must compete with an obligation of benevolence (311–12). All of these balances reflect a natural law perspective which views partial commitments to the political community as fulfilling of the person, yet also prescribes universal obligations.

Finally, in the Confucian perspective, it is universal obligations that seem to govern cognate areas of justice. While it is true that familial relationships constitute the good of the person, the scope of the family is infinitely elastic, and the world of the ancient Confucian tradition is one without borders. With respect to ownership and distribution, few distinctions between groups are to be made; the obligations derived from *ren* apply everywhere. On the issue of diversity, Chan notes the tradition's assertion of Chinese superiority. Yet a benevolence that comes from a recognition of the common humanity of "barbarian" outsiders eviscerates any logic of conquest or second-class citizenship. "[P]eaceful edification and persuasion rather than violent or military domination should be the strategy to deal with the barbarians," writes Chan (103). Exceptional for full theories of the good, the Confucian perspective calls for little distinction between insiders and outsiders, members and nonmembers, when making determinations about justice.

What Do We Learn from Diverse Ethical Perspectives on Boundaries?

Prior to reading this volume, one might suspect that the eight ethical traditions have little to do with each other, and perhaps not much to do with boundaries. But in fact, they all turn out to have something to say about boundaries; and, if what I have argued is correct, their conclusions are patterned. They divide into two broad categories, depending on how they treat the question of partial commitments. It is not hard to see that partial commitments are the central moral question evoked by borders. What borders do, after all, is partition, categorize, and separate people, creating, or at least demarcating, distinct political communities. For many of its members, the political community may be the largest horizon of justice; they may have little considered obligations to outsiders. The moral question, then, is whether the members of such a bordered political community are justified in restricting ownership, distributing goods, treating minorities and outsiders, sealing borders, and governing in a way that gives those within the borders more weight, value, and recognition than those outside.

The traditions return two broad answers to this question. Some justify partial commitments, if at all, as instrumental to the good of their members. The other kind of tradition treats these commitments as ends in themselves, as instantiations of communal ties which in fact promote the very good of humans. Partial commitments, here, are not instrumental to goods, or at least not *merely* instrumental to goods; rather, they *are* a good. The two answers are, in turn, rooted in two different conceptions of the person which the traditions consider relevant to politics. The first is a person whose thin, political good is realized when she enjoys civil rights and liberties and a just allotment of wealth; her full good is realized (or not realized) in the way that she chooses to pursue it. The second is a person whose good includes membership and participation in the political community—a full good which is relevant for politics.

Which tradition ought we generally to endorse? I doubt that anyone's answer to this question will ride on a tradition's treatment of borders and partial commitments, although it is certainly possible that one's attraction to a tradition might be enhanced or diminished by this treatment: an appearance of exclusiveness might repel; one of inclusiveness might attract; perhaps a tradition's rich communal ties or deep historical roots will sway. But most likely, one's decision for a tradition will depend on prior questions about its truth, beauty, and goodness. If that is the case, then what is the value of this comparative inquiry? It is manifold. First, members of the traditions will understand better what their commitments imply for the question of boundaries. If one is a Jew, for instance, how ought one to regard the question of immigration? Second, we all learn what we can expect from the thought of other traditions, helping us to understand them and to relate to them more constructively. Finally, we learn what general type of tradition is likely to yield what general type of answer. Broadly speaking, a tradition rooted in natural law, religion, or ancient cultural tradition is more likely to endorse partial commitments robustly as an element of their members' good, while variants of the liberal tradition are more reluctant toward, even embarrassed by, partial commitments, and more likely to endorse them as instrumental and provisional. This, though, is a broad conclusion. Full theories of the good have their universal claims; thin ones sometimes value nation and culture quite highly. It is the discovery of broad patterns among the traditions that makes a volume such as this valuable; it is respect for the complexity of the traditions that makes it credible.

Notes

1. For an excellent exploration of the issue of partial commitments in the context of nationalism and the state, see the essays in Robert McKim and Jeff McMahon, *The Morality of Nationalism* (Oxford: Oxford University Press, 1997). For a helpful exploration of partiality and impartiality, see Thomas E. Hill, Jr., "The Importance of Autonomy," in his *Autonomy and Self-Respect* (Cambridge: Cambridge University Press, 1991).

2. He actually uses the terms "thin" and "full" to denote theories of the good. John Rawls, *A Theory of Justice* (Cambridge: Harvard University Press, 1971), 395–99, 433–39.

3. See Charles R. Beitz, *Political Theory and International Relations* (Princeton: Princeton University Press, 1979), 125–76.

4. The works of the leading lights of the liberal tradition—Locke, Kant, Mill, Bentham, and Rawls, to name a few—deal only secondarily with politics toward the outside world. When they address it, they usually treat it as a problem of relations between states or, occasionally, as one of groups and states, rather than the obligations of the people within a set of borders to those outside it.

5. John Gerard Ruggie, "Territoriality and Beyond: Problematizing Modernity in International Relations," *International Organization* 47:1 (1993): 139–74.

6. In Kymlicka's case, this idea is found in writings outside this volume. See Will Kymlicka, *Liberalism, Community, and Culture* (Oxford: Oxford University Press, 1989).

Index